# MY
# GRANDFATHER'S
# MILL

# MY GRANDFATHER'S MILL

## JOURNEY TO FREEDOM

### ANDREW MELNYK

**To order additional copies of this book, contact:**
Xlibris Corporation
1-888-795-4274
www.Xlibris.com
Orders@Xlibris.com
49544

*When I despair, I remember that all through history the way of truth and love has always won. There have been tyrants and murderers and for a time they seemed invincible, but in the end they always fall.*

—**Gandhi**

# DP (Displaced Persons)

At the end of World War II, several million refugees from Eastern Europe found themselves in Germany, Austria, and other parts of Western Europe. They were victims of forced labor, prisoners of the Soviet Army, survivors of Nazi concentration camps, people evacuated by force from battle areas, political refugees from the Bolshevik-occupied lands, soldiers from various military formations, and those who left the war zones temporarily, planning to return as soon as the war was over.

Among them were some two to three million Ukrainians. When the war ended, however, most of them were repatriated—sent back to their homelands against their will—to an uncertain future. Those who were in the Soviet zones at the end of the war were sent back immediately. They were arrested and either sent to Siberian labor camps or summarily tried and executed. Their simple act of leaving had demonstrated that they were enemies of the motherland. Those who were in the American, French, or British zones fared somewhat better, although they still had to prove to the authorities that they were not the enemy and that they had no connection with the Nazis during the war.

At the Yalta Conference in 1945, Stalin had argued that, by definition, refugees were people who wanted to return home, and he managed to convince his allies that they should cooperate by returning all former residents to "their" lands. When reports of the treatment of the refugees by the Soviets reached the West, the Americans, first, and eventually, the French and British, slowed the process of repatriation of the refugees. Eventually, the Allies were convinced that refugees should receive legal protection, that is, the right to live in displaced persons (DP) camps and free passage to countries of permanent resettlement.

At the beginning of 1946, only about two hundred thousand Ukrainians remained in Allied-controlled territory. The United Nations Relief and Rehabilitation Administration (UNRRA) and, later in 1947, the International Refugee Organization (IRO) were formed to coordinate the relief efforts. Although UNRRA, at first, confused legal state citizenship and nationality, it eventually recognized Ukrainians as a distinct national group and allowed them to form separate DP camps, chiefly in Bavaria and western Austria.

By the summer of 1949, virtually all the residents of DP camps, having survived four or more years of uncertainty, boarded requisitioned ships and made their way to Canada, the United States, or Australia.9

The characters in this book were among the fortunate ones who made the journey to freedom.

# Contents

## Part Eight: The Littlest Exiles

## Postscript: To Leave a Legacy

## Epilogue: Tributes, Memoirs and Documents

*For our grandchildren*

# Prologue

I have always had a passion for history.

Maybe it's because I was born just a few kilometers from the Soviet-Nazi front lines during the most brutal days of World War II and was forced to leave the country of my birth as an infant.

Maybe it's because, as a child, I overheard stories—often in hushed tones—about what it was like "back then."

Maybe it's because of the gentle indoctrination I received at Saturday-morning Ukrainian language classes and as a member of the Ukrainian Boy Scouts.

Maybe it's because as a young student I was never able to find a history book whose description of the war remotely matched the stories I had heard.

When I was growing up in Montreal in the 1950s and 1960s, it upset me that most of my classmates had a country of origin they could clearly identify and I did not. They could fly off to England or Ireland or Italy or Germany to visit their families. I could never do that. The country of my birth was somewhere behind the iron curtain. It might as well have been on another planet. I could never go there.

When I told people I was born in Ukraine, their reaction was often, "Huh?" or they'd say, "That's in Russia, isn't it?"

So often I searched for information about Ukraine and found its existence was almost totally ignored by mapmakers and historians.

Maps of Europe would abruptly stop at Poland's eastern border and fade into the pink vastness of an endless Russia or Soviet Union. Sometimes, it seemed someone had come along and airbrushed away any references to Ukraine or Ukrainians from all maps.

How could they ignore a country the size of France with a population of fifty million? It's not as if the maps only had room to note major countries. Tiny Liechtenstein was always squeezed in, even if in abbreviated form. And Monaco, with an area of only a few square kilometers, somehow managed to be listed—a dot on the map with its name floating in the Mediterranean. But there was never room to write "Ukraine."

Though Ukraine had been occupied by various colonial powers for the previous three centuries, the nation still existed, the language survived, Ukrainians maintained a separate identity, and the land hadn't changed.

Historians must have gone through severe contortions to avoid the *U*-word.

The Soviets insisted the Ukrainian SSR should be included as a separate country and a founding member of the United Nations, but they did not necessarily feel the country should be included on maps. Moscow found it inconvenient to have a separate Ukrainian nation at its doorstep since that country would, out of necessity, include Kyiv (Kiev), a city the Russians liked to claim as their own.

The year 1988 marked the one-thousandth anniversary of the acceptance of Christianity in 988 by Prince Volodymyr of Kyiv. In 1987, Moscow, the capital of an officially atheist state, tried to get some mileage on the international scene by mounting a huge campaign proclaiming the "Millennium of Christianity in Russia!" This was dutifully reported in the western press, ignoring the fact that neither Russia nor Moscow even existed in 988. (The first mention of Moscow or Russia in history books is in 1146.)

Winners write history . . . and they spin it to suit their agenda.

During the twentieth century, Ukraine was victimized by a long list of invaders with imperialistic ambitions. The old Austrian and Russian empires, which divided the country between themselves at the start of the century, were replaced by the Poles and Soviets after World War I and later by the Germans, and then the Soviets again. Each of the invaders caused death, destruction, dislocation, and severe misery for the Ukrainian population.

Sprinkled between each of these foreign occupations were brief periods when Ukrainians tried to create an independent state and rule themselves.

The historians of each of the imperialistic powers that invaded Ukraine were able to write their version of events, and each occupier believed that the "occupied" should have been happy and grateful.

It was not necessarily so. Between the euphoric moments of freedom and independence, throughout their history, Ukrainians resisted imperialistic advances at all costs and tried to maintain their separateness in language, religion, and government.

\*    \*    \*

In 1993, half a century after we had left the respective villages of our birth as infants, my wife, Chrystyna, and I had an opportunity to return to Ukraine following its declaration of independence in 1991.

At the time, I was the principal of a large high school in suburban Toronto and was also teaching a summer course at the University of Toronto, preparing aspiring principals for certification. My wife worked as a special education consultant with a local school board. We believed we had something to offer this new democracy.

We managed to connect with a group of educators with similar ideas from the Toronto area who had already made contact with educators in Ukraine. Some of them had been to Ukraine previously and were able to give us advice on what to expect.

For five months before our trip, we brushed up on our Ukrainian, read extensively, and spent hours with my then eighty-one-year-old mother, listening to her stories, trying to visualize what life was like during her childhood, and seeking her help as we translated key parts of the Ontario Principal's Qualification Program and special education documents into Ukrainian. It was exhausting, challenging but satisfying work.

Our first trip to Ukraine was one of the most incredible, most moving experiences of our lives. We were fortunate to find remnants of both our families still living in Ukraine. Each family received us warmly, with excitement, wonder, and tears. They provided us with new information about our past, showed us the places where we were born, and described their lives under communist rule. We were amazed that although we had been separated for fifty years and lived such different lives, we were so similar physically, socially, and emotionally.

After we returned to Canada, we spent hours listening to my mother's stories (much more intently now) and we encouraged her to write down everything. This remarkable woman was in her eighties, but her mind was still sharp as a tack. She remembered dates, names, and situations as clearly as if they happened yesterday. We also reread history books, periodicals, and the articles and letters published by Chrystyna's late father, Oleksander Tatomyr.

There were still so many loose ends. So little had been written about the war years from *our* point of view, and almost nothing had been written about the experiences of displaced persons (DPs) and the immigration of Ukrainians to North America.

Orest Subtelny, a history professor at Toronto's York University, filled in the information gap. In 1988, he published a highly successful and very comprehensive text: *Ukraine: A History*. In preparation for writing this book, I used his book to check my historical data and occasionally to quote him directly.

Another book that I used, *Europe: A History* (1997) by Norman Davies is, in my opinion, the best post-Marxist, post-Revisionist history book about Europe. This book clarified my thinking. I also reread articles and books written in Ukrainian, particularly books about the postwar years. One book, *Regensburg*, published in 1987, contained excellent source material about DP camps. Another book, *The Refugee Experience: Ukrainian Displaced Persons after World War II*, presents a detailed analysis of life in DP camps from the perspective of twenty-five historians, scientists, writers, and community leaders. This book helped me formulate my thoughts.

A few years ago, my brother, Roman, told me about a book by an Israeli professor, Shimon Redlich, who wrote about Berezhany (Brzezany), an important town in eastern Galicia, where he was born in 1935 (I was born in Pidhajci, a town some thirty kilometers away, nine years later.) Redlich had done extensive research, including countless interviews of people from this town, and used their experiences to present a picture of what was happening in the area at the time. I read his book eagerly because he was able to fill in certain pieces of information I did not have, especially the exact dates of events.

Reading Dr. Redlich's book, it was interesting to see how two people who experienced the same event at the same time could interpret the circumstances surrounding the event so differently. Professor Redlich's perspective is that eastern Galicia was always *Poland* and was populated by a large number of Ukrainians as well as Poles and Jews, and that this *Polish* area was at times *governed* by Austria or by the Soviets or the Nazis, and from time to time (briefly) by Ukrainians.

My perspective is that eastern Galicia was always *Ukrainian*. It was occupied by Poland for a number of years and then became part of the Austro-Hungarian Empire in 1772. After World War I, it was *occupied* by the Soviets, Poles, and the Nazis before finally being absorbed into the Soviet Union. Poles, Jews, and Germans lived in this fertile area, most by choice, although others were sent there as colonists by Poland or Germany to tilt the population balance in their favor.

Professor Redlich's reaction to the coming of the Red Army to Galicia in 1944 was that the Bolsheviks had *liberated* the area from the Nazis and that *some* Ukrainians and Poles fled.

Most Ukrainians did not see the coming of the Soviets as liberation. They remembered that just a few years earlier, in 1932-33, Stalin engineered an artificial famine in eastern Ukraine, and millions of their countrymen died. When it became obvious the Soviets would win the war, many Ukrainians fled to the west.

Despite our differing points of view, I highly recommend his book to serious students of the era.

# Place-Names and Transliterations

Invaders and foreign occupiers often change the names of cities, towns, and even streets to establish their "ownership" of the places they've occupied. The city of Lviv in western Ukraine was known as Lemberg before WWI when the Austrians occupied the area, and again from 1941 to 1944 when the Germans occupied it. It was Lwow when the Poles ruled the city between the wars, and Lvov when the Russians were in charge. It is called Lviv again, now that the Ukrainians have reclaimed it. Throughout this book I will use the current (2008) official spelling for all place names in Ukraine.

Thus, I will use *Kyiv* rather than *Kiev*; *Lviv* (Ukrainian) rather than *Lwow* (Polish), *Lvov* (Russian) or *Lemberg* (German); *Chornobyl* rather than *Chernobyl*; *Odesa* rather than *Odessa*; *Ternopil* rather than *Tarnopol*; and *Sambir* rather than *Sambor*. If in a particular case it is confusing to use the current name, I will use the more familiar, older name. Therefore, I will use Galicia rather than the Ukrainian *Halychyna*, except when referring to specific organizations or military units that use that name.

I accept the fact that the decision to use one name over another can be a political statement.

Still, Peking became Beijing and Bombay became Mumbai because China and India, respectively, decided to change the names of their cities. I will use *Kyiv*, *Lviv*, and *Odesa* because that is how the current administration in Ukraine refers to these places.

NOTE: The country I write about is Ukraine, never "the Ukraine." The latter reference has colonial implications that are no longer relevant.

# Author's Note

Oral history is elusive. Family stories are told and retold and sometimes, this may result in discrepancies. The same incident, described by two relatives, often will contain slightly different information and will have a slightly different interpretation. I have done my best to compare family lore with descriptions of events that took place at that point in time by checking history books written by respected historians. Sometimes, different historians saw things differently as well. Passages taken directly from history books are listed in "Sources" near the end of the book. These passages helped put things into context for me. I hope you will find these passages interesting and informative as well.

In most cases, I am confident that my dates are accurate or very close approximations. Events that took place in the distant past (pre-1900) and those that took place in the heat of war are sometimes hazy. At times, I needed to fill in information from other reliable sources, and in a few cases I made a best estimate. I tried my utmost to make this a true account of events. Any inaccuracies are unintentional. Please enjoy the story.

**EUROPE**

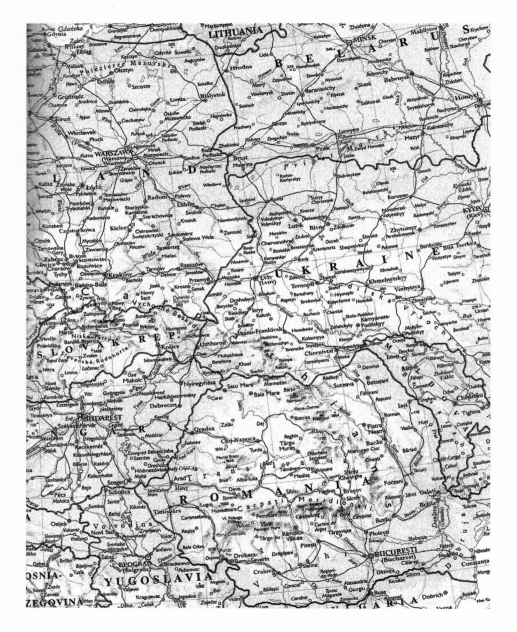

**WESTERN UKRAINE**

# Melnyk and Tatomyr Family Trees

# THE MELNYKS

**1. 1820's** — **IVAN MELNYK**

**2. 1850's** — Ivan Mochulskyj*-Anna Zelynska — Katerina Mochulska*—**MYKHAJLO**
(Maria's parents) — (1850's-1920's)

**3. 1880's** — —Mykhajlo Martyniuk—Justina — **MARIA** Mochulska—**PETER**
(1875-1941) (1882-1969) — (1881-1954) (1881-1944)
(Bronyslawa's Parents)

**4. 1910's** JULIA, EMILIA, ROMAN, JOSEPH, OLGA, EMILIA** — Bronyslawa—**BOHDAN**
(1902-57) (1904-21) (1906-81) (1912-44) (1914-05) *1922 — Martyniuk (1910-1965)
(1912-)

**5. 1940's** IRENE, TAMARA; DARIA, OKSANA; CHRYSTYNA; ROMAN; **ROMAN,** **ANDRIJ**
(Nenych) (Stulkowsky) (Mychalewsky) 1941- 1944-
1927- 1933- 1944- 1947- 1946- 1949- **Tania Boyko**
1944-

**6. 1970's** Myroslaw, Bohdan;
Roxolana, Sonia; Nadia, Alexander; Petro, Urij; **MARICHKA, MELANIA** **MARKIAN**
1973- 1982- 1978- 1981- 1965- 1968- 1970- 1974- 1970-
**John Stetic** **Kristine Chandler**
1974- 1974-

**7. 2000's** Andrij — Nicholas — **WILL KATYA** **ANYA** **AVA**
2006- 2004- 2007- 2004- 2006-

---

* Line 2: Katerina Mochulska, Peter's mother and Ivan Mochulskyj, Maria's father were siblings.

** Line 4: Emilia Melnyk, born in 1922 was named after her sister, Emilia, who died the previous year of tuberculosis.

# THE TATOMYRS

Rev. Nicolaj Pobuch-Nestorowycz

(1792-1842)

**1. REV. EVHEN SAS TATOMYR**          Rev. Olexander Pobuch-Nestorowycz

(1815-1870)                                      (1817-1895)

**2. REV. IVAN SAS TATOMYR**—Karolyna Nestorowycz Rev. Petro Khomytsky

(1842-1925)                                      (1845-1905)

Rev. Martyniak

**3. REV. JULIAN**—Olha Khomytska          Antin Tereshkevych—Rosalia Martyniak

(1883-1946)            (1888-1968)                       (Sophia's parents)

*: Rev Mykkajlo Sas Tatomyr* (Julian's brother)

(1876-1930) (Volodymyr and Evhen's father)

**4. OLEKSANDER**—Sophia Tereshkevych     **JAROSLAV, EVHEN**     Volodymyr Evhen

(1913-1987)            (1915-1983)          (1910-1994)   (1906-1908)

Luba Fedewych

(1910-1989)

**Bishop Ivan Martyniak*** (1939-1993)

**5. CHRYSTYNA,**     OSTAP          LESYA          MARTA

1944-            (1949-2005)      1953-          1943-

Christina Holubinsky   Roman Horodysky    Omelan Lukasewycz

1946-          (1942-2006)

**6. ROMAN**     DANIEL, MELANIE     ANDRIJ, LARYSSA          ANN, STEPHEN

1974-       1982-       1986-        1978-       1981-         1973-       1979-

—Tammy Jones                                                            —Kristi

1974

**7. JULIA**                                                        ANDREW

2007-                                                            2006-

---

*      Line 4: Chrystyna's mother's first cousin, Bishop Ivan Martyniak, became a priest in 1964, and was appointed vicar-general for Ukrainian Catholics in Poland in 1981. In 1989, he was consecrated as the first Ukrainian Catholic bishop in Poland since 1945. In 1991, he was appointed bishop of Ukrainian Catholics in Peremyshl, Poland. He died in 1993 and is buried in the village of Spas, Chrystyna's mother's hometown. Centuries earlier, legendary Prince Lev, for whom the city of Lviv is named, kept his hunting lodge in this picturesque sub-Carpathian village.

# PART ONE

# Grandfather's Time

# Chapter 1

# My Own, My Native Land

*Breathes there the man with soul so dead,*
*who never to himself hath said,*
*"this is my own, my native land";*
*whose heart has ne'er within him burned*
*as home his footsteps he has turned*

—**Sir Walter Scott, 1771-1832**

## PRAGUE, Summer 1993

As we boarded the Czech Air shuttle flight from Prague to Lviv that hot summer afternoon, my wife, Chrystyna and I were overcome with emotions neither of us could contain or verbalize.

Almost half a century had passed since we, as infants, left our respective villages in western Ukraine in 1944. The Red Army was approaching and, without any doubt, the Bolsheviks would have murdered all members of both our families because of their political beliefs and because they were educated professionals.

We had no choice. We had to leave our homeland.

I peered out the window of the plane, looking for some sign that we had crossed into Ukraine. I half expected to see a line defining the border. After all, the iron curtain had stood here just a few years ago. Out of the plane's right side to the south I spotted the foothills of the Carpathian Mountains and somehow knew we had finally entered Ukrainian airspace.

It was just seven years since the horrible nuclear accident at Chornobyl, and for some naive reason, I had expected that the countryside would be scarred, that there would be little vegetation, that all the trees would be defoliated, that the land would be blackened, and that there would be no sign of life. To my surprise, the countryside was green and lush, and we could see tiny villages surrounding domed churches. The fields were almost ready for harvest. I felt a little silly just then, that we had packed dried food, chocolate bars, and even a dozen cans of Coke, just in case there was nothing edible to be found in Ukraine. If necessary, we reasoned, we would be able to survive for three weeks on what we brought.

My wife took my hand. I had slumped back in my seat, and my eyes welled up. We were both having trouble assimilating the reality that after all these years, we were returning to the land of our birth.

We were coming to Lviv, along with six other Canadian teachers, to teach a three-week summer course. Chrystyna and I were scheduled to teach a group of principals and other school administrators from all parts Ukraine. I would give them an overview of North American leadership theory and Chrystyna would give them an overview of special education practices.

As our plane started its approach into Lviv, questions and doubts raced through my head.

My Ukrainian was a little rusty. Even though I spoke Ukrainian with my family members, attended events where Ukrainian was spoken, and occasionally read Ukrainian newspapers, I never really had to speak at the technical level required to teach, especially to teach school administrators.

We were preoccupied with other doubts.

Would the school administrators we would be teaching dismiss us because of our poor grasp of the language? Would they think us presumptuous—coming here to teach *them*? Would they be hostile? Would there be any latent communists among them who would consider us capitalist opportunists? Would any of them consider us traitors because we "escaped" fifty years ago, leaving them behind to face the Bolsheviks? Would we be allowed to travel? Would we be able to visit our birthplaces?

We also wondered whether our parents, in their stories to us as children, had glamorized this country of their youth. Was Lviv as beautiful as my father had described? Were the mountains that much more beautiful than the mountains back home, as he had insisted? Was the land as fertile as they had bragged?

Friends who had traveled to Ukraine in the past came back with some unsettling stories. Many came back depressed, vowing never to return.

But for us, the desire to come here was too great. We gladly gave up our precious summer holidays and spent countless hours preparing our course materials for the opportunity to come here to work—for no pay. We steeled ourselves for the challenge. We were determined that no matter what, we would come out of this with our heads held high.

Some of the passengers cheered and applauded loudly as we touched down, and the plane finally came to a stop just inches, it seemed, from the end of the runway. Alongside the runway, we could see a dozen or more camouflaged military aircraft, rusting in the high, uncut grasses. The terminal appeared much too small for a city of almost a million people.

Three story high Ionic columns supported the roof of the terminal building. They seemed incongruous, but the blue-and-yellow flag of an independent Ukraine fluttered at the highest point. On the side of the terminal building that faced the runway, a large sign read LVOV.

I shook my head, turned to Chrystyna, and let out my frustrations, "It's LVIV, dammit! Haven't they heard this city is now Ukrainian? Why is this sign the first thing one sees upon entering Ukraine, written in Russian? Couldn't someone just get some paint and paint it over?"

"Take it easy," Chrystyna cautioned me, "you're a guest here. Let it go!"

Among the passengers on our flight were many first-time visitors to Ukraine, just like us. As we disembarked onto the tarmac, we congratulated each other and exchanged good wishes for a successful visit. We made it! For a moment I felt I should do the "Pope thing" and kiss the ground, but didn't.

An old man in a tired-looking military uniform approached the plane and stopped us from proceeding to the terminal. After an unusually long delay, considering that ours was the only flight arriving or departing that afternoon, an old rusty bus belching putrid black smoke approached, and we were ushered aboard. We drove no more than twenty meters towards the terminal when the door opened, and we were again ushered off and directed through a narrow door into a much-too-small waiting area.

It was sweltering inside the terminal. The aroma of a backed-up washroom assaulted our nostrils. With our passports and visas in hand, we shuffled through another doorway where another official-looking clerk stopped us. The sign over his head read Customs in Russian and Ukrainian. There were no signs written in English or any other Western language.

I was prepared for a long interrogation and started to rehearse a plausible explanation for the emergency food we had brought. The official took my passport, flipped to the visa, and greeted us in English, "Ah, Kanada! Velcome to Ukraina!"

To our surprise, our luggage had already been delivered to the area beyond the booth and was left in a huge pile in the center of the room.

We picked up our bags and made our way through another waiting room where several hundred people were waiting for friends and relatives. They held signs, flowers and, pictures, and called out names of people they were expecting but perhaps had not seen in decades or, indeed, had never met. We pushed our way outside.

Hundreds of people were milling around the terminal entrance, and a few beat-up Ladas were parked by the door. Otherwise, the parking lot was empty.

This did not resemble any airport we ever had experienced.

Finally, we spotted a familiar face: a Canadian teacher who had arrived a few days earlier was waiting to take us to our hotel. Several local school board officials accompanied her. They welcomed us with flowers and kisses on both cheeks and thanked us profusely for coming. They spoke Ukrainian with the same accent as our parents. (What did I expect?) They were warm, friendly, and polite, almost to a fault. They could not have been more welcoming.

We packed into the Ladas and drove past endless stretches of shabby, identical, and unimaginative Soviet-style apartment buildings. So far, Lviv was not very impressive and a bit of a disappointment. Finally, we stopped in front of a four-story building set back from the street a little more than the rest of the buildings. This unmarked building, our hotel, would be our home for the next three weeks.

As we walked in, an attendant handed us our room keys. We had already been pre-registered. Our bags were taken, and before we could unpack or even see our rooms, we were steered into a large dining room. The walls were decorated with Ukrainian embroidery, and the long wooden tables groaned with hot food, vodka, and champagne. We were treated to a hearty Ukrainian feast, and after the meal, there were speeches and lengthy toasts, and then the music started to play and the dancing began. We were definitely made to feel at home.

*    *    *

The "hotel" selected by the local board of education was an old Soviet-era hostel originally designed for visiting communist youth. Young, up-and-coming communist leaders, the *Komsomol Youth* could stay here free of charge when they were in Lviv. The somewhat spartan rooms were reached by a tiny rickety elevator. Each room had two heavy wooden single beds and a bathroom. The bathroom was actually just a small enclosure, perhaps one square meter, with a commode, a sink, and a shower all in one. It took us a while to figure out how to take a shower. But at least everything worked, more or less.

Because of the water shortage in Lviv, water was only available for a few hours in the morning and two or three hours at night. It was important to schedule bathroom stops well in advance.

We only had a few days before our course started, and there was so much we wanted to do. We were scheduled to travel to Odesa for a two-day meeting with officials in that city, we had to visit the school where we would be teaching the following week, and we wanted to try to find the villages of our birth.

But first we had to call home to tell our sons we were OK.

The desk clerk would only speak Russian to us even though I strongly insisted that she try to speak to me in Ukrainian in this Ukrainian city. She understood everything I said to her but answered only in Russian. She informed us that if we wanted to call outside the city, we would have to go to the main post office downtown.

We spotted a taxi parked outside our hotel. We approached the driver and asked him to drive us to the post office. To our delight, the driver was a personable young man who spoke Ukrainian. He could see we weren't locals and wondered what we Westerners were doing staying in this "communist" hotel instead of in a comfortable hotel downtown.

He introduced himself as Victor and talked with pride about his city, told us about his family and how hard it was to make a living. He said that he desperately wanted to come to Canada and offered to be our guide for the duration of our stay in Ukraine.

The trip into town lasted twenty minutes. The meter was running and had reached an amazing sum of $62.50. I was preparing to negotiate aggressively when he said, "Don't worry about that, I have to have the meter running in case I'm stopped. If you give me one American dollar, it will be enough." I paid him and asked him to wait.

The main post office was a huge imposing building. Inside, a crowd of people mingled and waited in long lines. Handwritten cardboard signs in Ukrainian covered the elaborately engraved Russian signs. A blue-and-yellow flag hung from the ceiling. Almost everyone spoke Ukrainian. We got into a line that appeared to lead to a phone. Just then, Victor, our driver, appeared and ushered us into another shorter line, the line for overseas calls. With incredible difficulty, and after a very long delay, we connected with our sons and explained to them that it might be difficult to call often. "Tell everyone we're fine!"

Victor gave us a brief tour of the old town, but jet lag was starting to affect us. We asked him to take us back to the hotel.

I liked this young man and asked him how much he would charge to take us to Sambir and to stay with us for a full day.

He said, "For forty American dollars, I'll take you anywhere you like."

That, I thought, was a bargain.

We arranged to have him pick us up at the hotel at seven the next morning. We needed some sleep.

## SAMBIR

We wanted to visit our respective birthplaces. I was born in Pidhajci, southeast of Lviv, and Chrystyna was born (we thought) in Starij Sambir, a suburb (we thought) of the major city of Sambir, southwest of Lviv. We decided to try to find Chrystyna's birthplace first.

The next morning at seven, Victor was waiting.

We set off through the same suburban Lviv streets, past block after block of the same dull Soviet-era apartment buildings we had seen the day before. Before long we found ourselves on the outskirts of the city on our way to Sambir. The roads were narrow but not in as bad a condition as we had expected, and car traffic was light.

We passed a dozen or more villages with neat, freshly painted houses, all with flower gardens in their front yards. It seemed that almost every village had a major construction project in progress: new churches, municipal buildings, and schools were being built. We were impressed.

After about an hour, we came to an intersection with a sign written in Ukrainian, Russian, and English: "Sambir . . . Sambor." We told Victor that we really wanted to go to Chrystyna's birthplace, Starij Sambir (Old Sambir), which was just a few kilometers southwest of Sambir.

Victor mentioned that Starij Sambir was in the "closed zone" and that until recently, outsiders could not enter the area. He took a sharp left turn just before the next major intersection, and thus avoided a long delay at what appeared to be an inspection post just ahead. He seemed to know where he was going. We traveled south for a few kilometers, and then just outside the town of Starij Sambir we came to our first checkpoint.

I was puzzled and mockingly asked Victor what was happening.

"Why are there so many checkpoints?"

Victor explained we were now very close to the border with Poland, and the police were looking for smugglers.

A young man in the uniform of the border militia waved us over to the side of the road. He asked for Victor's "papers," but his eyes were on Chrystyna and me. Even though we tried to dress like the locals, we really did not blend in very well, and we knew it. It was obvious we were Westerners. The guard came over to us and gruffly asked for our travel papers.

We had none. We had left our passports in the hotel as this was supposed to be a short ride in the country. We never expected anyone would want to check our identities.

Chrystyna decided to get involved. She stepped out of the car, put her hand on the young soldier's shoulder, and started to tell him in detail that she was looking for the village where she was born, that we were from Canada, that this was just a day trip and so on and so on.

The soldier told us to wait as he went back to confer with an older guard. A few minutes later, he returned and politely told us we were free to go on. He returned the papers to Victor. We were on our way.

Before reaching Starij Sambir, we passed a long, high, stone wall on the left side of the road. It seemed to stretch for several kilometers. We couldn't see over the wall, but Victor informed us this was once a secret Soviet Army base. A little further down the road we passed an airfield. In the distance, we could see a number of military jets parked on the runway. We understood why this was a closed zone during Soviet times.

A small sign by the road indicated that we were within Starij Sambir's town limits. I asked Victor to take us to the church in town because we wanted to see if we could find a record of Chrystyna's birth.

He glanced at me, gave a funny look, then smiled and drove on.

When we finally reached Starij Sambir, our hearts sank. This was not a small village. This was a town with a population of perhaps thirty thousand people, the provincial capital. This is not what we had expected.

A few minutes later, we arrived at the town's main square.

The most prominent building on the square, slightly raised on a hill, was a large impressive Gothic-style church.

"This certainly is not a Ukrainian church," I thought. "It looks like a Polish *kostel*—on the best site in town of course. Let's move on."

Our spirits rose as we came to the next block. A domed church, obviously Ukrainian in style, was just ahead. As we approached the church and read the sign, we found it was a Ukrainian Orthodox church.

We stopped a passerby and asked where the Ukrainian Catholic church was located.

"Which one?" the man asked. "There are several in this town."

Frustrated, Chrystyna and I sat on a bench by the church.

"We don't have enough information. We'll never find your church."

But Chrystyna was disappointed and upset for another reason. "My mother told me I was born in the foothills of the Carpathian Mountains. I don't see any mountains here."

Chrystyna pulled out a faded envelope containing a letter from a woman named Oksana with whom Chrystyna's father corresponded until his death five years earlier. We weren't sure who this woman was, but we knew she was related to Chrystyna's mother and that she had nine children.

Victor came over, looked at the envelope, and found the faded postmark: "Selo Tershiv."

"It's a village about twenty kilometers south of here. That letter was mailed from Tershiv. I can take you there," Victor said.

Tershiv didn't sound at all familiar to Chrystyna from the stories she heard as a child. How she wished her parents were alive today. She would have simply called them and asked for directions.

\*     \*     \*

A half hour further south on a narrow unmarked two-lane highway, the foothills of the Carpathians appeared, and in the distance we could make out the peaks of the higher mountains, perhaps another hour's drive away.

"This is more like it," said Chrystyna.

We were getting very excited. The road turned slightly to the right as we approached a small bridge. The sign read Dnister River. Just beyond the bridge, a sign read *Selo Tershiv*, the village of Tershiv.

We spotted an old man walking on the side of the road.

I asked Victor to stop the car. "It's more likely an old man would know someone named Oksana who had nine children. Surely there would only be one such woman in this small village."

The old man was startled as we pulled up. I rolled down the window.

"Slava Isusu Khrystu [glory to Jesus Christ]. Do you know someone named Oksana who has nine children?"

"Of course I know her. She lives just down the road."

I asked the man to get into the car and to take us to her house. He was glad to help us. "Just go left at the church and take a left down the narrow lane."

A small herd of cows blocked the road. We waited patiently as children gathered around our car. I guessed they didn't have too many visitors here, and we were quite a novelty. Finally, we stopped in front of a small gate and stepped out of the car.

A woman appeared at the door of a very humble cottage. The old man yelled out, "Oksana, you have visitors from Canada."

Oksana, who was Chrystyna's niece, once or twice removed, looked older than her forty-eight years.

As we stepped out of the car, Oksana yelled, "Chrystyna, it must be you. You look so much like your mother, God rest her soul."

There were children everywhere, some were hers, and some had just drifted in from the neighborhood. Oksana invited us into her humble home. Within minutes, a feast was on the table and we were invited to eat.

Chrystyna and Oksana were hugging and crying and telling each other stories. The house began to fill with more and more people, each introducing themselves and explaining how they were related to Chrystyna.

The family tree that Chrystyna's father had prepared for us before he died was much too complex to remember. We didn't really know who these people were and how they were related to Chrystyna.

Oksana was the only person with whom Chrystyna's father corresponded. When he left in 1944 with his wife and baby daughter, he was a wanted man. The Bolshevik secret police, who had already infiltrated the town several weeks before the Red Army came to the area, knew of his anti-Russian views and his membership in the partisan underground. He would have been among the first to be arrested and shot. For forty years, he still feared that members of his family would be found and persecuted, especially during the repressive Khrushchev era. He sent Oksana ten or twenty dollars and care packages from time to time, hoping she would receive them and share the contents with unnamed family members.

The village grapevine was working overtime. Within a half hour of our arrival, there were more than twenty people in the house and yard. An old woman walked through the door, crossed herself and whispered, "Guests from Canada, praise God."

The woman introduced herself as Maria, Chrystyna's first cousin. She was only ten years older than Chrystyna but when she stood beside her, Maria looked as if she could have been Chrystyna's grandmother. The house filled with more people, each explaining their relationship to Chrystyna. They knew so much about us. How careless and arrogant of us to know nothing about them. The stories they told about the days after the war made our heads spin.

During the conversation, Chrystyna learned that in spite of what was written on her birth certificate, she had not been born in Starij Sambir. In the turmoil surrounding her birth, it was simpler to register her as being born in the provincial capital, and perhaps this was just another way to further hide her father's whereabouts. In fact, she was born in a small village named Topilnicia, a few kilometers south of this village.

"That was where your father was a teacher," explained Maria. "I'll take you there if you like."

"Yes, absolutely." said Chrystyna. Chrystyna also told her we wanted to see her grandfather's church, if it was still standing, and her mother's village and anything else that pertained to our family.

"Today, I'll take you to the church and then to your mother's village. That should be enough for one day," Maria replied.

Maria, Oksana, Chrystyna, and I got into Victor's car and drove south along the road that ran parallel to the Dnister River. We were very close to the source of the Dnister, and here the river was only a few meters wide.

I felt a little guilty that we had an agreement with Victor to take us only to Sambir. We had already gone a long way further, but Victor seemed to take it all in stride, as if he had expected this all along. Perhaps a kilometer further down the road, we crossed another bridge.

"This is the Dnister River, and on your right is Spas, your mother's village." Maria informed us. "Your mother's nephew, your cousin, still lives in the house. This is where your mother was born. We'll stop there on the way back."

We were well into the foothills of the lush Carpathian Mountains. Chrystyna remembered her mother's stories about how their house stood near a small river at the bottom of a hill. Often her mother would climb this hill with her brothers and sisters. She had described it so exactly that Chrystyna felt she was watching a movie.

We had come with such low expectations. This was already well beyond our wildest hopes.

The road followed the Dnister River upstream for about two kilometers until we came to another village, Luzhok. This sounded familiar to Chrystyna as she remembered that name from her father's stories. This is where her grandfather had been the parish priest on and off for twenty-three years.

Grandfather Julian Tatomyr's beautifully restored church stood at the center of the village.

"We'll go up to the priest's house to get the key," said Maria. "Driver, pull over at that lane."

Maria, Oksana, and Chrystyna started up the hill to the priest's house as I gathered my camera and searched my knapsack for some gift we could bring the priest. I stopped to admire the scenery and took a few pictures of the mountains.

Just then, a car pulled up behind us and a uniformed militia man stepped out. He gruffly demanded Victor's travel papers. He then came towards me and demanded I give him my camera.

"This is a restricted area. No pictures are allowed!" he snarled.

I had no intention of giving up my camera. "What are you talking about?" I yelled at him, forgetting I wasn't in Canada where this type of demand by a policeman would not be tolerated.

"Haven't you heard the Soviet Union is dead, that this is now a democracy?"

I glanced over at Victor. He looked worried.

Seeing I was not intimidated by him, and obviously an "outsider," the militia man turned to Victor and ordered him to surrender his papers and car keys.

I felt terrible. I had really gotten this poor man into a mess. And how would we get back to Lviv if we had no car?

At that very moment, out of the corner of my eye, I saw Oksana and Maria running across the road toward us. They descended on the militia man. They yelled at him, threatened him with their purses, and shoved him against his car.

"Uh-oh, what have I started," I thought. "Yelling at a cop is one thing, but attacking him is quite another. We're in big trouble now."

To my surprise, the militia man lost all his bravado, took off his hat, apologized to the women, returned Victor's papers, got into his car and drove off.

"He still thinks we're in the 1950s," explained Maria. "Don't worry about him."

I was still a little shaken as we walked up the hill to the priest's house, but I was so proud of these women. Some people were still intimidated by policemen, but these women, perhaps because they had nothing to lose and knew they would have nothing to gain from being nice to government bureaucrats, or perhaps because women generally are treated with such regard here, paid little attention to pompous authority figures.

We walked slowly up the hill, past an orchard in full bloom, a carefully planted vegetable garden, and lovely flowers planted along the path. As we passed the edge of the orchard, we spotted a large well-kept house built on the brow of the hill. As we approached the house, Chrystyna stopped and sat down on a tree stump at the side of the road.

"I have a picture of my father standing by that house, holding me in his arms. It must have been taken when I was just a few months old," she whispered. Tears were streaming down her face.

After a few minutes, Chrystyna composed herself, and we walked up to the main house and knocked on the door. A young man answered.

"Slava Isusu Khrystu," she said. "My name is Chrystyna Tatomyr-Melnyk. My grandfather was the parish priest here before the war."

The young man, wearing a clerical collar but casually dressed, was visibly surprised. "This is a miracle! Please, come in. I have pictures of your grandfather."

We spent the next two hours looking at books and listening to the priest's stories about the old days, with Maria filling in the details. I observed this and said little. Chrystyna looked so young and beautiful sitting in the priest's living room, the sun shining brightly through the windows.

"This was your grandfather's house," he explained. "He came from a family of priests that went back many generations. His property once stretched down the valley, across the river, and halfway up the mountain on the other side. If you look carefully, you can see the Sokil Rock.

"It stands at the edge of his former property. It was a famous meeting place for the partisans who first fought against the Poles, then against the Russians, then against the

German invaders, and then for many years after the end of World War II, against the Russians again. The partisans were finally wiped out by the Soviets in the early fifties, and we've waited all these years for independence. Your grandfather and your father were great leaders during our most difficult times."

*     *     *

The young priest then took us to the church. The grounds were tidy, the flowers were planted neatly along the walk, and the wood trim was freshly painted. Inside, newly embroidered traditional linens covered the altar and side tables. The walls were painted with traditional religious scenes, and a beautifully carved wooden *iconostas** covered with freshly painted icons stood at the front of the church. Several old icons hung in front of the altar, and all the wood trim was freshly gilded.

"How did you manage to decorate the church so beautifully in such a short time, and where did all the old icons come from?" I asked the priest.

Slowly, and with some emotion, the priest explained, "When the Bolsheviks came during the forties to destroy the churches, the villagers all gathered to protect them. The icons and all the sacred items were distributed among the trusted parishioners, who hid them in their homes or buried them in their gardens. They took it upon themselves to safeguard all the precious items at great risk to themselves. When the bandits came, they tried to burn the church, or at least to destroy the roof so that the church could not be used by the villagers. But the parishioners, carrying pitchforks, circled the church and wouldn't allow the Bolsheviks to destroy their sacred place.

"The priest was arrested and sent off to Siberia. We never heard from him again. The church was locked for more than thirty years, but when things got better in 1990, we reopened the church. One by one, the villagers brought back all the sacred articles they had kept hidden all these years, and everyone helped restore the church. It was the first building to be restored. For thirty years while the church was closed, mass was celebrated secretly in people's homes—never in the same one twice in succession. We kept the faith. We knew someday this church would reopen."

It was getting late. Before we left, the priest told us he would celebrate a Mass the following Sunday in honor of Chrystyna and her grandfather.

We promised to return.

On our way back to Oksana's house, we stopped in the village of Spas, Chrystyna's mother's home village. This village was also famous because several centuries before, this was where Prince Danylo, a beloved thirteenth-century ruler of this area, had a hunting lodge on top of this mountain.

Victor parked his car just behind the little chapel by the river in Spas, next to the cemetery. Many members of Chrystyna's family were buried there, including her

---

*    *Iconostas*: a screen separating the altar area from the congregation.

mother's first cousin, Bishop Martyniak, who had died recently. Bishop Ivan Martyniak (1939-1993) was the bishop of the Ukrainian eparchy in Peremyshl, Poland, and until recently, served the needs of Ukrainians in this part of western Ukraine. They took us to the small cemetery beside the little church by the river. Carved into tombstones were several familiar names like Tereshkevych and Martyniak and others Chrystyna recognized from stories she heard as a child.

When we arrived at the house where Chrystyna's mother was born and lived her early life, we were greeted by Chrystyna's cousin, Osyp. He invited us into his tidy little house. Food was on the table, and the children in their best clothes were lined up to meet us.

The house was just as Chrystyna's mother had described it: the river and the hill were just meters from the garden.

We tried to reconstruct what happened that summer in 1944 just before grandfather Julian, his two sons and their families, including babies Chrystyna and her cousin Marta and his nephew Volodymyr left for the safety of the West.

"Why did some people leave and some stay behind?" we wondered.

"What happened to those who stayed?"

We went back to Oksana's house, where more people had gathered to see the visitors from Canada.

An hour or so later, a well-dressed man in his mid forties entered the room. He walked up to me, introduced himself as Ivanko Luts, and asked me to step outside. It seemed a little dramatic, but I did what he asked. He pointed to the car where our driver, Victor, sat patiently reading a newspaper.

"Who is that man?" he whispered.

"He's a taxi driver we hired in Lviv," I answered. "Why do you ask?"

"How did you meet him? How did he contact you?"

"He's a taxi driver," I repeated. "We hired him outside our hotel."

Ivanko became very serious. "He's with the secret police. You must get rid of him right away!"

This sounded like something out of a spy novel. Was he paranoid or was I naive?

He pointed to his sleek new Audi parked behind Victor's old Lada and told me he would drive us back to Lviv.

Now *I* was getting paranoid. The day's events flashed through my mind.

Were we unusually lucky on our first day in the country to find such a personable, cooperative young guide who knew his way around the Closed Zone, who charged us only forty dollars for the whole day with the price of gas being what it was here? And how did we get through that checkpoint so easily? Did Chrystyna really charm the young guard? And who was this Ivanko? Maybe *he* was with the secret service!

Maria came outside, explained that Ivanko was her son, that he was a doctor in Lviv, and that she had telephoned him as soon as we arrived in the village.

"Send your driver away," she urged.

Nobody could have faked all of this. I paid Victor, thanked him, and said we wouldn't need him any longer. He shrugged, started his car, and drove off. Ivanko watched the car disappear down the highway and finally relaxed. He hugged me and kissed me on each cheek. He walked up to Chrystyna, crossed himself, took her hand gently as if afraid she would shatter like a piece of crystal, and kissed it.

After many hours and many stories, tears and toasts (although I noticed that Ivanko drank only water), things started to become more clear. Maria did most of the talking. She told us about Chrystyna's mother and about her father, their passionate views about a free Ukraine; about her grandfather, Julian Tatomyr, the parish priest, and how he was loved and respected; about those terrible days when the Nazis came, burning homes, murdering people in cold blood; and how the dreaded Russian army arrived just days after Chrystyna and her family had escaped. She spoke sadly about the forty years that followed—the deaths, the persecutions, and the deportations of family members to Siberia.

Slowly, slowly, things began to come into focus.

It was well past midnight. We were all exhausted and emotionally drained.

Maria stood in the center of the room and demanded everyone's attention. "Chrystyna, I will never forget that awful day when you left. It was July 25, 1944. That day, your grandfather said his final mass in his church. We hitched the wagons and helped load your belongings. All the villagers came to say good-bye and gave you what little food they could spare. We could not decide whether we should stay or go with you."

Her voice was trembling.

With tears in her eyes, she said, "Chrystyna, you were just six months old. I was your babysitter. I was the one who placed you in the wagon."

$$*\qquad*\qquad*$$

It was well past midnight when I got into the back seat of Ivanko's Audi. We had to get back to Lviv. In the morning we had to report to our school and then in the evening catch the train to Odesa.

Ivan threw the Audi into gear and raced toward Lviv, periodically checking to see if anyone was following us.

# Chapter 2

# *The Melnyks of Ternopil*

## Galicia / Halychyna*

In 1991, the Soviet Union crumbled and a new country, Ukraine, started to appear on world maps.

Ukraine, as it appears today, represents almost all the Eastern European lands where Ukrainians live and where Ukrainian is spoken.

Before the Soviet Union incorporated all the present day lands into the Ukrainian SSR after World War II, the borders shifted back and forth from year to year, or even week to week, as various occupying armies fought over this fertile and strategically located territory.

The capital, Kyiv, was first settled in the 5th century and during the 10th, 11th and 12th centuries was the center of a powerful kingdom; Kyivan Rus. Invasions by the Mongols in the 13th century and later by the Russians, Poles, Lithuanians and Tartars left the territory under foreign control for the next four centuries.

During the 1640's a powerful army of Cossacks, led by Bohdan Khmelnytsky, marched from their fortresses along the Dnipro River and conquered most of the northern half of present-day Ukraine, pushing the Polish armies right up to

---

\*    Halychyna: According to the *Primary Chronicle*,Prince Volodymyr of Kyiv first conquered this area in 981. His descendants, specifically descendants of Jaroslav the Wise, ruled this area for four hundred years. Galicia/Halychyna was located directly along the international trade route that connected Kyiv with Poland, Bohemia, and the rest of central Europe. This territory was also valuable because near the city of Halych (located perhaps 100 km south of Lviv) salt mines were located. Salt, as a preservative, was one of the most valuable commodities in medieval times, and the subsequent salt trade transformed Halych into a leading city. Some scholars have argued that the very name Halych is derived from the Indo-European word for salt, *hal*. Galicia, the Latin name derived from Halychyna, could be considered the "land of salt."

the gates of Warsaw. In 1650 Khmelnytsky marched triumphantly into Kyiv as 'Hetman'—Head of the new Ukrainian state. Ukrainian national identity was rekindled. Pressures from all sides, however, gradually deteriorated the territorial holdings of Khmelnytsky's Cossack Hetmanate. Within a few years he was forced to concede the western portion of his territory to the Poles and in 1709, at the Battle of Poltava, his successor, Hetman Mazepa, who had allied himself with the Swedish king, lost a crucial battle against the armies of Muscovy. Kyiv and the surrounding lands fell under Russian control.6

When Poland was first partitioned in 1772, the Austrian province of Galicia was created. The area of land that lies north and east of the Carpathian Mountain range and west of the Zbruch River became part of Austria.

The western half of Galicia (most of present-day southern Poland) was inhabited mostly by Poles, although a substantial number of Ukrainians lived in the southeastern Lemko region. In the eastern half of Galicia, Ukrainians were in the majority, although they were in the minority in larger cities and towns like Lviv, Ternopil, and Sambir, where Poles and Jews outnumbered Ukrainians.

Lviv, named for the medieval Kyivan prince Lev, was populated by Poles, Ukrainians, Jews, Germans, Russians, Armenians, and others. At the turn of the last century, Poles were in the majority in that city. Poles considered "Lwow" their eastern city, part of greater Poland.

Ukrainians considered Lviv their western capital. Friction between Poles and Ukrainians was constant and significant.

Poles held a strategic advantage in their relationship with Ukrainians in Galicia because, since the middle of the nineteenth century, the emperors in Vienna consistently appointed Polish aristocrats as governors of their easternmost province.

> In general the Poles treated Ukrainians poorly. Ukrainian institutions were banned, Ukrainian language schools and use of the Ukrainian language was discouraged and Ukrainians were kept out of important government positions. Only the Ukrainian Uniate Church (now called the Ukrainian Catholic Church) avoided persecution as it was under the special protection of the Austrian emperor.
>
> Polonization was government policy during the 19th century and continued with even greater enthusiasm in the interwar years (1922-1939) when Poland again controlled eastern Galicia. 6

The Austrians knew when they created this new province back in the eighteenth century that it was composed of two distinct peoples with two distinct languages, two distinct alphabets, and two distinct religions.

How different might the history of this area have been had the emperor decided to divide this area into two provinces, one with a Polish majority and another with a Ukrainian majority, with two separate administrations?

Undoubtedly, the existing arrangement suited the Austrians and was part of a shrewd, deliberate plan on the part of the emperor. His logic was that internal tensions between Ukrainians and Poles would prevent either group from challenging the authority of Vienna. Since the Austro-Hungarian Empire consisted of a dozen or so distinct ethnic groups, it was in Vienna's interest that "all nationalities be kept in a balanced state of mild discontent."

So it was in Galicia.

For centuries, Ukrainians in Galicia were separated by the Zbruch River from their Ukrainian speaking brothers and sisters in the Russian empire to the east. Despite the tensions that existed between Poles and Ukrainians, Ukrainians generally fared much better in the Austrian empire than did Ukrainians in the Russian empire. On the eastern side of the Zbruch, 'Russification' was in full force. During the Stalin era, repression against Ukrainians was severe. In the 1930s an artificial famine initiated by Stalin led to the death of millions in eastern Ukraine. 6

# THE MELNYKS OF TERNOPIL

*My great-great grandfather:*

**IVAN MELNYK**
**(1820s-1880s)**

*My great-grandparents:*

**MYKHAJLO MELNYK—KATHERINA Mochulska**
**(1850s-1900s)**

*My grandparents:*

**PETER (PETRO) MELNYK—MARIA Mochulska**
**(1881-1944)              (1881-1963)**

*My parents:*

**BOHDAN MELNYK—BRONYSLAWA Martyniuk**
**(1910-1965)              (1912- )**

*My aunts and uncles:*

| | |
|---|---|
| Julia | 1902, married name, Nenych |
| Emilia | 1904-1921 died of tuberculosis |
| Roman | 1906-1981 married ~1929, ordained ~1930 |
| Joseph | 1914-1944, married Bronyslava ~1940, both killed, 1944 |
| Olga | 1914-, married Dmytro Stulkowky (1916-1996), living in Philadelphia |
| Emilia | 1922-2005, married Nicholas Mychalewsky (1907-1977). |

My grandfather's grandfather, **Ivan Melnyk**, built a mill on a small river in the village of Varvarenci in eastern Galicia sometime during the 1850s. The surname *Melnyk* means *miller*. We're not sure whether Ivan was called *Melnyk* because of his chosen trade or if he decided he might as well become a miller since his name was already *Melnyk*.

Ivan's father may have also been a miller but, since Ivan was not the oldest son, he would not have inherited the family mill. Ivan practiced the trade, and, perhaps with a little help from his father, set off to build his own mill on the river that runs through the small village just a few kilometers south of the provincial capital, Ternopil.

The small river, named Svyntukha, almost always had a good flow as it meandered through the rich farmlands of Galicia. Eventually, the Svyntukha empties into the Seret River and, further south, the two rivers join the Zbruch River, which flows into the Dnister River. The Dnister starts as a small spring in the Carpathian Mountains near the Slovak border, flows north through Starij Sambir, through Sambir, then curves south, gathers strength, joins with several other smaller rivers, and eventually reaches its full and mighty two-kilometer width when it empties into the Black Sea, just west of Odesa.

Ivan dammed the river with huge squared logs from a nearby forest, carefully quarried the heavy millwheels, and practiced his trade. He was personable and outgoing, worked hard and delivered the flour on time. Peasants from nearby villages brought their wheat to his mill because they trusted him and because they appreciated his high quality product.

The business prospered. Eventually, Ivan passed the mill to his oldest son, my great-grandfather, **Mykhajlo** (Michael).

Mykhajlo married a local girl, **Katherina** Mochulska. They moved into the house adjoining the mill and started a family. Katherina's older brother, Osyp Mochulsky, married Anna Zilinsky from a neighboring village, and the young couple moved into a house next door to Mykhajlo and Katherina. The two couples were close friends and eventually, Osyp started to work in Mykhajlo's mill.

Mykhajlo and Katherina, had five children, all boys.
Their third son, **my grandfather, Peter** (Petro), **was born in 1881.**
Within a few weeks, Osyp and Anna also had their first child, **Maria**. Peter and Maria grew up together, played together, and went to school together. They were best friends.

# PETER AND MARIA

Because the families were reasonably well-off, Peter and Maria were able to stay in school longer than some of the other children from the village. They both completed grade 4 at the local school, and one or both may have continued their education at the gymnasia in Ternopil for a year or more, although neither completed their *matura* (Grade 12 graduation).

Peter stayed in the village and worked with his father at the mill. He also continued his close friendship with Maria. Not long after their twentieth birthday, in 1901, Peter and Maria were married.

In the spring of 1902, Maria gave birth to a healthy baby girl, **Julia.**

Peter, Maria, and the baby moved into Grandfather Michael's comfortable house by the mill. Grandmother Katherina would help care for the baby, and Peter continued to work with his father and older brother at the mill.

In 1904, Maria gave birth to their second daughter, **Emilia.**

In 1906, Maria gave birth to their first son, **Roman.**\*

Although Peter was able to support his family by working at the family mill with his brother, he knew that with the income he was receiving, he would never have enough money to buy his own mill.

At that time, in the nearby village of Ladychyn, about four kilometers upstream from Varvarenci, a Polish merchant was building a mill on the same Svyntukha River. The Polish merchant's intention to build a large modern mill intrigued Peter and because there was a need for at least one more mill in the area, the building of a new mill was not considered a major threat to the Melnyk mill in Varvarenci.

Peter contacted the merchant, and because he was an experienced miller, he easily convinced him that he should be hired to help build the mill.

Peter worked two jobs. He would ride his father's horse to Ladychyn every morning, put in a full day's work building the new mill, and then would return at night to help his brothers at the Melnyk family mill in Varvarenci.

The arrangement worked well, and Peter slowly started to accumulate some money. As work progressed on the new mill in Ladychyn, and the owner saw that Peter was trustworthy and competent, he placed Peter in charge of the project.

Peter and the merchant got along well, and Peter joked that he would one day like to own that mill. The owner promised that if Peter had the money, he would sell the mill to him. Peter saved his money but realized that, even working at two jobs, it would take him a lifetime to save enough for the asking price.

On April 8, 1910, in the family mill in Varvarenci, my grandmother Maria gave birth to their second son, **my father, Bohdan.**

---

\* A note about Romans: My uncle, Roman, born in 1906, is the first of many Romans to enter the family. My parents named my older brother Roman when he was born in 1941, and my father's sister, Emilia (Lucia) Mychalewsky, named her son Roman. In 1974, my wife, Chrystyna, gave birth to our second son. We named him Roman. He has five Uncle Romans: Roman Melnyk of Toronto, Roman Mychalewsky of Philadelphia, Roman Horodysky of New Jersey (married to Chrystyna's sister, Lesya), Roman Lukasewycz of Philadelphia, and Roman Perih of Colorado (+2006). There are also a lot of Ivans in our two families.

Grandfather Peter announced that his first son, Roman, would become a priest and his second son, Bohdan, would take over the mill in Ladychyn—the mill that Peter, now more than ever, was determined to own.

Two years later, in 1912, Peter and Maria's third son, my uncle, **Joseph**, was born. On March 5, 1914, their sixth child, **Olga**, was born.

A year later, when Maria announced she was again pregnant, Peter decided he had to do something significant to improve their economic situation.

Shortly after Olga's birth, my grandfather, Peter, made a decision that would dramatically change his life and the lives of all the members of his family. He decided that the only way he would ever improve his lot significantly was to go to America to get a job and earn some money.

In May 1914, Peter said good-bye to Maria and his children and set off for Lviv to book passage to New York.

\* \* \*

Three months later, in another part of the Austrian Empire, in the town of Sarajevo, a Serbian nationalist, unhappy with the Empire, assassinated Archduke Ferdinand of Austria and started a chain of events that dramatically changed Europe, and the world, forever.

**My grandparents, Maria and Peter Melnyk by their Mill, Ladychyn, c.1935**

# Chapter 3

# *The Tatomyrs of Sambir*

## Union of Brest—A Short History of Religions in Ukraine

In 988, Prince Volodymyr of Kyiv, urged on by his grandmother, Olha accepted Orthodox Christianity from Byzantium (Constantinople) on behalf of his realm. Until that time, Volodymyr was a heathen, but politics dictated that he accept some form of religion.

He was christened, and then he ordered his people to the banks of the Dnipro River, where they were baptized en masse.

Volodymyr's church would use the Old Slavonic liturgy along with the Cyrillic alphabet and accept the preeminence of the Patriarch of Constantinople. The Orthodox religion, with its unique liturgy, spread northward into present day Russia and Byelorussia. It differentiated these Slavs from the Poles, and Lithuanians to the west, who accepted Roman Catholicism at about the same time.

During the sixteenth century, much of Europe was preoccupied with religious wars between Catholics and Protestants. The Vatican, under Pope Gregory, tried to convince Eastern Europeans to join the Roman Catholic Church.

In the meantime, in 1589, Ivan the Terrible's son, Fedor, founded the Moscow Patriarchate of the Orthodox Church, creating the Russian Orthodox Church and claimed jurisdiction over all Orthodox churches. Fedor also laid claims on the Kyivan heritage.

In Ukraine, bishops and priests had always looked to the Patriarch of Constantinople for spiritual leadership, and those not wanting to accept the Patriarch of Moscow as their leader now sought the protection of Rome. In 1596, at the Union of Brest, most of the Orthodox churches in western Ukraine and Byelorussia and churches from as far east as Kyiv, created the Uniate, Greek Catholic Church of Slavic rite. They retained their church rituals and their married clergy, while accepting the supremacy of the pope.

Moscow never accepted these developments and maintained a furious determination to punish and forcibly reconvert the Uniates.

Poland, on the other hand, tried to convert the Uniates to Roman Catholicism feeling that it could then more quickly assimilate the Ukrainians under its control.

A constant irritant among the Poles was that Ukrainian Uniate clergy retained the right to marry. Another was that the Uniates refused to accept the new Gregorian calendar, (adopted in 1582), wishing instead to retain the old Julian calendar to determine ecclesiastical holidays.

Today, the vast majority of Ukrainians are either Orthodox or Byzantine Catholics. Conversion attempts by Rome and Moscow continue, but Ukrainians continue to resist these moves and instead are making plans to unite the Ukrainian Orthodox and Catholic churches in Ukraine into one Ukrainian Church with one patriarch in Kyiv.

## THE TATOMYRS OF SAMBIR

*Chrystyna's great-great grandfather:*
### REV. EVHEN SAS TATOMYR
(1815-1870)

*Chrystyna's great-grandparents:*
### REV. IVAN SAS TATOMYR—KAROLYNA Nestorowycz
(1842-1925)        (1845-1905)

*Chrystyna's grandparents:*
### REV. JULIAN SAS TATOMYR—OLHA Khomytska
(1883-1946)        (1888-1968)

*Chrystyna's parents:*
### OLEKSANDER SAS TATOMYR—SOPHIA Tereshkewych
(1913-1987)        (1915-1983)

*Chrystyna's uncles and aunts:*
*(Sons of Julian and Olha)*

### EVHEN SAS TATOMYR
(1906-1908)

### JAROSLAV SAS TATOMYR—LUBA FEDEVICH
(1910-1994)        (1910-1989)

*(Sons of Rev. Mykhajlo Tatomyr, Julian's brother)*

| **VOLODYMYR** | **ELEANORA** | **EVHEN** |
|---|---|---|
| (1902-1962) | (1905-1942) | (1914-1940) |
| | **(Married to Rev. Y. Turyansky)** | |

# TATOMYR DYNASTY

During the eighteenth and nineteenth centuries, and perhaps before then, Tatomyrs lived in the picturesque foothills of the Carpathian Mountains of western Ukraine, along the upper Dnister River valley south of Sambir.

The first mention of the name *Tatomyr* in the *Primary Chronicles of Rus* occurs in the year 1263. The Tatomyr family was listed among the ancient Boyar families of that era. Boyars were the senior members of aristocratic houses, the ruling class of Kyivan Rus in the court of the *kniaz* (prince). They were a major force in eastern Galicia from about 981 (when the lands were first conquered by Prince Volodymyr of Kyiv) until 1349 (when Galicia fell to the Poles).

The particular Tatomyr mentioned in the *Primary Chronicles of Rus* likely served in the court of Prince Danylo of Halych. The Tatomyr family was one of about one hundred families considered minor nobility. As such, they were permitted to add the title *Sas* to their name. Designated families in Hungary, Poland, Lithuania, and other parts of Eastern Europe also carried this title. 13

The next mention of the name in genealogical records is in 1650:

**Ivan Tatomyr**, *Lieutenant, Cossack cavalry.* 4

This Ivan may have been a direct descendant from Boyar times, but because of the scarcity of records from that era, it is difficult to substantiate this. He may have joined Bohdan Khmelnytsky's Cossack army as it moved westward during the late 1640s, reconquering the Ukrainian lands that had been held by the Poles for three centuries.

As an officer in Khmelnytsky's army, Ivan would have been granted a tract of land at the conclusion of the victorious campaign against the Poles. Since Tatomyrs were known to live in the area south of Sambir in Galicia in the eighteenth century, it is possible that this Ivan settled and started his dynasty there.

Shortly after his triumphs, Khmelnytsky became entangled in treaties with the Russians, Poles, and Tartars, and eventually lost control of lands he had conquered. Eastern regions of the Ukrainian lands were absorbed into the Russian empire and the western parts again came under Polish rule.

The Sas-Tatomyrs may have lost some of their status and lands but stubbornly retained their title *Sas* well into the twentieth century and maintained their claim to status as members of the nobility, the *shlachta*.

Tatomyrs believed that education and literacy determined their status. They insisted their children learn to read and write, and taught them that as adults, they had an obligation to continue the family legacy of public service.

During the late 1700s, a male, possibly a descendant of the same Ivan and still a Sas-Tatomyr, entered the seminary and became a priest.

In his memoirs, Chrystyna's father notes that his grandfather, Ivan Tatomyr, a priest in the town of Siletz, had traced the Tatomyr family back to the early 1700s. These records, however, have either been lost or are still somewhere in the church vaults in Siletz or elsewhere.

Nevertheless, the current known branch of the Tatomyr family starts with the birth of **Reverend Evhen Sas-Tatomyr** in 1815.

*   *   *

To Ukrainians, it made perfect sense that priests should be married and should have the experience of family life in order to be good counselors and pastors for their congregations. There was also the assurance that a good wife would be able to take care of all the priest's needs and thus he would be less likely to stray. The priest's wife was also an important link in the chain of rural life. Her role was to ensure that the highest moral standards were followed, not only by her spouse, but also by everyone in the parish.

Ukrainian priests and their families enjoyed a very good life in rural Ukraine. Priests usually held substantial tracts of land near the church. Parishioners took turns tilling and harvesting the fields for their priests and tended their horses and cattle. In return, the priest baptized the children, married young couples, and buried the dead.

As many of the parishioners could neither read nor write, priests were often called upon to co-sign documents and write letters and read any mail the parishioners received. Village priests were not only the keepers of religious customs and traditions, they were also the ones who defined morality and manners and monitored every form of social behavior within their parish. Often, they were the only ones who regularly traveled to the distant city and thus, they were also the ones who transmitted news. They operated schools and reading rooms for adults, and organized church choirs and children's activities. All in all, it was a fair exchange of services.

Life in Austrian Galicia during the late nineteenth century was generally quite good. Serfdom was abolished in 1848 and the Ukrainian Uniate clergy was recognized and protected by the empire. Uniate priests even received a modest salary from the Austrian government to supplement their income.

By the middle of the nineteenth century, the Sas-Tatomyr priestly dynasty was solidly established. The oldest son was expected to enter the seminary, to marry well (usually to a daughter from another priestly family), and to continue the tradition of Tatomyr priests.

In 1841, another **Ivan** was born into the Sas-Tatomyr family at the family estate in the village of Siletz. Like his father, Evhen, Ivan became a priest, married Karolyna Nestorowych, a daughter of Rev. Pobuch-Nestorowych from another well-established priestly dynasty, and was given a parish in the village of Sprynia. After a short time, he was given a parish in the larger town of Cherkavi, where he was pastor for forty years. He died in 1925, at the age of eighty-four, and was buried next to his wife in the church cemetery. The town of Cherkavi, and especially Ivan's residence on a hill overlooking the church, became a "mecca" for the Tatomyr family during the late nineteenth and early twentieth centuries. Ivan and his wife, Karolyna, hoped their sons and grandsons would become priests and would carry on the Tatomyr priestly traditions.

Ivan and Karolyna had two sons. **Mykhajlo**, their eldest, was born in 1875, and became a priest at the turn of the century. (He in turn had two sons, **Volodymyr,** born in 1902, and **Evhen,** born in 1914.)

A few years later, on January 3, 1883, when Ivan was already forty-one years old, Karolyna gave birth to the couple's second son, Chrystyna's grandfather, **Julian Sas-Tatomyr**. He too was destined to become a priest.

Ivan and Karolyna also had three daughters, Eleonora, Olena, and Maria. Two of them married priests. (Please see *Tatomyr Dynasty* later in this chapter and Memoir 7, *The Tatomyr Clan, Letter to his Children,* in the Epilogue.)

Father Ivan's two sons, Mykhajlo and Julian, were groomed for the priesthood from an early age. They were tutored, taught to play musical instruments, and instructed in the writings of Shevchenko and other nationalist writers including Ivan Franko, who came from a town just a few kilometers south of Siletz.

The two boys traveled extensively with their father: to Lviv, to Peremyshl (long the seat of the Greek Catholic eparchy with rich libraries and home of some of the most patriotic members of the Ukrainian Catholic clergy), to Sambir, the largest city in the region, as well as to major cities in the Austrian empire including Vienna and Prague.

*    *    *

Like his older brother before him, Julian entered the seminary in Sambir in 1902, at the age of nineteen. At the turn of the century, seminarians were being prepared not only to take care of the religious needs of their parishioners but also to be leaders in the Ukrainian revival that was sweeping western Ukraine. The emphasis of their studies was on religion and the liturgy, but they also had to prepare for the political aspect of the priest's role in the new political reality developing around them.

In spring of 1905, after three years of theological studies in Sambir, Julian returned to his father's village for a rest, but also to look for a wife. (In the Uniate Church, married men may be ordained to the priesthood, but once a man accepts Holy Orders and is ordained a priest, he can no longer marry and must remain celibate.) Julian wanted to make sure he had a wife before he became a priest.

Julian's father, Reverend Ivan, decided this would be a good time to have a family reunion to which he would invite a few of his fellow priests and their families from neighboring villages.

He was particularly careful to invite priests who had eligible young daughters. A large get-together was planned, as always, on Ivan's name day, June 7, the feast of St. John.

Whether through good luck or perhaps because of good planning, Father Peter Khomytsky and his family were among those invited to the feast. Father Khomytsky's daughter, Olha, had just turned seventeen. She was petite and beautiful, had blue eyes and blond hair, and a wonderful disposition. She was well educated, played the piano, and was deeply religious—the absolutely perfect choice for any eligible young bachelor-seminarian. Julian and Olha were introduced to each other and seemed to get along very well. Within a few weeks, the marriage was arranged.

## JULIAN AND OLHA

Julian and Olha were married during the summer of 1905 in Olha's village, with the two proud fathers, Father Peter Khomytsky and Father Ivan Tatomyr, co-celebrating the wedding mass. The wedding festivities lasted three days and people in the area talked about them for months.

Julian spent his final year of seminary studies in Peremyshl, a largely Polish town on the San River in western Galicia (now in Poland). After his ordination, Julian was assigned to his father-in-law's church as an auxiliary priest.

He had expected to get his own parish right away, but the bishop knew young Julian needed some polishing. He was also concerned that Julian's bride, still only eighteen years old at the time, was much too young to take on the role of a village priest's wife. While serving at his father-in-law's parish, Julian could mature and practice his vocation, and Olha's mother could take her daughter under her wing and teach her to adapt to her new position as a priest's wife. Also, the bishop reasoned, since Father Khomytsky was in poor health, he would need an assistant.

Julian settled into his new role with a passion. He organized a church choir and taught them to sing the mass the modern way, as they did in Lviv. He organized a kindergarten and primary school for the village children and opened a reading room for adults. There he taught them to read and write and introduced them to nationalist ideas. Meanwhile, at her mother's side, his young wife was perfecting her role.

In June 1906, at the age of eighteen, Olha gave birth to their first baby, a boy. Julian and Olha were ecstatic. The Tatomyr priestly dynasty would continue.

Ivan brought his whole family for a visit as soon as he heard the good news, and the two proud grandfathers performed the baptismal rites. The boy was named **Evhen**, after his grandfather. Everyone naturally expected that Evhen would one day enter the seminary and would become a priest.

But life doesn't always work out exactly as planned. During the summer of 1908, tragedy struck the young family. An epidemic of typhoid fever swept Eastern Europe. Evhen, just two years old, became infected and died.

Julian was devastated. He blamed Olha for his son's death. He reasoned it was her duty to take care of their son and she should have been more careful, especially knowing an epidemic was spreading.

Olha's world changed dramatically. Her husband, never particularly affectionate or considerate, was now morose and irritable. Olha fell into a deep depression. She had to bury her baby son and also bear the guilt her husband placed on her young shoulders. Julian lost some of his former enthusiasm after his son died. Life in the village was no longer attractive. More and more, he left his wife in the village as he traveled to Sambir, where he became involved in political organizations. He pleaded with the bishop to transfer him.

In 1909, the bishop agreed to transfer Julian and Olha to Sambir. Julian was comfortable in the larger city setting, and because he was energetic and well-traveled, he would be an excellent assistant to the bishop. Lviv was the centre of extensive Ukrainian nationalist movements, and, as a priest, Julian enjoyed easy access to news and free movement around the territory. Julian immersed himself in nationalist causes and established an extensive network of friends who kept him informed about political activities in Galicia and beyond.

Before long, Julian decided that life must go on and that he and Olha should try to have more children. Olha, still depressed, did not feel the same enthusiasm, but she submitted to her husband's will. Soon she became pregnant and in 1910, she presented her husband with another son, **Jaroslav.**

Little Jaroslav resembled their first son, Evhen. Olha doted on him and was very vigilant in keeping him from any harm. Olha and Julian decided Jaroslav would now be the one who would become a priest, and the process of grooming him for the priesthood started in earnest.

Three years later, on June 9, 1913, another boy was born to Olha and Julian, Chrystyna's father, **Oleksander.**

# Tatomyr Dynasty

Rev. Ivan Sas Tatomyr was born in 1842, the son of an Eastern Rite Catholic priest, Rev. Evhen Sas Tatomyr, who was born in 1815.

Before his ordination, Ivan began to search for a suitable wife. Ivan married into one of the oldest and most influential priestly dynasties in western Ukraine, the Pobuch-Nestorowych family. His bride, Karolina Nestorowych, was the daughter of Rev. Olexander Pobuch-Nestorowych (1817-1895) and the granddaughter of Rev. Nicholaj Pobuch-Nestorowych (1792-1862).

The Pobuch-Nestorowych's were members of the Ukrainian *shlachta* (nobility), as were the Sas-Tatomyrs.

Karolina's brother, Peter Nestorowych, became a priest and later became pastor in the town of Ilnyk. Her sister married Rev. Lev Kozanowych, pastor of Mistkiw. Her nephew, Lev Nestorowych, became a priest in Peremyshl, and two of her nieces married priests, Rev. Steven Makar and Rev. Antin Sawchyn.

Ivan and Karolyna had five children, two boys and three girls. Two of the three daughters married priests: Eleonora married Rev. Rudkash of Kurilo; Maria married Rev. Oleksander Bereznysky, and they were posted to Cherkavi, after the death, in 1925, of the church's longtime pastor, Reverend Ivan Sas Tatomyr.

Ivan and Karolyna's oldest son, Mykhajlo (1876-1930), became a priest and married Sofia Pashichniak, a daughter of a priest. Mykhajlo became pastor in Strij. They had two sons, Volodymyr and Evhen, and a daughter, Eleonora.

Their other son, Julian (1883-1946), Chrystyna's grandfather, married Olha Khomytsky, daughter of Rev. Peter Khomytsky of yet another family of priests.

Chrystyna's grandfather, Senator Rev. Julian Sas Tatomyr, had a long and distinguished career as a political leader, a senator, and a pastor in Luzhok for more than twenty years until the forced departure of the family from Ukraine in 1944.

Rev. Julian and his wife, Olha, had three sons: Evhen, Jaroslav, and Oleksander. They had hoped that one, two, or all three sons would become priests. It wasn't to be.

**Fiftieth Anniversary of the priesthood of
Rev. Oleksander Pobuch-Nestorowych.
Family compound in Sambir, 1892.**

Future priests, Julian Tatomyr, age eleven, and his brother, Mykhajlo, age sixteen, are sitting in the front row, left. Most of the males in this picture are priests and are related through marriage. Most of the women in the picture are daughters of priests or are married to priests.

The bulge in the guest of honor's cheek is chewing tobacco.

Chrystyna's great-grandfather Rev. Ivan Sas-Tatomyr (standing),

Chrystyna's grandmother, Olha Tatomyr (second from right) is holding her two-year-old son, Jaroslav, and is pregnant with Chrystyna's father, Oleksander (born 1913).

Outside Reverend Ivan's garden house, Spryni, 1912

# PART TWO

# The War to End All Wars

# Chapter 4

# *Lviv, 1993*

*There is nothing more difficult to take in hand*
*More perilous to conduct*
*Or more uncertain in its success*
*Than to take the lead in the introduction*
*In the new order of things*
*Because the innovator has for enemies*
*All those who have done well*
*Under the old conditions.*
**—Machiavelli, *The Prince*, c.1500**

The school the Lviv Ministry of Education reserved for our courses was just a ten-minute walk from our hotel. The first morning, all the Canadian teachers walked to school together. On the way, we received some last-minute instructions and answers to last-minute questions, and gave each other some last minute encouragement and moral support.

Chrystyna and I were a little nervous as we were preparing to meet our class of administrators. We didn't know quite what to expect. Although we were both seasoned teachers, and we both had experience teaching adults, we had always made our presentations in English. Today, for the first time, we would be teaching adults—in Ukrainian.

We introduced ourselves and asked each of the twenty-four administrators in our group to do the same. When we do this type of warm-up exercise in Canada, it usually takes about fifteen minutes. Here, in Lviv, it took more than two hours. Our administrators didn't just introduce themselves, they added their philosophy, their experiences, something about their town (we had participants from all parts of Ukraine), their school, and their impressions of Lviv and of us. Each participant tried to be entertaining and original, and each tried to show they had a great sense of humor.

To our great relief, they welcomed us warmly, seemed genuinely interested—even honored—to be able to participate in this course and were grateful that we were offering these workshops for them. One of the participants commented how impressed he was that even though we had lived in a foreign country all our lives, we had managed to retain our Ukrainian language! That made us feel very good.

We relaxed and from that point, we started to enjoy this teaching experience. We knew if we were ever stuck for a word or made a mistake, the participants would be more than willing to help us out. If we mispronounced something, they would forgive us.

This workshop was probably the most pleasant teaching experience we had ever had. After all these years, Chrystyna and I were doing what we loved—teaching—and doing it together. It felt great.

The three weeks passed very quickly. In some respects, it felt like summer camp. We became close friends with our students, we were invited to their homes, we exchanged addresses, we went for drinks, we sang songs, and we danced. We surprised each other that we knew the same songs even though we had lived in very different places for the past fifty years. We maintained a very busy social schedule. Something was planned for us every evening. In addition to the usual planned school and after-school events, we had recently connected with Chrystyna's family. Chrystyna's new found nephew, Ivanko lived in Lviv, and was very interested in spending time with us.

Soon after our courses started, he invited us—no, he *insisted*—we come over to their flat for dinner. We enthusiastically agreed.

---

## FLOWERS, FLAGS, and FREEDOM

Before going to dinner at Ivanko's house, we stopped to buy flowers from one of the vendors that can be found on street corners everywhere in Lviv.

As the flower lady was wrapping our flowers, she asked what color of ribbons we preferred. We hesitated and shrugged. With a twinkle in her eyes, she suggested the blue and yellow ribbons, the colors of the Ukrainian flag, would look best with the red roses we purchased. We agreed.

As she handed us the flowers, she proudly informed us that had she used blue and yellow ribbons just a few years earlier, she would have been arrested.

---

When we arrived at Ivanko's flat in an upscale part of Lviv not far from downtown, we were greeted by his wife, Lesya, and by his sister, Ola, and by Ola's husband, Ivan (not another Ivan, we thought!), who was a successful businessman and owner of a factory just outside Lviv. Chrystyna immediately hit it off with Ola while her husband, Ivan, had such a positive and infectious personality that he and I felt like old friends in no time.

That evening was just the first of many, many get-togethers we had that summer and in years to come.

Over the next few weeks, we had a chance to tour Lviv with our newly discovered family. They showed us around the old part of town with its historic buildings, they took us to some of the nicer restaurants in town and to a performance at the Opera House.

The highlight for us, however, was our visit to Lviv's St. George's Cathedral. Ivanko was a prominent member of the Ukrainian Catholic hierarchy in Lviv. As a layman, he was one of the few who kept the faith throughout the communist era and who quietly supported the underground Catholic Church. As a doctor working in the main training hospital in Lviv, he was often pressured to join the Communist Party. He is very proud that he never lost his resolve. His career may have suffered but he never joined the Party.

When Ukraine declared its independence, Ivanko became a leader in Lviv's Ukrainian Catholic diocese. He helped negotiate the return of churches to the Ukrainian Catholics, and he was one of the advisors to the new major archbishop of the Ukrainian Catholic Church and Metropolitan of Lviv, Cardinal Lubachivsky.

Ivanko arranged for us to have an audience with the cardinal.

That audience was a very moving experience for Chrystyna and me. Although we had not been particularly active in Catholic Church matters over the years, we were nevertheless fascinated by the courage of some of the Ukrainian church leaders in the face of cruel and vicious oppression by Bolsheviks, and by the work done by these leaders during the repressive Stalin, Khrushchev, and Brezhnev eras. Most of all, we were impressed they survived and kept the faith.

For me, meeting Cardinal Lubachivsky was also déjà vu.

Many years before, during the late 1960s, I was hitchhiking through Europe and found myself in Rome with little money and no place to stay. I had a phone number of an old friend from Montreal who was studying at the Ukrainian Seminary in Rome. He found me a place to stay for a few days and, more importantly, he brought me to the seminary where the new director was a former parish priest from our parish in Montreal. Bishop Datsiuk remembered me from my altar boy days and after some begging on my part, agreed to arrange a private audience with the first Ukrainian cardinal ever appointed by the Vatican, Cardinal Joseph Slipyj. Cardinal Slipyj succeeded Metropolitan Andrij Sheptytsky as Metropolitan of Lviv after Sheptytsky was poisoned by the Soviets in 1944.

Cardinal Slipyj had spent eighteen years in Soviet prisons and in Siberia, never giving up his faith. He was released in 1963, old but unbroken, thanks to the intervention of Pope John XXIII and President John F. Kennedy. (The main character in the 1968 Hollywood movie, *Shoes of the Fisherman*, starring Anthony Quinn, was based loosely on Cardinal Slipyj.) That meeting with Cardinal Joseph

Slipyj, being in his presence, in his Vatican office in 1967, was the highlight of my European trip.

After our visit with Cardinal Lubachivsky, Ivanko gave us a tour of the hospital adjacent to the cathedral. This hospital was built by Metropolitan Andrij Sheptytsky early in the century. During the Nazi occupation, this hospital, with its series of tunnels and alcoves, was used by Sheptytsky to hide Jews disguised as patients, or to hide them in the tunnels through which they were later able to escape. Hundreds of Jews were saved through his efforts.

After the Chornobyl disaster of 1986, the hospital was used to care for children who had been born with serious defects. The nun, who took us around the aging but still efficient structure, introduced us to some of the children. It was a heart-wrenching experience for us.

Lviv is a beautiful old city. Its central part was designated a national architectural preserve and the city is on the UNESCO World Heritage List. The downtown area consists of narrow cobblestone streets, elegant homes of wealthy merchants, beautifully restored churches, the university (renamed Ivan Franko University where the language of instruction is now Ukrainian), the Opera House, and large public squares and parks, hotels, and restaurants.

Lviv is also now very much a Ukrainian city. After the Chornobyl accident of 1986, it was here that protests against Soviet and Russian rule were loudest. Lviv sustained the revolution of 1990 and was looked upon for leadership in Ukrainian causes ever since. After the 1991 declaration of Ukrainian independence and the establishment of a new Ukrainian state, Lviv was the first city in Ukraine where citizens and local leaders tore down Lenin's statue from its pedestal in front of the Opera.

Lviv was also the first city to change street names which left reminders of Soviet times.

Street names honoring Marx, Stalin, Lenin, the Soviet Constitution, the Red Fleet, May 1, and Moscow were quickly removed. More than half the street names in Lviv were changed after 1991.

The people responsible for the name changes must have had some fun while they deliberated their choices for new street names. The street named after Artem, the former head of the KGB, was changed to honor the Ukrainian Sich Riflemen who fought against the Russians during World War I. Lenin Street became Bohdan Khmelnytsky Street, Kirov Street became Andrij Sheptytsky Boulevard, Red Army Street was changed to Vasylkivska and the World War II anti-Soviet Ukrainian nationalists, Stefan Bandera and Andrij Melnyk, had their names placed on streets formerly named Chernavski and Soviet Peace.

On our very first tour of downtown Lviv, we easily found Andrij Melnyk Street.

# OPERA

When I was about ten years old and much too young to appreciate it, my father took me to see a performance of a Ukrainian opera in Montreal: Artemovsky's *Zaporozhetz Za Dunajem* (Cossack Beyond the Danube). It's a sad tale about a Cossack captured by invading Turks and sold into slavery. After years of captivity, old and broken, the old Cossack sings the final aria, *Vladyko Neba I Zemli* (Lord of Heaven and Earth). This lovely prayer ends with the phrase, "Lord God, Please give us back our Native Land."

This opera was banned by the Soviets because of its underlying anti-occupation and thus anti-Russian messages, and because it is a prayer. Ukrainian patriots love this opera for the same reasons.

This haunting aria, sung by a powerful tenor, was my father's favorite song. One of my fondest memories of my father was hearing him sing this aria in his best, but not exactly perfect, tenor voice, as he worked around the house.

Chrystyna and I were fortunate to be in Lviv in late July, the traditional end of the Lviv opera season and to get tickets to the sold-out final performance. This concert consisted of a review of the best performances of the previous season by members of the Lviv Opera Company. It was an excellent display of talent and a most enjoyable evening.

At the end of the concert, the lights went down, the curtain opened, and a lone performer stood at the center of the stage—the lead tenor of the Lviv Opera. As the lights went up he started to sing—of all things—my father's favorite aria, Vladyko Neba I Zemli. As he sang, one by one, the rest of the Opera Company, perhaps one hundred strong, walked onto the stage and joined him in singing the prayer. It was a very powerful moment.

Chills ran up and down my spine. My body was covered in goose bumps. My eyes filled with tears as I remembered my late father.

Some people at the front of the hall stood as the song began.

Of course! This was a prayer!

There was an awkward moment as people realized this was a once-banned aria from a once-banned opera. A public prayer was being sung in a once—officially atheistic society.

People also realized that if this had happened just a few years earlier, all the people who participated in the performance would have been arrested.

I jumped to my feet along with more and more of the audience. Within seconds, almost everyone in the audience was standing.

It occurred to everyone that things had changed significantly in Ukraine during the last few years.

# GRANDFATHER JULIAN'S CHURCH

Early Sunday morning after we completed the first week of our course, Ivanko and Ola drove us to Chrystyna's grandfather's church in Luzhok. The priest told us he'd celebrate a mass in our honor so we knew we couldn't be late. We felt honored to be remembered by the priest and the congregation in Chrystyna's grandfather's former church, but we did not expect the extent of the celebration they had prepared for us.

Word had spread through the villages that Father Julian Tatomyr's granddaughter was coming to church that Sunday. When we arrived, the church was already full, and some people were unable to get in. Women dressed in their best embroidered blouses and men wore crisp white shirts and ties.

We squeezed to the front of the church where the priest welcomed us publicly. In his sermon, he spoke about all the accomplishments of Father Julian and how excited he was to have met Chrystyna and to discover what had became of the little girl who left forty-nine years before when she was only six months old.

After mass, Chrystyna was mobbed by old women who remembered Father Julian and Chrystyna's father, Oleksander. One woman brought a picture of Chrystyna's grandfather and herself when she was a member of his choir during the 1940s.

Everyone wanted to be photographed with Chrystyna and many just wanted to touch Chrystyna. It was quite a scene.

After the mass, I asked the congregation to come to the side of the church to take a picture. I remembered a picture Chrystyna had of her grandfather blessing Easter baskets on that very spot in 1944—under very different circumstances.

# TOPILNICIA

After church, Ivanko's sister, Ola, and her husband, Ivan, decided they would show us the place where Chrystyna was born.

Nestled in a valley just off the main road, about ten kilometers south of Luzhok, was the village of Topilnicia. We drove to a building located on a small hill just across the river that runs through the town. This building was once the school where Chrystyna's father served as director back in 1944, and where Chrystyna's mother was a teacher. It was also here, in the small apartment adjacent to the school, that Chrystyna was born on January 28, 1944.

Shortly after the war, the school was converted into a hospital, and in 1950, when it served as the local birthing facility; it was here that Ola, Chrystyna's niece, was born.

During the 1960s, the building became the town's administration building.

As we drove up, a couple was standing outside the building. When Ola explained that she and Chrystyna were born in that building, the couple cheerfully invited us inside. They took us into the room they said would have been the school director's bedroom fifty years before.

Only a few weeks earlier, Chrystyna had vague knowledge that she was born somewhere in Starij Sambir, somewhere in Ukraine. For the first time she saw the exact location of her birth, in a small village of Topilnicia.

As we were leaving, Chrystyna remembered that just before her family left in 1944, her parents placed valuables in a metal trunk and buried it under a tree. At that time, they thought they would return after a year or so to dig it up. They never did. Years later, thinking they would never be able to return to Ukraine, Chrystyna's parents never bothered to tell their children the exact location of this trunk.

Now Chrystyna's parents, and anyone else who may have had information about where that trunk was buried, were dead.

As we stood by the house, we tried to imagine where they might have buried the trunk. Just behind the director's apartment, out of sight of the road, stood an old oak tree. We guessed this is where they would have buried the trunk.

We promised ourselves that we would return someday, bring a metal detector, and find that trunk. (We still hope to do that someday soon.)

We returned to the priest's house for afternoon tea. He again showed us around Grandfather Julian's house and grounds and told us more about Julian's work and his resistance to the occupying Polish and Bolshevik authorities.

The priest took us behind his house to an orchard higher up the hill. He pointed westward across the Dnister River, to the other side of the valley about halfway up the mountain. Just visible from behind a thick growth of pine trees was a large rock.

"That's Kamin Sokil," he said. "When the Soviets occupied this area in 1944, members of the underground Ukrainian Insurgent Army, the UPA, used that rock as their base. From that strategic defensible position, they could see anyone approaching them. At the same time, they were close to the villages below and could easily get needed supplies. If necessary, they could retreat further up the mountain and even cross westward into Poland, less than an hour away on foot. These insurgents remained in that area for years after World War II ended, staging raids on the Bolsheviks."

Later that afternoon, Ivanko took us to Kamin Sokil. We waded across the Dnister River and crossed the fields on the other side. Just before we entered the forest, we disturbed several pairs of nesting storks. The huge birds circled us menacingly, occasionally swooping down very near us. We wondered if storks acted as early warning sentries for the UPA soldiers years ago by creating a disturbance whenever someone came too close to the trail head. We climbed the steep narrow trail up to Kamin Sokil. From there the view across the valley was breathtaking.

We could see the tiny villages strung out along the river, and we understood how and why the UPA resisted the Soviets for so long.

Topilnicia, 1993: Chrystyna stands in front of the house in which she was born in 1944. At that time this was a school where her father, Oleksander, was the director. (The director's quarters were to the right of the front door.) It was converted into a hospital after the war and Chrystyna's niece, Ola, was born here. In 1993, it served as the administrative offices for the village of Topilnicia.

**Chrystyna and her niece, Ola touring Lviv, 1993.**

**Tram stop on Andrij Melnyk Street in Lviv, 1993**

**Meeting Chrystyna's family in her mother's former home in Spas, forty-nine years after infant Chrystyna escaped with her family for the West.**

**Chrystyna surrounded by well-wishers in the church where her grandfather, Julian, was pastor for more than twenty years.**

**Luzhok, 1993**

**In front of Grandfather Julian Tatomyr's newly renovated church with Maria who was Chrystyna's babysitter in 1944,and Dr. Ivan Luts, Chrystyna's nephew.**

Kamin Sokil.
To the left, over the mountains, lies Poland; below, the Dnister River and villages.
This rock stands at the edge of the old Tatomyr estate. During the 1940s, the
Ukrainian Insurgent Army often conducted raids against Nazi and Bolshevik forces
from this spot.

Outside Lviv Opera House before the final concert of 1993 season.
During the Soviet era, a statue of Lenin stood in the grassy area behind Chrystyna.
It was torn down shortly after Ukraine's Declaration of Independence in 1991.

(Below)
Canadian teachers, Nadia Luciw, Oksana Wynnyckyj, and Chrystyna with young
Ukrainian soldiers during intermission.

**(Above)**
**Audience with Cardinal Lubachivsky, major archbishop of the Ukrainian Catholic Church and Metropolitan of Lviv. In his offices at St. George's Cathedral, Lviv, 1993.**

**(Right)**

**Andrij Sheptytsky Hospital Where many young victims of the Chornobyl nuclear disaster receive treatment.**

Stopped by Border Patrol near Slovak—Ukraine border. The encounter quickly became quite pleasant as both patrolmen told us how much they wanted to come to Canada.

Canadian teachers and Ukrainian hosts in front of a freshly constructed burial mound commemorating soldiers who fell fighting for Ukraine's freedom. These mounds appeared in western Ukraine shortly after independence in 1991. The sign on the right reads, "Slava Ukraiini" (Glory to Ukraine).

**Picnic at Ivan Samoylenko's estate north of Lviv. (From left) Ola and Ivan; family friend, Dr. Ivanko Luts, and wife, Dr. Lesya Luts; visitors, Andrew and Chrystyna.**

**Seeing us off, on "*Grand Tour*," Lviv to Kyiv train.**

# Chapter 5

# *Ellis Island, 1914*

Between 1892 and 1954, more than twenty two million ship passengers came through Ellis Island and the Port of New York. Among them were some twelve million steerage and third class passengers. These immigrants traveled in crowded, unsanitary conditions near the bottom of steamships with few amenities, often spending up to two weeks seasick in their bunks during rough ocean crossings.

Upon arrival in New York City, ships would dock at the Hudson or East River piers. First—and second-class passengers would disembark, pass through Customs at the piers and were free to enter the United States. The steerage and third-class passengers were transported by ferry or barge to Ellis Island where they were legally and medically inspected.

Before the outbreak of World War I, up to four million immigrants from the Austrian Empire were admitted to the United States, but after the outbreak of war in 1914, American attitudes toward immigration began to shift. Through the early 1920s, a series of laws were passed to limit the flow of immigrants.*

My grandfather, Peter Melnyk, arrived at Ellis Island from the German port of Bremerhaven in 1914, just days before the outbreak of World War I.

## CHICAGO

In the spring of 1914, my grandfather, Peter Melnyk, said good-bye to his family and boarded the train for Lviv. An agent would arrange his travel to Germany, and from there, he would board a boat to America. He joined hundreds of other Galicians who

---

*     www.ellisisland.com

found themselves in similar circumstances. Since there was little land left in Galicia and few opportunities for employment, the only way to escape the abject poverty was to emigrate.

When they arrived in America, Ukrainian immigrants from Galicia were usually classified as Austrians. Among the four million immigrants registered in the United States as Austrians before World War I, many probably were actual Austrians or Hungarians, but most were Ukrainians, Poles, or Jews who were fleeing poverty and oppression and looking for a better life for themselves and their families.

After they arrived in America, some of these Galicians stayed in New York, where there were already established Ukrainian, Polish, and Jewish communities and where jobs were readily available. Others flocked to locations where jobs for unskilled laborers were easy to find: to the mines of Pennsylvania or Virginia. Some went further west to the booming town of Chicago.

From Lviv, my grandfather, Peter, traveled by train to Bremen, Germany, and waited for a freighter heading for New York.

The agent in Lviv had arranged for him to pay part of his passage by working in the engine room. Though he still had to pay a small fee for the passage, he would receive a meager ration and would have a bunk in the lower part of the ship.

Two weeks later, just a few weeks before the start of World War I, my grandfather, Peter, arrived in New York.

His goal was to find a job, make money, and perhaps convince my reluctant grandmother, Maria, to pack up the children and join him. If that didn't work out, he was determined to save enough money to return to his home village and buy that mill in Ladychyn. He also planned to have enough money left over to ensure a better life for himself and his family.

Along with all the other Galicians, Peter would have been ferried to Ellis Island and would have to submit to a standard medical examination. After several hours, he received all the required stamps on his entry application.

We're not exactly sure why Peter decided to go to Chicago. We know that he wrote often and that he sent money to Maria, but all the letters were lost. My mother remembered that in Chicago, he worked as a butcher. Maybe she meant that he worked in the Union Stock Yards.

Prior to World War I, the Union Stock Yards on Chicago's South Side were booming. This was still the "Slaughterhouse to the World." More than twelve million heads of cattle passed through these yards every year. The economy was strong, and there was always a need for unskilled labor—no experience necessary, no questions asked.

Immigrant workers of all nationalities lived near the Union Stock Yards and most worked in the yards. Within days of his arrival in America, Peter would have had a job, but he would have started at the bottom, the same as every other newcomer.

The custom in the stockyards was that the most recent arrivals were given the most menial and most undesirable job in the slaughterhouse: cleaning the slippery floors of the blood and guts of recently slaughtered animals, shoveling them onto the cemented outside chutes, and pushing the bloody wastes directly into the Chicago River. In the summer heat, the smell was unbearable.

The various ethnic groups who worked in the yards didn't often mix with each other. Each group, the Poles, Lithuanians, Germans, Italians, Ukrainians, and others, kept to themselves, rarely interacting.

Occasionally, tensions would boil over and fights would break out, but by and large, Peter managed to avoid confrontations. Most of the fights took place after the men had a few too many drinks.

Like everyone else, Peter would have worked ten—to twelve-hour shifts, six days a week. He did not have a chance to spend the money he earned, and that was fine with him. Although, after their shifts, many of the workers went for a drink at one of the many bars in the neighborhood, Peter stayed away. He was a nondrinker and by not socializing too much, he would save his money and reach his goal sooner.

Peter estimated it would take him two years to earn enough money to return to his village and buy the mill, or some land, and live comfortably.

When World War I broke out in August 1914, American attitudes towards foreigners changed. Tensions increased. Germans, Austrians, and, by association, Galicians, were looked upon with suspicion or even as enemies. The U.S. government slowed immigration from Eastern Europe to a trickle and eventually made it very difficult for anyone from Eastern Europe or Austria, including those with family members already in America, to gain entry.

But Peter soon learned that war creates opportunities.

With the United States preparing for war, equipment and uniforms would be needed for the soldiers. According to my Aunt Olha, Peter was offered a job as a tailor. Someone he knew, perhaps someone he met at the Ukrainian church he attended, owned a small business and received an order to supply uniforms for the U.S. military. He was expanding his business and was looking for help.

Peter quit his job at the stockyards, joined his new friend and became a tailor. The hours were long, but he was able to earn more as a tailor than he ever could at the Union Stock Yards, and he didn't have to work at menial, backbreaking jobs.

Along with many of the other newly arrived Ukrainians, Peter attended church regularly, if not for religious reasons, then certainly for social ones. Since it was the only Ukrainian Catholic church in Chicago at the time, it is very likely that he became a member of St. Nicholas Church on Rice Street, and that he saved his money in their credit union. He wrote Maria regularly and sent her money to support the family.

Two years turned into three, then four, then five.

The war ended in 1918, and travel was again possible, but immigration was still restricted, especially for Austrians and Germans.

Peter had more or less mastered the English language, made a number of friends and connections within Chicago's Ukrainian community, and was quite comfortable in this new country. By 1920, my grandfather had saved a substantial amount of money, set up his own business as a tailor, and had applied for U.S. citizenship.

He wrote Maria and asked her to pack the children and come to America to join him, but Maria did not want to leave her village. Their second daughter, Emilia (nicknamed Milya), was very sick with tuberculosis, and Maria simply couldn't imagine leaving her family, friends, and everything that she had known all her life. She begged Peter to return to Varvarenci and reminded him the Polish merchant was still willing to sell him that mill in Ladychyn for the agreed-upon price.

Peter was torn. In spite of the hardships and loneliness he faced every day in Chicago, here, in America, he was a free man. He had made friends and, most of all, he was living in a democracy. After six years of living in a free country, he didn't know if he could live in subservience again.

He hoped the war had changed things for the better back home in Galicia. In any case, he reasoned he owed it to his family and his nation to come back and fight for their freedom.

In the fall of 1920, Peter packed his few belongings and returned to Europe. If things didn't work out in Ladychyn, he reasoned, he could always try to convince Maria to return with him to America.

## MY GRANDFATHER'S MILL (1)

Although World War I in most of Europe had ended two years earlier, it still raged on in Galicia. Ukrainians had declared their independence in 1918, but the Poles did not give up. Hostilities between Ukrainians and Poles continued. When Peter arrived back in his village in 1920, he found there was even more chaos and uncertainty than when he left. It wasn't clear who was in charge.

Nevertheless, Peter and Maria decided they should try to buy the mill in Ladychyn.

Peter visited the Polish merchant, inspected the mill, saw that it was in excellent shape, and, after some tough negotiations, he bought it.

Finally, he had attained his dream.

Peter moved his family into the spacious house adjacent to the mill in Ladychyn.

In the midst of all the excitement, however, there was also sadness. Peter and Maria's daughter, Emilya, who had been very ill for several years, died, at age seventeen, of tuberculosis.

Just days after they buried her in the Ladychyn cemetery, Maria announced she was pregnant again. The following year, in 1921, Maria gave birth to their last child, another baby girl. They named her Emilia in memory of her older sister. Her nickname was Lucia.

*       *       *

Even after the mill purchase, Grandfather Peter was still a relatively wealthy man. He had enough money to provide for his family's needs; he bought a team of matching chestnut horses, a special Sunday carriage, and new clothes for his wife and all his children. Even after all that, he still could afford to send his children to the best schools.

Peter and Maria's oldest son, my uncle Roman, decided to become a priest. My grandparents were thrilled. It would be an honor to have a priest in the family. Their three daughters, Julia, Lucia, and Olha attended primary school in nearby Terebovla and, later, boarding school in Ternopil.

In 1920, when he was ten years old, my father, Bohdan, joined his older brother, Roman, at boarding school in Ternopil. Their younger brother, Joseph, would follow a few years later.

My grandfather's mill, Ladychyn, c.1920s

Melnyk Children: Roman, Julia, Bohdan, Olha, Joseph, Emilia. Late 1930s

# Chapter 6

# *Quadrangle of Death*

## SAMBIR, 1914

The First World War was Europe's first shocking experience with modern warfare. The dimensions of the struggle are mind-boggling: thirty-four countries eventually participated, 65 million soldiers were mobilized, of whom 10 million died and over 20 million were injured. Civilian casualties were almost as high. Not only was the war massive, it was total. As losses mounted, the tremendous pressures they created, both at the battlefront and at home, exposed the weaknesses of Europe's old imperial order. For the German, Ottoman, and Austro-Hungarian empires, which constituted the Central Powers, and for the Russian Empire, which along with Britain, France, and America, constituted the Entente, the war eventually became an exercise in self-destruction.

There are shades of barbarism in twentieth century Europe, which would once have amazed the most barbarous of barbarians. During World War One, Europeans armies destroyed more human beings than in all other previous wars. 6

During the summer of 1914, Rev. Julian Tatomyr and his young family were living in Sambir. Julian was the auxiliary pastor in one of the largest Uniate parishes in this predominantly Polish town. Julian also spent a lot of time in Lviv, where Ukrainian nationalist activity was rampant. His wife, Olha, and two young children, four-year-old Jaroslav and one-year-old Oleksander, were left alone for long periods of time.

Julian had become passionately involved in various organizations and was one of a number of young men who spread revolutionary spirit throughout Galicia. He was becoming more and more involved with nationalist causes and, for the first time, came into close contact with émigrés from eastern Ukraine, where, under the Russians, conditions were very much worse for Ukrainians than they were in the Austrian empire.

Germany declared war on Russia on August 1, 1914, and Austria declared war on Serbia on August 3. These political events created an opportunity for Ukrainians. Julian was one of the community leaders in Galicia who realized that with determination and luck, they might be able to achieve an independent Ukraine. He knew his world would change dramatically forever, but he could never imagine how terrible the next thirty years would be for him and his family.

> The outbreak of World War I in August 1914 ushered in a period that, over five years, would have a profound impact on Ukrainian lands. During those few years, Ukraine witnessed the conflicts of World War I, the Russian Revolution, the Russian-Polish War, and the breakup of the old empires. There were also several attempts to establish Ukrainian statehood—in an extremely complex environment, that included the advances and retreats of several armies, changes in alliances, and struggles between competing Ukrainian governments, peasant uprisings, foreign invasions, and civil war.
>
> For more than a century before 1914, Ukrainian lands were divided between two states, the multinational Russian and Austro-Hungarian empires. By early 1920, these empires had disappeared, and most Ukrainians found themselves within the borders of four new states: the Ukrainian SSR, Poland, Czechoslovakia, and Romania. 6

As the Russian armies clashed with the Austrians east of Lviv, Julian contacted his friend, Kost Levytsky, a trusted parliamentarian who was in the process of setting up the General Ukrainian Council. Their goal was to take advantage of the chaotic situation and declare independence. Stating that *the victory for the Austro-Hungarian monarchy will be our victory, and the greater the defeat of Russia, the sooner will come the hour of liberation,* the council called on Ukrainians to fight for Austria, their best friend, against autocratic Russia, their worst enemy.

When the council issued a call for volunteers for an all-Ukrainian military unit, thousands of nationally conscious young men responded and formed the first Ukrainian military formation in modern history, The Ukrainian Sich Riflemen (*Ukraiinski Sichovi Striltsi.*) Julian and his older brother, Mykhajlo—also a priest—joined a Ukrainian Sich Riflemen unit as chaplains.

At the same time, émigrés from Russian-ruled Ukraine also formed a political organization in Lviv, the Union for Liberation of Ukraine—the SVU. Among their leaders was Mykola Zalizniak.* Their expressed unequivocal goal was formation of an independent Ukrainian state throughout all Ukrainian lands. They too resolved to cooperate with Germany and Austria against Russia.

Unfortunately, before these organizations had begun to fully function, and before the Austrians and Germans had a chance to mount their defenses, the Russians broke through into Austrian Galicia and occupied Lviv and most of northern Galicia.

---

* A personal footnote: Mykola Zalizniak was the grandfather of George Wesolowsky, my lifelong friend. Please also see *Growing up in Montreal* in the Epilogue.

Anarchy was the order of the day. Various armies were soon fighting throughout the region. The Russians, who a few years earlier had strengthened their hold on Eastern Ukraine were set to take over all of Galicia. The Ukrainian Sich Riflemen retreated to the friendly villages to regroup, while Romanian and Hungarian army units fought for control of the southern regions. Galicia was the scene of the biggest, bloodiest battles fought on the Eastern front. Its populous suffered terribly from the dislocation and destruction that resulted from the fighting, as well as from the brutal wartime administrations of both Russia and Austria. 6

Julian made his way quickly to Sambir, gathered his family, and traveled south to Starij Sambir. They stayed with Julian's sister for a few days, hoping for a reversal of events, but it was not to come soon. On September 7, 1914, as word came that most of the political hierarchy of the Union for Liberation of Ukraine had fled to Vienna to set up a government in exile, Julian hitched a one-horse cart and headed further south, deep into the familiar Boyko region, to the home of his in-laws.

Olha was happy to be reunited with her family even under these circumstances.

The war continued to go badly for the Austrians, and by mid-September, the Russians were pushing for full control of Galicia. As they advanced, Russian soldiers burned or otherwise destroyed Roman Catholic and Uniate churches and deported or murdered the clergy since the Russians only recognized the Russian Orthodox Church. They believed that it was the true church, and that Catholics, whether Roman Catholics or Uniate Catholics, were the enemy.

As the Russians approached, many village priests boarded up their churches, distributed the religious icons and church valuables among trusted parishioners, and either joined the Sich Riflemen or joined the exodus westward. Many people felt the Great War, which had engulfed Europe, would last only a few months and everything would somehow return to normal soon. Julian decided to take his family to the relative safety of Czechoslovakia.

Julian caught up on the latest news from both the eastern and western fronts and on September 25, 1914, he packed his wife, Olha, their two sons, Jaroslav and Oleksander, their trusted maid, and a few valuables into a wagon, hitched their best horses, and headed west. On the way, they stopped to pick up Olha's mother and younger sister and their maid in the village of Berech. The eight of them packed into two wagons and set off for the one train station where they knew they could find seats on a train headed west. They boarded one of the evacuation trains that had been requisitioned by the retreating Austrians and headed west to Belotz on the Polish-Czech border. They stayed there with friends for four weeks before moving south, deep into Czech territory.*

The war that was to last for only a few months now promised to last for a very long time. The political map of Europe was being redrawn, empires were lost, borders were changing, and new regimes were taking power.

---

*    Adapted from Julian Tatomyr's diary.

Traveling with a wife, young family, and in-laws was not an easy task for Julian, but they soon made it to the relative safety of Prague. In late November 1914, while his family slept in a guest bedroom in the home of a Ukrainian expatriate friend, Julian was playing chess and catching up on the news. His friend informed him of the struggles taking place in western Ukraine. Groups of young men and women had formed partisan groups to turn back the Russians and Poles and to try to establish an independent Ukraine.

Julian asked himself why he was here on foreign soil when his training, his leadership abilities, his organizational skills, not to mention his responsibilities as a priest to be with his flock, far outweighed his need for his personal safety. This war would not end soon, the political maps were changing on a daily basis, and it was time for him to go where he was needed.

The next day, he made arrangements to take his family back home. He returned to Sambir where he conferred with his bishop. The Russians were still in control of this city, but he quickly made contact with the Ukrainian Sich Riflemen and with the group of Ukrainian political activists who formed the Union for Liberation of Ukraine. To achieve their goals, these organizations resolved to cooperate with Germany and Austria against Russia.

During the first year of the war, the tsarist Russian army was in control of Lviv and much of eastern Galicia. By May 1915, the Germans broke through in Gorlici in Polish western Galicia and by August, the Russians were driven back east across the Zbruch River; most of Galicia was again in Austrian and German hands.

For the next two years, Julian divided his time between Lviv and Sambir, working with various Ukrainian political organizations and military groups with the goal of setting up conditions for the formation of an independent western Ukrainian state.

> In the spring of 1917, the tsar was overthrown in Russia and his imperial rule was replaced by that of a Provisional Government. By November of that same year, a second Russian revolution took place in which the Provisional government was replaced by a Bolshevik-led government. The upheavals in Russia were accompanied by an avalanche of national risings in each of the non-Russian countries which had been incorporated into the Empire, and which now took the chance to seize their independence.
>
> In November of 1917, in Kyiv, a central council or Rada, was formed by group of politicians sympathetic to the Ukrainian cause, and they declared first an autonomous and then an independent Ukrainian National Republic in January 1918. A similar process was taking place in Galicia. 6

In 1918, when the Ukrainian independence movement was at its height, Julian was one of the most visible and most vocal leaders in the Sambir region. He was a member of the committee that organized peasants and formed the ten thousand person strong group, which demanded Ukrainian independence. This group took over the Sambir administrative offices, raised the blue-and-yellow Ukrainian flag on top of the city hall tower, and declared Sambir's support for the creation of the Western Ukrainian Republic.

As the Austro-Hungarian Empire was disintegrating, and with nationalist feelings running high in eastern Galicia, where Ukrainians formed the majority of the population, a Western Ukrainian People's Republic was finally proclaimed on November 1, 1918. Julian took his two young sons to Lviv to witness the proclamation of the West Ukraine National Republic in Lviv's Ploshcha Rynok (Market Square). They declared unity with the Ukrainian National Republic in Kyiv led by Vynnychenko and Petliura. This republic claimed most of the land that comprises present-day Ukraine.

During the brief period of independence, Julian organized Ukrainian schools and was appointed the school inspector for Sambir.

> This new, all-Ukrainian united government didn't really have a chance to consolidate its power and control over the territory it claimed. Invasions by the Bolsheviks, White Russians, Poles, and others made it impossible for the fledgling government to function. By one count, eleven armies were active on Ukrainian soil in early 1919 and by spring 1919, both the Ukrainian Government in Kyiv and the one established in Lviv had weakened considerably. Petliura, the War Minister, and the Ukrainian Directory retreated south west to the town of Kam'yanets Podilsky. 6

## QUADRANGLE OF DEATH*

As the Polish armies led by General Hallera approached Sambir from the west, Julian again packed his family and traveled with the Ukrainian Galician Army, this time eastward to Kamia'nets Podilsky. Here, at least, he could be of some use. As a chaplain to the young soldiers and as a respected leader, he was called upon daily to help with the war effort. This was no place for a wife and young children, but Julian didn't relish the concept of being in the middle of yet another Polish occupation. He had little choice. By this time, he was well-known as a Ukrainian nationalist and as a strong opponent of both Russia and Poland. Life would likely not be very pleasant for him under the Poles.

In Kamia'nets Podilsky, the two Ukrainian armies tried to regroup while facing daily attacks from Bolshevik and Polish divisions, as well as new threats from Romanian army groups operating to the south.

Conditions under which Julian and his family lived were dismal. They bunked with local townspeople and tried to keep up the spirits of the young soldiers. The Ukrainian Halychyna Army was well disciplined and well organized, but following their retreat from Kyiv, Petliura's Ukrainian National Army was tired. Things went from bad to worse. By fall 1919, they were caught in the "quadrangle of death", surrounded by the Whites, Bolsheviks, Poles, and Romanians.

Conditions worsened as time went on. By October 1919, the exhausted and undernourished Ukrainian armies, with no supplies and inadequate shelter, were struck by a typhoid epidemic. Within a few weeks, the vast majority of these troops were dead,

---

*    Source: Julian Tatomyr's diary

dying, or incapacitated by disease. Those who were still healthy left to join partisan groups.

Petliura took refuge in Poland and, seeing no alternative, made an alliance with the Polish general, Pilsudski. This alliance was met with distrust by many of the peasants who saw the Poles as their *landlords*. Nevertheless, their goal was to conduct a joint war against Soviet Russia.

Petliura wanted to establish an independent Ukraine with its capital in Kyiv. Pilsudski wanted to weaken Russia and have a friendly nonbelligerent neighbor on Poland's eastern boundary. In 1920, Pilsudski marched his army through Galicia into Kam'anets Podilsky and joined with the remnants of Petliura's army and several thousand soldiers of the Galician Army. On May 7, 1920, they captured Kyiv.

The celebrations, however, were short lived. The Soviets regrouped their forces and counterattacked, and by November 1920, the Russians had again captured Kyiv.

In the chaos, Pilsudski took eastern Galicia and placed it under Polish control.

Ukrainian hopes for an independent state were shattered.

## Portrait of a Child Soldier: VOLODYMYR TATOMYR

Julian's nephew, Volodymyr Tatomyr, (oldest son of Julian's older brother, Rev. Mykhajlo Tatomyr), was born in 1902.

In 1913, just before World War I started, Volodymyr was eleven years old, attending the first year of secondary school (Grade 5) in Strij, a large town in the sub-Carpathian region of Western Ukraine where his father, Mykhajlo, was the parish priest. Although this was a time of relative peace in the Austrian Empire and in Europe, the spirit of Ukrainian nationalism and yearning for independence was very strong among Ukrainians. When a Ukrainian version of the world-wide Boy Scouting Organization was started in Ukraine, Volodymyr and his classmates were among the first to join the Strij chapter at their school. The Ukrainian Boy and Girl Scout groups called themselves 'Plast', and although the overall principles of international scouting were central in the Ukrainian group's philosophy, Plast had a decidedly nationalistic focus which permeated all their activities.

When World War I broke out in 1914, young men in Galicia were drafted to serve in the Austrian army. Many of Volodymyr's older schoolmates, however, joined the newly formed Ukrainian Sich Riflemen whose goal was the creation of a free, independent Ukraine.

Volodymyr and his classmates were too young to fight for their country but they regarded their older school mates as heroes and role-models and were determined to help them in any way they could. They were also determined to join their ranks as soon as possible. For the next four years, Volodymyr and his friends prepared themselves for eventual military service and whenever they could, acted as scouts for the Sich Riflemen in their area.

On January 22, 1918, Ukrainians in Kyiv declared an independent Ukrainian Republic although western Ukraine remained under Polish occupation.

Volodymyr and his classmates decided it was their time to get involved in the fight for independence. As sixteen year olds, they secretly joined the Sich Riflemen and later the newly formed Ukrainian Halytska (Galician) Army, UHA, as a Plast unit.

On November 1, 1918, after a bitter struggle on many fronts, Ukrainians in western Ukraine declared the West Ukraine National Republic in Lviv with the intention of forming a union with their brothers in eastern Ukraine.

Volodymyr was involved in the cause for the liberation of Ukraine from the age of 12 as a member of a Plast group, as a scout for the Sich Riflemen, and as a junior officer in the Ukrainian Galician Army (Plast-Youth Division) from 1919 until the end of the struggle in 1921. To get a sense of the mood, confusion, anarchy, patriotism and aftereffects of this struggle, please see Tribute 1 in the Epilogue, where several excerpts from Volodymyr Tatomyr's book, **Youth in Defense of Their Homeland** published in Philadelphia in 1960 are included.

*   *   *

By early 1921, the Tatomyrs returned to Galicia under Polish occupation. Julian asked the bishop in Peremyshl for a parish deep in the Carpathian Mountains, out of sight of the Polish administration. Weary from seven years of the long bitter war and eager to reestablish some semblance of family life, he was relieved when the bishop gave him a small parish in the village of Hrozova. There, he and his family would rest, regroup their strength and wait for the situation to stabilize. In time Julian was given a parish a little further north in the Dnister valley, in the village of Luzhok.

He remained there as pastor, on and off, for more than twenty years, until July, 1944.

**Senator Reverend Julian Sas-Tatomyr, Chrystyna's grandfather, c.1940**

# PART THREE

# The War between the Wars

# Chapter 7

## Stalin's Famine—Genocide and the Pulitzer Prize

In 1932 and 1933, millions of Ukrainians died in the largest famine of the twentieth century. (Estimates range that between 4.5 and 10 million people died.) This famine was not caused by a natural disaster such as a drought or epidemic or pestilence, but was engineered, orchestrated, and directed from the Kremlin. It was ordered by Stalin and brutally implemented by his lieutenant, Lazar Kaganovich, in order to complete Ukraine's total subjugation to Moscow. Starvation became the tool, and the Ukrainian farmers became the main victims.

Before World War I, eastern Ukraine had been under the domination of the Russian empire for more than two hundred years. With the collapse of the Russian empire in March 1917, it seemed that the long-awaited opportunity for Ukrainian independence had finally arrived. Optimistic Ukrainians declared their country independent and selected their ancient city, Kyiv, to be the capital.

But by the end of 1917, Lenin sought to reclaim all the areas formerly controlled by the tsars, especially fertile Ukraine. Four years of chaos and conflict followed, in which Ukrainian national troops fought Lenin's Red Army and Russia's White Army (troops still loyal to the Tsar), as well as other invading forces, including the Germans and the Poles.

By 1921, the battles ended with a Soviet victory. Eastern Ukraine again fell to the Soviets while the western part of Ukraine was divided among Poland, Romania, and Czechoslovakia.

When Stalin came to power in 1924, he was determined to once and for all eliminate all resistance to Soviet rule. To Stalin, the burgeoning national revival in Ukraine was completely unacceptable. Beginning in 1929, over five thousand Ukrainian scholars, scientists, and cultural and religious leaders were arrested and accused of plotting an armed revolt. Most of the leaders were either shot or deported to remote areas of Russia.

Stalin also imposed the Soviet system of land management known as collectivization. This resulted in the seizure of all privately owned farmlands. *Kulaks*, wealthy farmers who owned more than twenty-four acres, or employed farm workers, were branded "enemies of the people." Their land and all possessions were taken away and they were either deported or killed.

In 1932, there was adequate grain harvested to feed the population, but Moscow imposed draconian grain quotas on Ukraine, which caused mass starvation. Zealous Communist League members and armed troops were dispatched into Ukraine from Russia to guard the fields and warehouses. Troops entered every home, tore up the floorboards searching for hidden grain, and confiscated whatever food they found. Resisting farmers were shot or exiled.

Theft of food, now Socialist-state property, warranted a minimum of five years imprisonment or execution. Anyone caught picking up even a grain of wheat risked being executed on the spot.

The word *holod*, (famine or hunger) was forbidden and decreed a counterrevolutionary rumor.

The Soviets sealed the borders of Ukraine, preventing any food from entering. They also imposed internal passports, preventing anyone from traveling outside their villages.

Starvation spread quickly with the most vulnerable, the children and the elderly feeling the effects of malnutrition first. Mothers in the countryside sometimes tossed their children onto passing trains traveling toward cities in the hope that someone there would take pity on them. But in the cities, children and adults were dropping dead in the streets, their bodies carted away in horse-drawn wagons, to be dumped into mass graves. There were reports of cannibalism in the villages, and, in some instances, the residents of entire villages would die within sight of guarded food granaries.

Western journalists based in Moscow at the time knew of the forced starvation but most chose not to write about it or deliberately covered it up.

The journalist who played the most influential role in the cover-up was the *New York Times* correspondent, Walter Duranty. He, along with other Westerners, was a fan of Stalin, whom he described as the "world's greatest statesman." Duranty was granted the first American interview with Stalin and received privileged status in the Kremlin.

When other journalists traveling in Ukraine started to write about the famine, Duranty branded their information as anti-Soviet lies. When British journalist, Malcolm Muggeridge, wrote about what he saw while traveling in Ukraine in 1933, he was denounced by Duranty, as well as the British and American press, led by the *New York Times*. Privately, Duranty confided to a British diplomat that he thought ten million had perished in the famine.

Western governments adopted a passive attitude toward the famine, although most of them had become aware of the true suffering in Ukraine through confidential channels. In November 1933, the United States, under its new president, Franklin D. Roosevelt, formally recognized Stalin's communist government and even negotiated a sweeping new trade agreement. The following year, the pattern of denial in the West culminated with the admission of the Soviet Union into the League of Nations.

Robert Conquest, a British historian who first brought the tyranny to Western audiences in 1986 with the publication of his work, *Harvest of Sorrow*, believes that Duranty was being blackmailed by the Soviet secret police over his sexual activities, which reportedly included necrophilia.

In 1931, a year before the famine-genocide began, Duranty won the Pulitzer Prize for a series of articles about the Soviet economy.

When he was confronted with facts about the famine, Duranty was reported to have repeated a quote attributed to Stalin, "You can't make an omelet without breaking some eggs."

In 2003, the Ukrainian community in the West, led by Dr. Lubomyr Luciuk, professor of history at the Royal Military College of Canada in Kingston, Ontario, launched a campaign to have Duranty's Pulitzer Prize posthumously revoked. A spokesman for the Pulitzer Prize, Sid Gissler, said the board had considered withdrawing Duranty's prize on previous occasions but had decided against doing so because it had not been awarded for articles related to the famine-genocide. He said he sympathized with the Ukrainian campaign and added that the board would reconsider the question later that year.

As of this writing (2008), the Pulitzer board has not withdrawn the award and the *New York Times* continues to list Duranty as one of its Pulitzer Prize winners.

In 2005, memos written by Stalin in 1932 and 1933 were released to the public. Among them are memos that show that Stalin was very much aware of the famine and that, in fact, he was directing it.

Today, some apologists for Stalin still maintain that Stalin was a great leader, without whom the Soviet Union would not have been able to become the industrial powerhouse that it was. They maintain that Stalin's crimes were justified in the name of the class struggle theory and the principle of dictatorship of the proletariat. The interpretation of both principles legitimized the "elimination of people who were considered harmful to the construction of a new society and, as such, were enemies of the totalitarian communist regimes."[*]

*   *   *

As children growing up in North America in the early1950s, Chrystyna and I were aware that a *holod* (famine) had taken place in eastern Ukraine some time in the past, that millions had died and that the then ruler of the Soviet Union, Joseph Stalin, was

---

[*]   Report to Council of Europe, January 2006

    For a more detailed account of the famine-genocide (Holodomor), please see Robert Conquest's book *Harvest of Sorrow* or www.unitedhumanrights.org.

the architect of that famine. We were also told that Ukraine is a very fertile land, and that millions of bushels of grain are grown in the area every year.

But we couldn't understand how it was possible to have a famine on such a huge scale, how soldiers could stand guard over large supplies of grain and watch children in the same village starve to death and how the soldiers could prevent farmers from gathering their own grain.

Also, we could not understand how a crime of this scale could be covered up and denied by the communist state or why Stalin was not arrested and tried for his crimes.

The *holod* was in our consciousness but all the details seemed so vague, so distant, so removed from our reality.

Now, sixty years later, we were finally in western Ukraine and were about to travel to eastern Ukraine, to see first hand the area where the famine happened.

## BLACK SEA

Following the disintegration of the Soviet Union in 1991 and Ukraine's declaration of independence, Ukrainians in the Diaspora, notably in Canada and the United States, raised substantial amounts of money for various projects to help Ukraine get on their feet.

The Toronto branch of the Canadian Friends of Rukh, bolstering Ukraine's independence movement, had a history of supporting educational initiatives in Ukraine. A number of previous exchange projects led to an invitation by the Lviv Ministry of Education to send a group of Canadian educators to run summer seminars for Ukrainian educators.

The Institute for the Professional Development of Teachers, headed by Nadia Luciw, was formed in Toronto. Its goal was to prepare programs aimed at introducing Western teaching practices into Ukrainian schools. Because the Soviet regime had intentionally isolated Ukraine's educators from developments in Western teaching practices, the need for reform and updating was imperative.

Michael Bregin, the director of education for the city of Lviv, a highly progressive, knowledgeable Western-leaning educator, was our Ukrainian host.

The team assembled in Toronto in 1993 consisted of: Nadia Luciw, an elementary school principal with the Peel Catholic Board of Education; Valentina Kuryliw, a high school teacher of Canadian and world history and an expert on Ukrainian history from Toronto; Mirka Onuch and Halyna Dytyniak, two elementary teachers from Toronto who would offer courses to Ukrainian elementary teachers on classroom methods used in Canada; and George Zerebecki, a language consultant for the Saskatchewan Ministry of Education who would lead a course on language arts. Bohdan Kolos, a teacher from Toronto and a prominent Plast leader, and others joined our group the following year.

When requests came from Lviv to offer a course for their school administrators, Nadia approached me and asked if I could provide a Ukrainian version of the course I was teaching at the University of Toronto to Canadian administrators.

I was thrilled by the proposal but knew I would need a lot of help. We agreed that Chrystyna, an educational consultant who was used to giving seminars and one whose knowledge of Ukrainian was perhaps a little stronger than mine, would team-teach the course with me and provide information about how we teach children with special needs.

Joining us in Lviv was Oksana Wynnyckyj, a native Torontonian who was living in Lviv at the time. She would teach a course in Teaching English as a Second Language. She had come to Lviv a few years earlier, where she met and married the talented and urbane musical director of the Lviv Opera. Both of them were able to give us outstanding insight into life in Lviv.

Thinking a year in advance, the organizing group in Toronto had already obtained funding to offer a course the following year in Odesa, an area of Ukraine that was highly "Russified." Their Ministry of Education officials invited us to come to Odesa for a few days to "fly the flag" and to try to convince some skeptical members of the educational bureaucracy that we should be permitted to offer courses in that city in 1994.

That evening, five of our group, Nadia, Mirka, George, Chrystyna, and I, boarded the 7:00 p.m. overnight train to Odesa.

*   *   *

During the summer, the train to Odesa is almost always crowded with vacationers taking their holidays on the Black Sea coast so additional coaches are added to each train to accommodate the crowds. These ancient coaches, called *summer wagons*, are pulled out of storage every spring and added to existing trains. The standing joke is that these coaches have been around since tsarist times.

In their time, these coaches must have been quite elegant. They still had their brass fittings, velvet seats, and carved wood partitions. On the other hand, the windows didn't always open or close and the toilets were quite primitive.

The underpaid conductors on these trains, nevertheless, tried their best to offer reasonable service, perhaps hoping to supplement their salaries with tips. (They had quickly learned about this aspect of Western capitalism.)

Before we left Canada, we obtained fifty one-dollar U.S. bills to be given as tips or encouragement during our trip and, although Chrystyna and I were nonsmokers at that time (we had quit about fifteen years earlier), we bought two cartons of Marlboro cigarettes at the Toronto Airport duty-free shop before we left.

As we were boarding the Odesa train, the conductor assigned to our coach was taking the last few puffs from a short, strong-smelling cigarette. I reached into my knapsack and pulled out a pack of Marlboros and asked him if he wanted to try one of *my* cigarettes. He was, of course, delighted and thanked me. I told him to keep the pack.

We boarded our car and were pleased to see our assigned seats were in a four-passenger sleeping compartment. Unfortunately, we had to share our compartment with two scruffy-looking men who spoke only Russian. They had an open bottle of vodka between them and had already dented it before we arrived. They were eating sausages, drinking and talking loudly. As we entered the compartment, they both eyed Chrystyna. One of them said something I didn't understand.

It was hot and stuffy in the compartment but we decided to make the best of it. We didn't think we would get much sleep, so we decided we would spend most of our time on this overnight trip in the breezy corridors.

Just as the train was about to leave the station, the conductor entered our car. He surveyed the situation and asked the two men to step outside. A few minutes later, he returned and told us we didn't look like we would enjoy the trip with those two men. He had placed them in another car so that we could have this compartment all to ourselves; we could lock our door and have complete *privacy* for the whole trip. He winked at me as he left the car.

"Incredible," I thought. "All this for just one pack of cigarettes! Obviously, he's looking for a much larger tip." I was more than willing to provide one. I took out my wad of dollar bills but he waved me off, saying, "It's O.K., you already tipped me."

A good start to our Odesa odyssey, I thought.

About an hour into our trip, the train made a stop in Ternopil, the last stop in western Ukraine. The Ternopil train station building is a magnificent ornate structure, a mix of imperial Austrian, imperial Russian, and Soviet architecture.

I remembered stories my parents told about Ternopil. Ternopil was where they both went to school and where they met. They must have passed through this station dozens of times during the 1920s. I struggled to remember more of my parents' stories. Their hometowns were just a few kilometers south of here. I hoped the train would turn south and pass by one of their villages. (It didn't.)

A large number of people waited on the platform to get on our train.

"Oh well," I thought. "We won't be alone in our compartment for long."

But somehow, everyone got on this already crowded train and nobody came to our compartment.

We were off again, and the train was picking up speed as it headed east. In less than an hour, we crossed the Zbruch River, the old boundary between Austrian and Soviet Ukraine. We were now well inside eastern Ukraine.

Sixty years earlier, Stalin's famine took place here.

I remembered how agitated my parents became whenever they spoke of the famine. I remember the *panachydas* (memorial church services) and commemorative concerts held yearly when I was young, and how strongly Ukrainian immigrants in Canada and the United States felt about the famine and how occasionally people would break down in tears, remembering lost family and friends. My mother's village, Ivanivka, in the easternmost part of Galicia, was located less than twenty kilometers from the Zbruch River. On the other side of this gently flowing river was Soviet-controlled Ukraine. My mother was a young woman during the early 1930s. Everyone knew the Soviets had created an artificial famine just across the river, but they also knew they could do nothing about it. People who lived on the western side of the Zbruch River didn't fully believe a famine could actually be taking place, especially when the crops on the western side of the river were coming in normally.

Occasionally, someone would escape across the river from the east and would reveal what was happening there—stories of soldiers guarding grain supplies while children starved, of people being shot for trying to get food for their families. There was no drought, no unusual weather on the west side of the Zbruch.

As darkness fell, the conductor brought us two clean sheets and two pillows. A few minutes later, he brought two glasses of tea served in traditional Russian glass and silver goblets. I handed him two one-dollar bills. He thanked me, "No, but . . . maybe if you have another pack of cigarettes . . ."

*   *   *

It was unbearably hot in the compartment. We couldn't sleep, and we knew that no amount of cigarettes or other bribes would get us air-conditioning on this train. In search of relief, we left our hot compartment and joined a number of other passengers in the corridor. The windows were wide open, and a lovely soft breeze cooled us, if just a little.

A full moon illuminated the passing villages consisting of simple small houses with their tidy orchards and gardens. We could see huge expanses of wheat and sunflowers, orchards with apples, pears, and plums, and huge gardens planted right up against the tracks.

I asked myself, "How could there have been such a total famine in this fertile land?" "How could millions have starved?"

And more importantly, I considered, "How could this have been kept secret from the rest of the world?"

It was well past midnight when we went back to our very much appreciated private compartment. The rhythm of the train put us to sleep in minutes. We were awakened by the morning sun about an hour before our arrival in Odesa. The landscape was a little different but we continued to pass fertile farmland and fields heavy with wheat and sunflowers.

It was only six in the morning but it was already very hot.

We pulled into Odesa right on time at 7:00 a.m.

*   *   *

Svitlana, a local principal, met us as we got off the train. Another man collected our luggage and squeezed it into an old truck.

Nadia, George, Mirka, Chrystyna, and I squeezed into Svitlana's car. She was a principal at a large high school in Odesa, a Ukrainian living in an almost totally Russian environment. A few months earlier, when she heard about our courses, she immediately signed up for the course Chrystyna and I would be teaching to school administrators.

Svitlana said she had a surprise for us. After a brief tour of Odesa, we arrived at a grimy wharf on Odesa's waterfront. A number of small rusty commercial boats were tied up at the pier.

The water in the harbor did not seem particularly clean. An oily film surrounded the boats, putrid smoke belched from the stacks on the boats, and the smell of bunker fuel was overpowering. Svitlana announced she was taking us on a cruise on the Black Sea so that we could see Odesa from a more dramatic angle.

The Black Sea had always held a special fascination for me. Stories my parents and Ukrainian schoolteachers told us and the games we played as children always glorified this sacred body of water. Visions of Cossacks coming down the Dnipro River in their longboats and crossing the Black Sea on their way to raid Constantinople, stories about the naval battles which took place here over the centuries and about the beautiful beaches that stretched "all the way to Turkey" lived in my imagination. I had often looked at maps of the Black Sea and hoped one day I could see it. (A few years earlier, traveling in Europe, I ended up in Istanbul and thought of making the short side-trip from that city just to see the Black Sea coast but I couldn't arrange a ride in time. That was very disappointing.)

With all the other impressions I had experienced over the last few days, finally seeing the Black Sea turned into a near-religious experience.

The old boat Svitlana arranged for us was a converted World War II minesweeper. It was not really designed for leisurely cruising but it was all Svitlana could afford. Luckily, we had brought an overnight bag that contained our bathing suits. When we got out into the bay, we changed and asked the captain to stop the boat. We took a dip in the refreshing, warm waters. For me, it was a kind of rechristening.

We spent only two days in Odesa during that first trip in 1993, but we had a number of experiences that gave us a better understanding not only of Odesa but also of the difficulties associated with life in Ukraine. We returned to that city the following year, in 1994.

Odesa, located between the mouths of two important rivers, the Dnipro and the Dnister, was built and settled in 1794, and became an important naval base and commercial port for the Russian empire. A large majority of the population had always been Russian with a substantial Jewish community (about a third of the population before the Second World War). In 1991, Odesa found itself geographically in an independent Ukrainian State.

It is easy to understand why the Russians were not happy to give up to Ukraine their ports in Odesa and Crimea, along with part of the Black Sea Fleet. On the other hand, given everything else that happened over the centuries, and the brutality Moscow inflicted on Ukrainians over the years, it's hard to sympathize with their situation. For once, the Russians had to accept geopolitical realities.

The language on the streets and most of the street signs in Odesa were written in Russian. All the government buildings, however, had freshly installed blue and gold signs written exclusively in Ukrainian. When we, Ukrainian-speaking teachers, came to our meetings at the Ministry of Education in this Ukrainian city, we needed translators.

Many of the officials spoke only Russian. Ironically, these same Russian speakers were charged with the implementation of directives from Kyiv mandating that the language of instruction in all public schools in Odesa would be Ukrainian. In this situation, I sympathized, just a little, with the officials.

# ODESA SNAPSHOTS

The hotel selected for us in Odesa was a former Communist Party resort hotel on the Odesa waterfront, just minutes from downtown. Our room in this faded old hotel had a wonderful view of the Black Sea and the walled-off exclusive beach below. Inside, all signs and services were in Russian.

When Chrystyna and I came down to breakfast on our first morning in the hotel, we were seated at a table next to another couple: a stout man in a military officer's uniform and a much younger woman. The officer had a small white, blue, and red badge on his shoulder, indicating he was with the Russian military. The gold, glitter, and ribbons on his uniform indicated he held a high rank.

When our waitress came to take our order, I spoke to her in Ukrainian, hoping she would understand. To my surprise, she responded in hesitant broken Ukrainian. I continued the conversation in Ukrainian, but as I did, the Russian officer rudely bellowed to her in Russian. She jumped, blushed, and ran to him apologetically. He then started to bellow at me. "*Po Ruski!*" (Speak Russian!), he shouted. I understood enough to guess he was unhappy with my use of Ukrainian.

He was an out-of-shape, overweight little man who was obviously accustomed to getting his own way. I was taller, fitter, and younger and certainly not intimidated by him. I walked over to his table and yelling back in Ukrainian I let him know that he was not in charge here. For good measure, I repeated it all in English. I don't know if he understood the words but I'm sure he understood what I meant.

I went back to my table.

He finished his breakfast quickly and left the room.

\*     \*     \*

Later that afternoon, we went for a stroll around the port area of Odesa. A few blocks from our hotel, we spotted a small café with four small tables on the outside patio. There was a large sign written in English and in Hebrew over the door advertising: "Maccabee Beer, Israel's Finest Beer!" The place was empty except for a tiny older woman, probably in her eighties, sitting on one of the chairs and nursing a cup of tea. We decided to have a beer.

"Two beers," I said to the waiter in English.

He responded in reasonable English, asked us where we were from, and quickly brought us two ice-cold Maccabee beers. Chrystyna and I continued our conversation in English and Ukrainian.

After a few minutes, the old woman turned to us, leaned over and whispered in English, "I hate Jews."

I was taken aback. I had assumed this lady was the mother or grandmother of the owner/waiter of the bar and, also, that she, like the waiter, was Jewish. Was she a local who mistook *us* for Jews? If she hated Jews, why was she sitting in this obviously Jewish bar?

Was she baiting us? When the Nazis invaded Odesa in 1941, the Jewish population of more than 300,000 was almost totally wiped out. Today only about 50,000 Jews remain in Odesa. There was reason for bitterness.

But why was she picking on us?

I told her she shouldn't say hateful things about anybody, but she insisted and continued to tell us how much she hated Jews. We finished our beers and left. She went back to her tea.

*    *    *

As we strolled back to our hotel, we noticed a trailer parked not far from the entrance to our hotel. A few tables and chairs were set up beside the trailer. On the bar inside the trailer, I spotted a bottle of Labatt 50 ale. "Wow!" I thought. "Canadian beer, here in Odesa? I have to have one!"

"How much for the Labatt's?" I asked.

He gave me the price in *coupons*, the Ukrainian currency at that time. His price was equivalent to about fifty cents in Canadian dollars! Maybe he forgot a zero and meant five dollars. I asked again. He repeated the same price.

"Two Labatt's 50!" I said and handed him the equivalent of a dollar.

It really was Canadian beer. The label said, "Brewed and bottled in Montreal." How could he afford to sell imported beer at that price?

But then, Odesa is a port. I guess things sometimes fall off the back of a boat.

The next day the trailer was gone!

*    *    *

The following night, we discovered the restaurants on Pushkinska Boulevard and the upscale shops on Derybasivska Street. As we strolled along the street, window shopping the expensive shops, we noticed a small crowd had gathered on a corner. As we came closer we saw a neatly dressed young man, surrounded by other similarly dressed young men and women, speaking to the crowd in English. The speaker and his companions were obviously westerners and it soon became evident that they were part of a Christian group preaching the bible.

I approached a man in the crowd and asked, in English, what was going on. The man answered in Russian that he didn't understand me. I asked another person, and still another but none in the crowd seemed to understand English.

After the young missionary finished speaking, I approached him and asked if he knew that his audience didn't understand English. He said he did but that it didn't matter as they were giving out Christian bibles written in Russian.

We introduced ourselves and chatted for a while. He seemed to be glad to find someone who spoke and understood English. He said their group came from towns in the United States Midwest and that they had been in Odesa most of the summer.

I asked why they had chosen this street and this city for their mission. He answered that they came here because this area had been communist for so long and the people had not had an opportunity to practice any religion.

I asked whether he was aware that this country had been Christian for more than a thousand years and had a long Orthodox-Christian tradition. He shrugged and stated that he would continue his work in Odesa until the end of summer and then he and his companions would return home to the United States.

\*   \*   \*

Just a short walk from that corner, two Orthodox priests sat in a small booth in front of a very large church. They were collecting donations for the rebuilding of the main Orthodox cathedral in Odesa which had been partially destroyed by the Nazis in 1943 and had been left vacant and unused for almost fifty years. One of the priests eagerly took us on a tour inside the cathedral showing us the magnificent frescos badly in need of restoration, windows in need of replacement and walls that needed repair. He proudly informed us that church services had resumed and invited us to return for morning mass. We gave the priests some money for their rebuilding fund. When we returned the following year, we were impressed to see that significant improvements had indeed been made to the cathedral.

\*   \*   \*

Our favorite place in Odesa was the outdoor café area at the top of the *Potemkin Stairs* on Prymorskyy Boulevard overlooking the Black Sea. It also became our hangout the following year when we were teaching in Odesa.

Whenever we had some free time, we would climb the stairs, made famous by the 1925 film, *Battleship Potemkin* by Russian film director Sergei Eisenstein, and would enjoy a glass of local champagne and a caviar sandwich in the café next to Richelieu's statue located at the top of the stairs. Sometimes we would stroll into the nearby Londonskaya Hotel. The doorman at this hotel was instructed to prevent non-guests from entering the hotel but on our first visit we waved confidently and strolled past him, ignoring his pleas for identification. The next time we came, we were welcomed as guests. The Londonskaya Hotel has one of the prettiest interior courtyard restaurants in Odesa.

\*   \*   \*

When we returned to Odesa to teach in 1994, Odesa was celebrating two major events: the 200th anniversary of the 1794 founding of the city and, more importantly, the fiftieth anniversary of the 1944 defeat of the Nazis and liberation of the city by the Red Army. There were signs scattered throughout the city commemorating that event.

We were encouraged that about two hundred teachers and school administrators from the Odesa region had signed up to take our courses.

The first day, however, there was a bit of a fuss. All of our classes were conducted in Ukrainian, and most of the Canadian instructors had only passing knowledge of Russian. Unfortunately, a few of the teachers who signed up for our courses assumed they would be taught in Russian. One woman loudly insisted we speak Russian. We tried to explain that we did not know any Russian. Showing her displeasure in no uncertain terms, she left and never returned.

The most poignant moments during the courses occurred when we discussed the famine of 1932-33. Our history teacher, Valentina Kuryliw, had brought a documentary video about the famine by Canadian filmmaker Yurij Luhowy. I thought it would be important for the administrators in our course to see this documentary.

When I first mentioned the "Famine," there were blank stares.

The course participants, most of whom were in their thirties and forties and who were all from the Odesa area, claimed they had never heard of any famine in Ukraine. Politely, they tried to tell me that perhaps I was misinformed, and a famine, if it had taken place, had taken place somewhere else.

I asked Valentina to come to our class. She was the expert on the famine, could give precise details about it, and answer questions better than I could. Some of my class members continued to doubt our information; others insisted this was capitalist propaganda. We asked them to be patient, to watch the film.

After seeing the film with its original footage of peasants dying and stories by survivors, there wasn't a dry eye in the place.

Two participants stormed out of the room and never returned. I don't know what happened to them. Most of the rest of the participants were moved to tears and slowly, slowly, the discussion revealed that yes, they did remember stories their parents and grandparents had told them, but they had also been told by their teachers in school that these stories were lies.

The Soviets had blanked out any references to the famine in all history books and talk of it was prohibited.

Today, facts about the famine are taught in all public schools in Ukraine.

In 2007, the Ukrainian parliament declared that the 1932-33 artificial famine, officially called the Holodomor, was genocide.

*　　*　　*

On the trip back from Odesa to Lviv, our train was even more overcrowded. Our wagon was even older than the one a few days ago, and we couldn't find the nice conductor from the previous trip. Eight people were crowded into a compartment designed for four passengers, and it was even hotter than before.

But this was a day trip. Chrystyna and I decided to spend most of the trip sitting on the steps between two cars. This was not necessarily safe, and this certainly would never be permitted in North America, but it was cool there, and we could watch the incredibly beautiful landscape. We felt like kids sneaking a ride on a freight train, enjoying every delicious minute.

The train made several stops in tiny villages. At each stop, dozens of villagers mingled on the station platform waiting to sell their fruits, vegetables, and flowers to the passengers. At each stop, passengers could jump off the train, buy some apples or potatoes or ice cream or cooked *perogies*, and then jump back on the train before it moved on. A stop usually lasted about five minutes.

Chrystyna and I decided to jump off at one of the stops. We found a lady selling apples and started a conversation with her. She was old and poor and asked just a few pennies for a whole bag of apples. I gave her a few dollars and asked if I could take her picture. We continued our conversation and lost track of time. Suddenly, out of the corner of my eye, I noticed our train was moving. I grabbed Chrystyna's hand and we started to run. (She, of course, was wearing high-heeled shoes.) Reaching the moving train, I took hold of a car railing with one hand as I grabbed Chrystyna with the other. Somehow, I managed to swing her onto the train and pulled myself up behind her. Passengers who saw all this as it developed cheered us on.

We later wondered what an experience we would have had if we had been left behind in the tiny village and had to wait for the next train to Lviv . . . twenty-four hours later.

# Chapter 8

# Polish Occupation

By 1918 the War to end all Wars was over in most of Europe though it raged on in Ukraine until 1921. When it was finally over, eastern Ukraine fell to the Soviets and western Ukraine (Galicia) fell under Polish control.

During negotiations at the Treaty of Versailles after World War I, President Woodrow Wilson spoke eloquently in support of a policy of self-determination for all ethnic groups in war-torn Europe. Yet, in spite of repeated strong representations by Ukrainian delegates to allow Ukrainians to form their own government in eastern Galicia, Wilson looked the other way and allowed Polish demands to govern Galicia.

In retrospect, it was a bad decision for all concerned. Ukrainians who fought so hard for independence and had experienced it from 1917 to 1921 were frustrated, humiliated and angry and did not quietly submit to the rule of the outside occupying forces.

The Polish governance of Galicia from 1921 to 1939 was unnecessarily repressive and was very unpopular among Ukrainians. Constant squabbles between Ukrainians and Poles actually weakened Poland at a time when that fledging country needed to consolidate its territory. It caused Poles to become increasingly less democratic and more and more dictatorial. It sapped their resources and since Poles had to use their scarce military resources to "control" Ukrainians, Poland became more vulnerable to Nazi advances during the late 1930s.

Jews who lived in Galicia were caught in the middle of the two warring factions.

The official policy in Galicia was that all citizens of greater Poland had the same rights and privileges. Poles, however, did everything in their power to keep Ukrainians at a subservient level.

## MY GRANDFATHER'S MILL (2)

Grandfather Peter's dream of owning his own mill came at a price. Poles living in Ladychyn were jealous of Peter's position as owner of a successful mill. In Ladychyn, as in most towns in Galicia, businesses were owned and operated by Poles or Jews. Less than ten percent were run by Ukrainians. Poles did not want Ukrainians to have too much economic power, and my grandfather and his successful business represented a threat to their financial dominance of the population.

On several occasions, Polish hoodlums came to the mill at night and tried to damage the equipment or to start fires. They also attempted to harass customers during the day. The local Polish police did little to correct the situation when Peter complained, or even when he gave them the names of the intruders.

Eventually, Peter retaliated by hiring a few tough Ukrainian boys to protect his property. After a few one-sided battles, where the intruders were badly beaten, a semblance of peace was restored in town.

Some Poles never accepted Peter's presence in Ladychyn nor his position as a successful businessman. On the other hand, Peter's firm resistance to Polish pressures earned him the respect of Ukrainians from all walks of life. Business doubled and tripled over time.

Peter had experienced freedom while he was in Chicago. In spite of all the hardships he faced here in his own country, he was not going to give in to intimidation.

He felt his ownership of the mill, and its success was the best way to make a positive contribution to the Ukrainian nation and he could best help the fight for freedom by being able to financially support the cause.

Peter passed these ideals to his children.

**Maria and Peter with five of their six children, Ladychyn Mill, c.1930**
**Standing: Joseph, Olha, Emilia (Lucia), Bohdan. Seated: Recently ordained, Roman**

# MY FATHER, BOHDAN OMELAN MELNYK

My father, Bohdan, was born in Varvarenci, Galicia, on April 8, 1910, the fourth of seven children of Peter and Maria. He was also the second of three sons. When Bohdan was eleven years old, his father, Peter, bought the mill in Ladychyn and moved his family to the spacious new surroundings, four kilometers upstream from Varvarenci.

Since Bohdan's older brother, my uncle, Roman, decided to become a priest, my father, Bohdan, was destined to take over the mill. From an early age, however, my father didn't have much desire to be a miller like his father. He had other plans. He enjoyed school and he preferred to live in larger towns.

He inherited a passion for freedom and fairness from his father. He also inherited his father's nationalistic feelings and spent many hours discussing politics with his friends. He felt a strong desire to serve his nation and felt he could do it more effectively in an occupation other than the one his father practiced.

In 1922, Poles tightened their grip on Galicia. Thousands of Polish settlers were brought into eastern Galicia to dramatically increase the percentage of Poles in the area thereby minimizing Ukrainian influence. Ukrainian schools were closed or taken over by Poles. There were attempts to discourage attendance at Ukrainian Uniate churches and efforts were made to convert Uniates to Roman Catholicism, with very little success.

By 1926, the government in Warsaw took an even harder line with regard to Ukrainians. There were more restrictions on the use of the Ukrainian language: reading rooms were closed and the final *matura* exams at the end of grade 12 had to be completed in Polish regardless of the language of instruction used in the school. Children who were taught in Ukrainian had to learn Polish language, history and other subjects, in Polish, if they hoped to graduate.

The imposition of these harsh restrictions did nothing to improve relations between Poles and Ukrainians. More and more, aware and educated Ukrainians found ways to undermine Polish authority.

Although some Ukrainians found it easier to become *Polonized*, the majority practiced sullen passive resistance and, in some cases, outright violence against Poles.

# THE SCOUTING MOVEMENT—PLAST.

While still a teenager attending school in Ternopil during the 1920s, Bohdan joined the Ukrainian Boy Scouts. In western Ukraine, this organization was called *Plast*, and was loosely based on the same lofty principles that Baden-Powell laid out for British Scouts in 1908. (The word Plast is derived from an ancient Cossack word, *plastun*, meaning scout or sentry.) The Scouting movement spread quickly throughout Europe and around the world. By 1911, a group of Ukrainians in Lviv had already laid the groundwork for the establishment of a Ukrainian scouting group.

At about the same time, Poles in Lviv also started a Polish scouting organization called Harcerstwo.

Although, technically, the Ukrainians and Poles belonged to the same global scouting organization, the goals of the individual national groups differed significantly.

While the British scout's motto was "For King and Country," Ukrainian Plast's motto was "For God and Ukraine." Included in Plast's founding principles were the goals to "expand the spiritual, intellectual, social, and physical aspects of its members and encourage the understanding of Ukrainian history, culture, and national traditions in a Christian setting."

The Polish Harcerstwo group's motto was certainly not compatible with Plast's motto.

Plast groups were established in schools throughout Galicia for students aged eleven to eighteen. Soon ten-year-olds were admitted, and the upper age limits were ignored as the members grew older.

Plast membership gained momentum after 1920 when Polish rule in Ukraine was established, and membership increased even more dramatically as the Polish authorities became more authoritarian and tightened their control on every aspect of the lives of Ukrainians.

In the mid 1920s, when Bohdan was still in Ternopil, the Polish authorities banned Plast membership while the activities of the Polish *Harcerstwo* were allowed to continue. Plast was forced underground. The resolve and commitment of its members increased even more.

Clashes between Ukrainians and Poles were common in the larger towns, and clashes among young people involved in the respective scouting organizations increased, especially in schools.

In 1926, the Poles closed the Ukrainian Gymnasia in Ternopil, partly because they feared the activities of Plast would get out of control.

Bohdan remained a member of Plast, in one way or another, most of his life. During the 1930s, Bohdan and many of his friends in Plast joined the Organization of Ukrainian Nationalists (OUN). During the 1940s, Plast was resurrected and remained very active in the DP camps of Germany and Austria. During the 1950s, Bohdan was one of the founders of the Montreal branch of Plast and later became the *Stanychnyj*—the head scout of the Montreal branch, which, at its peak, had more than two hundred members. He was instrumental in the fundraising and purchase of Plast's first *Domivka* (clubhouse) on Rue Esplanade, overlooking a large park at the foot of Mount Royal in Montreal. This wonderful setting near the center of Montreal became a great meeting place for young people. Bohdan was also responsible for the purchase of a farm in the eastern townships about one hundred kilometers east of Montreal. This farm was designed to serve as a *Tabir* (a camp) where summer programs for Plast youth could be held.

When Bohdan died of cancer in 1965, his funeral and burial at the cemetery on Mount Royal was attended by hundreds of mourners. Present were family, friends, and work associates, but the largest component among the mourners was Montreal's Plast community.

Bohdan would have loved that tribute.

On his tombstone, a large Plast emblem, a fleur-de-Lis intertwined with a Ukrainian trident is engraved by his name.

Today, Plast remains a strong organization active in major cities in Canada, the United States, Australia, and other countries throughout the world. As of 1991, Plast has also been reinstated in Ukraine.

# THE ORGANIZATION OF UKRAINIAN NATIONALISTS

The Polish government's repressive and often violent actions in western Ukraine during the interwar period generated great resentment among the Ukrainian population and, in particular, among the young educated gymnasia and university students. In 1929, a group of young men founded the Organization of Ukrainian Nationalists (OUN) and encouraged gymnasia and university students to join. The group appealed to the youth who felt victimized by the Polish authorities and frustrated by lack of employment opportunities for Ukrainians. OUN organized massive patriotic demonstrations, student protests, and boycotts of Polish goods.

It was completely natural for older members of Plast to join OUN or to at least be very sympathetic to their cause. OUN's objective to overthrow the Polish government by any means attracted a large number of former Plast members.

An internal OUN publication in 1930 outlined its objectives as follows:

*Only with continually repeated mass actions can we sustain and nurture a permanent spirit of protest against the occupying power and maintain resistance of the enemy and the desire of final retribution. The people dare not get used to their chains; they dare not feel comfortable in an enemy state.*

In the summer of 1930, there was a wave of attacks against Polish property in Galicia. These attacks usually took the form of burning the produce on Polish estates. The government's response was massive and brutal. By fall, large Polish police and cavalry units descended on the Ukrainian countryside and commenced a pacification campaign intended to restore order.

The OUN gradually changed its tactics and started to concentrate on political assassinations of leading Polish politicians and government officials. In retaliation, the Poles abolished self-government in the villages and placed them under the administration of Polish officials. This further inflamed Ukrainian nationalists and resulted in increased membership in OUN.

In 1934, the Poles established a concentration camp at Bereza Kartuska near the city of Brest in present day Belarus, for about two thousand political prisoners, most of whom were Ukrainian. (Please see Chapter 9 for additional information about this prison.)

As time went on, Poland, which in 1922 started out as a democratic state, became more and more authoritarian with Marshal Pilsudski as leader. After Pilsudski's death in 1935, Poland became a totalitarian state.

Ukrainians increased their resistance and the underground movement became more intense.

When the leader of the OUN, and former commander of the Sich Riflemen, Evhen Konovalets, was assassinated by the Poles in 1938, his close associate, Andrij Melnyk (no relation), who was considered a moderate, was nominated to succeed him. A year later, the OUN broke into two camps: the more moderate *Melnykites* and the more radical followers of Stefan Bandera, the *Banderivtsi* (or as they were called by the Poles and Russians, *Banderovtsi).*

# THE UKRAINIAN COOPERATIVE MOVEMENT,
## *The Cooperativa*

In 1931, with his economics diploma from the Lviv Polytechnic Institute in his hand, Bohdan went looking for work but found his options were limited. The Polish authorities made it impossible for educated Ukrainians to find work in eastern Galicia. Their policy was to send Ukrainians from Galicia to work in Warsaw or Krakow or other Polish areas, hoping these young Ukrainian graduates would become Polonized in time. The best jobs in eastern Galicia were reserved for the Polish settlers who were being encouraged to colonize this territory in order to diminish the Ukrainian majority.

Bohdan applied to work with the Ukrainian Cooperative (*Cooperativa*). Here, he was warmly welcomed.

The Ukrainian cooperative movement originally started in the late 1800s. Its goal was to buy and sell products in large quantities from villagers, to eliminate the middleman and pass the savings to the villagers who, in most cases, were Ukrainians. At first, the cooperative gained its major successes in the banking industry by creating credit unions, which charged a significantly lower rate of interest for loans than the rates charged by Polish or Jewish bankers.

The movement didn't gain momentum in Galicia, however, until the 1920s, when the Poles increased their oppressive and restrictive practices toward Ukrainians. Many educated Ukrainians saw the cooperative movement as the best way to protect themselves economically from the Poles. Cooperatives came to view themselves as schools for self-government and instruments of economic self-defense. Many Ukrainians felt the cooperatives were a means for continuing the struggle for the Ukrainian cause.

Every cooperative that was organized, every product or service it provided, and every penny that landed in Ukrainian, rather than Polish, pockets represented for them a blow against the Polish enemy and a step closer to independence. With their motto, "*In unity lies the strength of a nation,*" villagers gained an awareness and desire to rebuild their lives economically as well as culturally, intellectually, and politically.

The growth of cooperatives also had serious repercussions for the Jewish community: the boycotts of alcohol and the establishment of credit unions and consumer cooperatives badly hurt the Jewish tavern owners, moneylenders, and shopkeepers, heightening tensions between Ukrainians and Jews and encouraging many of the latter to emigrate. 6

*    *    *

In 1931, after completing his studies in Lviv, my father, Bohdan, was working for the cooperative in Berezhany, a town located just west of Ternopil, with large Polish and Jewish populations. Only about twenty percent of the residents were Ukrainians.

His older brother, my uncle, Roman, was the auxiliary priest at the Holy Trinity Ukrainian Catholic Church in Berezhany. Each used the other for moral support during those trying times.

Bohdan's first job was as director of wheat acquisition. In that job, he had significant and constant contact with the local peasants. He quickly gained the respect of the peasants because he too came from a family of working people, and as a son of a miller, he knew what he was talking about. He was welcomed warmly whenever he visited farms in his area, and soon, many of the farmers sold their grain only to him and bought goods only from the cooperative.

A few years later Bohdan was promoted to the position of manager of acquisitions of the cooperative in the town of Pidhajci.

Bohdan was fortunate that his older sister, Julia, who was married to a local businessman, Mykhajlo Nenych, lived in Pidhajci. Bohdan was able to live in his sister's house during the first few months after he moved to that town.

A year later Bohdan became a member of the Directorate of the Cooperative Central Audit Committee (PSUK), in Pidhajci.

The Polish administration of Galicia saw the cooperative movement as a threat and did everything possible to disrupt its further development. Polish tactics included allegations that reports by Ukrainian businessmen were improperly filed and that building or hygienic codes were violated. Polish interference became most intense just as the Polish administration of eastern Galicia was about to come to an end in 1939.

*    *    *

On September 1, 1939, Hitler invaded Poland and only a few days later, the Bolsheviks entered Pidhajci.

Eighteen years of Polish occupation and repression in eastern Galicia/western Ukraine were over, but negative feelings between Ukrainians and Poles would continue for many more years.

Although the Polish occupation of western Ukraine during the 1920s and 1930s was a very difficult time for Ukrainians in Galicia, what followed would be significantly worse.

# YOUNG LOVE

In 1922, twelve-year-old **Bohdan Melnyk** from the village of Ladychyn was a third-year student at the Ukrainian boys' classical gymnasia in Ternopil.

At the same time, ten-year-old **Bronyslawa Martyniuk** from the village of Ivanivka was starting her first year at the only private Ukrainian girls gymnasia the Polish educational authorities permitted in the region.

That year, the girls' school building was taken over by Polish authorities and the girls' school was forced to share accommodations with the boys' school.

At two o'clock every day, the girls, including rosy-cheeked Bronyslawa (Bronia), her hair tied neatly into two braids, waited patiently at the bottom of the broad staircase of the school as the boys descended at the end of their school day. Young Bronia, who was always in the company of her two friends, Lana and Marucia, noticed the older and handsome Bohdan, who himself was always in the company of his two best friends, Slawko and Joseph.

Bronia recalls the first time their eyes met and Bohdan actually smiled at her, she blushed uncontrollably and almost fainted.

This scene continued almost daily—Bohdan glancing her way as he neared the bottom of the stairs while Bronia blushed and giggled with her friends.

During May, the month of the Blessed Virgin Mary, Ukrainian Catholic churches hold evening services, *Majivkas*, to venerate the Virgin. Bronia and her friends regularly attended these evening services at the Ukrainian Church of the Immaculate Conception on Ternopil's Ruska Street.

Bohdan, along with his friends, also started to attend—but it's not clear whether Bohdan was there for the Virgin Mary or for Bronia. After the service, Bohdan and his friends would walk Bronia and her friends to their residences.

The school year ended, and Bohdan and Bronia returned to their respective villages.

The following September, the girls' school had new accommodations, and Bohdan and Bronia could not see each other at school. In May, Bronia again attended *Majivkas* at the same church, hoping to see her Bohdan, but Bohdan never came. A few times Bronia, saw Bohdan around town, but she recalls that whenever she was in his presence, she would blush uncontrollably and couldn't bring herself to speak to him, even when she was a mature fourteen-year-old. She felt it was improper for a young lady to approach the object of her innocent desires.

In 1926, the Polish authorities permanently closed the boys' gymnasia and turned the building into a Polish academy. Bohdan left for Lviv to finish his last year of gymnasia. Bronia never forgot her handsome Bohdan. She followed his career and remained true to him even though she didn't see him for several years.

After graduating from the gymnasia in 1930, and after completing a home economics certificate program at the Institute in Ternopil, Bronia found work with the Ukrainian cooperative in her hometown, Ivanivka.

In 1938, by accident or maybe by design, she attended a summer seminar for cooperative employees in the picturesque village of Vorokhta in the Carpathian Mountains where Bohdan, by then a director of the cooperative in Pidhajci, was an instructor.

They renewed their acquaintance. A few months later, Bronia transferred to Pidhajci, and two years after that, on February 4, 1940, Bohdan and Bronia, my parents, were married.

**Bohdan Melnyk**                    **Bronyslawa Martyniuk c. 1930s**

# Chapter 9

# Polish, Bolshevik, and Nazi Terror

## SENATOR REVEREND JULIAN TATOMYR

Luzhok, a village nestled in the upper Dnister River valley in the Carpathian foothills, was an ideal location for Reverend Julian Tatomyr in the 1920s. He was reasonably close to Peremyshl, Starij Sambir, and Sambir, the towns he knew best and where he had many friends and contacts. At the same time, he was far enough away from the larger cities and thus out of sight of Polish administrators, politicians, and police. He organized farmers in the village, built a new and larger church, and operated his parish, nursery school, reading rooms and choirs. Some of these activities were considered subversive by Polish authorities and were restricted or banned.

It wasn't long before the Poles noticed his activities.

In 1923, he was arrested by Polish police on a charge of issuing birth certificates written in Ukrainian rather than Polish. He spent several months in jail but was released without any charges laid. Upon his release, he continued his activism, daring the Poles to arrest him again. They did. He spent more time in jail and was again released.

Father Julian soon became a well-known popular figure in the area. He passionately defended the Uniate rite and resisted any encroachment by the Roman Catholics. He was willing to serve time in jail for his beliefs.

The Ukrainian bishop in Peremyshl rewarded him by appointing him to an administrative post in the eparchy.

During the late 1920s, the Poles tried to give their administration a semblance of legitimacy by allowing Ukrainians to organize political parties and run delegates in elections to the Polish parliament, the *Sejm*.

Julian was one of the chief organizers of a Ukrainian political party, the Ukrainian National Democratic Alliance (UNDA), which ran candidates in several eastern Galician ridings. The UNDA ran a strong campaign and, in the predominantly Ukrainian areas, easily took the majority of votes.

In 1928, Julian was elected, along with a small number of other Ukrainians, to the Polish Sejm as a senator. Now he was called Reverend Senator Julian Sas-Tatomyr.

The Poles weren't particularly happy that someone they had previously persecuted and jailed was now a political leader—in *their* Parliament.

Julian and the other Ukrainians elected to the Sejm were under no illusion when they arrived in Warsaw. Some Poles tried to bar their entry to parliament but Julian and the others served out their terms and tirelessly worked for Ukrainian rights. Their words fell on deaf ears and the façade of democracy quickly came to an end. Nevertheless, Julian remained a popular and powerful figure in the small villages nestled along the upper Dnister River.

Reverend Julian's election to the Polish parliament (Sejm) was a coup for Ukrainians and an embarrassment for the Polish authorities. Along with Julian, his close associates, Ivan Makukh and Ostap Luczkij were also elected to the Polish Senate while Stepan Bilak, Ivan Blazhkevycz, Stefan Vytyzckyj, Pavlo Luciak and Mykhajlo Matchak, were among the Ukrainians from his area elected to the Polish Parliament. *

## JAROSLAV TATOMYR

Father Julian Sas-Tatomyr raised his two sons in a strongly nationalistic home, and when his older son, Jaroslav, completed his high school education in 1928, Julian tried to convince him to enter the seminary and to become a priest. Jaroslav, however, decided to go to Lviv to study at the Lviv Polytechnic Institute. During his time in Lviv, Jaroslav was imprisoned several times by the Poles for his nationalist activities and for membership in the banned Organization of Ukrainian Nationalists (OUN).

He returned to Sambir where he became a prominent leader of Prosvita, organized Ukrainian reading rooms in towns and villages and worked to minimize the government's attempt at Polonization. His activities were noted by the Polish administration.

By 1930, the Polish occupation turned into an open and ongoing war. Ukrainian nationalism was on the rise, and Polish oppression increased. Along with Jaroslav, Julian's younger son, Oleksander, and their cousins, Volodymyr and Evhen, took up the cause and all of them, at one time or another, spent time in Polish jails.

---

\*     Elected to the Polish senate along with Rev. Julian Tatomyr: Dr. Ivan Makukh (one-time member of Austrian parliament, died in 1946 in Germany and was buried alongside his friend Julian Tatomyr in Salzburg); Ostap Luczkij (journalist, poet. Arrested by Bolsheviks in 1939, died in concentration camp in Kotlas in 1941.

*Elected to Parliament:* Stephan Bilak (lawyer, died in USA in 1950); Dr. Ivan Blakewycz (deported to Siberia, returned to Lviv); Stefan Vytyzcky (lawyer, orator, died in USA in 1965), Pavlo Lysiak (lawyer, journalist, died in Germany in 1948); Mykhajlo Matchak (Colonel, Sich Riflemen, arrested in Vienna in 1947, repatriated by Soviets, sentenced to 25 years in prison, died in Zubnov, Ukraine in 1958.)

Jaroslav informed his father, Julian, that he did not have a calling for the priesthood. Instead, he wanted to study engineering. Father Julian reluctantly agreed and decided that the best place for Jaroslav to study would be far away in Paris.

While Jaroslav was studying in Paris, World War II was declared. When Jaroslav returned to Sambir during the summer of 1940, the Bolsheviks had taken control of Galicia. They refused Jaroslav a travel visa to continue his education. (Please also see the Tribute to Jaroslav in the Epilogue.)

## OLEKSANDER TATOMYR

Julian's younger son, Chrystyna's father, Oleksander, joined the OUN in 1930 while he was a student at the Sambir gymnasia. After his 1931 graduation, he decided to study law at the university in Lviv, named after the Polish hero, Jan Casimir.*

While in Lviv, Oleksander continued his political activities. Predictably, his law studies were interrupted several times. The first time, he was imprisoned for two months for activism and for OUN membership. He spent those two months in cramped quarters, taking a daily tally of cockroaches, making chess pieces from scraps of paper, and playing chess with other prisoners who were imprisoned for similar crimes.

After his release, he became an even more fervent activist and soon became the commander of an OUN cell at the university. Polish police constantly tracked his moves. He endured frequent, lengthy interrogations and more periods of imprisonment. In 1933, after completing his second year at the law school, he was again imprisoned, this time in Sambir. His stays in prison interrupted his studies but didn't diminish his spirit. He became an even more determined and passionate freedom fighter upon his release.

The 1930s were difficult times in Europe. By the middle of the decade, Hitler had begun to assert power in Germany, the Poles were becoming more and more oppressive in Galicia, nationalist feelings were being fanned among Ukrainians, and in the latter part of the decade, the Bolsheviks started to make significant inroads in the western parts of Ukraine.

Ignoring the Polish ban on leadership activities in the OUN, Oleksander helped to organize a massive rally in Lviv of the Ukrainian Youth for Christ. With thousands of young Ukrainians eager to participate in this celebration, the Polish government issued a ban on train travel for all Ukrainians.

---

\*      The university in Lviv that had been the subject of so much friction between Poles and Ukrainians
        for decades was named for a Polish grand duke, Jan Casimir, a Polish hero. Among Casimir's
        accomplishments was the destruction of Uniate churches in the seventeenth century. He also
        banned the use of the Cyrillic alphabet requiring all documents, including Uniate church service
        documents and prayer books, be written in the Latin script. Naming Lviv's university for Casimir
        was a significant irritant for the Ukrainian population.

        Today, that same university in downtown Lviv is named after Ivan Franko, a passionate
        Ukrainian nationalist and poet who wrote in Ukrainian using the Cyrillic alphabet.

To circumvent the Polish ban, Oleksander helped organize the pilgrimage to Lviv using horse-drawn wagons for transportation. This pilgrimage became a highly visible show of defiance and encouraged even more people to join the rally. One hundred thousand Ukrainians swore their allegiance to God and to their Uniate church at this massive 1933 demonstration, held in Lviv's Sokil Square.

This demonstration annoyed the Poles and was a major embarrassment for the Bolsheviks, as many of the speeches, including Oleksander's, were directed at the "godless Bolsheviks" who had created the man-made famine in eastern Ukraine. Bolsheviks and some members of the foreign press tried to suppress news about this rally and to suppress the news about the human disaster that was taking place just a few hundred kilometers to the east, in Soviet-controlled Ukraine.

Ukrainian nationalists, including Oleksander, sprang into action. They visited many villages in Ukraine to inform the population of the mass murders, by famine, being perpetuated in eastern Ukraine and to educate the people about the other atrocities committed by the Bolsheviks. Oleksander was now considered a troublemaker by the Poles *and* by the Bolsheviks who had infiltrated Galicia.

**Chrystyna's father, Oleksander Tatomyr, fourth from right, leading a protest demonstration in Peremyshl, 1935.**

To circumvent the Polish ban on gatherings such as the one pictured above, they were advertised as *religious processions*, although there was little doubt in anyone's mind about their true purpose. The organizers of these marches were routinely arrested and often jailed by the Poles.

Oleksander knew the authorities would arrest him at the first opportunity if he went to Lviv and he knew they would find a way to prevent him from returning to the university so he decided to abandon his law studies. Instead, he entered the seminary, hoping to be the one to continue the priestly tradition of his family. Oleksander also stated that he felt the best way he could help his countrymen was by becoming a priest like his father.

During his summer holidays, he continued to work with youth, organizing various festivals and theatrical productions and giving speeches motivating young people to take pride in their heritage. He encouraged them to protect their homeland by getting involved in nationalist causes.

In 1938, before he completed his fourth year in the seminary Oleksander was arrested once again by Polish authorities and sentenced to two years in prison. With time for reflection during his imprisonment, he underwent a deep personal crisis. He began to experience serious doubts about his commitment to the priesthood. His father, Julian, visited him in prison several times to discuss his personal difficulties and concerns, but finally, Oleksander decided the priesthood was not to be his destined vocation.

Julian was deeply disappointed.

Oleksander had served ten months of his sentence when the Germans invaded Poland, effectively ending Polish rule in Galicia. The jailers left their posts and Oleksander was released from prison.

## VOLODYMYR TATOMYR, Part II (continued from Chapter 6)

When western Ukraine again fell under Polish occupation in 1921, Volodymyr, a war weary nineteen year old war veteran, returned to his hometown, Strij. He resumed his studies, continued to be active in the now banned Plast organization and continued his associations with his comrades from the now disbanded Ukrainian Galician Army.

During the late1920's, Volodymyr married his sweetheart, Oksana, a fellow patriot. Tragically, she died of tuberculosis one year later. Volodymyr never recovered from his loss.

During the early 1930's resistance to Polish rule in Galicia grew as Polish authorities became more and more oppressive. Ukrainian students, Plast members and other aware adults secretly joined the Organization of Ukrainian Nationalists (OUN) and continued their passive resistance to Polish rule. Volodymyr was one of the leaders of OUN in the Sambir region.

In 1938, Volodymyr was arrested for his activities in the OUN and sent to the Polish concentration camp at Bereza Kartuska.

## BEREZA KARTUSKA, POLISH DETENTION CAMP

**The Bereza Kartuska detention camp*** Polish: Miejsce Odosobnienia w Berezie Kartuskiej, "Place of Isolation" was created on July 12, 1934, in a former Tsarist prison and barracks at Bereza Kartuska (in present day Belarus, near the city of Brest) on orders issued by Polish President Ignacy Moscicki. It was intended to accommodate persons "whose activities or conduct give reason to believe that they threaten the public security, peace or order."

The event that directly influenced Poland's de facto dictator, Josef Pilsudski, to create the prison was the assassination on June 15, 1934, of Polish Minister of Internal Affairs Bronislaw Pieracki by members of the Organization of Ukrainian Nationalists (OUN).

Individuals were incarcerated at Bereza Kartuska by administrative decision, without right of appeal, usually for a period of three months. The incarceration could be extended for another three months, or even up to a year. Some 16,000 persons passed through Bereza Kartuska over the period of its operation. These included members of the Organization of Ukrainian Nationalists (OUN), Polish Communist Party (KPP), National Radical Camp (ONR), members of the Peasant Party (SL) and Polish Socialist Party (PPS). The first inmates to arrive at the prison were Organization of Ukrainian Nationalist (OUN) members Roman Shukhevych*, Dmytro Hrytsai and Volodymyr Yaniv, on July 17, 1934.

From 1934-1937 the prison usually housed 200-500 inmates. In 1938 the number went to over 7,000 when the Polish government sent 4,500 Ukrainians to Bereza Kartuska without the right to appeal. Conditions were exceptionally harsh. In the prisoners' building, each cell initially held fifteen inmates. There were no benches or tables. In 1938, the number of inmates per cell was increased to up to 70. The floors were of concrete and were constantly showered with water so that inmates could not sit. Estimates of the number of deaths at the prison vary from official Polish records admitting deaths of 17 to 20, to unofficial Ukrainian statistics claiming 324 Ukrainians were murdered or tortured to death during questioning, or died from disease, while escaping or otherwise disappeared without a trace. Most were OUN members.

OUN members who were incarcerated at Bereza Kartuska have testified to the use of torture. There were frequent beatings (with boards being placed against inmates' backs and struck with hammers), forced labor, constant harassment, the use of solitary confinement without provocation and punishment for inmates' use of the Ukrainian language.**

Volodymyr, and thousands of other Ukrainians, were released from Bereza Kartuska in September 1939 when the Nazi armies invaded Poland and the Polish prison guards

---

\*     Roman Shukhevych (pseudonym, Taras Chuprynka) was the supreme commander of the Ukrainian Insurgent Army. His capture and imprisonment was a major coup d'etat for the Poles.

\*\*    Yurij Luhovy, a member of the Academy of Canadian Cinema and Television, has completed a documentary film about the prison based on authentic photographs, documents, archival footage and eyewitness testimony from survivors. His father was a 1938 inmate.

      Compiled from Wikipedia, the Free Encyclopedia and other Polish and Ukrainian sources.

abandoned their posts and fled. Far from being repentant, the former prisoners became even more determined to fight for the freedom of their country.

*    *    *

Ten days after Hitler invaded Poland on September 1, 1939, the Red Army invaded eastern Galicia. By November 1, they entered Lviv and soon the Bolsheviks were in total control of eastern Galicia.

Although life under Polish administration was difficult, most Ukrainians in Galicia, aware of the way the Soviets treated their brothers in the east, feared things were about to get much worse.

The second occupation of Galicia by the Bolsheviks (1939-41) was even more brutal than the earlier one during World War I and significantly more deadly than the nearly two decades of Polish occupation which had just ended.

The next nineteen months under the repressive heel of the Soviets would prove to be extremely brutal for Ukrainians in eastern Galicia.

The Tatomyrs—Julian, Jaroslav, Oleksander, and their cousins, Volodymyr and Evhen knew they would not survive long under Soviet occupation. With the help of the bishop in Sambir, Julian was transferred to Peremyshl, a city located just across the San River in German-controlled Poland. A large number of Ukrainians lived in Peremyshl and had established a significant community there. Jaroslav, Oleksander and Volodymyr decided to go along with Julian. They felt they could provide a useful service to that community. All three were known to the Poles and the Bolsheviks, but the Germans had little reason to bother them.

Their cousin, Evhen Tatomyr, however, decided to stay in Sambir and to continue their fight for Ukrainian independence, this time against the Bolsheviks.

---

## TORTURE (NKVD 1)

Julian's nephew, **Evhen Tatomyr** was twenty-six years old when he was arrested by the Soviet Secret Police, the NKVD, in late 1939.

He was a handsome, educated, athletic young man. He was single, charismatic, popular, and an eloquent, inspirational speaker.

His father, Rev. Mykhajlo Tatomyr (Julian's older brother), had died in 1925 when Evhen was just ten years old, and his mother died a few years later. His uncle, Julian, and Evhen's older brother, Volodymyr, took care of him until he came of age. Like his uncle, his brother, Volodymyr, and his cousins, Jaroslav and Oleksander, Evhen was a Ukrainian patriot, nationalist, and activist. He resisted Polish occupation, and when the Soviets arrived in 1939, he spoke openly against their occupation as well.

His previous incarcerations by the Poles were relatively mild and he endured them defiantly and effortlessly. He would patiently serve his term and would wait for his inevitable release. He would then return to his previous activities. He knew the Poles, for the most part, had a sense of justice, even if they applied it unevenly.

The Bolsheviks were not as kind.

Evhen was arrested in Sambir soon after the Red Army entered the city. The NKVD had a file on all the Tatomyrs; Evhen was the first to be captured.

He was charged under Section 10 of the Soviet Criminal Code:

*Propaganda or agitation containing an appeal for the overthrow, subverting or weakening of the Soviet power or possession of literary material of similar content.*

Also, he was "too educated, too well-to-do, too independent, too influential" and a son of a Uniate clergyman. He represented everything the Soviets wanted to stamp out.

Evhen did not challenge the charges against him. He remained defiant and admitted to his captors he was against their occupation.

He was tortured mercilessly. He was starved, beaten, deprived of sleep, threatened, isolated, and burned. They demanded he reveal names. He refused.

After months of unspeakable torture, he died in the Sambir prison.

The NKVD didn't bother to hide the fact that they had murdered him. On the contrary, they used him as an example to intimidate the population.

When Evhen's older sister, Eleonora, came to claim his body, she reported it was so badly mutilated she barely recognized her beautiful little brother.

## SOPHIA TERESHKEVYCH

Chrystyna's mother, Sophia, was born May 29, 1915, in the village of Spas in the foothills of the Carpathian Mountains, the youngest of seven Tereshkevych children.

Sophia was a bright, reflective child and from an early age it was evident that she did not have the physical strength to work in the fields as she often fainted from exertion. Her family decided the best course of action was for Sophia to get an education and to work as a professional. She attended a local school and then a teacher's college in Sambir. While there, she became a member of an underground cell of the Organization of Ukrainian Nationalists.

Upon completing her studies in 1937, Sophia discovered that under Polish occupation, no teaching jobs were available for Ukrainian Greek Catholics. Sophia was devastated by the blatant discrimination.

Determined to find employment, she found jobs in nursery schools in neighboring villages. She was creative and artistic and excelled in preparing recitals and dramas for her talented tots. Eventually, aware of her keen intellect, the bishop's chancellery employed her as an administrator in Peremyshl.

---

## INTERROGATION, NKVD (2)

In September 1939, when Sophia was twenty-four years old, World War II broke out, the Poles lost power, and the Bolsheviks occupied Ukraine. Sophia returned to her home village, Spas, and finally found employment as a teacher. She loved music and taught her students Ukrainian songs, Cossack songs, and patriotic songs of the Ukrainian Sich Riflemen. Soon, a Bolshevik official paid Sophia a visit and warned her to discontinue the nationalistic education or her life would be in danger for opposition to authority.

He said, "*Tovarysh*, your teaching is counterrevolutionary and you will be deported to the labor camps in Siberia. Cease this type of teaching immediately!" Although shaken by this visit, Sophia, a rebel by nature, continued to teach her Ukrainian program.

Not long before the German invasion of 1941, the NKVD began lengthy and frequent interrogations of Sophia and other suspected nationalists. The Bolsheviks placed Sophia under arrest and demanded she provide them with a list of all subversive nationalists in the village of Spas.

Sophia gave the NKVD a list of all people living in the village of Spas: Ukrainians, Poles, and Jews. This outward defiance enraged her interrogators and they threatened to execute her on the spot.

Sophia returned from these interrogations pale, visibly shaken, and emotionally exhausted. However, she vowed she would never give the NKVD the information they wanted. She decided that in order not to betray the nationalists in Spas, she was prepared for imprisonment, deportation to Siberia, or death. Those who knew Sophia claim that she was never quite the same after these interrogations. Only the outbreak of the German-Bolshevik war saved Sophia from further persecution by the NKVD.

---

On June 22, 1941, the Germans invaded eastern Galicia. Many Ukrainians hoped this occupation would not be as oppressive as the one they endured under the Bolsheviks and that the Germans would free Ukraine from the Soviet tyranny they had suffered.

A formal Declaration of Independence was proclaimed in Lviv and other major towns in western Ukraine on June 30, 1941. In attendance were countless Ukrainians, including Sophia.

The elation of independence was short-lived. The German invaders arrested and deported the leaders of the newly independent Ukraine and brutally curtailed the freedom of all Ukrainians.

# PART FOUR

# World War II

# Chapter 10

# *Genocide in the Twentieth Century*

*"Thus for the time being I have sent to the East only my 'Death's Head Units' with the orders to kill without pity or mercy all men, women, and children of Polish race or language. Only in such a way will we win the vital space that we need. **Who still talks nowadays about the Armenians?"***

—Hitler speaking to his commanders, August 22, 1939

The world did not condemn the brutal extermination of Armenians during World War I, and little attention was paid to the Holodomor (murder by starvation) that Stalin had inflicted on Ukraine in 1932-33. Both genocides were covered up and ignored in the West.

For Hitler, two excellent precedents had been set. He felt justified to act on his plans to exterminate anyone else in his way.

The term *genocide*, derived from the ancient Greek word *genos* (race, kin, or tribe) and the Latin word *cide*, to kill, was coined by a Polish-Jewish jurist named Raphael Lemkin in 1944.

Genocide, as defined by the United Nations, means any of the following acts committed with intent to destroy, in whole or in part, a national, ethnic, racial, or religious group, including the following:

a. Killing members of a group
b. Causing serious bodily or mental harm to members of a group
c. Deliberately inflicting on the group conditions of life calculated to bring about its physical destruction in whole or in part
d. Imposing measures intended to prevent births within a group
e. Forcibly transferring children of the group to another group.

## Major Twentieth Century Genocides:*

- 1915-1918     Armenia                  1.5 million deaths
- 1932-1933     Ukrainian Holodomor      4.5-7 million deaths
- 1938-1945     Jewish Holocaust         6 million deaths
- 1975-1979     Cambodia                 3 million deaths
- 1994-         Rwanda                   1 million deaths

There were other genocides. Among them, the Rape of Nanking (1937), 300,000 deaths; Bosnia-Herzegovina (1992-1995), 200,000 deaths; as well as Pakistan (1971); Uganda (1971-79); Manchuria (1930); Iraq (1980-88) and in this century, Darfur.

*     *     *

In May of 2008, Ukrainian President Victor Yushchenko visited Canada, addressed Parliament in a joint session of the Commons and Senate and spoke, among other things, of the Ukrainian Famine-Genocide, the Holodomor.

On May 29, 2008, Parliament unanimously passed a resolution declaring that the artificial famine in Ukraine in 1932-33 was indeed an act of Genocide.

A week later, on June 2, 2008, I joined a delegation of Ukrainians requesting the inclusion of the Holodomor in the new Toronto District School Board course on Genocides.

Our group of presenters included Ukrainian Canadian Congress president Markian Schwec, Genocide Committee chair, Gene Yakovitch, former Toronto school history teacher Valentina Kuryliw, former school trustee Alexander Chumak, and parents Luba Terepatska and Christine Bidak.

Although we presented eloquent arguments and had the support of leading political leaders from the municipal, provincial and federal levels, our proposal was met with resistance at first. With strong support from the community and persistent lobbying, however, the Board finally supported our position, voted to commemorate the Holodomor and to honor those who died by setting aside the fourth Friday of November each year as a board-wide Day of Remembrance. They also encouraged staff to include the study of the Holodomor in all schools in the coming year.

It took seventy five years, but this terrible crime against humanity is finally being recognized.

---

*     *The History Place: Genocide in the 20th Century*, www.historyplace.com
    For more information about twentieth century genocides, the eight stages of genocides and genocide denial, please visit the following sites: www.genocidewatch.org/eightstages.htm www.faminegenocide.com   www.ucca.org

# THE MARTYNIUKS OF IVANIVKA

Chrystyna and I were busy teaching our courses in Lviv and enjoying a very active social life. We explored Lviv almost every evening, either with our fellow teachers, our course participants, or with our hosts from the Lviv Ministry of Education. We also spent a lot of time with Chrystyna's newfound relatives both in Lviv and in villages south of Starij Sambir.

We had not yet made contact with anyone from my side of the family, however, even though I had family living less than two hundred kilometers from Lviv. We simply had no time.

Finally, after the courses ended and we recovered from our good-bye parties, we asked our newfound cousins, Ivanko and Lesya, to take us to visit my mother's side of the family, the Martyniuks, who lived in Ivanivka, a village about twenty kilometers south of Ternopil and just east of Terebovla.

Before we left Toronto, my mother had given us some precise information and directions and even asked us to pass on letters and envelopes filled with money to people with whom she had maintained contact. Her sister, my aunt Stefa, still lived in the same house where my mother was born in 1912.

As we approached Ternopil from the north, we saw the *staw*, a lake created by a dam on the River Seret. I remembered my mother's stories about picnics by the staw when she was a student in Ternopil.

We drove down the main streets of the city, and I tried to visualize my parents living here more than sixty years before. On Ruska Street, the main avenue in town, we passed a large Polish Catholic church, and further down, a large Ukrainian Catholic church, which I suspected may have been the one attended by my parents in their youth (it was). Further down the road, we passed a Jewish synagogue. I tried to visualize this town in the 1920s—unpaved roads, few cars, small shops on the main road, people strolling and going about their business.

I wondered what life had been like back then and wished my mother could have been there with us at that moment.

From Ternopil, we drove south toward Terebovla, an ancient city, which, at the time, was preparing to celebrate its nine-hundredth anniversary. (This town is the regional capital and one of the few cities that survived from ancient times when the princes of Halych ruled this area.)

A crumbling but still impressive old castle stood on a hill on the west side of the town. We wondered who had lived there. Was it once the home of one of the Boyars from ancient times? Or had a Polish nobleman lived there more recently?

Sixteen kilometers east of Terebovla, and not that far from the Zbruch River, lay the prosperous village of Ivanivka, my mother's hometown.

We turned east off the main road toward the town, and although I had never been here and could not remember ever seeing pictures of this village, I felt I knew this place.

As we came to a row of houses on the left side of the road, I asked Ivanko to stop the car. It somehow felt like my mother's house was nearby.

I don't usually get these *feelings* but maybe my mother's stories were exceptionally vivid, or maybe I *had* seen a picture, or maybe it was sheer luck, but the very first house I approached in the village was the house where my mother was born.

My mother's youngest sister, Stefania Kuzyk, whom I had never met, answered the door. She recognized me immediately from pictures my mother had sent her.

For the second time in two weeks, Chrystyna and I were at the center of a long lost family reunion.

## THE MARTYNIUKS

## (MY MOTHER'S SIDE OF THE FAMILY)

*My great-great-grandfather:*

Ivan Martyniuk
1820s

*My great-grandparents:*

Mykola Martyniuk—Ahaphia Hryniak
1850s

*My grandparents:*

Mykhajlo Martyniuk—Justina Mychajluk
1875 1881

*My parents:*

Bronyslawa—Bohdan Melnyk
(1912-) (1910-1965)

*My aunts and uncles:*

Ivan, Pavlo Vasylko, Stefania
1905 1908 (1915-1993) 1917

*Four of my mother's first cousins, all males and all Martyniuks, emigrated to Canada in the 1930s and 1940s. They were our sponsors when we immigrated to Canada in 1949.*

My uncles (once removed) Vasyl, Stefan, Mykola, and Mykhajlo
Their children: (my second cousins) John, Anna, Vera, Andrij

My great-grandparents on my mother's side, **Mykola** and **Ahaphia Martyniuk,** inherited this small piece of land from my great-great-grandfather. They, in turn, passed it on to their oldest son, my grandfather, **Mykhajlo,** when he married my grandmother, **Justina Mychajluk.** Mykhajlo and Justina had five children.

The already small piece of land was divided among the two older brothers, Ivan and Paul, and the youngest daughter, Stefania. Mykhajlo and Justina's other two children, my mother, Bronyslava, and my uncle, Vasylko, left for Canada during World War II.

Stefania and the children of Ivan and Pavlo and their families lived in three adjoining houses that were built on this tiny property.

Just a few minutes walk down the same road in Ivanivka was another Martyniuk property, that of my mother's uncle, who also had five children—all boys. The oldest stayed on the property, the next three sons (Vasyl, Stefan, and Mykola) left for Canada in the 1930s and settled in Montreal after spending some time in northern Quebec.

The youngest, Mykhajlo, was too young to leave home with his three brothers. He stayed with his parents, went to school, and, when the Germans invaded in 1941, joined the Ukrainian underground. Two years later, in 1943, when the Red Army started to advance westward toward Galicia, he joined the Ukrainian First Galician Division of the German Army, thinking that was the only hope to liberate Ukraine. His unit was sent west to Czechoslovakia. They were captured by the Allies and spent time in detention camps near Rimini, Italy. Mykhajlo was released when the war ended, and in 1946, somehow found us in a DP camp in Germany. He ended up in Canada in 1949 at the end of a harrowing decade.

My aunt, Stefania, invited us into her home, where my mother was born and spent her younger years. After the customary hugs and kisses and the compulsory food, we caught up on as much news as we could all absorb. Aunt Stefania and her husband took us to the local Ukrainian church where my mother and all her brothers and sisters had been baptized, and where my parents were married in 1940. Then they took us to the cemetery at the edge of the village.

At the very center of this large cemetery was what seemed to us to be an exclusive Martyniuk section. There were no less than twenty gravestones engraved with the name Martyniuk. We tried to keep up with the descriptions of the relationships of each of my relatives buried here, but it was all too much to process.

One gravestone, however, caught my eye.

It read:

> ***Bohdan Martyniuk, son of Vasylko and Maria***
> ***1940-1943***
> ***Three years old***
> ***Murdered by the Nazis***

## BOHDANCHYK'S SHORT LIFE

I read the faded inscription on the gravestone and struggled to remember.

In this grave lay the remains of my first cousin, little three-year-old Bohdanchyk. I remembered as a child hearing about my uncle, Vasylko, and his first wife and his son, who died at an early age. Aunt Stefania told us the rest of the story.

Vasylko was born in 1915. During the 1930s, as a young man, he joined the Organization of Ukrainian Nationalists. In 1938, he married his sweetheart, Mary (Marynia), also an active member of OUN. Both of them were active in the anti-Polish and later in the anti-Bolshevik underground movement.

In 1940, a baby boy was born to Vasylko and Marynia. They named him Bohdan (Bohdanchyk). The three of them lived with my grandmother who took care of little Bohdanchyk whenever Vasylko or Marynia were away.

A few days after the Nazi armies crossed into Ukraine on June 22, 1941, the Bolsheviks received orders to withdraw eastward. They were also given orders to kill any political prisoners they had in their jails, and to arrest any suspected nationalists or anti-Soviet agitators and to load them onto trains headed for Siberia.

Early in July of 1941, the Bolsheviks were watching the house where Marynia and baby Bohdanchyk were staying with grandmother.

Early one morning a group of Bolsheviks carrying guns kicked down the door and charged into the house. When they couldn't find Vasylko, who was with his underground unit, they took Marynia and Bohdanchyk and placed them in a carriage along with other prisoners they had collected in the village. Grandmother Justina cried and pleaded with the Bolsheviks to let them go but they just pushed her aside.

As the carriage filled with prisoners started toward the Terebovla train station, grandmother and many other villagers ran screaming and crying after them. When they reached the station, the Bolsheviks loaded the prisoners onto cattle cars.

Just as the train was pulling out of the station, Marynia threw baby Bohdanchyk out of the train into his grandmother's arms. Grandmother covered the baby with her apron and ran back to Ivanivka.

Days later, when Vasylko returned to the house, he found his baby safe but neither he nor anyone else ever saw or heard from Marynia again.

When the Germans arrived a few days later, everything was just as bad as when the Bolsheviks were in charge. There were killings, beatings, and arrests of people, and stealing of food. In 1942, Vasylko, angry and desperate, left little Bohdanchyk with grandma and joined the Ukrainian Insurgent Army (UPA). He and his comrades had captured guns and ammunitions from the Bolsheviks and were making raids on the Germans. In 1943, Vasylko was captured by the Germans and sent to the Buchenwald concentration camp in Germany.*

Little Bohdanchyk was left in the care of grandmother. One day, when he was three years old, Bohdanchyk was playing in the front of his grandmother's house. He found a piece of shrapnel from a recently exploded German bomb, accidentally cut himself and the wound became infected. Medical help was not available, he developed a high fever and a few days later, he died.

Grandmother never forgave herself for that.

---

*Please also see Chapter 16, *Buchenwald*, and the Epilogue, *Vasylko and Erna Martyniuk*.

We still wanted to see Pidhajci, the town where I was born, and Berezhany, where my uncle Roman served as a priest and my father's village, Ladychyn, only about twenty kilometers away, but I didn't think I could emotionally handle seeing where my grandfather's mill stood. Not today.

After lengthy good-byes and promises to come back to visit, we set off for my birthplace, the town of Pidhajci, an hour's drive west of Ivanivka.

As we drove into the town, I became excited. Pidhajci had always been the word I wrote after *Place of Birth* on passport applications and other documents. For most of my life, I neither knew where it was nor ever expected to see it.

As we turned off the main road and approached Pidhajci from the south, the very first building we saw was a large Gothic-style church—a former Polish *kostel*. Unlike most other churches we had seen on our travels, however, this one was in a very poor state of repair. It appeared to have been bombed during the war but no one really expended any energy to repair it. The roof was badly damaged; birds nested in the steeples, and where once there must have been glorious stained glass windows, now there were open spaces.

Just past the kostel, we came upon a lovely town square. The buildings around the square were uniformly high but each had its own character and each was covered with brick of a different color. The overall effect was quite pleasing. On one corner of the square, we spotted a sign over the door written in Cyrillic script: *Pizzeria*.

I thought that looked incongruous and asked Ivanko to stop so I could take a picture. When we returned to Canada, I showed that picture to my mother. She recognized the building right away. That pizzeria was located where the cooperative offices my father managed had stood and where my mother worked during the late 1930s and early 1940s. The second window on the right, over the store, had been my parents' apartment and the room where I was born. That was an incredible circumstance!

We found a Ukrainian Catholic church just up the street. I suspected it was the church my parents attended and where I was baptized (it was).

We drove the twenty kilometers north to Berezhany. On the main square we saw a church we suspected was the church where my uncle Roman had been an auxiliary priest during the 1940s (again, it was).

Ivanivka. In front of house where my mother was born in 1912. Her younger sister, my aunt, Stefania, (third from left) still lives in the house with her son (far right), her daughter-in-law, and their children. My grandnephew stands next to me (far left).

In front of the Immaculate Conception Ukrainian Catholic Church where my mother was baptized in 1912, where my parents were married in 1940 and near where my three-year-old cousin, Bohdanchyk died.

**Ivanivka Cemetery. At my Grandmother Justina Martyniuk and uncle, Pavlo Martyniuk's, gravesite. Next to it was the grave of my cousin, three year old Bohdanchyk.**

I took this picture of a Pizzeria on the main square in Pidhajci in 1993. When we returned to Canada, my mother recognized this as the location of the cooperative offices where my father and mother worked during the 1940s.

I was born above the store in the apartment on the second floor (right) on February 28 or 29, 1944. Eleven days later, we left for the West.

Wading in the Zbruch River just a few kilometers from my mother's village, Ivanivka, 1994.

Before 1914, this peaceful small river formed part of the border between the Austrian Empire and the Russian Empire: Austrian Galicia on the left (west) and *Velyka Ukraina* or Russian-controlled eastern Ukraine on the right (east). After 1921, the left bank became Polish-occupied eastern Galicia, while the right bank was heavily fortified Soviet Ukraine. In 1932 and 1933, the harvest in Galicia was normal. In Soviet Ukraine, millions starved to death in Stalin's artificial famine—the Holodomor.

As of 2008, many civilized countries, including the United States of America and Canada, have recognized this famine as genocide.

There are still a few people who deny that genocide took place. One is Prime Minister Putin of Russia.

# Chapter 11

# *Stalin and Hitler*

The two most brutal, murderous dictators of the twentieth century, or perhaps ever, Hitler and Stalin, found themselves in power at the same time, in capital cities separated by only a few hundred kilometers. Millions were murdered on their direct orders, and millions more died as a result of their policies.

Between these two demons lay Poland, Ukraine, and the Baltics. Both dictators had designs on these lands. Hitler looked eastward to the rich farmlands of Ukraine to create *Lebensraum*, or "living space," for his people; Stalin looked westward to increase the size of his empire. Though their politics were very different, and they mistrusted each other, in August 1939 they signed the Molotov-Ribbentrop Pact. The Germans received promises of much needed grain and oil imports, and the Russians got a few more nations to add to their empire. Both made promises that they would not attack each other. Ten days after this pact was signed, on September 1, 1939, the Nazis invaded Poland and precipitated World War II. Seventeen days later, the Bolsheviks invaded eastern Galicia, Polish-occupied western Ukraine. As a result, all the Ukrainian ethnic lands were now in Soviet hands.

The Polish occupation of Galicia during the twenty years between the wars was brutal and very unpopular among Ukrainians. With memories of the murderous Soviet policies in eastern Ukraine still fresh in people's minds, however, the Russian invasion was even less welcome.

For the next nineteen months, eastern Galicia was subjected to bloody, senseless Bolshevik control. The Polish government structures were demolished. Roman Catholic and Uniate churches and priests faced persecution, resisters were jailed or summarily shot, and the Russian language was imposed on the Ukrainian population. Eastern Galicia became part of the Ukrainian SSR.

On June 22, 1941, Hitler launched Operation Barbarossa against the Soviet Union. German armies invaded Soviet western Ukraine and crushed the Soviets. After a brief period of hope among Ukrainians, who believed that nothing could be worse than the

Bolsheviks, the full extent of Nazi brutality became evident and Ukrainians faced yet another inhumanly brutal oppressor.

Three years of Nazi terror followed.

# BARBAROSSA, June 1941

Hitler never had any intention of honoring the non-aggression pact his minister, Ribbentrop, signed in August 1939. He was simply too busy in the west and just needed a little more time before launching his attack to the east.

Stalin, on the other hand, was a fool to have believed Hitler—or perhaps it was hubris.

When the massive German armies crossed into Soviet-occupied Ukraine on June 22, 1941, Stalin was unprepared. He was so surprised that he didn't react for several days. The Germans destroyed the Soviet defenses and Soviet aircraft and marched into eastern Galicia virtually unopposed.

When the Germans marched into Lviv, they were warmly welcomed by Ukrainians.

The simplistic analysis of this event was that Ukrainians were supporters of the Nazis and their policies. Lost in this line of thinking is that Ukrainians held a profound enmity towards their Soviet occupiers.

After months of Soviet rule in Galicia, and the mass murder of their brothers in eastern Ukraine in the forced famine-genocide just a few years earlier still fresh in their minds, most Ukrainians felt that anything would be better than the Bolsheviks.

Ukrainians remembered the pre-World War I days under the Austrians when relatively speaking, their situation was so much better. They also remembered that Germany politically supported an independent Ukraine in 1918. Many thought, the Germans would support an independent Ukraine again.*

On June 30, 1941, eight days after Operation Barbarossa began; Ukrainians declared an independent West Ukraine National Republic and the blue and yellow flag was raised on government buildings throughout eastern Galicia.

---

\* "For some reason, Ukrainians are usually stereotyped as Nazi collaborators, as concentration camp guards or as volunteers in the Galizien Division of the Waffen SS. These stereotypes are extremely unjust. Given the appalling repressions inflicted on Soviet Ukraine before the war, the surprising thing is how very few Ukrainians signed up for Nazi service. There were far more Ukrainians in concentration camps as prisoners than were as guards, and there were far more Dutchmen, Scandinavians and Hungarians in the Waffen SS than there were Ukrainians. And there were far more Ukrainians fighting against the *Wermacht* than for it. Unfortunately one rarely hears anything of the countless Ukrainian soldiers of the Red Army or the millions of Ukrainian civilian casualties. It's a well-known dodge. Whenever Ukrainians did bad things during the war they were called Ukrainians. Whenever they did good things they were called Russians."

—Davies, Norman. *Europe East and West*, Random House, 2006, p.236

The euphoria lasted only a few days. The Ukrainian government was soon disbanded, the leadership jailed, and Ukrainians suffered through a three-year Nazi reign of terror.

Any "honeymoon" period the Ukrainians enjoyed following the German invasion was quickly dissipated by the unspeakable brutality the Germans imposed on the population.

# PIDHAJCI, June 1941

My parents, Bronyslawa and Bohdan, had been living and working in Pidhajci since 1938 when eastern Galicia was still under Polish occupation.

When the Germans invaded Poland on September 1, 1939, and the Bolsheviks invaded eastern Galicia two weeks later, things began to get more difficult for Bohdan and Bronyslawa and the cooperative movement.

The Cooperativa was a little too capitalistic an enterprise for the Bolsheviks, and there were ongoing attempts to disrupt the operation. Inspections, new regulations, and intimidations were the order of the day. As well, Poles who remained in Pidhajci were still fighting old battles and, though out of power, tried to disrupt anything the Ukrainians had accomplished. In 1940, my father, Bohdan, and his coworker, Mykhajlo Kletsor, another manager of the cooperative, were arrested by the Bolsheviks after a complaint by a group of Poles. Bohdan and Mykhajlo spent time in a Bolshevik jail.

After a while, because there was no evidence, the charges against them were dropped, but the intimidation continued.

While eastern Galicia was under Bolshevik occupation, on February 4, 1940, Bohdan and Bronyslawa were married in a quiet ceremony at Bronyslawa's parish church in Ivanivka. The Melnyks of Ladychyn and the Martyniuks of Ivanivka, and their closest friends were in attendance.

A few days later, my parents returned to Pidhajci and took up residence in a small apartment on the main square in town, directly above the cooperative offices.

A year and a half later, in the midst of all the uncertainty, they were expecting their first child.

In mid-June 1941, my mother, almost nine months pregnant, made plans to travel to Ivanivka to have her baby. Ivanivka was a familiar setting, the local birthing facility was new and clean, and the midwife she hired was a family friend. She would be able to give birth to her first child just steps from her home. Her mother and her sisters would be close by to help her.

But things don't always turn out as planned.

Early in the morning on June 22, 1941, confusion reigned. News reached Pidhajci that the Germans had smashed eastward across the border on several fronts with overwhelming military might, and the Bolsheviks were retreating. The prospect of ridding their country of Bolsheviks was hopeful news to Ukrainians. Surely, the Germans would not be as brutal as the Bolsheviks. When they arrived in Lviv, the Germans announced they had "liberated" Galicia and would allow local representation in the new regime. Rumors circulated throughout the countryside that Stephan Bandera*, the Ukrainian nationalist leader, was making plans to form a government.

On June 28, just a week after the German invasion, with the Germans in Lviv and the Bolsheviks in disarray, Bohdan decided it was time to bring his very pregnant wife, Bronyslawa, to Ivanivka. He packed one of the cooperative trucks, and with Bronyslawa in the front seat beside him, headed east to Ivanivka.

\* \* \*

As he drove along the deserted roads, he thought of his father, Peter, and his mother, Maria, in Ladychyn. His parents already had two granddaughters but no grandsons.

A few weeks earlier, anticipating the birth of another grandchild, Peter had given orders that the baby *must* be a boy. He offered to have Bronyslawa come to Ladychyn to give birth at the mill but understood that she felt more comfortable in her own village, closer to her mother.

When Bohdan and Bronyslawa reached Ivanivka that evening, however, everything seemed different. Bronyslawa's house was dark, the curtains were drawn, and there was no one to welcome them in the yard as they drove in. Bohdan knocked on the door. Bronyslawa's father opened the door a crack and whispered, "You can't stay here. The Bolsheviks are watching the house. Ivanivka is not safe. You must leave."

Bohdan knew that this had something to do with my mother's brother, Vasylko, and his wife, Marynia, and their anti-Bolshevik activities. Bohdan quickly caught up on the news, took a small basket of food from his mother-in-law, and backed the truck out of the yard. They would go to Ladychyn after all. Bohdan's parents, Peter and Maria, would take care of them.

Peter was delighted they had come. His grandchild—no, grandson—would soon be born right here in the mill. He paid a visit to the most experienced midwife in the village, ordered her to be ready, had the house cleaned as if it were Christmas, and proudly informed his neighbors he would soon be a grandfather again!

On Sunday July 1, everyone in the village was nervously anticipating news from Lviv. Finally, an announcement was made that the day before, on June 30, an independent Ukrainian state had been declared in Lviv, and an important meeting would take place in the Prosvita Reading Hall that afternoon. Bronyslawa was huge and felt she would deliver at any moment but insisted she would go to the meeting with Bohdan.

---

\* Stephan Bandera, a powerful and legendary political leader in Ukraine. In 1934 he was sentenced to life imprisonment by Poles, in 1941 he declared independence of Ukraine, was arrested by Germans and sent to a concentration camp until 1944. In 1959, he was assassinated by the Bolsheviks in Munich.

A man from Lviv had come to deliver the news. He announced that the Germans had taken Lviv, and had permitted the Bandera faction of the Organization of Ukrainian Nationalists to convene a National Assembly. They proclaimed an independent Ukrainian state and were about to form a government. Everyone in the meeting hall cheered and celebrations began. Someone found a blue-and-yellow Ukrainian flag and hoisted it on the roof of the town hall.

But then, the man from Lviv gave the bad news. Just before the Germans arrived, hundreds of political prisoners, mostly OUN members being held in Soviet prisons, had been killed by the retreating Bolsheviks in Lviv and in nearby Ternopil.

As they slowly walked back to the mill after the meeting, Bohdan and Bronyslawa paused at the top of the hill overlooking the mill. They heard a dull droning sound, looked up, and saw a squadron of German planes flying eastward.

"Will we be OK?" Bronyslawa asked.

"I hope so," said Bohdan.

Bronyslawa worried about her favorite little brother, Vasylko, and his baby son, Bohdanchyk.

"Vasylko and his wife, Marynia, are very resourceful. They should be OK," she thought.

Bohdan had to return to Pidhajci that evening. He escorted Bronyslawa back to the mill and left her in the care of his father, Peter, and mother, Maria.

## BIRTH AT THE MILL

A few days later, on July 5, 1941, Bronyslawa announced, "It's time!"

The midwife was summoned, the women donned fresh white aprons, and the men were sent outside. Grandfather Peter didn't know what to do with himself. He was too nervous to just wait. He had to have a gift for the baby. He could find nothing in Ladychyn, so he hitched his horses and drove to Varvarenci looking for something special.

When he returned an hour later, he could hear the cries of a newborn coming from his bedroom. The midwife stepped outside and announced, "Mr. Melnyk, you have a grandson."

Peter was holding a huge basket of strawberries he had brought from the old Melnyk village. His eyes filled with tears of joy.

Word of the birth did not reach Bohdan until the next day. He hurried back to Ladychyn and found Grandfather Peter fully in charge.

"Someday the boy will take over the mill," he announced. "He's healthy, he's strong, and he looks just like me. We must make plans for the christening."

Bohdan held his baby boy for the first time. "What shall we name him?" he asked Bronyslawa. "How about Roman, after your older brother, and Peter after your father?"

**Roman Peter Melnyk.** That sounds good!"

At the time of his birth, the blue and yellow flags of Ukraine were flying over major public buildings all over eastern Galicia. By the time the baptism was arranged, however, the Germans had decided they had had enough of an independent Ukrainian state. They arrested newly appointed Premier Jaroslav Stetsko and his newly formed cabinet and sent them to concentration camps.

Technically, however, my brother, Roman, was born during the time of the short-lived West Ukrainian National Republic.

The Nazis were now in charge of Galicia but the Bolsheviks were not leaving quietly. Orders had come down from Stalin that before they left, the Bolsheviks were to arrest all suspected Ukrainian resistance fighters and their families, pack them on any available trains, seal the cars, and ship them east. The NKVD Secret Police went from house to house and dragged away hundreds of villagers—anyone who had any association with Ukrainian nationalists—packed them onto trucks, and drove them to Terebovla.

News reached Bronyslawa in Ladychyn that there was of a lot of activity in the train station in Terebovla, and prisoners were being loaded onto cattle cars. The next day, news reached her that her brother, Vasylko, had escaped, that little Bohdanchyk was safe but that Vasylko's wife, Marynia, had been captured and was on a cattle train heading east.

The joy of giving birth to a healthy baby boy was tempered by the terrible news from Bronyslawa's village.

## HOLOCAUST

Bohdan again packed Bronyslawa into the cooperative truck, this time with a brand new baby in her arms, and they headed back to Pidhajci. The Bolsheviks had quickly left Pidhajci, and things seemed relatively peaceful there.

When Bohdan, Bronyslawa and newborn Roman arrived, news that the Germans were about to enter Pidhajci greeted them. The next morning, as Bronyslawa sat by her second-floor window, feeding her baby son, and Bohdan stood at the front door of his cooperative office, a squad of motorcycles, each with a sidecar, entered the main square. Moments later, several cars loaded with officers circled and stopped near the center of the square. Marching behind the cars were several hundred German soldiers.

After the din of the motorcycles subsided, the only sound one could hear was the rhythmic pounding of boots on cobblestones. All other activity stopped. The Germans had entered Pidhajci unopposed and within minutes were in total control.

My mother remembers when she first saw the soldiers, she thought they looked so young—perhaps sixteen or seventeen. They stopped at the fountain in the square, stripped to the waist and washed. Bronyslawa remembers they looked so cheerful and confident. My mother marveled at their discipline. They knew they were in charge.

Within minutes, they were back in formation, a young officer bellowed out orders, and the soldiers dispersed—but with purpose and determination.

It was obvious they had scouted the town before arriving. Everyone knew exactly what they were doing and where they were going. One group moved toward the grand Polish church. This would be the soldiers' quarters. Another group moved toward the town hall. The red, black, and white swastika flag was raised on the flagpole. The most exquisite house on the square, owned by a wealthy Jewish merchant, was requisitioned for use as officers' quarters.

Groups of soldiers were sent to each of the churches and synagogues in town. All records were seized and brought to the town hall. The town's Soviet administrators had left, and only a few minor Polish bureaucrats remained. They were put to work.

Other soldiers were stationed at every business on the town square and beyond.

A young officer walked into my father's cooperative offices and announced to my father that he was assigned to "protect" the business.

My mother remembers that by noon, the town had been totally secured by the Germans. Loudspeakers were set up in the square and an announcement was made in German and Polish.

1. Pidhajci is now governed by the Army of the Third Reich
2. Everyone is to cooperate with all orders issued by the Army
3. All Jews are to report to the town square at six o'clock this evening.

That evening, almost the entire Jewish population of Pidhajci had gathered in the square. An officer called for attention and started reading names, one by one, ordering them to step forward.

One hundred names were called, but only ninety-two people stepped forward.

The ninety-two who were present were told they were being resettled and were immediately marched out of the square surrounded by almost as many armed soldiers.

As they were being marched out of town, Bohdan noticed that among the German soldiers were a number of Poles, Ukrainians, and Jews wearing armbands, indicating they were auxiliary policemen. Most of these people were familiar to Bohdan. They were among the unsavory, unemployed dregs of the town. Now they wore armbands and had that smug look of authority.

That night, just after sunset, gunfire was heard north of the town.

The following morning, the bodies of the eight men, women, and children who had ignored the previous day's roll call were hanging in the square.

A few days later the process was repeated.

Within a few weeks, there were no Jews left in Pidhajci. Some had escaped, but most had been "resettled."

In 1997, Toronto Star reporter Olivia Ward interviewed survivors of the Nazi terror in Ukraine. Below is part of her report:

---

*SELIDOVO, DONETTSK REGION, EASTERN UKRAINE*

*1941-43. THE NAZI TERROR*

*The Nazis crossed into Ukraine in June of 1941 and had occupied most of the territory by October. They invaded to seize control of the food and energy resources of the region.*

*Auxiliary police, local units were set up to assist the Germans in "keeping order"—aiding the Nazi genocide against the Jews and Gypsies, and violently repressing the Ukrainian and Soviet resistance.*

*"Those henchmen who threatened people both physically and morally were anathema here," says one local resident.*

*"Ukraine was ravaged by two brutal reigns of terror: the boots of murderous Soviet officials and Nazi invaders have trampled over millions of lives, leaving only a chilling silence.*

*"Many things happened during the war," recalls another.*

*"The fate of the Jewish residents was worse. There were repeated scenes of shootings, beatings and mass burials. They were pulled out of their homes, one by one, shot and thrown into a local mine shaft.*

*"During the German occupation there was a prison in the village," recalls one resident. "Nobody was allowed to enter, but we heard terrible noises coming from there. And people were taken to the mine shaft and shot. No one knew their names. All we knew was that they were killed."*

*It was a terrible irony that the region's natural wealth made it an irresistible prize for the century's most monstrous dictators, Joseph Stalin and Adolf Hitler.*

*Stalin coveted the area for its coal and its rich black soil, which guaranteed prosperity.*

*When Ukrainians resisted the Soviet dictator's campaign to strip their land and property, he took ruthless revenge, systematically starving millions to death by confiscating huge stores of grain. By 1934, at least 15 million Ukrainians were dead or deported.*

*In 1941, the rustic villages were unprepared for the onslaught of the German army. When the tanks arrived, a few people joined the resistance, but the majority just tried to co-exist with an occupation that was relentlessly organized and geared for terror. Some locals greeted the*

*Germans with short-lived hope for better times. A few, still simmering with hatred from the days of the Soviet starvation promptly joined the Nazis. These, along with some professional criminals and a few hungry opportunists, made up the notorious auxiliary police, charged with guarding strategic areas, but also cooperating in the Nazi's ethnic extermination campaign. The terror was directed by Hitler's merciless lieutenant Erich Koch, who saw Ukrainians as slaves to be beaten and subdued.*

*"We were in the fields. People came running, saying the Germans were here. They came to the villages in carts. There were chickens running around squawking, and they started shooting them," recalls another villager. "Soon they were shooting people. The executions were relentless and systematic—every Tuesday and Friday."*

*Up to 10,000 people arrived every day by rail. They came to the train station, freezing, and some already dead from cold. They were taken to a camp where they were fed rotting vegetables. Inmates who were not starved or frozen to death were shot in the mass executions. The full horror didn't surface until years later when a mine shaft containing more than 75,000 of their bodies was opened up, one of many sites for mass burial in the region.*

*It was impossible to tell who they were. No one even knew exactly how many had died. They just calculated how many corpses it would take to fill that space. Most of the targets for the systematic slaughter were Jews. The region's 64,000-strong Jewish population was the first to perish.*

*It was impossible to resist. Everything was completely organized and controlled.*

*Throughout Ukraine the pattern was chillingly similar. Ethnic classification of all the residents was done immediately, and Jews who tried to avoid identification were often turned in by the auxiliary police. Their property was confiscated and "fines" were imposed on trumped up charges. Red Army servicemen and Ukrainian partisans were arrested and shot.*

*The Ukrainian population was ordered into labor gangs or farm work to feed the German soldiers. "I was working on a road gang," said another villager. "They stood over us with whips and guns. If we stayed too long in the toilet they'd start to shoot. And they beat us with whips."*

*The penalty for defying the Nazis was death, but a few people in the village were prepared to face it.*

*Young girls, some as young as 12, were sent to Germany to work in industrial plants. Some were rounded up by "zealots" in the auxiliary police and thrown into trains without so much as a farewell to their parents. Both boys and girl were threatened, but especially girls. Some went into hiding, others leapt out of train windows to escape.*

# Chapter 12

# *Soviet / German Occupied Galicia, 1939*

When the Germans invaded Poland on September 1, 1939, they advanced only to the San River which divided eastern and western Galicia. The eastern part of Galicia, where the majority of Ukrainians lived, was occupied within days by the Soviets but Polish western Galicia, home to some half-million Ukrainians, remained under German control.

German General Hans Frank was in charge of occupied western Galicia and, in studied contrast to his treatment of the Poles, General Frank sanctioned several Ukrainian organizations including the Krakow-based Ukrainian Central Committee social welfare agency, Ukrainian schools and he ensured freedom for the Orthodox and Uniate Churches in the area. Ukrainians were also inserted into lower official positions in overwhelmingly Polish areas in a clear policy of divide and rule. 13

The Tatomyrs were already across the San River in the relative safety of Peremyshl in German-occupied western Galicia (present day Poland) when the Soviets invaded. Julian assumed his position as an assistant to the Ukrainian bishop of Peremyshl, and organized and headed the Ukrainian People's Aid Society there. Julian's nephew, Volodymyr Tatomyr became the head of the Ukrainian Central Committee (a social welfare agency) in Krakow. Oleksander, his younger son, helped organize Prosvita reading rooms in Peremyshl and the surrounding villages where Ukrainians lived. Julian's older son, Jaroslav, was in school in Paris studying engineering.

Julian and the bishop perhaps hoped that Oleksander, who was young, single, and energetic, and had almost completed his seminary studies, would still consider the priesthood, but Oleksander insisted he wanted to become a teacher. During his time in Peremyshl, Oleksander completed a one-year course in pedagogy.

In June 1941, when the Germans invaded Ukraine and pushed out the Bolsheviks, Julian, Olha, and Oleksander returned to their home villages in eastern Galicia. Julian was again posted to his parish in Luzhok. Oleksander also returned to Luzhok and worked as a teacher and youth organizer.

On June 30, 1941, Julian and Oleksander traveled to Lviv to witness the proclamation of an independent West Ukrainian National Republic.

---

## GESTAPO

**June 1941.** Sophia Tereshkevych was happy to see the Bolsheviks scurrying to leave as the Germans approached. She returned to her teaching and hoped the Germans would leave her and her students alone. Unfortunately, not all the Bolsheviks left the area. Some remained and blended with the general population.

Sophia traveled to Sambir on June 30, 1941, to witness the formal declaration of the West Ukrainian National Republic, then returned to her classroom and happily told her students the great news. When the Germans arrested the leaders of the independence movement and established their strict rule over the population a few days later, Sophia continued to teach her children patriotic songs and, importantly, continued to be active in the OUN. But now, the focus of the OUN was to defeat the German occupation.

One day, an informant accused Sophia of subversive activity and directed the German Gestapo to her home. The soldiers burst in, scattered family belongings, searching for anything valuable such as beautifully embroidered Ukrainian blouses, new clothing, kitchen appliances and utensils. As it happened, the Gestapo found a small handgun hidden behind a painting. At the time of this home invasion, a rather unpleasant forestry engineer happened to be living in Sophia's home, and the family insisted the gun belonged to him. No explanations were acceptable to the Germans. They arrested Sophia's brother, Osyp, and told her the family would never see him alive again. In despair, Sophia rushed to Sambir to find help for her beloved brother. Fortunately, the forestry engineer appeared and showed the Gestapo official permits for ownership of the handgun. Osyp was released and returned home. After this terrifying incident, it took Sophia a long time to overcome her anxiety and foreboding of future events.

---

In 1943, Oleksander completed agricultural studies in Berezhnytsi and Chernyzy in the region of Strij. The diploma he received enabled him to open a regional agricultural middle school in the small town of Topilnicia, nestled off the main road on the banks of a beautiful small tributary of the Dnister River, just ten kilometers south of Luzhok.

Oleksander was not only a teacher but also the director of the school, which, at one point, had as many as five hundred students from all over the Sambir and Starij Sambir regions. The school consisted of a large main building and a smaller two-story stone building with three classrooms and a small two-room apartment for the director.

As the school started to expand, Oleksander was in the position to hire additional teachers. One day, a dynamic, intelligent, beautiful young woman arrived for an interview. She was from the village of Spas, not far from Luzhok, and though she had received her pedagogy degree in Sambir in 1936, she had been unable to find work as a teacher under Polish occupation.

Her name was Sophia Tereshkevych. Oleksander hired her on the spot.

**Sophia Tereshkevych Tatomyr, c. 1938**

Oleksander and Sophia fell in love and, a few months later, were married in Father Julian's church in Luzhok. They moved into the spacious apartment near the school in Topilnicia and soon Sophia was pregnant with their first child.

# CHRYSTYNA

On a cold and snowy Friday, January 28, 1944, Sophia dismissed her class early and told Oleksander to summon the midwife. That evening Sophia gave birth to a healthy baby girl on the big bed in the director's quarters.

Nine days later, on Sunday, February 6, Oleksander and Sophia bundled up their new baby, hitched a team of horses, and made the short trip to Luzhok to Grandfather Julian's church for the christening.

The baby girl was named **Chrystyna (Xrystia** for short) and was given the middle name, **Olha**, in honor of her grandmother.

Perhaps to confuse authorities, or to protect the little child from possible retributions, the birth was not registered in Topilnicia where Chrystyna was born, nor Luzhok, where she was baptized and where her grandfather was the parish priest, but in Starij Sambir, a larger center and provincial capital some twenty kilometers north of Luzhok.

For a few months, the young family tried to have some semblance of a normal life. Oleksander, Sophia, and little Chrystyna made frequent trips to Luzhok, where she could enjoy her Grandfather Julian's spacious house and grounds and be cared for by Grandmother Olha and their servants.

In June of 1944, the Nazis were still technically in control of eastern Galicia, but with the German defeat at Stalingrad, and the slow retreat of their armies and advance of the Red Army westward, the Tatomyrs started to make some painful decisions. They would not survive another Bolshevik occupation.

Uncertainty and confusion reigned in eastern Galicia. On July 22, 1944, the Red Army crossed the Zbruch river and were advancing toward Lviv. By late July there were rumors the Bolsheviks had already taken Sambir, other rumors that they were already in Starij Sambir, just twenty kilometers to the north. In any case, it became obvious that the Bolsheviks were getting closer.

As the Bolsheviks approached their respective towns and villages in the summer of 1944, many people, especially the more educated, had to make a decision—to stay or to leave. In particular, the Soviets targeted community leaders and the clergy.*

The Tatomyrs had no choice. They were definitely *persona non grata* and would surely be arrested, and perhaps summarily executed or, at the very least, sent east to Siberia if they were captured by the Red Army.

Their decision was obvious.

---

\*    The most prominent churchman to be executed by the Soviets was Metropolitan Andrij Sheptytsky, on Nov. 1, 1944 though many others were murdered as the Bolsheviks advanced.

**Martyrs**: "The Greek Catholic Church of Western Ukraine was persecuted. It was sorely pressed by the Soviet occupation of 1939-41, tolerated by the German occupation of 1941-44, then savagely suppressed after 1944 by the return of the Soviets. It's martyrs include Father Zynovii Kovalyk (1941), who expired during a mock crucifixion, Father Emilian Kovch (1944) who died in Majdanek for helping Jews, Sister Tarsykiia Matsiw (1944), who was shot by the Red Army at the door of her convent, Father Romen Lysko (1949) who was walled up by the NKVD alive, Archpastor Nykyta Budko (1949) who had worked as a priest in Canada (and as bishop laid the cornerstone of St. Michael's Church in Montreal in 1916. Please see *"Growing up in Montreal"* in the Epilogue section of this book), and Bishop Gregory Lakota (1950) who was sentenced to ten years' hard labor in Vorkuta. Most martyrs, of course, are nameless." 14

Father Julian Tatomyr blessing Easter baskets at his church in Luzok, Spring, 1944. This would be last the time that he would bless Easter baskets. He died in March 1946 in Austria.

Rev. Julian Tatomyr's church choir, Luzhok, 1944. When we visited the church in 1993, a woman gave Chrystyna this picture to show that she was a member of the choir forty-nine years earlier. She is sitting on the floor in front of Julian.

# PART FIVE

# Escape

# Chapter 13

# *Chornobyl Means Wormwood*

*And the third angel sounded, and there fell a great star from heaven, burning as it were a lamp. And it fell up on the third part of the rivers, and upon the fountains of waters: and the name of the star is called Wormwood; and many men died of the waters, because they were made bitter.—Revelations 8:10-11*

April 26, 2006, marked the twentieth anniversary of the Chornobyl nuclear accident.

On April 26, 1986, reactor No. 4 at the Chornobyl nuclear power station, 120 kilometers north of Kyiv, exploded after numerous safety procedures were disregarded, creating a series of explosions and a fireball. Nearly nine tons of radioactive material, ninety times as powerful as the Hiroshima bomb, spewed into the sky. Thirty people died immediately, and hundreds more as a result of the sloppy and primitive clean-up efforts. 135,000 people were evacuated and an estimated five million people in Ukraine, Belarus, and Russia were adversely affected.

Some people, especially the elderly, refused to leave, and even tried to live off the small gardens they had planted by their homes. The most tragically affected were the young and unborn children. The incidence of thyroid cancer increased tenfold. The effect on young women of childbearing age is uncertain.

Repercussions from the Chornobyl accident were still being felt more than twenty years later by some five million people in the contaminated areas of Belarus, Russia, and Ukraine. The population of these areas continues to cope with the ongoing political, social, environmental, and health consequences of that event.

Chornobyl has become a metaphor not only for the horror of uncontrolled nuclear power but also for the collapsing Soviet system with its secrecy, deception, disregard for safety of workers and their families, and their inability to deliver basic services.

It also became the rallying cry for Ukrainian independence.

Note: For more information on the tragedy, please see the UN Report, *Chernobyl's Legacy*. Various organizations in the west stepped in to help following the explosion. One group which provides outstanding support for orphaned children in Ukraine is,

> Help Us Help the Children
> and the Children of Chornobyl Canadian Fund
> 2118-A Bloor St. West, Suite 2000, Toronto, On M6S 1M9,
> Phone: (416) 604-4611.

This group has done some incredible work with children in Ukraine. They merit everyone's support.

# KYIV

With our teaching duties over, and with only a week left before our scheduled return to Canada, we were invited to visit our other newfound relatives in Lviv.

Ivanko's sister, Ola, was married to another Ivan—a successful Lviv businessman. Although they were both named *Ivan*, there was no problem differentiating these two Ivans. Ivanko was short and slim, he didn't smoke or drink and was usually quite serious.

His brother-in-law, Ivan, was a big man who smoked and drank heavily, was gregarious, and always in a jolly mood. Ivan was also extremely generous. (We found out that the Audi Ivanko was driving was actually a gift from Ivan.)

Ivan was a true entrepreneur. When Ukrainian independence became inevitable in 1990, he pooled all the savings he had accumulated over the years, including the dollars he had exchanged for rubles in the old days when the value of the ruble was artificially inflated, sold his wife's jewelry, and somehow convinced a Swiss bank to lend him enough money to buy a Tetra-Pac franchise and start an apple juice packaging business. He bought a large apple farm near Lviv and promised other farmers who owned apple orchards in the area that he would buy all their apples if they sold them to him at a good price. He bought the latest packing equipment and built a factory in a village twenty kilometers north-east Lviv.

By 1993, just about everyone in that village was working for Ivan, and his apple juice was being sold throughout Europe. He had just moved into the not-yet-completed house he was building near the factory.

He proudly showed us around his enormous, immaculate factory and the huge new home he designed for his family and announced we would have a barbeque that afternoon. After a few drinks, he asked us to follow him outside. We expected to see a North American style gas barbeque but instead, we walked to a small wooded area at the side of his house. A few meters inside this little forest was a meadow. On one side, partly hidden by a few trees, was a long fire pit. Tending the fire and already cooking large quantities of meat on the grill was the chef from Ivan's factory who, we were told, was the best cook in the area. A row of tables—enough to seat thirty or more people were located nearby. By the time we sat down and all the family and guests with husbands and wives showed up, all the seats were filled.

Back home, Chrystyna and I rarely drink hard liquor, and I only have wine at formal occasions—when someone is likely to make a toast. But here we were downing full glasses of straight vodka in addition to wines and liqueurs. We ate much more than usual, we talked, we sang songs, and we drank and made toasts.

Someone offered me a cigarette. I declined, explaining that Chrystyna and I had quit smoking about twelve years earlier. An hour or so later, however, I took just one cigarette for old time's sake. Chrystyna looked at me in shock but by the end of the evening, she too had had a cigarette. We promised ourselves we would quit as soon as we got on the plane heading home. We kept our promise. The next year we tempted fate again and quit successfully again. After our third trip to Ukraine, however, we were hooked, and eight years passed before I finally quit smoking again—this time for keeps!

We told Ivan we were planning to go to Kyiv for a few days. He picked up his phone and in no time handed us two tickets, Lviv-Kyiv, on the upscale *Grand Tour* coach owned by the Grand Hotel in Lviv. This coach is attached to the regular overnight Lviv-Kyiv train and costs a few dollars more but it boasts fresh clean sheets and excellent service.

Kyiv is a beautiful ancient city that in 1993 had not yet been fully discovered by tourists. Our Canadian teaching colleague, Valentina, let us have the key to a Kyiv apartment owned by her uncle. She said it would be empty for a few days and we could use it. The apartment is located in the best part of town, on Volodymyrska Boulevard, right between two important tourist areas: the eleventh century St. Sophia Cathedral and Andrijivsky Road, where the eighteenth century St. Andrew's Church, designed in the Rococo style by Italian architect Rastrelli, commands a great view of the lower town and the Dnipro River. Located nearby are some of the most interesting shops and bars in town.

Embassies and government buildings are just across the street, and just down the hill is Kreshchatyk Boulevard, the main street in Kyiv. As a bonus, when Valentina's uncle returned, he took us to see some of the other outstanding highlights of Kyiv and gave us an excellent insider's view of his city's history.

From him we learned about the various Orthodox churches and some of the politics surrounding their histories. Valentina's uncle was a member of the Autocephalous Ukrainian Orthodox church, but here the predominant two Orthodox churches were the Ukrainian Orthodox Church of the Moscow Patriarch and the Ukrainian Orthodox Church of the Kyiv Patriarch.

Each patriarch controls a number of church properties in Kyiv and throughout Ukraine and, although Moscow is no longer in control politically, the Russian Orthodox Church still holds significant power and has refused to relinquish its churches and properties in Ukraine.

One of the first things we noticed in Kyiv was that, unlike Lviv, the majority of the people in Kyiv spoke Russian. They all seemed to understand our Ukrainian but would answer us in Russian even when we protested that we didn't understand. Sometimes they spoke to us in a very heavily accented mixture of Russian and Ukrainian. All the signs in Kyiv, however, were in Ukrainian.

As we walked along the elegant clean downtown streets, we noticed how well dressed the local citizens were. Men, even in the summer heat, wore long-sleeved shirts and, of course, long pants. (European males over the age of eight would never be seen wearing shorts in public, especially not in the city. Only tourists and schoolboys wore shorts.)

Women wore the latest fashions: crisp summer dresses, high-heeled shoes, designer handbags. Chrystyna commented on how gorgeous they all looked.

Photographs sent to North American newspapers from Ukraine inevitably feature toothless old babushkas huddled in an alley. (We did see old people, babushkas, begging in the subway entrances because their pensions had been so radically reduced after independence, but they were in the minority.)

Our guide took us to the most unique and spectacular attraction in Kyiv, *Pecherska Lavra*, literally, "the Cave Monastery," a complex of forty magnificent old structures representing eight centuries of art and architecture. The complex covers some seventy acres along the Dnipro riverfront within walking distance of downtown.

In 1051, it was founded by two monks who built the first church above the caves. The church and the attached monastery were supported by the Kyivan princes and boyars and grew into one of the largest religious and intellectual center in the Orthodox world.

When we approached the *Lavra*, we noticed the huge array of golden-domed churches next to each other. Each church was built in a different style and likely of a different era. In the center of the complex is the Refectory Church. This is one of the newer churches in the complex (only one hundred years old), and is the lead Ukrainian Orthodox church that still recognizes the Moscow Patriarch.

Some of the older churches have spectacular frescoes while others were destroyed by various invaders and were being rebuilt. The total effect was spellbinding.

We climbed the 239 steps up the eighteenth-century bell tower, and when the monk assigned to ring the many bells came to ring the bells, I volunteered to help him. He agreed to pose for a picture but declined my offer to ring the huge bells.

The caves for which the monastery is named are the main attraction.

They consist of two labyrinths of tunnels ranging from five to ten meters underground, with corridors, some of which are so narrow and low that a large person cannot pass, while others are up to two meters wide. Excavated in these soft sandstone catacombs are small burial niches containing remains of monks and saints naturally mummified due to the chemical composition of the soil and the constantly cool temperatures.

Our guide took us to the distant caves as he felt that the 'near' caves would be crowded. These distant caves were harder to get to and were often closed to visitors by the monks whenever they were conducting special services.

As we arrived near the caves, our guide politely told us not to speak as our accents would reveal that we were not locals and the monks may not let us in as they were trying to protect this small corner of their monastery from nonbelievers and tourists . . . or perhaps Catholics.

When we arrived at the entrance, a very tiny monk (although it seemed all the monks here were unusually short) stopped us and told us the caves were closed. Our guide told him he knew his way around the caves, that Chrystyna and I were very important visitors, and that he would take us down. He also handed the monk a small wad of bills to help pay for the renovations of the church. He insisted that we couldn't pass. I handed him more bills and gently pushed my way past him. He stepped back and let us through, perhaps fearing a confrontation in this holy place or maybe because he thought we had made a sufficient contribution to the church restoration fund.

## EXORCISM

We each lit a tall thin candle, cradled it in one hand, and slowly, one by one, we descended down the narrow earthen stairs carved into the cave. It quickly became very dark and we stopped to accustom our eyes to the darkness. (Knowing many monks were buried below made it a little spooky.) We climbed further down, around corners and down corridors until we knew we couldn't go back—we were totally dependent on our guide. After a few more minutes, as we approached the deepest part of the cave complex, we heard a woman's scream.

We turned another corner and reached an intersection where another monk was stationed, barring the entrance to the tunnel from where the screams seemed to be originating. He nervously directed us down the other corridor. Our guide asked what was going on. The monk told him that an exorcism was taking place in one of the underground chapels.

I looked down the corridor and caught a glimpse of a priest in full regalia, holding a cross in one hand and swinging an elaborate gold-covered brass *kadylo* (censer) in the other. He was waving it rhythmically, spreading incense throughout the tiny chapel but specifically directing the incense toward the poor woman kneeling on the earth floor. The priest incanted prayers as he held the cross on the woman's head. She again started to scream.

The monk ushered us down the other tunnel.

Chrystyna and I never thought we would ever witness an exorcism. Our guide told us it still happens here occasionally, and that this was the second time he had come upon an actual exorcism.

Further down the tunnel, we encountered another intersection and another monk who was guarding an entrance to a small room carved out of the clay where the remains of a long-dead monk lay on a raised platform. He allowed our guide into the room, but as I tried to follow, he stopped me. (I must have looked too much like a foreigner.)

When I persisted, he held his hand on my chest and asked, "*Virujuchij?*" (Are you a believer?") I nodded. He asked me to make the sign of the cross—perhaps to see whether I would do it the Roman Catholic way (left to right) or the Orthodox way. I crossed myself (right to left) three times. I passed the test and moved closer to the mummified monk, his blackened face and hands exposed. The monk then instructed me to kiss the hand of the dead monk to prove I really was a believer. I hesitated, but since I had gone this far . . .

The experiences of that day will stay with us forever.

*     *     *

The next day, we crossed the footbridge across the Dnipro River to the public park and beach. We were aware that the recently exploded Chornobyl nuclear plant was located just a few kilometers upstream and that this river carried all the radioactive pollution from that disastrous plant.

People were bathing and frolicking in the river. At the edge of the beach, a sign next to a water fountain read "Wash After Bathing."

At first we shook our heads and decided to simply watch the people in the water, but eventually we thought, "What the heck!" We waded into the Dnipro for a few refreshing minutes. As we washed in the fountain later, we wondered from where *that* water was flowing. Did it not come from the same Dnipro River?

The next day, Sunday, we went to church at St. Volodymyr Cathedral, the main Ukrainian Orthodox church of the Kyiv Patriarchate.

Patriarch Filaret was celebrating mass. He gave an excellent patriotic sermon in Ukrainian, and even though we are not of that faith, we took communion from him.

Maybe one day, religion will become a little less political.

# Chapter 14

# *Insurgency*

During the Iraq War, which started on March 19, 2003, and may last for many more years, the word "insurgent" was often used by the media to describe the various groups that fought against the Americans.

"Insurgent" soon became a dirty word.

But it all depends on your point of view.

During World War II, there were a number of insurgent and partisan groups operating in Eastern Europe.

"Nazi rule fostered resistance movements like rain encourages mushrooms . . . The earliest and the largest, underground army began to operate in Poland before the end of the September Campaign in 1939. It was supplied and trained by the Polish Section of Britain's Special Operations Executive (SOE), and acted as the military arm of a fully fledged underground state. From 1942, it assumed the name of the Armia Krajowa (the Home Army), and recruited 300,000 to 400,000 men and women. It engaged in widespread sabotage, in the assassination of SS and Gestapo personnel, and in brilliant intelligence work.

In Ukraine, an independence movement surfaced in 1941—as in the First World War—only to find its leaders cast into German concentration camps. From then on, the Ukrainian Insurrectionary Army (UPA) attempted the impossible by fighting in multi-sided conflicts with Poles, Soviet partisans as well as with the Germans. 14

"When the Bolsheviks and Nazis invaded Ukraine and showered death and destruction on the population, Ukrainians with no standing army of their own discovered that one way to fight the invaders was by becoming insurgents. The *Ukrainian Insurgent Army (UPA)* was formed in 1942 when the extent of the Germans' brutality, mass murders of Jews and Ukrainians became evident and when Ukrainians, notably the OUN leader Bandera, realized the Germans had no intention of helping Ukrainians secure independence, but instead had invaded in order to rape the land and to enslave the people" 6

Ukrainians applauded the young men and women who resisted occupation and joined the insurgency. They were heroes. Villagers supported, fed, and sheltered insurgents at great risk to themselves. Thousands died for their country as members of the Ukrainian Insurgent Army.

Three of my uncles, Vasylko, Mykhajlo, and Joseph were members of UPA. Several of Chrystyna's relatives were members of UPA, and our parents supported the Organization of Ukrainian Nationalists, the political branch of the Ukrainian Insurgent Army.

# LEAVING PIDHAJCI, February 1944

During the very cold winter of 1942-43, the Red Army won a decisive battle against the Germans at Stalingrad. By February 1943, the Germans were frozen, starving, and demoralized. They accepted defeat. The newly energized Red Army was determined to avenge all their previous losses and to take back all the territory they had lost since 1941. The Red Army methodically started to take back previously lost territory, pushing the Germans westward across Ukraine.

Just as the Soviets had done when they were retreating eastward in 1941, destroying and burning everything in their path, leaving nothing of value for their pursuers, the Germans now practiced their own version of the "scorched earth" policy as they retreated slowly westward across Ukraine.

With the Nazis still firmly in charge in Galicia, my mother's youngest brother, Wasyl (Vasylko) Martyniuk, and their first cousin, Mykhajlo Martyniuk, who was also the youngest in his family, joined the Ukrainian Insurgent Army soon after it was formed in 1942. They had little to lose. Both were members of OUN and would likely be found out before long. Neither would inherit land from their father and neither had a steady job. They were in their mid twenties, and since they were strong and healthy, they were exactly what Germans were looking for as slave laborers. Better to go into the woods and fight honorably than to be arrested or captured and enslaved.

Vasylko and Mykhajlo participated in a number of raids against the Germans and had several close calls. One night, in the summer of 1943, their group of insurgents came upon a German patrol. A battle ensued—Vasylko was shot and captured by the Germans, Mykhajlo got away.

Vasylko was not seriously hurt. The German captors took him to the interrogation center in Lviv where they tortured him and tried to obtain information about the UPA leadership. After several months of beatings and interrogations, he was transferred to the Buchenwald Concentration Camp.

News of the capture of her favorite little brother, whom she played with as a child and protected for so many years, hit my mother very hard.

By the start of 1944, it was obvious to my father that whoever won this war—Germans or Soviets—our family was going to be in danger. Stalin's policy was to eliminate all intellectuals, clergy, teachers, doctors, and anyone of influence. The Germans, on the other hand, were bitter, tired, and poorly supplied. They would brutally take anything they needed from the population and had no difficulty killing anyone who remotely resisted them or was of no use to them.

As well, the Soviets were particularly brutal with anyone suspected of past anti-Soviet activity and anyone who supported Ukrainian nationalist causes. Bohdan was starting to formulate plans to take his family out of Ukraine and to travel west. His father, Peter, had been to America and had done well. Bronyslawa had family in Canada and they seemed to be prospering. It wasn't safe for them here in their own country. Bohdan and Bronyslawa didn't want to raise their family under these conditions. Besides, there was little chance that they could safely survive the Soviet advance. There was no future for them here. In early January 1944, Bronyslawa was eight months pregnant with her second child. Her firstborn, my brother Roman, was born at the start of the German invasion, and it was beginning to look more and more that her second would be born at the end of it.

On January 6, 1944, Bronyslawa, Bohdan, and little Roman traveled east to Ivanivka to celebrate Ukrainian Christmas Eve with Bronyslawa's family.

They had the traditional twelve-course meal and attended midnight mass at the village church where Bohdan and Bronyslawa were married four years earlier. When Bohdan told Bronyslawa's parents of their plans to leave the country, they were devastated. They had lost Vasylko, his wife Marynia, and their grandson, Bohdanchyk, and now they were about to lose their daughter and their grandson, little Roman.

Resigned to the inevitable, Bronyslawa's father gave Bohdan some money he had saved and wished them luck. They could not believe this may be the last time they would see them.

The next morning Bronyslawa, Bohdan, and Roman drove to Ladychyn to spend Christmas Day at the mill with Bohdan's family. Grandpa Peter was quite sick. He was diagnosed with stomach cancer and was unable to work. Bohdan's younger brother, Joseph, and his wife, Slava, were running the mill.

Peter tried to change Bohdan's mind though he understood it was best that they leave. To add to the pain, Bohdan's two younger sisters, Olha and Lucia, announced they had also decided to leave with Bohdan. This was a very hard day for Peter and Maria. Peter asked Bohdan to promise that after a few years in North America, he would return to the mill. Grandfather Peter again announced that when he came of age, little Roman, would inherit the mill.

By mid-February, the Red Army was only a few kilometers east of the Zbruch River and their leaders were making plans for their final push on Lviv and the takeover of all of Galicia, and perhaps more. Bronyslawa again stated she wanted to give birth to her baby in familiar Ivanivka, her home village, with friends and family around her.

But it wasn't safe to go to Ivanivka. It was too close to the Zbruch River, and if the Soviets broke through, there would be little time to retreat. It was safer in Pidhajci, a few kilometers further west, where Bohdan's sisters lived and where they had the support of the cooperative and all their friends. If nothing else, should the Red Army cross the Zbruch, it would give them more time to prepare for a flight to the West.

Almost as soon as they returned to Pidhajci after Christmas, Bohdan and Bronyslawa began to pack their most precious possessions. No one could predict how long it would take the Red Army to fight its way back or if the Germans would send reinforcements and take the fight to them. The Germans were still in control, but Galicia was slowly beginning to slip into anarchy.

By mid-February 1944, it was hard to tell who was in charge of the town, but Bohdan was still running the cooperative, or what was left of it. In the apartment above the store, everything was ready for the move West, except that Bronyslawa was still not ready to deliver her child. Bohdan's sisters, Olha and Lucia, moved into the vacant apartments above the cooperative, and everybody waited for the baby.

Bohdan decided to make a final trip back to visit his ailing father in Ladychyn to let him say his final good-byes to his beloved grandson, Roman, who would never work in his grandfather's mill. Grandfather Peter promised to try to stay alive long enough to see his next grandchild.

A few days later, on February 18, 1944, with only his wife and youngest son, Joseph, at his side, Peter died at his mill. He never saw his next grandchild who would be born just ten days later.

Bohdan returned for the funeral without Bronyslawa. My grandfather Peter was buried in the most prominent spot in Ladychyn's Ukrainian cemetery behind the Catholic Church. Even though these were very tense times, with the Bolsheviks already quite active in the villages in anticipation of the arrival of the Red Army, the funeral was attended by hundreds from Ladychyn and the surrounding villages. They knew the Bolsheviks were watching, but they came anyway to pay tribute to Peter. Perhaps for some, it was their only way of showing defiance in the face of an anticipated Soviet victory.

What our family did not anticipate was that danger would not come from the approaching Red Army but from an enemy already well established and well known within the town.

Bohdan said good-bye to his brother, Joseph, and his wife, and returned to Ladychyn.

The Red Army was already in control of the area east of the Zbruch River, just a few kilometers away, and Bohdan wanted to get his family to safety but Bronyslawa, was in no condition to travel.

Several times a day, he would ask her, "Is it time yet?"

The answer was always, "No."

Bohdan was getting more and more anxious. All the plans had been made: the office would be closed and the cooperative truck was partly packed with supplies, ready to leave on short notice.

Finally, on February 28, 1944 (a leap year*), with the help of her two sisters-in-law, Bronyslawa delivered a sickly baby boy amidst the luggage in their cramped apartment. As he was not expected to live, a priest was called immediately. The child was baptized, but with all the confusion and with no civil government in place, his birth was never registered. What would be the point?

They had already discussed a possible name for the child should it be a boy. Bronyslawa was a great admirer of Metropolitan Andrij Sheptytsky, and my father was an admirer of OUN leader Andrij Melnyk. So Andrij it would be.

In their haste, my parents never gave me a middle name. (Again, what would be the point?)

I'm still just **Andrij Melnyk** (no middle name), sometimes Andy, and usually Andrew in formal occasions. And whenever anyone asks me my middle name, I explain my parents were poor and couldn't afford one. It's not that far from the truth.

Conditions in Pidhajci had deteriorated badly. Four distinct groups, with distinct agendas were fighting for supremacy:

The **Germans,** who had been so completely in charge, who kept such strict order in Pidhajci, who had wiped out the Jewish population and had arrested or executed so many Ukrainians and Poles during the previous two and a half years, were now worried about their own safety.

Some **Poles**, particularly members of the Polish underground *Armia Krajowa* (Home Army), still smarting from their defeat in 1939, were looking for revenge and still hoping to somehow win back eastern Galicia for Poland. For the moment, they directed their frustrations against Ukrainians.

The **Bolsheviks**, who had infiltrated Pidhajci, and who had kept a very low profile for two years, now smelled victory for their side and were making lists of people who they considered the enemy.

**Ukrainians** formed the last part of this circle of hatred. Against all odds, they just wanted to rid their country of the three other groups.

On March 11, 1944, when I was just eleven days old and still very sickly, my mother announced that she was ready to travel. Although my parents worried that I may not survive, it was no use holding up all the others.

My father packed suitcases and supplies into the back of the cooperative truck and gathered the group that would be leaving Pidhajci. It consisted of our family of four,

---

* To this day, I'm not sure whether I was born on the February 28 or 29. My mother was an educated woman, but one of her superstitions was that it was unlucky to be born on February 29. One of my aunts, who was present at my birth, told me years later that I was really born on the twenty-ninth. The birth certificate I finally received four years later, in 1948, from a Ukrainian priest in Germany, indicates I was born on the twenty-eighth. I've asked my mother about this several times, but she always avoided the question.

Bohdan's sister, Olha, (who was six months pregnant at the time) and her husband, Dmytro Stulkowsky, and Bohdan's youngest sister Emilia, nicknamed, Lucia.

Bohdan and Dmytro locked the cooperative office and the seven of us set out on the trip. The men sat in front while my mother, my two aunts, my brother, and I were in the rear cab with the luggage.

Our first stop was the town of Berezhany, about an hour's drive northwest of Pidhajci, where my uncle Roman was a priest. Although he was also vulnerable, he had a large house next to the church and he felt our families would be safe there for a short time. After we were settled in Berezhany, my father returned to Pidhajci to take care of the cooperative for as long as he felt it was safe, and to try to earn as much money as possible before our inevitable departure.

After a few weeks, my parents, aunts, and uncles decided it was time to start their trip west. The Red Army had made significant advances and was poised to cross the Zbruch River into Galicia.

They loaded the truck once again and set off to the town of Strij, where we stayed for three weeks with the Bihus family. The Bihus family later joined us on the westward journey and eventually settled in Toronto. As things became increasingly more dangerous, the group packed the truck again and headed for Sambir. They visited the cooperative office in Sambir to try to return the truck they had borrowed in Pidhajci and to get some supplies, but the Sambir cooperative and offices had been abandoned. With supplies running low and with the roads becoming more and more dangerous, the family continued west, to Peremyshl, on the other side of the San River in Poland. My mother's best friend from her school days, Vlodka Cybushnyk, lived in Peremyshl. They hoped to find refuge with her.

My parents hoped the Soviets would be happy to recapture eastern Galicia and reasoned they would never go further west. German General Hans Frank was still in charge in Peremyshl and he still maintained his policy of *divide and rule* by favoring Ukrainians over Poles for some lower official positions.

The usually short trip from Sambir to Peremyshl was fraught with dangers and challenges. Many Ukrainians were leaving for the West, and the Germans were trying to maintain control while also planning their own retreat. Hungry, injured, and discouraged, but still armed, German soldiers retreating from the eastern front limped through this area. Gasoline was very difficult to find since all supplies and all the available gasoline were reserved for the German army. There were numerous checkpoints along the way, and German officials demanded passes (or in most cases, bribes) to travel on the main roads. As well, various partisan groups roamed the woods and infiltrated villages. A truck would be a valuable prize for any insurgent group.

The Germans were still officially in charge, but Bolsheviks, Polish AK units, and UPA units fought for control in many areas.

As we approached the San River, I was all of two months old, still jaundiced and underweight, but improving slowly. This was not an ideal situation for a sickly infant. With all the tension and anxiety my mother experienced, she could not always produce milk, and food for infants was difficult to prepare. It was crowded; I cried constantly and was still relatively underweight. Quite honestly, my parents were surprised I was still alive.

My parents cut up old sheets to use as diapers and, whenever possible, my father would stop the truck by a stream so my mother could wash the dirty diapers as the men watched for anyone who might present a danger. When it rained, the diapers would not dry quickly so my father often placed the wet diapers on his chest as he drove, hoping to dry the diapers using the heat of his body.

After they left Sambir, it was still another thirty kilometers or so to the San River and a few kilometers more to Peremyshl. They knew there would be sentries and checkpoints as they got closer to the border.

My father bought a few liters of gasoline from someone in an alley at the edge of town and hoped it would be enough to get them to their destination. They waited for darkness.

When they reached the bridge a few kilometers before Peremyshl, they were forced to stop at a checkpoint. Four young German soldiers, looking tired and scared, pointed their rifles at my father and asked him where he was going. In his best German, my father told them he was making a small delivery to Peremyshl. He took out a handful of German money and offered it to the soldiers. They took the money and waved him on. They never bothered to check the "cargo."

Vlodka Cybushnik and her husband, Volodymyr, welcomed us warmly when we finally reached Peremyshl early the next morning. They also had two young children, two-year-old Christine and their three-month-old baby girl, Oksana, but somehow, we all managed to find a place to sleep in their tiny apartment.

We thought we had reached safety, but we found we could only stay with Vlodka for a few days. They were being forced out of their apartment and had already made plans to leave for Vienna the following week.

We rested, caught up on news, and, with few options remaining, my father and Uncle Dmytro made a decision to keep driving west. Our destination was the town of Gorlice, a few hundred kilometers west.

My father bought a little more gasoline on the black market, filled up the truck's gas tank, and prepared for the next leg of our journey.

## MY GRANDFATHER'S MILL (3) Lost Dream.

Poles formed the Armia Krajowa (AK) in February 1942, at about the same time the Ukrainians formed their underground Insurgent Army, the UPA. At one point, the AK had more than 300,000 members. The original goals of the AK and the UPA were not that dissimilar: to defeat the Germans who had invaded Galicia (and Poland proper). Unfortunately, there was so much bad blood between the Poles and Ukrainians that the two underground groups often fought each other rather than their common enemy.

In 1944, when it became clear that the Soviets were unstoppable, the AK started to retreat westward, but first, they decided to settle old scores.

Early one morning, a group of AK members came to my grandfather's mill. They knocked on the door of the living area. When my uncle Joseph answered the door, they shot and killed him. As his wife, Slava, ran to help, they shot and killed her as well.

Grandmother Maria was the only one left in the mill. She was unhurt.

No one was left to run my grandfather's mill so Grandmother Maria locked the mill and went to live with her son, Roman, in Berezhany.

When the Red Army finally liberated Ladychyn in 1945, the Bolsheviks decided the mill was an example of capitalist free enterprise and decadence. They burned the mill to the ground and then bulldozed what was left of it.

My grandfather's mill and his dream were no more.

Today, all that remains is a grassy area by the Svyntukha River. Some older locals still remember the mill and the AK attack and my Grandfather Peter and Grandmother Maria.

Before she died in 1954, my grandmother erected tombstones in a prime spot in the cemetery of the Ukrainian Catholic Church in Ladychyn. Four Melnyks—my Grandfather Peter, Grandmother Maria, Uncle Joseph, and Aunt Slava are buried there.

# HORLYCI / GORLICE

Gorlice, a large Polish town in western Galicia, site of several major battles during both world wars, lies in the foothills of the Carpathian / Tatra Mountains, not far from the Czechoslovakian border.

Osyp Boyko, a family friend, lived in Gorlice. Osyp was a lawyer who married Helena Spunder of Pidhajci, a descendent of German settlers in Ukraine. Both of them had lived in Pidhajci before the war. Osyp found work and settled in Gorlice, though he continued to do business with the cooperative in Pidhajci.

Osyp Boyko was fluent in German, Polish, and Ukrainian and mixed freely in all three cultures. When the Germans invaded Poland and occupied western Galicia, he was given a position in the town administration.

When we arrived at Boyko's doorstep, we found several other families, escapees from the east had already arrived in Gorlice. Boyko nevertheless happily found housing for everyone and took care of all the Ukrainian escapees who made it that far. When we arrived, he found living accommodations for all of us, either in his own home or in homes nearby. We stayed with the Boykos in Gorlice for two months, May and June of 1944.

Among the people in Osyp Boykos's house were two very pregnant ladies, Osyp's wife, Helena, and my aunt, Olha.

On May 30, 1944, my aunt Olha gave birth to a baby girl, my cousin, **Daria Stulkowsky**. Shortly thereafter, we made arrangements to continue our travel westward. The Melnyks and Stulkowskys, including newborn Daria, and our aunt Emilia, boarded a train for Vienna in early June 1944.

Osyp and Helena Boyko, our former hosts in Gorlice, were anxiously awaiting the birth their first child. Originally, they had planned to escape to the West with us, but they decided to wait until their baby was born before leaving.

It wasn't to be.

In late June, the Soviets recaptured Lviv and were marching steadily westward towards Warsaw. At the same time, the Polish Home Army, with the support of the Allies, consolidated their forces in defense of Warsaw. Their stated mission was to defeat the Germans, but as they did in eastern Galicia, they also took revenge on Ukrainians who were in positions of power.

On July 29, Osyp received a warning. Painted on his front door were the initials "AK." A Polish friend informed him that the AK was planning to attack his house imminently. They decided to leave immediately.

Osyp managed to get train tickets to Vienna leaving the morning of July 29.

Though not completely packed, Osyp and a very pregnant Helena boarded the train along with other Ukrainians, including, their good friend, a doctor, who also decided it was no longer safe in Gorlice.

Just as the train was crossing the Czechoslovak-Austrian border, Helena Boyko gave birth to a baby girl, **Tania.** Her birth was registered a few hours later, on July 30, when they arrived in Vienna. Our paths would cross again.*

---

*   The Boykos emigrated to Canada in 1948 and settled in Toronto. Years later, my brother, Roman, was traveling in Paris and ran into Tania Boyko, who was also touring Europe. They spent time together, continued their courtship in Canada, and were married in Toronto in June 1970. Paris is still their favorite city. (Please see their stories in part eight of this book.)

# Chapter 15

# *Tatomyr Escape, July 1944*

NOTE: Much of this chapter is an excerpt from the handwritten diary kept by Rev. Julian Tatomyr from 1914 to 1946. The document was transcribed and collated by Chrystyna's sister, Lesya Horodysky, and was translated into English by Chrystyna.

Chrystyna's grandfather, Julian, had a great sense of history and of his place in it. He kept a detailed record of events because he believed it might be used some day as a historical record of a very difficult time.

Because this material stands quite well on its own, it is presented in almost unedited form. There are some small gaps in the diary, and at times some words in the original diary were illegible. On these rare occasions, additional information from the memoirs of Julian's son, Oleksander, were added to clarify incomplete passages.

The defeat of the German Army at Stalingrad in February 1943 was the beginning of the end of the German invasion of Ukraine. The Red Army gained the upper hand and with victory after victory over the retreating German army, moved relentlessly westward. By November 1943, the Red Army had cleared Kyiv of Germans, by April 1944 they recaptured Odesa, and on June 22, 1944—precisely three years after the original German invasion—the Red Army crossed the Zbruch River into Galicia.

The Red Army didn't stop there. The Russians were determined to take back all the lands they had occupied before 1941 and to chase the Germans all the way to Berlin. By July 1944, they were in Lviv and started to move south toward Sambir.

The Tatomyrs were well known throughout the region as anti-Polish, anti-Soviet, anti-German, Ukrainian nationalists, and activists. At one time or another, Tatomyrs had served time in Polish, Soviet, and German prisons for their views and activities. In addition, Julian was a high-profile community leader, a former senator, and a Ukrainian Catholic priest.

Of the three recent occupiers of Ukrainian lands, the Soviets displayed the most brutal behavior toward clergy, teachers, professionals, and the educated among the Ukrainian population. Should the Soviets control this area, the Tatomyrs would be among the first to be executed or exiled.

As the Red Army approached, the Tatomyrs and thousands of other Ukrainian nationalists and members of the intelligentsia prepared to leave.

Since the retreating Germans denied train passes to refugees, the Tatomyrs packed as many valuables as they could carry, along with food and other supplies, into four horse-drawn open wagons, tethered a cow to one wagon so they could have milk for the babies, and prepared to join the caravan traveling from Sambir to the Slovak border. They did not know how long they would be away or if, indeed, they would ever return.

In July of 1944, Julian was a sixty-one-year-old grandfather, the undisputed patriarch of the Tatomyr clan. His wife, Olha, was a frail fifty-six-year-old. His oldest son, Jaroslav (Slavko), and his wife, Luba, were thirty-four years old. Their baby daughter Marta was not quite a year old.

Julian's younger son, Oleksander (Oleksa), was thirty-one, his wife, Sophia (Sonia), was twenty-nine, and their baby daughter, Chrystyna (Xrystia), was just six months old.

Joining them was Julian's nephew, forty-two year old Volodymyr (Vlodko), who was recently widowed (his wife died of tuberculosis), and three servants from their household: Yevka, her daughter, Slavka, and "the driver."

Julian's diary describes their incredible journey.

# DIARY OF REVEREND JULIAN TATOMYR

**L**uzhok, July 25, 1944. Our group awaited the arrival of 38 wagons from Sambir that were organized by the Ukrainian Relief Committee. When the wagons arrived we did not leave immediately because family, friends and parishioners came to say their farewells to us. We all had tears is our eyes because we did not know when we would be reunited. Suddenly we heard the sounds of gun shots. Germans were forcefully gathering people to dig rifle trenches. We could no longer delay our departure. The wagons began to move.

Our first night was spent in Rosluch in abandoned villas. On a reconnaissance mission, Markovsky, an engineer, and Stryletsky left our group and traveled rapidly south to Turka. When they returned to Rosluch, they gave us the bad news that the German Army was not allowing civilians to travel through Turka. Our only solution appeared to be to divert our journey westward, over the mountains to Limna. Stryletsky was rather angrily urging everyone to move immediately.

We decided to stay in Rosluch and appointed a night watch. So that we would not be detected, we also turned out all lights. The night was bitterly cold. Remnants of German Army units walked silently down the road past the villas in which we were staying. The night watch asked the soldiers where the Bolsheviks were located. We did not receive a definitive answer from them. Some of the soldiers thought they may be near Sambir, while others felt they may be advancing toward Starij Sambir.

I felt responsible for the well-being and safety of our group, so I spent the night checking the villas and the surrounding area. In the morning our group had a conference to decide whether to head south to Turka or west to Limna. The majority of our group indicated they would head toward Limna.

I expressed my opinion that to travel through Komancha on the way to Limna would take four days and the Bolsheviks, who were simultaneously advancing toward Khyriv-Sianok, may intercept us at some point. I advised the group the only logical choice would be to head for Turka, because I did not believe there was a travel ban for civilians through this village. Following our deliberations eight wagons, under the leadership of Holovchak, left for Limna. Thirty wagons, including our family, headed in the direction of Turka.

**July 27:** The morning was very cold. A heavy mist settled over the mountains. On our route the wagon train was interrupted by army trucks, followed by a massive force of artillery moving toward the south.

We faced great hardships in crossing the steep mountain, Petrykiv, to reach Turka. My pair of horses had to descend the mountain three times to help those wagons pulled by weaker horses. At 10 a.m. it became extremely hot. When we finally reached the peak of the mountain, our route was blocked by heavy artillery that was hastily left behind by the army. We waited and rested on the peak of Petrykiv for three hours because our route was also jammed with wagons of other escapees. If, at that moment, enemy aircraft had flown over the peak, they could have easily killed all of us—mowing us down as a thresher mows down all grain in its path. When the other wagons moved on, we by-passed the strewn artillery and continued south toward Turka.

By evening we arrived in Turka and set up camp in the estate of the mayor of the village. Prominent nationalists had left Turka earlier: Rev. Levitsky, director of a school in Sheremeta, members of OSK, and other refugees who had stayed in Turka for several months (Dr. Antin Lutsky, Dr. Maksymchuk and Roman Kulchytsky, a teacher). Members of the Ukrainian Relief Committee from Staryj Sambir, Rev. Monchak and his wife, arrived in Turka on July 30. We were also joined by Dr. Martyniuk and his family on July 31. Dr. Martyniuk was the head of the Ukrainian Relief Committee in Drohobych.

**August 2:** In the morning we learned there was going to be an evacuation of all refugees, so to avoid incarceration we left Turka immediately. Our group now included my family (four wagons), the Martyniuks, the Marushchaks and the Voryk family. We rested in the village of Boryn and arrived in Turochok in the afternoon. Our group stayed at a local school.

On **August 8**, my wagon and my son Oleksa's wagon left before dawn to cross Sokolyk. On our journey, as we were approaching the train station, an enemy aircraft flew overhead. Oleksa, who was traveling very fast, overturned his wagon and blocked the road.

As the wagon overturned Sophia, Oleksa's wife, fell out of the wagon clutching her baby, Chrystyna. Sophia was shaken and bruised but the infant was uninjured. The contents of the wagon was scattered along the roadway. It was impossible to lift the wagon upright, because the harness had broken. This was a critical moment in our journey. Nearby a regiment of Hungarians, who were assigned to guard the station, was hiding among the boulders at the train station.

As the aircraft flew over the station again, we immediately abandoned our wagons and ran for cover to a nearby forest. Only my nephew, Vlodko, remained by the wagons to guard the horses. The bomber circled the train station several times and then departed.

Afraid that the aircraft would return again and spray us with machine gun fire, we immediately returned to our wagons. Fortunately, several other wagons came upon the site of our calamity, helped us to raise my son's wagon and reloaded the spilled contents. We departed instantly. It was only after we had taken shelter in a pine forest that we thanked God for helping us avert disaster.

Our subsequent route to Benova was very difficult, because the heat was oppressive. Oleksa's wife Sophia fainted several times during this journey. Upon our arrival in Benova we settled in the home of a forest ranger. In the town we met other escapees from Galicia—Professor Shankovsky, operatic singer Raynarovych, Levytsky, an engineer, and Semkiv from Drohobych. Daily, enemy aircraft fired their machine guns on Sokolyk and Syanok. Benova lies between these two villages, so we were caught in the middle of the air assault.

**August 12:** We were joined by refugees from Luzhok, who were traveling from Rosluch: the Holovchaks who were turned back from Limna and followed us through Turka, the Fusiaks, Mykola Luzezky and Dmytro Hurin. On Sunday we were joined by Hnat and Yakiw Luzetsky, Ivan Volyansky and Myron Kovalsky, an engineer.

On the afternoon of August 13 our group consisting of 23 wagons left for Syamka and Uzoka. We paused to admire the exquisite scenery of the Uzoka mountain range. By twilight we arrived in Uzoka, where we joined a 100-wagon caravan of refugees. It was an unpleasant site in which to spend the night. Rain poured upon the caravan incessantly through the night. We stayed in Uzoka for another day, where we were given food for the first time. We took the opportunity to hang our soaked blankets and wet clothing on nearby bushes to dry.

**August 15:** The massive convoy of wagons continued its journey. By evening we arrived at a camp in Stavnichna. There was a large field between a mountain and the road. Skirting the edges of the field were several huts. It was decided to house mothers with young children in these huts. At nightfall enemy aircraft approached our camp. With the deafening sounds of bombing and gunfire, we all fled in panic to the mountain to find shelter among the trees. Fortunately after a few moments the planes departed.

Following this attack we learned that on the other side of the mountain, workers were building bomb shelters. They had been the main target of the enemy aircraft and mercifully none of us were injured during their mission.

On **August 16** we left Stavnichna. As the convoy moved out onto the road we were again approached by enemy aircraft. People cried out *fiefflieger* and everyone ran for cover. Luckily the aircraft departed, we returned to our wagons and continued our journey. Toward evening we camped in a huge field near a demolished factory. This was the ugliest, dirtiest and most uncomfortable place we had spent a night since we began our journey. We stayed there for one day and left on August 17.

Shortly before noon we met a battalion of Hungarians on horses. Suddenly enemy aircraft flew directly overhead and there was general panic among the soldiers and escapees. Miraculously the aircraft departed and no one was injured.

As we crossed the river Berez we finally approached the border of Czechoslovakia. We all took a last look back at our Ukraine and wondered when, if ever, we would return to our homeland.

## Czechoslovakia:

That afternoon we arrived in Ubla in Slovakia. We camped in a field near a creek surrounded by mountains, a beautiful site. Here we were given rations for the refugees and feed for the horses.

**August 18:** We crossed into the town of **Humenne** and camped in a beautiful park near a deep river. The following day everyone went swimming, including the horses. Luba and Sophia bathed their babies in the clear waters of the river.

It was the holiday of Spassa. In groups, young Slovak children in their bright national costumes (with wide crinolines) wandered into the park for the Spassa celebration. There was a Mass for everyone at a nearby church. It was a happy and festive occasion.

The following day, after Mass, we all went swimming again. In Humenne we sold our pretty mare, the half-Arabian Chira, her 15-month-old foal Irka, and 5-month-old foal Yurko for 7,000 kronas. We bought two horses: a chestnut horse and a pretty mare with a fiery and high strung temperament.

We resumed our journey on August 21. My wagon was pulled by one of my existing horses, Lysym (handsome and strong), and the new mare. Vlodko's wagon was pulled by two old strong chestnuts, a wonderful pair of horses. In beautiful weather, we passed lovely villages and glistening fields of wheat and grain. Spending the night amidst birches near a stream, we went swimming that night.

**August 22:** We traveled through another scenic region. In the afternoon we stopped in a lovely city, Seviziach, and bought essentials. There was a wide variety of goods available in the city. We purchased clothing, two knapsacks, two pairs of shoes, baked goods and some fruit.

During our stay at Seviziach I met Hnativ, a friend from Sambir. He introduced me to the local priest. Both the priest and Hnativ advised me to remain in Seviziach. I was undecided because I had observed that revolutionary strife was beginning in this country. With four wagons it would be difficult to remain unnoticed in Seviziach. During my deliberations I had to sadly say good-bye to a good friend, Pokotylom, a teacher who had traveled with us from the beginning. Pokotylom made a personal decision to leave the caravan and join the partisans in Ukraine as a freedom fighter.

Deciding not to remain in Seviziach we continued our travels to a small village where we bought some items to maximize the value of the coronas we had acquired previously. This village, whose name I do not remember, lies at the foot of a very high mountain. We traveled for two kilometers up the mountain and camped in a large meadow amidst a lovely forest. We placed our wagons under a large oak tree and gave the horses a well-deserved rest.

In the morning we learned that a German convoy had escaped from partisans and hid in the small village. Apparently the partisan battalion had approached within three kilometers of our camp site. We thanked God the soldiers had not dropped in for a visit.

We left our site and continued to scale the steep mountain. Briefly we rested at the peak and then began our descent, crossing the Hungarian border and arriving at a group camp in the village of Seplak-Apati by nightfall. The group camp was located in a large park shaded by numerous towering trees near a river. We chose to set up camp in the park.

Here I met many priests from the Stanoslavivsk dioceses. Our group of clergy discussed the possibility of priests with families gaining permission to stay in Hungary. The bishop of Koshuziach supported our proposition. The mayor, who was German, also supported our request to remain in Hungary.

During our deliberations our cows and horses were removed and registered by local officials. Yevka, our cook, managed to regain our registered cow. A local man in the village took the cow across the river and sold it to a villager, giving Yevka the money. When my son Oleksa asked Yevka to retrieve our cow, she succeeded in her task. However, when the local man took the second cow across the river and sold it, he pocketed the money. This left us with only one cow to provide milk for the babies, Marta and Chrystyna.

Regarding the matter of settling in Hungary, I was summoned to the mayor's office in **Kosice**. My younger son, my friend Rev. Tarnavsky and I traveled on our horses to Kosice. The Commander wanted to settle the matter of foreign priests remaining in Hungary. To our great disappointment the Hungarian commander denied our request to settle in his country.

The bishop and mayor, who had shown strong support for our request, were greatly offended by the commander's decision. In farewell the mayor assured us he would reserve seats for our group on a train to Austria. We were very grateful for his concern and efforts on our behalf.

It was a very hot and humid day. Feeling great disappointment at this turn of events, Oleksa and I stopped for a few beers, snacks and watermelon before returning to our family.

The following day I did not feel well. I experienced symptoms of severe indigestion. That night I joined my family in the school for the night. That night I had a severe attack of diarrhea that left me feeling very weak. A Ukrainian doctor tried to help me. Nevertheless, by Monday I was so debilitated and dehydrated that I could hardly speak. That evening Oleksa and the local priest took me to a clinic in Kosice. Until Friday I received only tea and some nutrition in powdered form. On Friday I had a divine extravagance-soup and crackers. Each night Oleksa and various parishioners came to visit with me at the clinic.

**On Monday, September 11**, Oleksa informed me that our train headed for Austria would be departing on the next day. The head of the clinic allowed me to leave the hospital by car. Joining our group, I told them the doctors and nurses had been very kind to me during my time at the clinic and that I was grateful for the kindness shown by the Hungarians.

I was very weak but in good spirits. On Tuesday morning, September 12, I sold one pair of horses for 2,000 pentivs. From this money I bought 25 kilograms of flour, potatoes and other essential supplies.

At four o'clock in the afternoon, laden with our earthly belongings, we left for the train station. Since early morning my elder son, Slavko, had been loading our luggage onto the train. While we waited for the departure of the train, the army bought our second pair of horses for 700 Deutche marks. We had to leave our wagons behind, for which we received no remuneration. When we boarded the train our group occupied one-half of a wagon, while the other half was occupied by other Ukrainian refugees. In total, the train consisted of 40 wagons.

After much waiting, the train finally left for Hungary in late evening.

## Hungary:

**September 13** That night there was a significant invasion of Budapest by Bolshevik air craft. Waves of enemy aircraft flew over our heads for about an hour. Suddenly the train stopped. Rockets exploded around us. Everyone in the train ran for their lives into the fields. We chose to remain in the wagon on the train. Finally the horrific drone of the aircraft subsided and the train continued its journey.

At noon on the next day, English planes hovered above us. The train stopped again. In a panic many people fled into the fields. Others tried to find refuge in a bomb shelter.

The planes departed, we reboarded the train and continued our challenging voyage toward Austria.

**September 14:** The train stopped at the western outskirts of **Budapest**. The conductor announced the train would remain in this location for the night. Everyone was unnerved by this announcement. Since we were sitting in an open field there would be no escape if enemy aircraft approached us. We were preparing to go to sleep when sirens blared mercilessly. AIR RAID!!! Where to run? I thought it would be safer to remain on the train. The two babies, Marta and Chrystyna, who were suddenly awakened from their sleep were crying uncontrollably. Their mothers tried to soothe them. After a few moments Slavko rushed toward me and said the conductor advised us to leave the train immediately.

Opening the door of the train we saw the dark sky illuminated with a myriad of searchlights. The sirens blared their urgent, shrill cry once again. I helped all the women off the train. In terror, my horseman and Yevka refused to leave the train.

With people fleeing from all 40 wagons of the train in panic, it was a chaotic scene. We headed in the direction of some homes surrounded by orchards at the outskirts of Budapest. In the darkness I lost sight of my sons and Slavka among the teeming escapees. Someone yelled that they had headed for the nearest gate. We followed in search of them. The sirens stopped abruptly, but Scheiriwerfer (searchlights) continued to flash across the sky.

Then we heard the horrendous roar of approaching enemy aircraft and the high-pitched whistle of bombs exploding around us. We ran toward an orchard . . . I called for my loved ones, but there was only silence. Exploding bombs were directly overhead. As the explosions became more and more frequent, I told my wife to lie down under a stone wall and continued to call the names of our missing family and friends.

Suddenly a trap door opened next to a stone house. I ran back to get my wife. By the entrance a huge man lowered us into a basement with three small windows. We walked down three steps and lay down hastily on the floor of the basement . . . the whistle of bombs was heard again. Trying to look around in the dark basement I could not see my sons or the others.

Suddenly we heard a terrifying scream in the field. Did the bomb hit the train? I raised my head to one of the small windows and saw our train glowing from the illumination of searchlights . . . a perfect target for enemy aircraft. People were running in fear and panic: some crawled under the train, while others scattered in all directions. Would a bomb fall? How many of our people would die in this foreign land tonight? What had become of Vlodko and Yevka? If bombs hit the train we would lose all of our provisions, papers and belongings. Yet material loss seemed inconsequential at this time in terms of loss of life.

Bombs continued to explode near us and total darkness descended as the searchlights ceased to play across the sky.

Exhausted, we lay down on the floor of the damp basement to avoid shrapnel from the bombs. Blessedly, for a moment, we fell asleep. Waking from a short slumber, I continued to hear the whistle and explosion of bombs. This air attack lasted from 10:00 p.m. to 1:00 a.m.

Finally, the air raid warning ended and I climbed out of the basement to search for our family and friends. I found them in a very primitive shelter in the orchard. Miraculously, their lives had been spared. Assured they were safe, I immediately went to the train to investigate the state of our luggage. Upon entering the train, I spotted Vlodko and Yevka. Our group had survived this massive air attack! I thanked God for protecting our family. Surviving passengers reboarded the train. Physically and emotionally exhausted by these traumatic events, we all managed to fall asleep.

In the early morning of September 15 the train left the station. All passengers gave a collective sigh of relief. In the evening we arrived in Komarno. At the station I bought some groceries, French pastries and sweets. It was a great treat for our group after a harrowing train ride.

On the morning of September 16 we paused at a large station. Here we again bought biscuits, plums, candy, tea, soap and other sundries. As a consequence of poor nutrition during our journey, I began to experience severe stomach pains again. I was fearful of being incapacitated, searching for another clinic and becoming separated from my family. Luckily the stomach pains subsided. On that day we traveled over the beautiful Danube River. We marveled at the scenes of countless boats, luxurious resorts and lush vineyards. We imagined spending a few days in this "Garden of Eden," free from the daily obstacles facing us. Further on our trip, ancient stately castles appeared on hilltops. It was truly a glorious panorama! Crossing the border I exchanged 600 pentives for Deutsche marks.

# Tatomyr Escape to the West - July - September 1944

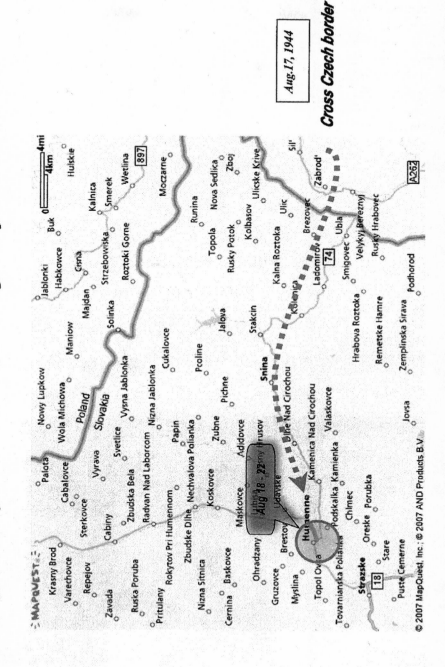

Aug.17, 1944

**Cross Czech border**

Aug 18 - 22

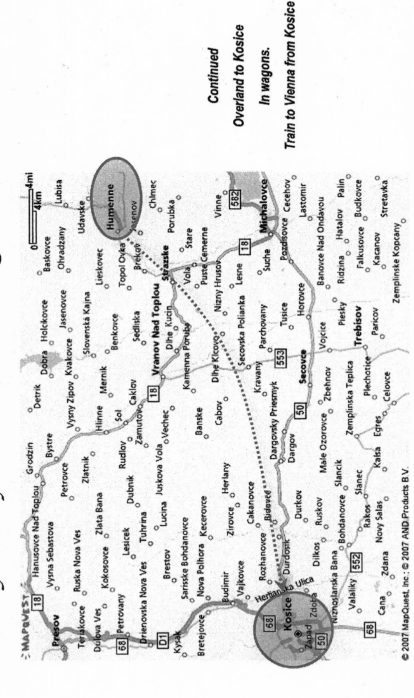

*Tatomyr Escape - Humenne - Kosice 9/22 -23*

Continued

Overland to Kosice

In wagons.

Train to Vienna from Kosice

Tatomyr Escape - Train to Vienna

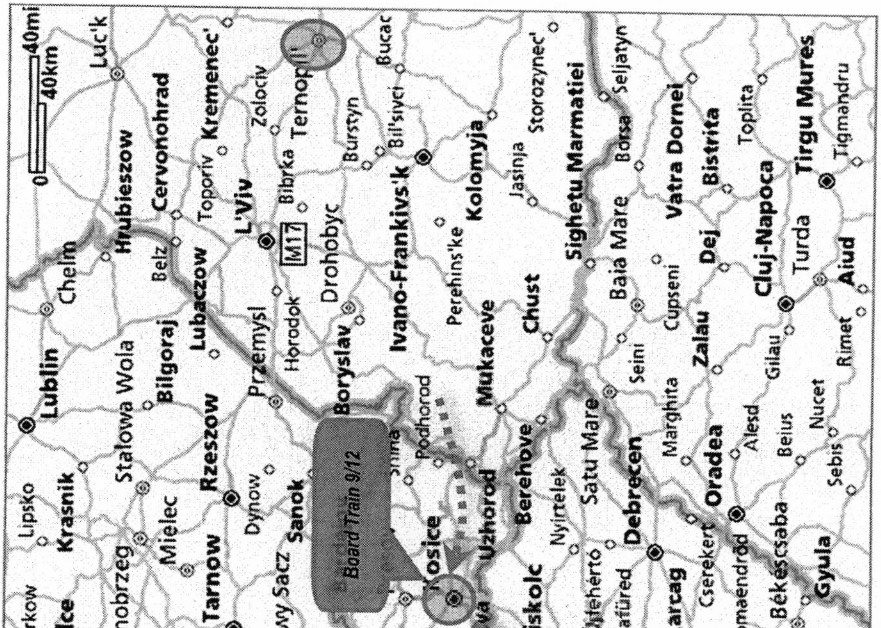

## Tatomyr Escape - Advancing Russian Army Spring 1944

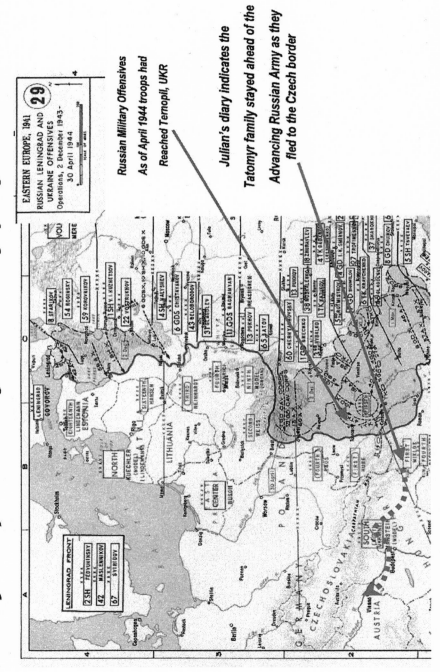

*Russian Military Offensives As of April 1944 troops had Reached Ternopil, UKR*

*Julian's diary indicates the Tatomyr family stayed ahead of the Advancing Russian Army as they fled to the Czech border*

# *Russian Spring Offensive 22 June – 19 Aug, 1944*

*Major spring offensive moves into Czechosolovia with the Tatomyrs just ahead of the advancing army*

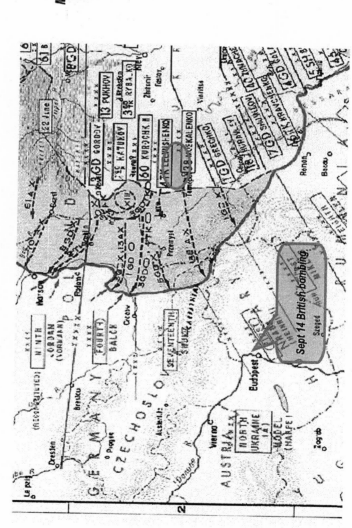

## Austria

**September 17:** We traveled through the beautiful city of **Vienna**. On the outskirts of the city we saw the destruction wreaked by countless bombings. Before noon our train stopped in Strasshof. The station was immense as was a train carrying refugees from the east. Not far from our train we saw a huge transition camp. We disembarked from the train and met many Ukrainian refugees. In the evening I visited a friend, Rev. Kukusha, from our seminary studies. In the front yard of his home the Baranyk family, brother of Senator Baranyk, had settled in for the night. We were all embittered by the behavior of the Germans who were hostile to foreigners and refused them shelter in their homes.

Oleksa and I went to Vienna on Monday, September 18, by train. We visited Rev. Hornikevych of the Ukrainian Relief Committee. At the committee meeting Mr. Polyansky strongly advised us not to leave the train because it was imperative to escape as quickly as possible. Also, escapees who came to seek assistance from the relief agency would find the organization lacked resources to help them.

Following our discussion, I returned to Strasshof while Oleksa traveled two more stops to search for work. In Strasshof I learned our train would be leaving momentarily for Nuremberg. Immediately we went to remove our belongings from the train as we had decided to remain in Strasshof. Initially my friend Fusiak had wanted to stay in Strasshof, but he eventually changed his mind and left on the train for Nuremberg.

To my parishioners I repeated the advice from the Ukrainian Relief Committee in Vienna and personally stated that without any concrete evidence, I could not counsel them. They needed to make decisions based on personal instincts as my decision to remain in Strasshoff was personal and unique to my family. My parishioners decided to continue their journey by train.

Vlodko managed to requisition a wagon and Slavko went in search of a home for us. After one hour the wagon arrived. The wagon was delivered by two young men, one of whom claimed he was a former mayor in Galicia. I doubted the truth of his sudden elevation in position. For one kilometer of transport they demanded 20 kilograms of sugar, 20 kilograms of potatoes and flour. I stated I would give them what had been initially agreed upon between Vlodko and the owner of the horses.

While we were loading the wagon the young men had loftier schemes and made even greater demands for payment. One of the shyster's spoke, "You cannot remain in a field. You must pay us for our services because you left the train illegally." Infuriated by their arrogance and greed, we unloaded our belongings from the wagon.

Fortunately, a Rusyn with a one horse-drawn wagon appeared and transported our belongings to the train station in two trips. His price for transport included one-half liter of whiskey and some meat. Upon arrival we settled in a small yard in the train station building.

My sons, with their wives and children, Chrystyna and Marta, spent the night on the veranda. The rest of us slept outside on our belongings. We slept peacefully, unconcerned about the possibility of an air attack.

**September 19** We all went to a DP (displaced persons) camp with the exception of Oleksa who traveled to Vienna. My wife and the Stebelsky family left the DP camp in Strasshof after receiving information from Oleksa that one could spend one day in a transitional camp in Vienna. In the interim I ran into the commander of the **Strasshof** camp.

We began to converse more freely after I offered him some champagne and he promised that after two days in the Strasshof camp he would provide us with a permit and lodging in the area of Linz. The next day we returned to the Strasshof DP camp. There I was reunited with professor Boytsun, Dr. Mykhajlo Rabij, a relative, and Rev. Klonskum.

**September 22**: The commander of the DP camp left for a new placement in Vienna, while our family and the Stebelsky family were assigned as *arbeiters* (workers) in Znojmo.

On Saturday morning we loaded our belongings onto a train bound for Znojmo. Slavko remained in Strasshof as he had been assigned to work in St. Polten. We parted from Slavko with sadness and then we had to wait all day for the train to leave in the evening. On Sunday in Znojmo, *arbeitsamt* officials gave everyone information where they could obtain work. We were assigned to Ausi Edlungs Geselshaft in **Aufspitz**. We arrived by train in Nicolsburg in late afternoon. On Monday a transport truck arrived to take us to Aufspitz. It was an extremely cold day and the bitter winds blowing through the cracks in the truck chilled us to the bone. We were worried about ill effects on the babies in this inclement weather. Finally, our family arrived in Aufspitz.

For the time being we were assigned to one room, where we slept on the hay. We stayed there until September 28. We were then transferred to a rooming house on Erfurherstrasse No. 10 and were assigned to one large room. It contained a steel stove, four beds, a table, two chairs, a bench and two closets. It also had electricity.

The officials immediately assigned work to all refugees. Young children were assigned to kitchen work, men did household and outdoor work and women were assigned to work in the kitchen. Volkdeutscher, the owner of this dwelling, was fairly accommodating to his 56 workers (Russians, Ukrainians and Poles). I insisted that we receive *Lebenseniffel karten*, which meant we could manage our own kitchen. The request was approved. The approval was greeted with great joy by the women who had declined to cook in the communal kitchen. We installed a brick stove in our room and cooked our meals on it. The meager allocation of coal per month proved insufficient, but we supplemented this with wood and hay. This combination of heating sources proved adequate for our needs. The women were finally able to provide more nutritious meals for the babies.

In Auspitz there were forty people of the Ukrainian intelligentsia. Among them were Sheremeta, a director of a school in Turka, Komarnysky, an administrator of a school in Turka, Dr. Hura, a veterinarian with a large family, Dr. Oleksyshyn, a businessman with a large family, Shalabavka, an artist and others. In the early days of November Kovalysko, a businessmen from Starij Sambir, arrived with his family and Matkowsky from Bergzhnycicj. Rev. Adrian Levitsky, formerly a priest in Turka, lived in a nearby village. We enjoyed a pleasant social life with this group of people under less than ideal circumstances.

Personally I was gratified to be granted the status of "resident-celebrant" from Cardinal Ilinzer of Vienna and the title of "apostolic delegate" from Rev. Berhun in Berlin. This enabled me to celebrate Mass almost every day in Auspitz. The intelligentsia faithfully attended my masses. I had the opportunity to travel to Vienna several times and often to Nicolsburg.

I received payment for my horses and exchanged 2,000 zloti into Deutche marks after a government course. I petitioned the National Bank of Vienna for payment but, although I received approval, I was unable to contact Krakow for approval to exchange the funds.

**November 28:** Vlodko left to work in the mines in Najzizlar-see. As well, on December 12, Oleksa left to work in the mines. Slavko wrote that since December 15 he was also a miner. Sophia and Luba missed their husbands but the babies, Marta and Chrystyna, kept them busy and buoyed their spirits.

**Christmas, January 7, 1945:** Slava decorated the Christmas tree in our room. Our tiny Chrystyna, who was then just three weeks before her first birthday, a great enthusiast of dance, immediately began to dance in the Boyko style when we sang *kolomyjky*. Prior to Christmas Oleksa came home for a three-day holiday. He became ill and stayed with us through the Christmas holidays.

After the holidays I went to Dr. Felsman to plead and find a pretext for releasing Oleksa from the mines. At the same time, following an x-ray, the doctor told me I had an ulcer. Concerned with the state of my health, I went to an army doctor the following day. After a very thorough examination, he stated I had stomach cancer. This was a major personal blow to me, as we had been through so much thus far and I knew my family depended on me.

We petitioned the *Ortsgruppenbeiter* to release Oleksa from the mines and the petition was granted. I then went to a clinic in Felsberg on **January 11, 1945,** for another opinion on my cancer. There I had a four-day evaluation and obtained differing diagnoses. It stated I had neither an ulcer nor stomach cancer. On January 16 I returned to Auspitz. I chose to be optimistic about the state of my health.

Vlodko returned from the mines on **January 21** and Slavko wrote he had also been released from his job as a miner. Good news for the family!

In February I again went to the clinic in Felsberg for a follow-up visit. After four days the clinic informed me I had a shrunken stomach as a result of a healed ulcer in 1943. At this point I had a variety of diagnoses, but I felt hopeful as this latest diagnosis was the most positive one to date.

At the **end of February** I bought a wagon and horses. The owner of our dwelling, Hudechka, housed and fed my horses without a request for payment. I was grateful for his kindness in this regard. Upon repair of the wagon and reins, Oleksa and Vlodko left Auspitz on March 20 with a heavily laden wagon. We said farewell to our friends and colleagues and left for Nicolsburg on March 20 by train. In Nicolsburg we were reunited with Oleksa and Vlodko, said good-bye to Dr. Rabij and left for Naydof on March 22. There we settled in a hotel. Oleksa and Vlodko continued to travel by wagon, while we traveled by train to Schatz, walked three-and-a-half kilometers to Naydof and again settled in a hotel. Immediately, I went to visit Dr. Hur to give him a letter from his brother. There I encountered Barnuchir, a friend.

After two hours our wagon arrived and was housed on the premises of Dr. Hur's residence. The Hur family was extremely gracious and welcoming. They invited all of us to stay with them, but only Oleksa, Sophia and baby Chrystyna accepted their invitation. We stayed in Naydof until March 23, preparing for our journey to Ernstburg.

On **March 24**, a Saturday, we continued our journey in the early dawn to **Schatz**. In Schatz we took a train, while Oleksa and Vlodko continued the trip by wagon. From the moment we left Auspitz the weather had been beautiful. Mornings were cool and the rest of the days resembled late spring.

At 9:00 a.m. we boarded a train in Mistelbach because the train to Ernstburg was scheduled to leave in late afternoon. Wary of air raids, we walked ten kilometers from Mistelbach to Ernstburg, pushing Chrystyna in her carriage. After our lengthy walk, our wagon caught up with us. There was a sudden air attack but we managed to survive it without any injuries.

Before entering Ernstburg we met Dr. Levitsky who was traveling by car to Mistelbach. He invited us to come and visit him. Ernstburg is a small pretty town, but it had been heavily bombed (over 200 bombs had fallen on this town). Visiting the Levitskys, we found then to be generous and gracious hosts who prepared a generous meal for us and provided a lovely room for rest and recuperation.

On **March 26** I left with the women and babies by wagon, while Oleksa went to the train station for our belongings. The St. Polten train station did not accept parcels and luggage because its route was frequently bombed. Oleksa caught up to us by foot, and Vlodko followed us on horseback.

We traveled to Rev. Benutne's house on the outskirts of the next village. This priest was extremely hospitable. Although he had little to share with us, he gave us ten eggs and clover for the horse. We were forced to delay our departure until a strong air attack had passed. We repacked our luggage and left nonessentials with the priest. Saying our farewells and thanking him for his generosity, we left Rev. Benutne's home at 4 p.m.

We stopped for the night at Gellabrun (14 kilometers from Ernstburg) at a gasthaus. The proprietor, a German woman, was very gracious. We slept on benches in the dining room and left at 4 a.m. At 7 a.m. on March 27 we crossed a dangerous point at Schtokerav. At noon we rested in an abandoned gasthaus and continued our journey.

There were no air raids that day. It was such a rare blessing. In the evening we passed Tuln, which was heavily bombarded, and stayed the night at a gasthaus in Uudenburg, three kilometers beyond Tuln. It was an extremely cold night so we were fortunate to have obtained lodging.

At dawn on **March 28** we entered a dangerous zone. Near the main road we counted 50 homes that had been demolished in an air invasion. At noon we rested in a gasthaus, but the owner was very disagreeable and sullen. Leaving early we traveled within 15 kilometers of St. Polten, where we spent the night in a gasthaus in a small village.

As we departed for Harland in a steady downpour on March 29, we were determined to avoid traveling through St. Polten. At a factory in Harland we met Tymko Slipec and his wife from Luzhok. While we rested, Oleksa went in search of lodging for us. A gasthaus was found where we settled in an inviting room and the horses spent the night in the stable. We stayed in Harland for four days and shopped for food supplies and grain for the horses.

**April 1:** There was a strong air attack over St. Polten that lasted for a long time. Many Germans in Harland escaped to our gasthaus by bike or on foot. Countless bombers flew over us. We sought shelter in the basement with the exception of Vlodko and me. We decided to remain in the lobby of the gasthaus. We shook with fear from the deafening explosions of bombs around us. The bombings left us shaken, but luckily no one was injured. During our stay in Harland, Oleksa managed to visit Slavko, and his wife Luba and baby Marta in St. Veit. It was a joyful reunion.

On March 31 and April 1 we listened to the radio for news about the Bolshevik offensive, their advance on Bern (Czechoslovakia), Vienna and Viner-Nachtigalt. In light of rapidly developing events it was vital we travel to St. Veit and join Slavko and his family, and then change our route to the west. We were worried that with Slavko's family and their additional luggage, our horse would not be able to pull the load. Ignoring our concerns, we immediately left for St. Veit at daybreak on April 2.

In our travels we met a large number of escapees from Burgenland. Their wagons were in very good shape and their horses were strong and healthy. Passing Vilgelmeburg, we met a refugee from Sambir who told us the German High Command had reached an agreement with the Ukrainians. It had appointed Colonel Shandruk the leader of the Ukrainian division and asked him to transform his unit into the Ukrainian National Army. At last the Germans had come to their senses.

As we approached St. Veit we encountered long columns of German troops on motorcycles. They were headed for Vilgelmeburg, which meant the German army was retreating. Based on these developments it was imperative we reach Slavko and immediately head west. At the outskirts of St. Veit, we stopped our wagon because the radio was warning people of an imminent air attack. Oleksa and Sophia, carrying Chrystyna in her arms, immediately ran into the forest. The rest of us remained near the wagon. The threat of an air attack passed and after some time we spotted Oleksa and Slavko approaching us. (Oleksa had found his way through the forest to Slavko's home). At last we were all reunited. We drove to Slavko's home and loaded their belongings onto the wagon.

While Vlodko and I repacked and reorganized the wagon, we were approached by a column of wagons. We were very happy to see the Maruschaks and their relative Surokivsky. They waited for us as we finished repacking our wagon and in the evening we joined their column. Slavko and Oleksa, with their families, were to join us as soon as possible. Our column was moving very slowly past some large factories when an air raid alarm was sounded. This was a very critical situation because the road and a nearby field were jammed with cars. If the enemy aircraft had turned on their searchlights there would have been a massacre. After an hour the cars managed to disentangle themselves and moved on. We were fortunate to begin to move from a very treacherous place, at last.

The weight on our wagon was immense and the wheels began to creak from the load. Luckily, our horse managed to pull this daunting load forward. There were no signs of my sons and their families. For some reason they were late and this caused us great anxiety.

We managed to reach Vilgelmeburg and drove off the main road in the direction of Kirgeberg. It was here we stopped to await our family. Everyone went to sleep on blankets laid on the ground while I went back to the main road. I sat down on a large slab of rock and carefully watched the passing wagons. I was getting increasingly more concerned when I finally spotted Oleksa and Slavko at midnight pushing the baby carriages containing Marta and Chrystyna, with Luba and Sophia walking behind them. To my great relief, Slavko was also leading a dilapidated army horse. The horse was scrawny and weak, but we now had a second horse to help pull the wagon.

My sons explained they were late because they had to 'shoe' the horses. They also said their arrival was delayed by waves of army columns. It was difficult to break through the columns while pushing the babies in their carriages. Although I was greatly relieved by their arrival, I did not sleep that night. I fed the horses and guarded my loved ones and the wagon.

In the morning we prepared the wagon while Slavko decided to return to St. Veit to complete unfinished business, collect possessions left behind and obtain some Reisemarken for us. He promised to catch up to us on the following day.

Our wagon left directly west, aiming to avoid main routes and larger cities such as Melk, Perg and Lunz. Shortly we faced the formidable challenge of crossing a very steep mountain. Our newly acquired horse was not up to this daunting task. Slavka and I fed the army horse in the hopes it would provide him with some energy. The journey up the mountain was extremely difficult. With the babies in the wagon, we pushed with all our waning energy to help the horses pull the wagon. With God's help we managed to cross this mountain and arrived in Kirgeberg ad Pielach at 11:00 a.m. After a much-needed rest at a hotel, we bought some supplies. As we were leaving in the evening, we left a note for Slavko at the hotel that we were heading north. We had to change our route because, with a heavy wagon and a weaker pair of horses, we did not want to attempt to challenge the big mountains in the south.

As we began our route north on April 3, we met Rev. Leshkevych from Stanislavivshchyna who was traveling in a southerly direction. We continued north to Rabinsteire. Arriving in the evening through rain showers, we found a place to sleep in abandoned barracks. We went for an unappetizing meal in a nearby inn and then returned to the barracks, pulled out our mattresses and went to sleep.

**April 4** : It was cold and rainy as we headed for Oberrndorf Beorgstall. Since we parted with Slavko, we continued to leave notes for him in hotels and on signposts. I was becoming very concerned because Slavko was now late in rejoining us. We found shelter in Kouderheim. We left our horses with a generous Bavarian who not only fed the horses and Vlodko, but also brought us several liters of coffee in the morning.

The sun shone brightly on April 5. We went shopping for food and a dress for Slavka and left in the afternoon. I think we slept in a barn in Pyhrafold. It rained continuously through the night. We were very lucky the children had stayed healthy most of the time.

All of us were worried about Slavko's whereabouts but we had no choice but to continue our journey to Euratsfeld. The weather was very inclement with rain mixed with snow. In Euratsfeld we came upon a battalion of prisoners.

Though the weather was cold and snowy, the prisoners wore light shirts and sandals, and many walked in their bare feet. Starving and pale, these prisoners resembled skeletons. One prisoner of muscular physique, reduced to a skeleton, fainted and fell on a stone slab at the side of the road. A German woman approached the fallen prisoner with a piece of bread. The head of the battalion did not permit the woman to give the starving man food. Another official approached the fallen man and removed his watch. I sadly witnessed the reaction of the prisoner toward his "masters." There was no fear in his eyes, no begging for mercy . . . he looked embittered, his eyes totally overcome with resignation. Since there was no way I could help him in this situation, I left with a heavy heart.

In an hour conditions had deteriorated badly. The roads had turned to mud. As Oleksa and Vlodko tried to push the baby carriages, their ankles sank in the mud and snow. Further along the route we discovered murdered prisoners lying in pools of blood by the road. Our women quickly crossed to the other side of the road to avoid seeing this carnage.

Since the weather was so harsh we decided to head for Ulmerfeld to rest. We saw a house by the side of the road and pleaded with the owners to let us enter to heat some food for the babies. The owners began to squirm and ultimately refused to let us in. In despair, we told them off in no uncertain terms regarding their inhumane treatment, particularly toward the infants. The woman looked guilty, but we left this home in frustration and rage.

By afternoon we managed to reach Ashbach. A wealthy and kind Bavarian opened his doors to us. Soaked, chilled and muddy we warmed ourselves in their house. We washed, prepared some food and set up our *samovar* to make tea. After this respite the babies were permitted to sleep in the warm house with their mothers while the rest of us slept on some hay in their barn. In particular, I remember the sister of the Bavarian, a teacher by profession, as a very kind and pleasant woman.

**April 7:** We left for St. Peter and by late afternoon had arrived in Steyr. This was the boundary of Nicoberelorian. The city was under army control. We heard entry into Steyr was forbidden and the army formed columns of refugees and marched them to DP (displaced persons) camps. Oleksa went to explore the situation, while I managed to find a pretty gasthaus on the outskirts of the city. Upon Oleksa's return, he said he had heard there was a possibility of obtaining permits for further travel. Oleksa and I returned to Steyr and were reassured that permits could be granted. We returned to the gasthaus, gathered our family and headed back to the city.

Speaking to the army control unit, we learned we would be permitted to leave Steyr under the condition we would be assigned to travel with a specific group. Hoping that things would look brighter in the morning, we began to look for a place for the night. Divine Providence intervened—as we walked through the city we suddenly came face-to-face with Slavko who was standing by the roadside desperately searching for us. In celebration, we found an inviting gasthaus and sat around a table in the dining room. Slavko said that in attempting to trace our route, he had lost his way. He did not find any of the messages we had left for him. It appeared someone had consistently removed all of these significant notes. During his journey Slavko lost two pieces of luggage, but ultimately he had found us by divine intervention. He brought us *Reisemarks* that would last us several days.

Traveling to Steyr at dawn we were immediately assigned to a Hungarian group by an army official. We did not want to be assigned to any particular group because we felt we would be safer on our own. At the next village, the Hungarians stopped to shoe their horses. I approached the *Treikfuhrer*, an elderly, solemn and intelligent official, and told him I needed to fix my wagon wheel. Since the blacksmith in Steyr was very busy "shoeing" the horses of the Hungarians, I would need to find another blacksmith and asked his permission to go further to find one. The Hungarian official replied that permission was granted, but we would have to return by nightfall to rejoin the group. My plan had succeeded and he knew we had no intention of rejoining the Hungarians at nightfall. It was an act of human kindness amidst the brutality of war.

On our way to Kremsmunster we were stopped by army gendarmes who wanted to know why we were not part of an assigned group. I replied that the group was ahead of us and we were trying to catch up with them. "Who are you?" he asked. We replied that we were Ukrainians. "You must be in the fourth group of Ukrainians who had passed this checkpoint some time ago." "Of course," we replied. The gendarmes told us our route would lead us to Lyamgan.

After this encounter we traveled freely to Lyamgan, arriving in the evening. The town was teeming with refugees. Eventually we found a large group-lodging for refugees in a theatre. Although we were in tight sleeping quarters in the gallery, we enjoyed the warmth.

**April 9:** We headed for Voklabriok in much-improved weather. Upon arrival we parked our wagon in a lot and spent a long time looking for shelter for the night. Eventually we settled in a local school and slept comfortably on the porch. We stayed there for one more day while Slavko obtained food ration coupons to last us several days. In the meantime I visited the commander of the town to request a permit, because we did not want to travel with the others to Harnahav (where we would be assigned to barracks). We wanted to head toward Salzburg. I was told by the commander that no permits were required and we could travel with no restrictions. This good news was followed by yet another air raid.

On **April 11** at 8:30 a.m. we left for **Salzburg**. We spent the night at a gasthaus in Frankenmarkt. We were welcomed warmly by the Germans in this town.

On **April 12** frost blanketed the countryside as we continued our journey. Going up hills on icy roads, our horses fell repeatedly. My sons, with the babies in their carriages, pressed ahead quickly. Vlodko and I also walked to lessen the load on the wagon and the horses. At 7 a.m. we stopped at a roadside inn, had breakfast and continued our journey. We had traveled only a few kilometers when we were stopped at a check point. We were informed that all wagons were forbidden to enter Salzburg. At that moment a car drove up with some officials. In my conversation with them, the mayor informed me travel bans had been issued for army transport but that civilians could travel to Salzburg on secondary roads.

This was both good and bad news . . . my sons and their children were somewhere ahead of us and we needed to return to Frankenmarkt and search for alternate roads. We turned back and settled in a forest, allowing our horses to graze. We were very concerned about the fate of my sons and the babies. Time passed slowly . . . With growing concern I returned to the check point to get permission to look for my sons and grandchildren. Just at that moment, I glanced up to see Oleksa walking toward me. He said Slavko and he had passed the check point in the early morning before the restrictions were imposed and had traveled about eight kilometers when they heard the news about the travel ban. While Slavko stayed with the babies, Oleksa backtracked to find out what had happened to us. We decided Oleksa would return for Slavko, while we waited for them near a forest. The weather was very pleasant and we rested and tried to relax awaiting their return. Slavka took the opportunity to shop for food in a distant grocery store. In the afternoon my sons returned with their babies.

Reversing our direction, we came across a group refugee camp. Suddenly we heard machine gun fire and screams of *Fiefflieger!* We and looked up to see enemy aircraft directly over us. We hid among trees in a dense forest. After the aircraft left we took a narrow path through the forest and came to a clearing. We stayed there for one more day because we had to fix a wagon wheel.

On the next day we continued to travel in scenic areas. Just as we were approaching a large forest, we saw enemy aircraft overhead. We freed the horses to graze while we fled into the forest, made a fire and spent the afternoon in this sheltered area. After this respite we continued toward the pretty town of Feldkirchen. We stayed there for two days in a gasthaus, April 15 and 16. The owner of the gasthaus was very kind to us.

On **April 18** we headed for the Bavarian border in very inclement weather. It poured steadily until we arrived in Laufen. By order of the army commander we were forbidden to cross the bridge into Bavaria. We were forced to retreat again. Salzburg had denied us entry and we did not want to go to Bravnav. We went to the gendarme office and received *Marschbefe* for Tyrol, based on the most current information from army commanders.

We turned in the direction of Salzburg. It continued to rain and conditions were poor for travel. By nightfall we arrived at a village where there was no room in any of the inns. Finally a local, riding a bicycle, directed us to a gasthaus beyond the village. While the owners were unfriendly, they allowed the babies to sleep in the house. The rest of us spent the night in a cold, damp barn.

Although the weather continued to be cold and rainy, we did not want to remain in this unfriendly inn. As we left the sun came out for a short time, but then we were once again drenched by an unrelenting downpour. In the evening we approached Salzburg cautiously. We had learned from news reports that all refugee wagons were to be checked and supplementary food confiscated. We asked other refugees if there were any alternate routes to by-pass Salzburg, but we could not receive any helpful information.

As evening descended, rain began to fall. We entered Salzberg through steel gates. At this inopportune moment, our horse weakened and we had to stop to feed him. As we stood on a road under a tree suddenly sirens began to blare their dire warning of impending doom. Salzburg had been bombed repeatedly and it was happening again. Slavko ran ahead to find a gasthaus for shelter while we walked wearily behind him. I thought at any moment the enemy aircraft would appear and "all hell would break loose."

Finally we found a gasthaus, but there was nowhere to shelter the horses. Quickly we placed the horses under the jutting roof of the barn. We pleaded with the owner of the gasthaus to let us in, but she refused on the orders of the police. The only shelter remaining was an open veranda in the yard. We spread out our mattresses and blankets on the veranda and placed the babies in their carriages. It was a cold, damp, miserable night for sleeping outdoors.

Suddenly we heard the droning sounds of approaching aircraft. Overtaken by exhaustion and numbed by the cold, we fell asleep, leaving our survival in the hands of God. At 3:00 a.m. Vlodko and I fed the horses and hitched the wagon. After one hour we awoke everyone and headed out. The rain that had stopped momentarily began to fall in earnest. We tried to stop at a shelter, but there was no room for us. We ate our breakfast in the teeming rain outdoors and continued on to another wayside gasthaus where there was no room for the night. However, the owners allowed us to spend the afternoon in the warmth of their inn and that helped us regain some of our ebbing strength. This couple helped us to find night lodging with their neighbors, where my sons and families slept in a room, while the rest of us slept on the hay in their attic. The horses were housed in their barn and we obtained feed for them.

In the morning we reorganized our belongings and ate breakfast at the gasthaus. The American army was not far from us, so it is possible they had survived the onslaught of the Bolsheviks. Praise the Lord! We continued our journey toward Halant that day, April 21. It was a beautiful, frosty morning. When we arrived in town, the sirens began their familiar, terrifying warning. It was imperative for us to find immediate shelter because we were traveling on a main thoroughfare. Again the sirens announced the imminent arrival of enemy aircraft. Trying to reach Halant, my sons, with their families, sprinted ahead of us and the enemy bombers.

We heard the hiss of a detonated bomb, followed by more frequent detonations. We stopped the wagon in front of a gate and tried to find shelter there. Hearing the tremendous roar of exploding bombs, we had to focus on saving at least one of our horses. Vlodko and I unleashed our horse and led her to the nearest shelter. Above us the shelter was very sparse. A small caliber bomb could destroy this building instantly. We heard one, then two, explosions.

People were running down the street trying to reach the nearest bomb shelter. Yevka was overcome with panic, convinced we should run somewhere for cover. I tried to keep our group calm, reiterating it was very risky to move during a bombing. Totally unnerved, Yevka, my wife and Slavka bolted onto the main road. Knowing we shouldn't be separated under these circumstances, Vlodko and I chased after the women. In the lead, I glanced back and lost sight of Vlodko.

At this point, sprinting to outrun whistling bombs falling around us and the staccato sound of machine gunfire, I couldn't turn back. At last we reached a shelter, a huge salt mine. In the winding corridors of the mine countless refugees sat on benches. We searched for Slavko and Oleksa and their families, and finally found them in a corridor assigned for women and children.

We sat in the salt mine for five hours while overhead the skies exploded with deafening sounds. The earth shook from the impact of the bombs. During this relentless attack some refugees fainted from lack of air. At 3:15 a.m. the sirens signaled the end of the enemy invasion. Stepping outside, I was relieved to see Vlodko approaching me. At once we noticed a barn nearby where we intended to "shoe" the horses. At that moment the sirens signaled the beginning of another air attack. We hurried back to the salt mine while the air attack continued for another hour.

What were we to do next? Should we remain here? When we were told we could circumvent Salzburg by a dirt road, we knew this was the only option open to us. As we approached the dirt road near the train station we were informed the road near the tracks had been demolished. Attempting to change our course, I put pressure on the horses. On the most difficult section of the alternative road, one of our horses fell. We were frozen in our tracks. At this precise moment the sirens announced yet another air attack. If we had been near the train station at this time, there would not have been any salvation for us. One of the locals quickly pointed out a narrow path through which we could escape. Ten Germans came to help us turn our wagon around. We were eternally grateful to these strangers for helping us in our time of need.

Halfway through our journey we heard the urgent warning of sirens again. From Salzburg, soldiers and civilians were fleeing toward bushes in the foothills of a mountain. Immediately Vlodko unhitched the horses and began to run through the meadow in search of shelter. I was unable to run for great lengths and Slava did not want to abandon me. The sirens continued their death wail but it was still a long distance from the foothills. At that moment we still could not hear the bombers. Running with countless soldiers through the open meadow, there was no safe haven. It would take only one shot to end a life in this foreign land. Eventually we reached the foothills and collapsed for an hour until the sirens signaled the end of the air raid.

As evening descended, we returned to our wagon. Stopping for a short time to warm food for the babies and the rest of us, we then continued onward. Finally we escaped the "hell" we experienced in Halant. The stress, fear and trauma of these repeated air raids had left all of us in various states of emotional distress. It took some time for our nervous exhaustion to abate. After traveling three kilometers we came upon a gasthaus and several homes. The heartless owner of the gasthaus refused us entry. As evening descended we finally found a place in which to spend the night. We spent the night in a barn sleeping on hay and prepared tea on the inn owner's porch.

Sleep eluded us because for ten hours we heard the roar of countless detonations of bombs in the nearby mountains. The sky was illuminated by countless searchlights looking for a most important target: Hitler's residence in Berchtesgaden.

On **April 22** there was a bitter chill and frost covered the ground. We approached Golint, a pretty town. As we were approaching the main thoroughfare the sirens declared a *voralarm*, but this warning passed quickly. In Golint I met two German officers who told me battles had begun in the outskirts of Berlin. In their opinion Berlin could only withstand these alien attacks for four to five days.

In the afternoon we moved toward the challenging and steep Lueg Pass. We experienced incredible difficulties climbing the steep mountain; the horses were not strong enough to pull the wagon. We were very fortunate to find help in unexpected places. For one hour the wagon was pushed up the mountain by a car filled with Hungarians.

German forest rangers helped us to cross another challenging mountain. After what seemed like a long time, we reached the peak of Pass Lueg, where we had a rest.

Descent was a more formidable undertaking and we devised a braking system for the back wheels of the wagon, while Oleksa and Vlodko manually braked the front wheels. This was a very harrowing descent, for if we had lost control, we would have plummeted to our deaths or drowned in the river Salz. Luckily our braking system held and our descent was a success. We followed a narrow mountainous ridge along the river Salz.

Crossing through Bishovshofen, sirens signaled an air raid. We heard that previous air raids had ravaged the city, but we were fortunate to have had safe passage as the warning quickly passed. The babies spent the night in a gasthaus, while we slept in the barn and cooked food on bricks outside.

On **April 23** we passed through Mark-Poshtov. A heavy downpour began in the afternoon, so my son chose to stay in the village with the babies. Looking for shelter for all of us, we discovered a shed at the side of the road. Soaked to the bone and exhausted, we slept on the hay. What to do next?

I went to the city of Svarzach, where I found a comfortable gasthaus. Returning for our group, we walked to Svarzach to give the horses some relief. Covering the horses with double blankets outside, we hurried into the warmth of the inn. After half an hour, my sons joined us with their families. Here we took a brief rest, while Oleksa and Vlodko found the home of a rich landowner in a forest on a hill. There we spent the night. We put the horses in an uncovered shed while we slept in the barn.

Slavko and Oleksa and their families hurried ahead while the wagon slowed perceptibly, as did the rest of us. As I staggered down the road due to an injury to my left leg, Slava refused to leave my side. Crossing a dangerous point in our journey, the industrial town of Lend, we came to a stop beyond the town and rested in a field by the road. The sun warmed our wearied bodies and souls. As we rested we saw troops of Cossacks passing by. They were going back because they were ordered not to proceed any further. While we were observing the retreat of the Cossacks, one of our horses was grazing in a meadow near the river Salz. Unfortunately, he had a misstep and fell heavily and awkwardly to the ground. We had great difficulty in helping the horse get back on his legs and had to shoot him to put him out of his misery.

With this misfortune we had only one horse left to pull the wagon. We struggled through rough terrain to Tachsenbach. For night lodging we found an abandoned barrack. Entering a dirty and revolting room by an outside staircase, we were soon joined here by a division of young Ukrainian boys under the leadership of Germans. They slept on the dirty floor of the barrack.

While the babies, Marta and Chrystyna, slept in the barracks with their parents, the rest of us slept in the barn. That night a huge snowstorm developed and by dawn we were frozen and stiff from the cold. We stayed in Tachsenbach April 26 and 27. During that time Slavko went in search of a home for us in the nearby areas. He managed to find a house in St. Georgen, whose owner was Mudryk. Happy to be approaching a final destination, we left for St. Georgen. On the way we stopped in Hraz, warmed ourselves and pressed forward.

After much negotiating, we obtained a horse when we arrived in **St. Georgen.** With great difficulty we scaled the mountain on the outskirts of St. Georgen. We stayed at the home of a Bavarian named Shvarubachera, while my sons and their families found a warm and clean barn in the nearby area for the night.

On **April 29**, the next day, we decided to make an attempt to scale the steep mountain, where Mudryk resided. The weather was unfavorable for our ascent . . . snow mixed with mud was under our feet. Our first attempt up the mountain was unsuccessful. In the afternoon we made a second attempt to climb the mountain, but we had to again retreat as the horses could not pull the load under these hazardous conditions.

In the evening our group and Oleksa and his family left for the home of Mudryk's brother on the opposite shore of the Zalzach River. There we established residence in an unheated room (no available oven) on an upper floor. The next day Slavko and his family managed to successfully scale the mountain to Mudryk's home where he established residence with another Ukrainian family, Stefan Petyk, his wife and two sons.

Politically, it had become obvious the German Army had capitulated. Bavaria had declared its independence from Hitler. In desperation, the Germans offered the Allies an olive branch. The Allies refused their offer and demanded immediate unconditional surrender from the Germans.

Over a short period of time a few Ukrainian refugees from Galicia established roots in **St. Georgen**, Austria. The group eventually numbered 100. We managed to establish contact with other Ukrainian refugees in Bruck, Fush, Zell am See and neighboring towns and villages. With difficulty we succeeded in moving the Ukrainian Relief Committee to **Zell am See**. Three hundred Ukrainian refugees registered with this agency.

After a long, dangerous journey under harrowing conditions and life-threatening circumstances . . . crossing three countries and over 90 towns . . . and experiencing countless air raids, we were prepared to settle in St. Georgen for a longer period of time.

I became increasingly debilitated by my stomach disorder and began to suspect that the original diagnosis of stomach cancer had been accurate.

# PART SIX

# Displaced Persons

# Chapter 16

## Strasshof Austria, Summer 1944

*. . . . For the world, which seems*
*To lie before us like a land of dreams,*
*So various, so beautiful, so new,*
*Hath really neither joy, nor love, nor light,*
*Nor certitude, nor peace, nor help for pain;*
*And we here as on a darkling plain*
*Swept with confused alarms of struggle and flight,*
*Where ignorant armies clash by night.*
*"Dover Beach", Matthew Arnold (1822-1888)*

Strasshof, a suburb of Vienna, was one of the major Austrian refugee camps and registration centers for the thousands of escapees from Eastern Europe.

In July 1944, the Germans still believed they could win the war. They did not view this avalanche of frightened humanity as victims of the suffering they had caused by their 1939 and 1941 invasions. Instead, they saw them as a nuisance to be tolerated or, better still, to be used for their own purposes.

The Strasshof camp was a clearing house for refugees. Everyone passing through Vienna was registered, and the healthy and able ones were assigned work for the German war effort.

When our family, the Stulkowskys, and my aunt Emilia (Lucia) Melnyk, arrived in Strasshof, German officials immediately separated us into two groups.

My father, uncle, and older brother were sent to the men's area while my mother, my two aunts, and the two nursing infants, Daria and I, were sent to the women's area. Everyone was ordered to remove their clothing. My mother, along with most other women, found this to be the ultimate humiliation and refused, but the female guards, who carried guns and menacing batons, directed them to undress and to place their clothes into piles. We were then marched to another room where other guards shoveled a white disinfectant powder on us before being moved to another area where we were hosed down with cold water. When the powder was completely rinsed away, we all had to return to have the process repeated a second time. The women were ordered to wash all their clothing with a strong soap.

We were kept naked for two days.

My father, uncle, and brother faced a similar ordeal in the men's area.

Finally, we were reunited in the "general area" and were lined up to receive work and travel papers.

We were assigned cots in a large dormitory and were given food coupons. My father was issued papers that permitted him to travel specifically to the town of Erfurt in Thuringia in central Germany. He was assigned to work in an underground munitions factory. After two weeks in very uncomfortable and unsanitary conditions in Strasshof, we boarded another train and headed north, again across Czechoslovakia to Erfurt, Germany.

The town of Erfurt is located just a few kilometers from Buchenwald. Although we had no way of knowing it at the time, my uncle Vasylko was imprisoned in this concentration camp and assigned to perform slave labor just a short distance from where my father was forced to work in the underground munitions factory.

The conditions in Erfurt were even worse than in Strasshof. My father, in spite of his appearance, was not accustomed to manual labor. After three weeks working in the mines, my father was able to "buy his release."

When they left Pidhajci so many months before, my parents took with them the silver service they had received as a wedding present. It proved to be useful now. My father separated the solid silver service for twelve in half and presented a military official with a service for six, as a gift. In return, my father was released from his work in the munitions factory and received a new travel pass.

We crossed Czechoslovakia once again to Austria, where we stayed for a while with friends in Klein Heflein.

In the meantime, Osyp Boyko and his family had traveled to Zell am See* in central Austria, where Osyp found work as a manager of a textile plant. My father obtained work there for several months as well.

# DRESDEN

In December 1944, my parents received a letter from their good friends, the Sawchaks, also refugees from Pidhajci. They had found work in Valda, a small town on the outskirts of Dresden in eastern Germany. They invited us to join them.

We traveled there for Christmas and within a few days, my father found work in Valda.

Dresden is the seventh largest city in Germany, and was considered by many as the most beautiful. It was one of the few cities that had not been bombed, perhaps because it had little military significance. The British decided to change things.

---

*    The Tatomyrs eventually settled in Sankt Georgen, a few kilometers from Zell am See. Chrystyna's
     father, Oleksander, found work in the same plant a few months after my father had left.

On February 13, 1945, the British flew eight hundred bombers over Dresden, partially to show the approaching Soviets what they could do, but officially to destroy German morale at a time when the Allies had just about won the war.

More than thirty-five thousand people lost their lives in the firebombing of Dresden. Most of the victims were women, children, older people, and refugees from Eastern Europe.

Some consider the firebombing of civilians in Dresden a war crime; others felt it was "a necessity," justified in order to bring the war to a quicker end.

Just before midnight on February 13, we were awakened by the sound of bombs. Dresden was on fire. Even though we were more than ten kilometers from the edge of the city, the night sky was lit up as if it was noon.

A week after the bombing of Dresden, just a few days before my first birthday, my father managed to find a train going west that bypassed Dresden. The Sawchaks and our family traveled to the relative safety of Bavaria, to the town of Kulmbach.

A few months later, Dresden and Saxony fell under Soviet control and, after the war, became part of East Germany. Most Ukrainian and other East European refugees who were found in that area were quickly repatriated by the Soviets. Those who were not summarily executed were sent to work camps in Siberia or eastern Russia. Had we not left when we did, we might have been among those unfortunate souls.

## FRÄULEINS

In Kulmbach, we found a small apartment, and again, eight people, four Melnyks and four Sawchaks, shared a small space. Before the war that apartment, as well as the upstairs apartment, was occupied by two young couples. The husbands went off to war in 1939, and both were killed on the eastern front. The two young widows moved in together to save money, leaving one apartment empty and available.

The apartment we took was on the ground floor. The two fräuleins, Trina and Anna, lived upstairs. Living with them was Trina's mother, Fräu Webberfals, also a widow. She lost her husband on the western front.

This situation was repeated countless times throughout Germany. Hitler's armies had killed millions of the enemy, but millions of his own citizens had died as well. Widows and empty homes all over Germany were a testament to Hitler's ambitions.

The three widows seemed to genuinely welcome us. Throughout most of our recent journey we were met with resentment and hostility, but these women saw us as victims of the same misguided policies that had changed their lives so dramatically and had brought them so much misery and grief.

Fräu Webberfals seemed to take a special interest in me. She brought me toys and books and called me her little *boobale*. She volunteered to babysit my brother and me, allowing my mother to go to work a few days a week. At one point, I was spending more of my waking hours with Fräu Webberfals than with my parents. Just as I was beginning to speak, I was exposed to German during most of each day, and as I approached my second birthday, my dominant language was German. I called Fräu Webberfals *oma* (grandmother) and preferred her apartment to our crowded one.

# BUCHENWALD

Buchenwald means "beech forest." The Buchenwald Concentration Camp, opened in 1937, was originally designed by the Germans as a Class 2 camp for hard-core political prisoners. At the beginning of World War II, many of the prisoners in the camp were Slavs. They were used as slave laborers in the nearby armament factories or on construction projects. In late 1944 and early 1945, when the Soviets approached Poland, many of the concentration camps scattered around western Poland were evacuated and the prisoners, mostly Jews, were transferred to Buchenwald. They were kept in a section of the camp called "small camp," where the conditions were much worse than those in the "main camp." Thousands of Jews were exterminated or used for medical experiments at this camp.

The prisoners were housed in cramped, unsanitary quarters and were fed so little; all of them were slowly starving to death.

When my uncle, Vasylko Martyniuk, arrived at the camp in late 1943, a number was tattooed on his arm, and for the next year and a half this formerly healthy young man slowly wasted away. He was assigned to a work detail along with other Ukrainians, Poles, Lithuanians, and other Slavs, building roads in the immediate area of the camp. The workers were beaten regularly, and if a German soldier felt someone was not working hard enough or if someone was unable to work, the person was shot. The other workers had to carry the body to a cart and pull the cart back to the camp for disposal.

Vasylko managed to survive in this horrific place until the camp was liberated by the American Third Army in April 1945. Weeks before the camp was finally liberated, the SS started killing non-Jewish prisoners, especially those deemed too weak to work. Each day names were called out and the prisoners, many barely able to stand, were "sentenced to death." My uncle was among the prisoners whose name was called out one day. Another prisoner, my uncle's friend, yelled out, "He died yesterday!" The SS officer crossed my uncle's name off the list and moved on.

Just before the Americans came to liberate the camp on April 11, 1945, many of the German guards fled. Several prisoners seized control of the camp and opened the gates. My uncle was among the hundreds who walked out of the prison. As they walked away from the camp, a convoy of American soldiers was moving in the opposite direction, toward the Buchenwald camp.

My uncle and other fellow prisoners raised their arms in surrender, not knowing what to expect. One truck stopped. The American soldiers were horrified at the condition of these men. Most were just skeletons covered with skin. (My uncle estimated that when he was released he weighed less than sixty pounds.) The Americans gave them food and water and sent them on their way. After the American commanders entered the camp and saw the killing ovens, the dead, and the condition of the survivors, they knew they were witnessing a major war crime. The soldiers were ordered to find the prisoners who had "escaped" so that they could be questioned.

My uncle was questioned about his treatment at the camp, photographed, given a basic medical exam, fed, and released to fend for himself.

# REFUGEES

The war in Europe ended in the spring of 1945, and UNRRA, the United Nations Relief and Rehabilitation Administration, took over the administration of war refugees in Europe. All refugees, or displaced persons, were registered and given assistance. Displaced Persons camps were formed for those who needed accommodation and, eventually, UNRRA agreed that these camps should be formed along ethnic and national lines. With so many Ukrainians among the millions of displaced persons in Europe, UNRRA formed several camps in Germany and Austria exclusively for Ukrainians. 9

After he was released from Buchenwald, my uncle boarded a train for Holland because he heard that work could be found in the construction trades in that country. He worked there for a few months and then he too registered with UNRRA. On a long shot, he asked if there was a family of a Bohdan and Bronyslawa Melnyk living anywhere in Europe. He had had no news from us for years and had no idea whether we had escaped or, indeed, survived the war. After a few months, he was notified that there was a Melnyk family with those names in a DP camp in Kulmbach, Germany. My uncle left his job and traveled back to Germany to search for us.

One day, during the fall of 1945, my four-year-old brother, Roman, was playing in front of our house in the Kulmbach DP Camp when a stranger approached and asked him if he knew where the Melnyks lived. My brother pointed to our apartment.

That stranger was my uncle Vasylko.

A very tearful but joyous reunion followed.

Our uncle, who was still badly undernourished, and surely weighed less than a hundred pounds, lived with us in Kulmbach until December 1945. In 1946, we were relocated to a DP camp in Bayreuth, where I celebrated my second birthday. The following year, we all moved to a large, almost exclusively Ukrainian DP camp in Regensburg. Here life for Ukrainian displaced persons was much more hopeful.

# Chapter 17

## *Sankt Georgen, Austria*

By the spring of 1945, the Soviet Army had muscled its way into eastern Austria while the Americans, British, and French moved in from the west. The race was on to see who would make it first to Berlin. The Red Army was by far the largest army in Europe at the time, and eventually took control of a large part of Germany and Austria. When the war finally ended, Central Europe was divided into four zones by the Allies; American, British, French and Soviet. The eastern parts of Germany and Austria, including Vienna, became part of the Soviet zone.

As the Red Army advanced deeper into Europe, over five million escapees from Eastern Europe found themselves trapped behind Soviet lines. They were deemed "Soviet citizens" and were repatriated—forcibly sent back to the Soviet Union.

But even those refugees who had made it farther west into the American and British zones were not safe. In February of 1945, a conference was held in Yalta, Crimea, attended by Franklin D. Roosevelt, Winston Churchill, and Joseph Stalin. The purpose of this conference was to establish an agenda for governing postwar Germany. Each leader, however, had his own agenda: Roosevelt was looking for Soviet support in the U.S. Pacific War against Japan, Churchill pressed for free elections and democratic governments in Eastern Europe, and Stalin demanded a Soviet sphere of influence in Eastern Europe as essential to the USSR's national security.

Since, at the time of the conference, the Red Army was only forty miles from Berlin and advancing quickly, Stalin felt that he was in a position to dictate terms. Among his many demands was one insisting on the total repatriation of all refugees. A secret agreement was finalized on March 31, 1945. It stipulated that all displaced nationals, found anywhere in Europe under Allied control, must be returned, by force if necessary, to their homelands.

Stalin had manipulated Roosevelt and Churchill at the Yalta meetings. The two Western leaders conceded much more than necessary in order to appease Stalin. Stalin made commitments but reneged on most of his promises, promises he never intended to honor.

What followed was a sad chapter in American war history. American soldiers were ordered to round up escapees from Eastern Europe who had made it to their zone and to deliver them, often kicking and screaming to the Soviets. The refugees protested, rioted, and some committed suicide when they were faced with forced deportation.

Finally, on September 4, 1945, General Dwight D. Eisenhower, appalled by what he was witnessing and facing significant pressure from his own commanders, ordered a ban on further forced return of refugees to their countries of origin.

Of the estimated two million Ukrainians who left their homeland, fewer than 250,000 remained in the western parts of Germany and Austria when repatriation finally ceased. The majority of the refugees who had avoided repatriation, through sheer luck in most cases, settled in displaced persons camps scattered throughout the American, French, and British zones. They were among the fortunate ones.

\*   \*   \*

The Tatomyrs were lucky to have made it to the American zone in western Austria by the spring of 1945, but they did not settle in a DP camp. They were concerned that even after the danger of repatriation had passed, Soviet agents were still active among the refugees. Some prominent Ukrainian anti-Soviet figures had been assassinated well after the end of the war.

After a harrowing nine months of very difficult travel by horse cart, train, and on foot, Julian, Jaroslav, Oleksander, and their families stopped at the tiny village of Sankt Georgen located off the main road, a few kilometers east of the picturesque town of Zell am See and some thirty kilometers south of Salzburg. Several other Ukrainian families settled there as well. Everyone knew everyone in the town. They reasoned that it would be difficult for Soviet agents to operate here.

Although they lived in Sankt Georgen, the displaced persons camp at Zell am See was the cultural center for the Tatomyrs. Oleksander found work in Zell am See, and Jaroslav and Oleksander and their families joined and led various Ukrainian organizations in that DP camp.

Some of the Ukrainian residents of St. Georgen, Austria, Summer of 1945.
Front row center, Chrystyna and cousin, Marta. Top row, third from left, Chrystyna's
mother, Sophia, and sixth from left, Marta's mother, Luba.

Cousins Chrystyna and Marta Tatomyr, St. Georgen, 1946

## JULIAN'S LAST DAYS

Reverend Julian Tatomyr suffered severe stomach pains almost continually since the family left Vienna, and over time he became more and more ill.

Although he was critically ill with cancer, he continued to head the St. Andrij Society which worked to increase cooperation between the Ukrainian Orthodox and Catholic Churches. He also continued to say masses in the DP Camp.

Reverend Senator Julian Sas-Tatomyr died at sixty-three years of age, on March 26, 1946, following an operation in Salzburg, Austria. He was buried in Salzburg at the Kommunal Friedhof Cemetery, next to Dr. Makukh, former minister of the United Ukrainian National Republic. The funeral was attended by thousands of Ukrainians. Some said it was the largest funeral ever held at that cemetery.

Through the efforts of his elder son, Jaroslav (Slavko), Rev. Julian Tatomyr's remains were transported to the United States of America and interred at St. Mary's Ukrainian Cemetery in Fox Chase, Pennsylvania, in 1978. He was buried next to his wife, Olha, who died on October 8, 1968, in Bristol, Pennsylvania.

## MOTHER OF EXILES

By 1948, as the refugee crisis in Europe became more and more urgent, and after much debate among the Allies, U.S. President Truman announced, "I urge Congress to turn its attention to this world problem in an effort to find ways whereby we can fulfill our responsibilities to these thousands of homeless refugees of all faiths."

Congress responded with the Displaced Persons Act of 1948, offering thousands of refugees entry into the United States.

Similar acts were passed in Canada and Australia, and within a few years, the DP camps of Austria and Germany were emptied.

Shortly after the act was passed, the Tatomyrs, sponsored by the American Catholic League, set off to Bremerhaven in northern Germany, where they boarded the SS *Marine Tiger* headed for New York City.

The journey to New York was harrowing as inclement weather battered the ship. Most of the refugees traveled in steerage in very close quarters near the bottom of the ship. They were frequently seasick and incapacitated by other illnesses that spread among the passengers. The women, Grandmother Olha, Luba, and Sophia were violently ill during the crossing, but the children, Marta and Chrystyna, were healthy and active. They spent many hours on the main deck of the ship playing and, as Chrystyna remembers, "annoying" other passengers.

As the SS *Marine Tiger* neared the coastline of the United States, there were feelings of elation and trepidation on board. The refugees were elated that they were finally in

America, the land of the free. But they were also filled with trepidation because they knew they would face examinations and interrogations upon entry; if they were deemed unfit, either mentally or physically, they would be denied entry and would be returned to Germany and, quite possibly, eventually to the Soviet Union. After all the suffering, narrow escapes, hunger, and close calls, the Tatomyrs had survived during their four-year journey, this outcome was unthinkable.

Finally, after a long and rough passage, the SS *Marine Tiger* steamed into New York Harbor on a May evening in 1948, just as the sun was setting. Chrystyna recalls that all the passengers were standing on the huge deck, and there was total silence as their ship approached the Statue of Liberty.

*       *       *

For the immigrants, the arrival in New York was a midpoint in the voyage of transformation that had begun thousands of miles away. The experience of these newcomers would be woven into the myth of America.

Standing in awe as their ships glided past the Statue of Liberty, the immigrants could almost hear the statue's welcome:

> *Here at our sea-washed*
> *Sunset gates shall stand*
> *A mighty woman with a torch . . .*
>
> *And her name, Mother of Exiles . . .*
>
> *Give me your tired, your poor,*
> *Your huddled masses yearning*
> *To breathe free . . .*
>
> *Send these, the homeless,*
> *Tempest-tossed to me,*
> *I lift my lamp beside the golden door!*

As the sun set over New York Harbor, most passengers on deck rushed to get a better view of the Statue of Liberty. The whole ship seemed to lean toward the "Mother of Exiles".

# Chapter 18

# *Displaced Persons Camps*

In 1947, camps in Germany and Austria held 1.6 million displaced persons. Among them were 200,000 Ukrainians.

About two-thirds of Ukrainian refugees eventually settled in one of five large displaced persons camps organized by UNRRA (United Nations Relief and Rehabilitation Agency) in Germany and Austria. They were Munich, Mittenwald, Regensburg, Berchtesgaden, and Ausburg.

Life was more tolerable in these cities thanks to the efforts of two people:

Lt. Colonel Jaromir Pospisil, the commander of the American forces in the area, the son of immigrants from Czechoslovakia, who was very sympathetic to the plight of the refugees; and a Canadian Salvation Army officer who was appointed welfare officer for the camps. Both are fondly remembered by the refugees. 9

As early as 1945, Ukrainian camps established their own local agencies of self-government. An active civic, political, cultural, educational, religious, economic, literary, and artistic life developed in the camps during their brief existence. 5

Below is a copy of a directive written by Lt. Colonel Pospisil, where he defined "displaced person" and established a basis for the treatment of refugees in his sector.

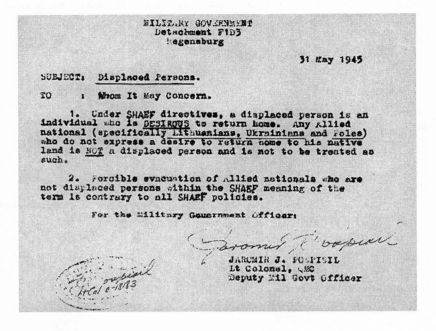

## Ganghofersiedlung Regensburg

Since leaving Pidhajci in March 1944, our family of four lived out of suitcases as we journeyed from town to town. We traveled from Gorlice, Poland, to Strasshof, Austria, to Erfurt, Germany, back to Klein Heflein, Austria, to Dresden and finally to Kulmbach and Bayreuth in Bavaria.

Although the conditions were not ideal, once the war ended, life for refugees in Germany improved. The American administrators of this zone reasoned that everything would be more efficient and everyone would be happier and easier to deal with if the refugees were allowed to settle in camps according to their ethnic backgrounds. The largest camp designated for Ukrainians was Regensburg, Bavaria. Between five and six thousand Ukrainians eventually settled there.

Approximately 20 percent of the Ukrainian refugees were members of the intelligencia. They rejected the Soviet system and, in turn, were not welcome in the newly acquired Soviet territories. They were well educated; leaders in their various professions in Ukraine and all were highly politicized. It was estimated that among the Ukrainian refugees were 1,000 teachers, 400 engineers, 350 lawyers, 300 physicians, 300 clergy, and more than 2,000 university students. 13

Putting all these people together in one place created a powerful dynamic. Every organization that had been active in Ukraine under Polish or Bolshevik rule was suddenly free to function without fear of reprisal. In most cases, people also had more time on their hands than ever before. Doctors, lawyers, teachers, clergy and other leaders from towns and villages scattered all over Ukraine, were now concentrated in small pockets in Austria and Germany.

The American military allowed Ukrainians to elect a camp administration, which organized all aspects of life in the Camp.

Churches, reading rooms, medical clinics, schools, (including a kindergarten, an elementary school, and a high school), music schools, youth organizations such as Ukrainian Boy Scouts (Plast) and SUM, women's organizations, political groups (including OUN Bandera faction and Melnyk faction), sports clubs, and other clubs and societies were organized by these ex-patriot Ukrainians. In 1948, a group of university and technical school professors even organized the Ukrainian Technical and Husbandry Institute (UTHI). My father, Bohdan, completed his studies at this institute and received a diploma in 1949—just before we left for Canada.

In 1947, our family moved to Regensburg, where we managed to find a modest apartment. My father was able to find work in a nearby factory and my mother found a job teaching in a kindergarten organized by the Ukrainian refugees.

**Ukrainian kindergarten class, Regensburg DP camp, March 1949. Little Andrij, standing top row, fourth from the right. My mother, Bronyslawa, is the fourth teacher from the left, at the center of the picture.**

By 1948, the Allies and the United Nations were desperate to get all the DPs out of Germany and Austria. The United States, Canada, and Australia agreed to accept several thousand refugees each. Those who had sponsors in any of these countries were usually processed more quickly, and by early 1948, a great many Ukrainians were on their way to a new country.

My mother's cousins, Wasyl and Stephan Martyniuk, were our sponsors to Canada. Earlier, they had sponsored their youngest brother, Mykhajlo Martyniuk, and my uncle, Vasylko Martyniuk, who preceded us. By the summer of 1949, with the number of displaced persons decreasing daily, we were ready to leave.

My mother had the foresight to try to learn English while we were waiting in the camps. She enrolled in a translator's program and became certified as a Ukrainian-English translator. This skill would serve her, and all of us, well in Canada.

**Regensburg Displaced Person's Camp.**
**We lived in the second building, ground floor.**

**Waiting. Regensburg, 1947**

## JUNE 21, 1949

In June of 1949, while our family was still living at the DP camp in Regensburg, we received the long-awaited invitation to come to a hearing regarding our application to emigrate to Canada. My two uncles, Vasylko and Mykhajlo, had left for Canada six months earlier.

As our family traveled to Amburg by train to attend a hearing at the immigration commission, my eight-year-old brother, Roman, leaned against the door of the train. With the train traveling at full speed, the door swung open. Roman fell out of the train onto the next set of tracks. When my father realized what had happened, he pulled the emergency brake and stopped the train about a kilometer down the track.

My brother was frightened but unhurt. Before the train even stopped, he got up and started to run after our train, just as another train was approaching on the track onto which he had fallen. My father jumped from the train to rescue my brother and pulled him to safety just as the train on the adjoining track passed. Everyone on the train cheered and marveled at the miracle that had just taken place.

We all took this as an omen that Roman was destined for great things.

My mother declared June 21 would be celebrated as my brother's other birthday.

## SS SAMARIA

A month after the hearing, we were notified there was room for our family on a ship heading for Canada. In August 1949, we traveled to Hamburg and then on to Bremen and the port of Bremerhaven to board our ship, the Samaria, a converted troop carrier pressed into service to accommodate the masses of immigrants heading to North America.*

We underwent lengthy medical screenings and interviews by Canadian immigration officials, and, with all our papers in order, boarded the ship. Cramped in tight quarters below the water line, we were finally on our way to Canada to freedom and to a new life.

The passage was quite rough. I was sick and developed spots all over my body. My parents feared that we would not be admitted to Canada and would be sent back to Europe.

As we approached the Canadian shore, the captain of our ship, the Samaria, was informed that Pier 21 in Halifax, the main entry point for refugees to Canada since

---

\* The Cunard White Star Line, SS Samaria was originally built in 1920 and along with her sister ships, the SS Scythia and the SS Laconia served as a passenger ship in the lucrative trans-Atlantic market. The Samaria had accommodations for 665 first and second class passengers and fifteen hundred third class passengers. In 1940 all three ships were converted to serve as troop carriers. The SS. Laconia was torpedoed and sunk by a German U Boat on September 12, 1942 off the coast of Africa with a substantial loss of life. After the War, the Scythia and Samaria were converted to accommodate the masses of refugees traveling from Europe to America. The Samaria was scrapped in 1958.

1928, was overloaded with other ships and would not be able to receive us. We were told to travel on to Quebec City.

My parents were relieved. We would have a few more days to recover from our illnesses in the calmer waters of the St. Lawrence River and would be better prepared for the anticipated medical inspection. As we approached Quebec City, my mother covered me from head to toe in a long sleeved shirt, buttoned to the top, and long pants, hoping to cover my spots and to somehow get me past the examiners.

We arrived at the port in Quebec City on August 15, 1949. We all passed our medical exams.

Penniless (though my parents still had a few pieces of their wedding silverware), we were welcomed to Canada. As we disembarked, a Salvation Army officer handed my father a ten-dollar bill and an immigration officer handed us train tickets to Montreal, which had been purchased by our sponsor, Uncle Steve Martyniuk.

The next day, on August 16, 1949, we arrived in Montreal, and with much uncertainty but great anticipation, began our new life in Canada.

Top: Roman, Bohdan, Bronyslawa, and four-year-old Andrij Melnyk.
Waiting at the Regensburg DP camp for clearance to come to Canada. Summer, 1948

Below: Four-year-old Chrystyna Tatomyr, recently arrived in the United States of America.
Second Street, Philadelphia. Summer, 1948.

# PART SEVEN

# Integration

# Chapter 19

# *Belonging*

In their lifetimes, our parents, not unlike many of the other thirty-something former DPs who came to North America in the late 1940s, had experienced many different governments and had been forced to pay allegiance to various regimes and rulers in different European capitals.

- Our parents were born before World War I when Galicia was a province of the Austrian empire. Their capital city was **Vienna.**
- When Austria collapsed after 1914, the Bolsheviks moved in and their government was based in **Russia.**
- In 1918, Ukrainians in Galicia joined the Ukrainian Republic with its capital in **Kyiv.**
- By 1922, Galicia became part of Greater Poland and their capital city became **Warsaw.**
- In 1939, Poland fell to the Germans, the Bolsheviks moved in again, and orders came from **Moscow.**
- In 1941, the Nazi's invaded Galicia and briefly, Ukrainians thought of creating a new state. A provisional Ukrainian government was formed, and the blue and yellow flag flew over major buildings in **Lviv.**
- Days later, the Nazi's took full control and now, orders came from **Berlin.**
- For five years, 1944-1949, our parents were stateless—refugees living in the American zone under the auspices of the **United Nations.**
- For five more years, they were landed immigrants in Canada or the United States but finally, the day came when they could confidently say they were Canadian or American citizens and their capital was **Ottawa** or **Washington.**

**The Tatomyrs** arrived in New York City in May 1948, without their patriarch, Reverend Julian Tatomyr. Julian's widow, Olha, was sixty years old and quite frail. Jaroslaw and wife Luba were thirty-eight years old, and their daughter, Marta, was four.

Oleksander was thirty-five years old; his wife, Sophia, thirty-three years old; and their daughter, Chrystyna, was four years old. Chrystyna's and Marta's uncle, Volodymyr Tatomyr, who was forty-six years old, arrived in Philadelphia a few weeks earlier.

**The Melnyks** arrived in Montreal, August 16, 1949. Bohdan was thirty-nine years old, Bronyslawa was thirty-seven, my brother, Roman, was eight years old, and I was five years old.

My father's sister, Olha (Melnyk) **Stulkowsky**, was thirty-five, her husband, Dmytro Stulkowky, was forty-two. Their daughters, Daria and Oksana, were five and two years old, respectively.

Lucia (Melnyk) **Mychalewsky** was just twenty-seven, her husband, Mykola Mychalewsky, was twenty-five, their daughter, Christina, was three, and son, Roman, was less than a year old. They settled in Philadelphia.

**The Tatomyrs** traveled from New York to Philadelphia, where a large number of Ukrainians lived and where jobs were available. They found a small flat on Second Street in South Philadelphia in a poor racially mixed part of town near Logan Street. Oleksander and Jaroslav found work, joined the Ukrainian church, and mixed comfortably with the local Ukrainian community. Marta and Chrystyna became members of the newly organized Plast youth group. As part of the Ukrainian community in the United States, the Tatomyrs were able to sponsor others still living in DP camps.

**The Melnyks** were greeted in Montreal by my mother's relatives, the Martyniuks: Cousins Vasyl, Mykola, and Stefan who came to Canada during the 1930s, and my mother's brother, Vasylko, and cousin, Mykhajlo, who arrived in Canada from Germany a few months earlier. For several months, we lived in Uncle Steven's tiny house on Twenty-Sixth Avenue in Rosemount, in northeastern Montreal, along with two other families. Eventually, we moved into our own apartment on Bercy Street in east-end Montreal. My father found employment, and we joined St. Michael's Ukrainian Catholic Church on Iberville Street and, soon after, other Ukrainian organizations. My father became a member of the church committee and was instrumental in organizing the Montreal chapter of the Ukrainian scouting group, Plast. He served on the committee that purchased the first *domivka* (clubhouse) on Esplanade Avenue and a hundred-acre farm in the Eastern Townships for use by Plast children for summer scout camps. My mother became quite active in the Ukrainian Women's League.

# FIRST GENERATION

Our parents, and most of the adults who left the DP camps and emigrated to Canada or the United States after the war, worked hard, stayed connected with other immigrants, and slowly began to make a life for themselves in North America, but in spite of their best efforts, their adopted country would always be somewhat foreign to them.

Most of the former professors, engineers, and doctors who arrived in North America with old-world credentials were unable to find work in their professions and most had to take menial jobs to survive. All of them struggled to learn English and many tried to become recertified in their professions. Inevitably, most of them compromised their dreams, abandoned the hope that they would ever work in their professions, and did whatever was necessary to make ends meet.

After spending four of five years in DP camps in Germany and Austria, it may have been difficult for our parents to adjust to the reality that their new city was not just another camp in another country, though many of the same activities available in DP camps in Germany or Austria were available in Canada and the United States.

The immigrants maintained very close ties among themselves and, ironically, perhaps tried to recreate the conditions they had just left in the displaced person camps. The organizations and clubs that flourished there were restarted, the concerts and other social events resumed, and the social interactions they had nurtured in Europe were maintained.

Honorary titles such as *Pan Professor, Pan Doctor*, or *Pan Engineer* were used in conversations among associates, even though the persons addressed were no longer practicing teachers, doctors, or engineers. (This occasionally caused confusion among the younger generations.)

But the adults knew their children would fit in much more easily in their new countries. They watched their children grow, learn a new language, get an education, and blend in easily with the local population. There was an expectation that all the younger immigrants would get the best education available, would attend university, and, if possible, become professionals.

While they encouraged their children to absorb everything that was good about their new North American culture, they worried that the children would become assimilated too quickly and would forget their own language, culture and heritage.

As time passed, our parents realized that they were never going back to Ukraine. Their "old country" was behind the iron curtain. The cold war had begun and, from what they heard, conditions in their homeland were terrible.

These immigrants knew they had made the right choice for their families. Their children would have a better life, and certainly, their children's children would prosper at an even faster rate.

When they arrived in their new cities, the first organization most Ukrainian immigrants joined was a church. Virtually all postwar immigrants were members of the Eastern Rite Ukrainian Catholic or Ukrainian Orthodox Church, and most cities in which they settled already had established Catholic and Orthodox parishes. These parishes welcomed the newcomers and helped them to get established in their new countries.

Next, because Ukrainian newcomers worried that their children would have difficulty retaining their native language, in every city where they congregated, newcomers established Ukrainian Schools.

# NEXT GENERATION

For the immigrant children, weekends were very tightly scripted. Ukrainian school classes were usually held on Saturday mornings, when the children were free, and, importantly, when the otherwise employed Ukrainian professors and teachers were available. Saturday afternoons were reserved for youth or scouting organizations such as Plast or SUM (Ukrainian Youth Association). Sunday mornings were reserved for church, and Sunday afternoons for concerts and festivals.

The "next generation" children lived in an English-speaking environment on school days, but on weekends, for the most part, they existed in a structured Ukrainian environment.

They were comfortably fluent in English and Ukrainian and were able to move easily from one group to another, to switch from one language to the other in mid sentence, and to instinctively understand subtle cultural differences between each group. They would grow up bilingual and bicultural.

They were comfortable living in two worlds.

# OUR MONTREAL BUBBLE

Webster's Dictionary defines a *ghetto* as "a quarter of a city where members of a minority reside as a result of social or economic pressure."

Although we didn't feel it at the time, and would argue vigorously that it was not the case, an objective observer might conclude that during the 1950s, most Ukrainian immigrants in Montreal lived in one of the self-imposed geographic ghettos surrounding one of the Ukrainian churches sprinkled throughout the city. If these were not physical ghettos in the technical sense, at the very least, we can safely say that many of our early experiences occurred in a "Ukrainian bubble."

Reflecting on my first twelve years in Canada (until I went to university), I realize that I knew very few non-Ukrainians and almost all my social interactions were connected almost exclusively to Ukrainian activities.

My life revolved around St. Michael's Ukrainian Church, St. Anselm School (where my closest friends were other recently arrived or Second Generation Ukrainians), and the Ukrainian Boy Scouts, (especially after Plast purchased a clubhouse on Esplanade Street adjacent to Mount Royal Park near downtown Montreal.)*

I'm not sure to what extent our early experiences in Canada were similar to those of other DPs, but it seemed that all my friends were in more or less the same situation, had the same expectations, challenges, and demands, and shared similar experiences.

---

\*    For an additional personal description of my experiences in the Montreal Bubble, please see *Growing up in Montreal* in the Epilogue.

My mother worked as a seamstress. Eventually, she was promoted to sample maker, joined the union, and enjoyed a steady salary. My father held a series of menial jobs: in a tannery, on construction, and, finally, at a factory where he worked the afternoon shift at the American Can Company for many years.

We didn't see much of my father during the week for the first few years. He would arrive home after midnight when we were already asleep, and when we got home after school, he was gone.

When I was in elementary school, my father tried to take every opportunity to maintain a connection with us. He took the "long way" on his way to work every afternoon so that he would pass by our school. He always timed it for when we would be in the schoolyard for afternoon recess. He would stand outside the fence and watch us for a few minutes as we played. Sometimes, I would run over to talk to him for a few seconds or just to say hello. Other times, especially when as I got older and was too busy playing with my friends, I would just wave to him. But we always connected in some way, if only for a moment.

Every night, at eight o'clock, when he had his lunch break, my father would call us from a phone booth at his factory. For several years, this was a very important family ritual. My father would dial our number and would let the phone ring once. He would then hang up and get his dime back. Whenever we heard the phone ring, we'd always wait. If there was a second ring, we'd answer and tell whoever was calling that we would call them right back. If there was no second ring, we knew it was my father. We would then dial the memorized number of the phone booth at his work. My brother and I would usually talk with my father for a few minutes, catch up on the news, and then we'd pass the phone to my mother and she would talk for a few minutes.

She also saw little of him.

I suppose we owe Bell Canada a whole bunch of dimes for all those calls—and after all these years, I still never answer the phone until the second ring—and when the phone sometimes rings only once and stops, for a fraction of a second, I think maybe it's my father calling . . . .

\*   \*   \*

In February 1956, after five and a half years in Canada, we obtained our Canadian citizenship. After being stateless for so long, it felt good to finally belong to a country. A few months later, we moved into our new house in Rosemont. For the first time in their lives, my parents were not only citizens of a country of their choosing, but also homeowners in their own right.

Three years earlier, in May of 1953, after being in Canada for less than four years, my father and two partners bought a large building lot on Second Avenue in Rosemont—a part of Montreal where many Ukrainian immigrants also settled. The building lot cost one thousand dollars. My father borrowed his $333 share from the Ukrainian credit union, and after he paid off this loan, he and his partners hired my uncle, Vasylko, to build a six-unit apartment building on the property.

Our three families lived in three of the units and rented the other three units to help pay off our mortgage.

In 1959, just ten years after we arrived in our new country, my father, Bohdan, was diagnosed with intestinal cancer. Our parents didn't talk about my father's illness, but my father stopped working at the factory and stayed home for more than a year. This caused financial hardship for our family as my mother became the sole breadwinner, but it gave my brother and me a chance to get to know my father a little better. After all those years when he worked the afternoon shift and we saw so little of him, we now had his company anytime we were home.

Every morning, during the time he was at home convalescing, he would wake us, make breakfast for us, and send us off to school. He then rested until we returned in the afternoon. When his cancer went into remission, he took a job as a bookkeeper at the Ukrainian credit union and again became fully active in the Ukrainian community. He knew his time was limited.

Five years later, the cancer returned. My father was home again during the year I was completing my teaching degree. He and I had a chance to spend a lot of time together. He was very pleased that I had become serious about school and earned my Bachelor of Science degree. He was also very proud that I had decided to become a teacher.

During the summer of 1965, my father's condition worsened. We contacted my brother, Roman, who was working at the Canadian Consulate in Stuttgart, Germany. He returned home in mid-August.

On September 3, 1965, at the age of fifty-five, my father died. He was buried at the Cote des Neiges Cemetery on Mount Royal the day after Labor Day—the day that was to be my first day of teaching.

More than forty years later, I still miss him.

## PHILADELPHIA STORIES

Philadelphia had an active Ukrainian community before the Second World War, and this city became a beacon for a large number of Ukrainian DPs during the late 1940s.

My father's two sisters, Olha and Emilia, and their families, who escaped with us from Pidhajci in 1944, found sponsors who brought them to Philadelphia. Their stories can be found in Part Eight of this book.

The Tatomyr families also settled in Philadelphia. Marta's and Chrystyna's accounts of their early life in Philadelphia and later in the suburbs can also be found in Part Eight of this book.

# Chapter 20

# *The Incredible Decade*

The most important decade in my life corresponded to (in my opinion) the most exciting decade of the twentieth century, the 1960s.

It's a tired old cliché, but those of us who were of a certain age during the 1960s in varying degrees feel that everything that came before 1960 was in "black and white" and everything after that date was in wonderful living color.

It wasn't just because photographs were more often in color or because movies and TV changed to color, and it wasn't just because of the psychedelic drugs that a few people tried, or because marijuana and other soft drugs were so easily available. It's just that so many amazing things happened during that decade. Our culture and the way we looked at the world changed so much.

(Most of us are also aware that those who didn't live through the sixties really don't like hearing our stories.)

The decade started with John F. Kennedy as president of the United States—Americans were living in glamorous Camelot; anything was possible. It ended with Trudeau-mania in Canada. In between, we had the Bay of Pigs, the Cuban Missile Crisis (many of us felt the end was near and we began to appreciate life a little more because every day might be our last). On November 22, 1963, we all lost our innocence and optimism when news reports from Dallas confirmed that JFK had been assassinated.

During that decade, the war in Vietnam consumed our lives. Too many young Americans, among them many of our friends, were dying. Many felt that that war—and all wars—were immoral. The Tet Offensive was badly handled, the government lied to the people, the My Lai Massacre showed how quickly good people could turn bad under the pressures of war. Almost every American knew someone who had been killed in that war. Young men refused, on principle, to participate in the draft. Many became draft dodgers. Young people all over the world took part in protests against the Vietnam War and fought for social change.

In April 1968, Martin Luther King was assassinated, and less than two months later, Robert Kennedy was shot and killed as he campaigned for the presidency.

Czechoslovakia had its Prague Spring and in Africa, the Biafra genocide was taking place.

We also had the Summer of Love, Woodstock, Expo 67 in Montreal, and, before the end of the decade, a man landed on the moon.

Music evolved. We moved from Perry Como, Frank Sinatra, and Doris Day to the Beatles, the Rolling Stones, and Janice Joplin.

During the 1960s, I graduated from high school, got my Bachelor of Science degree, became a chemist, earned my teaching credentials, started teaching, got my Master's, and took an extended trip to Europe as my own personal centennial project.

I also met the woman of my dreams.

# SKI CAMP

Our parents did their best to keep us occupied and involved throughout our teen years and tried hard to find ways to keep us out of trouble. It wasn't easy with all the wondrous distractions that Montreal offered.

During the late 1950s, some of our more imaginative Plast leaders decided to organize a winter camp. A dozen or so boys, including my brother, Roman, went to the Plast camp in the Eastern Townships during the Christmas holidays for a few days of winter "camping" and skiing. The camp was a success.

The following year, a bigger winter camp, to include boys and girls, was organized in the Laurentians. That too was a great success. At first, it seemed revolutionary that boys and girls would be encouraged to share their camping experiences. When nothing terrible happened that first year, the concept caught on.

In 1961, Plast members from Toronto, New York, Philadelphia, Cleveland, Chicago, and other cities were invited to come to the Laurentians for a truly international ski camp. A few adventurous pioneers, notably from Toronto and Philadelphia, came to this camp.

Among the first group of American participants were three adventurers from Philadelphia: Orest Subtelny, Omelan Lukasewycz, and Marta Tatomyr. (Marta writes about her experiences, later in this book.) Orest, Omelan, Marta, and many of us Montrealers became lifelong friends. Since I had close family living in Philadelphia, this created a second Philadelphia connection for me. I already had four cousins living there, and now I had all these great new friends.

The camps grew in size and popularity. It seemed that as soon as one camp ended, plans were being made for an even better and even greater camp the following year.

In 1965, I was twenty-one years old, and had just started my teaching career. Four of my very best friends, George Wesolowsky, Mickey (Lubomyr Mykytiuk), Bobby Hrycaj, Stefko Sawka, and I decided it was our turn to organize a ski camp. We were determined that it would be the best camp ever.

Two years earlier, the five of us were invited to join the international Plast fraternity "Burlaky." This fraternity for "older" scouts was originally formed in Ukraine in the 1920s. Their symbol is a beat-up, old, torn hiking boot and its motto is "*mandruj* (keep on traveling)." Of all the Plast fraternities, the Burlaky have always had a reputation for being the most fun-loving.

That was a good fit for us. Other chapters of this fraternity already existed in New York, Philadelphia, and Cleveland. Now there was a chapter in Montreal. (A Toronto chapter was started a few years later.)

We found a new location for our ski camp, the Ivry Inn in beautiful St. Agathe, an hour's drive north of Montreal. We negotiated a great price and assigned ourselves specific responsibilities: George would take care of registrations, Mickey would organize the ski hills, Bobby would purchase our food, Stefko would be our accountant, and I would be in charge of program.

George, Mickey, and I (we continuously argued about who among us was the best skier) would also be the ski instructors.

Just to add a little credibility, and to pacify the parents of the young girls we were hoping to attract from out of town, we asked a slightly older scout—a "Burlak" from Cleveland with a solid reputation (unlike us)—to be the camp leader.

During the early 1960s, the ski season didn't really start in Quebec until after New Year's Day. Snow making machines were not common and most skiers waited until January when good snow conditions were guaranteed. Hotels in the Laurentians had vacancies and offered lower rates during Christmas Week. (How different it is today.)

We decided to start our camp on December 24, and to end it before the prices went up on January 1. This way, we could end the camp with a great New Year's Eve Party.

In Canada, most Ukrainians celebrate Christmas according to the old Julian calendar, on January 7, and even though Ukrainian parishes in the United States had switched to the new calendar and celebrated Christmas on December 25, we five Montréalers were young and arrogant and reasoned that if they really wanted to come to our camp, the Americans would simply have to move their Christmas celebrations!

Over the years, these ski camps in Montreal had developed such a great reputation and were so popular that the usually overprotective Ukrainian parents in the United States were prepared to send their sons and daughters miles away to Canada (a country most had never visited), and would even rearrange Christmas just so that the children could be part of this event.

At six o'clock in the morning on December 24, 1965, George, Mickey, Bobby, Stefko, and I were at the downtown Montreal bus station waiting to meet the overnight bus from New York. The Philadelphia crowd had boarded their bus at six o'clock the previous evening; they switched buses in New York and from there, traveled overnight to Montreal. There was great anticipation and much celebrating on these bus rides. (Someone always managed to bring some special Christmas cheer.)

There was also great anticipation in Montreal as we waited for the New York bus to arrive. We were about to see friends we hadn't seen for a long time, and, this year, there were several new people coming to our camp. Regulars like Orest, Omelan, and Marta were coming, as were perhaps a dozen others who had been to these camps in previous years.

Among the new people registered for our camp was Marta's cousin. Omelan wrote to tell me Marta's cousin was coming . . . *and* he mentioned that she was really good-looking! (For some reason, I forgot to pass that message on to my buddies.)

## HAPPILY EVER AFTER

As they got off the bus, we met our visitors with hugs and kisses, songs, and lots of loud greetings.

In the midst of our celebrations, out of the corner of my eye, I noticed someone getting off the bus that I didn't recognize.

She was the most beautiful woman I had ever seen, the 'girl of my dreams', in a baby-blue ski jacket.

I felt light-headed, I could hear nothing, and my peripheral vision was gone. All I could see was this gorgeous girl, with her big blue eyes, stepping off the bus. I had never felt quite this way before.

I whispered a silent prayer. "Please God, let this be Marta's cousin—or at least, let her be one of our campers."

I approached her, welcomed her to Quebec, and gave her a hug. She hugged me back. I got up all my courage and kissed her. She may have been in shock after the long trip, but I swear she kissed me back. I asked her name. She said, "Chrystyna Tatomyr."

My prayers were answered.

I didn't want to lose her. I had the presence of mind, just in case one of my buddies would try to steal her, to go over to Mickey and George to tell them that this year I would instruct the *Beginners*. The two of them could fight over who would instruct the *Intermediate* and *Advanced* skiers.

If there is such a thing as love at first sight, this was definitely it.

We held a special Christmas Eve dinner the first night at our camp for our American friends since they were missing this very important holiday with their families. After dinner, we held a mixer dance in the hotel dining room. I approached Chrystyna. We sat on the stairs and talked for a long time. I found out that she too was a first year teacher, that we were born a month apart, and that during our early years we had fairly similar experiences.

She asked me to dance. I said I couldn't since my father had died just four months earlier and I was still in mourning. I thought she would go off to have fun with someone else. Instead she said, "Let's go for a walk."

The Laurentians in winter are as beautiful and romantic as any place on earth. The night was clear, the stars were out, and it was cold. The snow crunched below our feet. As we walked down the snow covered back road near the inn, a speeding car came around the corner towards us. I decided to take another bold move. I "saved" Chrystyna by pushing her into the snow bank and falling on her. After the car passed, I tried to convince her that we were safe only because of my heroic actions.

She reacted with a sense of humor and wit. She was not only beautiful, but also intelligent, sensitive and fun.

The next day, we divided all the campers into three groups according to their skiing ability. Chrystyna joined my *Beginners* group. When the formal instruction time ended, I asked her to stay behind for extra instructions.

After two days, I told my buddies that I was going to marry this girl. I was so sure of my feelings. They, of course, didn't believe me and told me to get over it.

This was, for me, the best ski camp ever. The New Years Eve party was memorable and the next day, before our Philadelphia friends left, I brought Chrystyna home to meet my mother. She was the first and only girl I had ever brought home.

As she was getting on the bus for home, Chrystyna asked me to be her date at the annual Engineers Ball held every January in Philadelphia. I, of course, said yes.

In return, I asked Chrystyna to come up for the Quebec Winter Carnival in March. She did. By this time we both knew that we were experiencing something special.

When she returned to her school in Philadelphia, Chrystyna had a hard time with her teacher friends. She told them she met a ski instructor in Canada and was in love. They tried to tell her that *everybody* falls in love with their ski instructor and tried to convince her to be more realistic.

I'm glad she didn't listen to them.

Four years after we met at the Montreal bus station, almost to the day, on December 27, 1969, with both our families and quite a few guests from that year's ski camp in attendance, we were married in Montreal at St. Michael's Church and held our reception at the brand new La Steppe Restaurant. Although Montreal was experiencing a record-breaking snowstorm, all 150 of our guests made it to the reception . . . . eventually.

We ended that fabulous decade on our honeymoon, in Mont Tremblant, with a number of our skiing friends, in particular, Marta and Omelan.

*     *     *

It's been more than forty years since the day we met, and the magic is still there. Chrystyna and I have a wonderful life together, had exciting and fulfilling teaching careers, traveled the world, and raised two wonderful sons who married wonderful women who gave us gorgeous grandchildren.

Now, whenever I read stories to our grandchildren and we come to the part, "and they lived happily ever after," I always read the lines with complete conviction.

I know it really *can* happen.

**Engineer's Ball, Philadelphia, 1966**
**A beautiful woman, a rye and ginger, and a ciggy.**
**Twenty-two and in love.**

# Part Eight

# The Littlest Exiles

## *The Littlest Exiles*

Below the radar of history, children consciously or subconsciously amass vivid memories of their war experiences . . .

Children can survive without comforts—they are amazingly adaptable . . . but the children will bear their war memories inside themselves into exile . . . they will carry the burdens of ethnicities, history, violence and politics, hunger and poverty, the past, present and future into adulthood . . .

Children manage the minefields of peace and recovery from trauma of war in radically different ways. Some engage directly with memories, some never think about them and others repress and avoid the war memories they carry with them.

As these children become adults and parents, they will work toward a society where opportunities will abound for their children and the next generation will, hopefully, inherit peace as their heritage.

> To all parents, alive or dead,
> who tried against the odds to protect us[*]

Members of our closest families, who came to North America after the Second World War, had among them a few "Littlest Exiles."

In addition to Chrystyna and me, the children who were born in Europe and came to North America from our families are:

**Roman Melnyk, Marta Tatomyr, Daria and Oksana Stulkowsky, Christine and Roman Mychalewsky, Tania Boyko, Omelan Lukasewycz and Roman Horodysky.**

Technically, we are *first* generation Canadians or Americans, but our parents are also first generation, and our younger brothers and sisters who were born in North America are considered *second* generation Canadians and Americans.

Do we classify these "Eleven Littlest Exiles" as Generation One and a Half?

These littlest exiles married and had children, (Generation 3), and some of these children have married and have had children of their own, (Generation 4).

To continue this history, I have asked the people who are in our generation (line 5 on the Melnyk and Tatomyr family trees at the start of the book) to write a little about themselves in a hope that one of several things may happen:

---

[*]    London, Charles. *One Day the Soldiers Came: Voices of Children in War.* NY Press: Harper Collins Publishers, 2007.

- Each writer will bring a unique perspective and recollections of his or her war experiences.
- Some of these writers will be inspired to write their own book for future generations or
- Someone from Generation six or seven will be inspired to pick up the torch that has already been lit.

**The people who have written their stories and are included here are the following:**

- Chrystyna Tatomyr-Melnyk

**Our brothers and sisters and their spouses:**

- Roman Melnyk and Tania Boyko-Melnyk—Toronto
- Ostap Tatomyr and Christina Holubinsky-Tatomyr—Toronto
- Lesya Tatomyr-Horodysky and Roman Horodysky—Bordentown, NJ

**Our American cousins and their spouses:**

- Marta Tatomyr-Lukasewycz and Omelan Lukasewycz—Duluth, MN
- Daria Stulkowsky-Kulchycky—Philadelphia
- Oksana Stulkowsky-Winstead and Ricord Winstead—Seattle
- Christine Mychalewsky—Bak-Boychuk—Philadelphia
- Roman Mychalewsky—Philadelphia

# Chrystyna Tatomyr-Melnyk

Of the three children of Oleksander and Sophia Tatomyr, I was the only one who was born in Ukraine, survived World War II, and entered the United States as a refugee. The five years following my birth on January 28, 1944, are best described in my grandfather's diary—periods of great danger and fear followed by periods of relative normalcy and tranquility.

For my cousin, Marta, and I, the sound of air raid sirens were often the "lullabies" to which we fell asleep at night. When we were lucky, a "gasthaus" would be our shelter at night, but mostly we slept in barns, bombed out buildings, underground bomb shelters, and the great outdoors. As we passed from village to village, there were times that there was "no room at the inn." As infants, Marta and I were fortunate that we remained healthy in spite of having to sleep outdoors on wintry or rainy nights. These circumstances, more or less, were the beginning of our formative years.

And what of childhood memories? It is difficult to anticipate which memories a "war baby" will absorb over an intense period of five years. My war memories in vivid images start at the age of two years.

- being in an underground cave with many, many people . . . hearing the horrific sounds of exploding bombs, droning bombers, pealing sirens, and crying babies
- living in a tiny two-room house on stilts in Sankt Georgen, Austria, and having to navigate dozens of steep steps to reach the front door. Playing with my cousin, Marta, my strong will surfaced at an early age—I always had to be the first one up the steps. "*Issya persha*" (Chrissy first), I would inform my patient cousin
- frolicking joyfully with my cousin in the meadows and pastures of Austria and, on one occasion, running faster and faster as we were chased by a herd of stampeding cattle, or maybe it was just one cow
- intently observing the inmates of the sanatorium in Sankt Georgen on their daily walks and being riveted by their appearance, odd gait, and bizarre mannerisms;
- moving to a DP camp somewhere in Germany prior to our resettlement to the United States, and getting lost amongst the barracks (they all looked the same)—a long period of time passed before my father found me;

- traveling in a very crowded train to somewhere (probably to Bremen) at eye level with a growling German shepherd.

From early childhood in the United States, I would become anxious when aircraft flew overhead, I disliked all types of dogs (particularly, German Shepherds), didn't like crowded places (like elevators), and became uncomfortable if I lost my way to a destination. I also devoted my career to working with special needs children for thirty years. Somehow, these feelings and decisions appeared to be related to my earlier, vivid, imprints during the war.

When I was four years old, we boarded the *Marine Tiger* in the Port of Bremen, steerage class, to make the voyage to New York City. This ship was built to transport soldiers, but when the war ended, it was converted to carry refugees on their voyage to America.

Most of the adults were very ill during the rough crossing, while my cousin and I chased each other on deck, annoying the exhausted refugees who had managed to struggle upstairs to find some fresh air—I accidentally stepped on someone's head and the person reacted by grabbing my leg in irritation. Screaming at the top of my lungs brought my father on deck to save me.

As young children, we did not understand where the ship was taking us, but then one evening, all the refugees from steerage climbed "on deck," scrubbed, and dressed in their Sunday clothes, as the ship approached the harbor of New York City.

There was silence as the ship glided past the immense Statue of Liberty and headed to Ellis Island. There was concern among the adults about being retained or rejected at Customs. I have no memories of Ellis Island or the trip to Philadelphia, but I do remember the Statue of Liberty. Unfortunately, I also do not remember the names of the people who sponsored us and gave us the opportunity to live in a free country. At this point, the process of integration and "culture shock" was about to begin for the refugees.

When we arrived in Philadelphia in May 1949, it was hot and humid. We shared one stifling room with several of our relatives for a short period of time. Soon, my father, mother, and I moved to a tenement on Second Street in South Philadelphia. That apartment was also stifling. I spent most of my time outside playing on the hot, concrete pavements with other children and cooling off in the icy water spraying from fire hydrants. On weekends, our family and other refugee families gathered in Fairmount Park near the Schuylkill River.

My father worked long hours at a butcher shop and would return home with his apron covered in blood. In the little time he had left in the evening, my father studied English and took courses.

I was very excited to enter kindergarten.

I loved school, but my idyllic life fell apart in October of my first year of school when I was the only one to arrive without a Halloween costume. After many anguished tears, my teacher improvised a costume for me and I felt less alien. It is interesting what one remembers.

The most dramatic memory of my life in Philadelphia was the night I was brought home in a police car in Grade 1. A friend and I decided to take a scenic tour of Philadelphia after school. As dusk descended and my parents became increasingly more frantic, they called the police. A long lecture followed, not once but twice, by the police and then my parents. The police were much more understanding and gentle than were my parents.

My greatest treat in Philadelphia was going to the Saturday afternoon matinees with my father. He loved the cinema, the silent movies, the old movie stars. My father passed on his love of movies to me, and I haven't missed an Academy Award show since I was eight years old.

My brother, Ostap, was born on March 3, 1951, and I was very happy to have a baby brother to take care of and baby-sit. He was a beautiful baby with huge eyes and curly brown hair. He had a gentle nature that endeared him to everyone.

My younger sister, Lesya, was born when I was nine years old. Like Ostap, she also resembled my mother's side of the family, the Tereshkevycz's. Since there was such a large age gap between us, and because I left for university when Lesya was just seven years old, we did not bond until we got older. With the death of our grandmother, father, mother, and brother, we comforted and supported each other during our losses. Her kindness and love of family is legendary.

Just before I entered Grade 2, our family moved out of the heat, pollution, and traffic of Philadelphia to the tiny hamlet of Edgely, near Bristol, Pennsylvania, where my cousin, Marta, had moved several months earlier. My mother had lived at the base of the Carpathian Mountains, and this new setting made her much happier. We had bought the tiniest house in existence (four small rooms and an unfinished basement). Years later, my sons visited this home as adults and could not believe that a family of four could have lived in such a small space.

School was my favorite activity. I enjoyed every aspect of learning and received straight As. I loved to read. Since our house was very small, I would read in the dark so as not to awaken anyone. The first book I read in Grade 4 was *Gone With the Wind*—all one thousand pages. I fell in love with Rhett Butler and spent the better part of my early life searching for him. Eventually I found him in the Laurentians. His name wasn't Rhett but Andrij had many characteristics of my childhood prince. I still have that original book. It is now very old and I am saving it for my oldest granddaughter, Anya, who is looking for her own prince.

I enjoyed my friends in school. My parents told me to be friends with everyone, but that dating was only permissible with Ukrainians. I think my parents were worried about rapid assimilation and loss of our native language, but I was highly incensed by the unfairness of their decision.

Outside of school, I was active in Ukrainian social life, attending Ukrainian school and dance classes on Saturday mornings, Plast (girl scouts) on Saturday afternoons, and violin (which I hated) on Saturday nights. One Saturday morning, I went "on strike," refusing to go to all of these activities while my American friends enjoyed leisure time. I told my parents I was suffering from hurried "child syndrome." Unimpressed with my self-diagnosis, my parents curtailed my personal activism, and I resumed my busy Saturday schedule. Summers were spent at Plast camp in East Chatham, New York. I really enjoyed this annual summer camp for its stimulating program, athletics and the handsome boys.

In secondary school, I was usually at the top of my class in academics. I participated in gymnastics, track and field, and baseball, but my parents did not give me permission to join the cheerleading squad because the skirts were too short and the movements were too provocative from their point of view. It's understandable that my perspective was somewhat different from theirs. All my arguments fell on deaf ears.

University spelled F-R-E-E-D-O-M for me. Although I managed to maintain good grades, I majored in dating. It is unforgivable that I lost a four-year scholarship because I did not maintain the required A average. My parents were so concerned about my metamorphosis that they considered putting me on the restricted list (in the dorm by 8 p.m.). Since I told my parents that I would be humiliated beyond words by this decision, they reluctantly relented. In my last year of university, I excelled in student teaching. I graduated from West Chester University in 1965 with a Bachelor of Science in Education and obtained a teaching job near my home with the local school board. Those were golden years in teaching—I had a wonderful offer to teach Grade 6 in Paoli, Pennsylvania but my parents put a lot of pressure on me to live at home. Reluctantly, I agreed to their demands.

That Christmas, I joined the Philadelphia Plast group going to ski camp in the Laurentians in Quebec. It was there that I fell madly in love with my future husband, Andrij. He was intelligent, handsome, witty, outrageous, and athletic, and happened to be my ski instructor. We were married December 27, 1969, in Montreal during the biggest blizzard in the province for years. Despite road closures and treacherous driving conditions, all our guests eventually arrived at the reception. We had a wonderful Ukrainian wedding, dancing until five o'clock in the morning, accompanied by the music of the most popular Ukrainian singing group in North America at that time, *Rushnychok*. We honeymooned at Mont Tremblant with a number of our friends.

**Chrystyna with her ski instructor.**
**Mont Tremblant, December, 1965**

Our oldest son, Markian, was born in Montreal on December 18, 1970 and the following year we moved to Toronto. Two years later, we moved to Barrie, Ontario, where our younger son, Roman, was born on March 16, 1974. Although we loved our life in Barrie on Lake Simcoe, and even bought a sailboat, our teaching jobs were too far from our home. We moved closer to Toronto, to Newmarket, where we've lived ever since.

Like all the other boys in town, our sons wanted to grow up to play hockey in the NHL. Luckily, our sons were excellent students, and when the NHL failed to call them, they continued their academic studies.

Mark graduated from Carleton University and McGill University with a degree in education. Later, he completed his master's degree at the University of British Columbia. Presently, he is the History department head at a large high school in Markham, Ontario. In 2005, he won the prestigious Governor General's Award for Excellence in the Teaching of History and was honored at a great reception in Ottawa, hosted by the governor general, Adrienne Clarkson.

Roman completed McMaster University and the University of Toronto, where he obtained a PhD in biochemistry. He completed his postdoctoral work at Harvard University and is presently doing leading-edge research at a pharmaceutical company in Montreal.

I loved research, and after I obtained my master's degree in special education at the University of Toronto, I was encouraged to continue my studies toward my doctorate, but I had to accept that I was not a superwoman. As a wife and mother working full-time, it was difficult to do postgraduate work with young children. I became a consultant in special education for a number of years in the Woodbridge area, where I was responsible for servicing special needs students in fourteen schools and supervising sixty resource staff. At that time, I was also invited to become a member of the Phi Delta Kappa society, an international association for teachers.

After thirty years of teaching, I retired and became a professional artist. I was fortunate to have had success in the field and participated in individual and group shows. I won a number of awards in juried shows and was chosen to show my work, along with other artists, at McMichael Canadian Collection Gallery in Kleinburg, Ontario.

**Art Exhibit, 1999**
**Displaying the "Millenium Series."**

In 2000, my husband retired from his board when he was offered a position as principal at an international school in Madrid, Spain. I was offered a position of special education teacher in the same school. We enjoyed every minute of our overseas placement, and after two years, moved on to work in schools in Trinidad, Tokyo and Cairo.

Our son, Markian, married Kristine Chandler in 2001, and Roman married Tammy Jones in 2005. Presently, we are proud grandparents of three princesses: Anya, Ava, and Julia. Their lives are so unlike our lives as refugees and we thank God for that.

When my husband and I were teaching in Egypt, our oldest granddaughter, Anya, at the age of three, and her mother, Kristine, came to visit us. Among other adventures, we took a cruise together down the Nile River. I remembered our voyage on the *Marine Tiger* sixty-three years earlier. It took that long to get promoted from steerage to first class!

In retrospect, it is hard to believe that my parents, on one salary, managed to put three children through university. Even though we all worked every summer, they still had to make great sacrifices to give us the opportunity to have a good education. In Ukraine, my father had been a principal of an agricultural school, had completed his theological studies, and could have become a priest. Here, my father worked on an assembly line at General Motors.

When I grew older, I asked my father how he coped on a daily basis with mindless, repetitive piece-work. My father smiled and said that these were the best of times because his body had to be alert and present on his job, but his mind was free to take wing, to return to his homeland, to develop ideas for articles and journals. My father was a "realist-idealist," he dreamed great dreams but he did what he had to do to provide for his family.

As my father approached retirement, his dream was to enjoy life with my mother and do some traveling. Unfortunately, my mother died in 1983 at the age of sixty-seven of a massive heart attack and my father died four years later after suffering a heart attack in his sleep. During his last four years without his beloved Sonia, he spent time with his children and grandchildren in Toronto and New Jersey. He never recovered from the sudden death of my mother—my parents were like lovebirds in their marriage, and lovebirds always travel in pairs.

My parents and grandparents had traveled a hard road, experienced the challenges of culture shock and integration and, to some degree, had suffered from posttraumatic stress, yet they managed to build a new life for themselves in an unfamiliar land and create a happy home for their children and grandchildren. For that, we are eternally grateful.

**Proud mom with son, Markian, at his graduation.**
**Carleton University, Ottawa, 1992**

**Proud mom with son, Doctor Roman A. Melnyk**
**Harvard University, Boston, 2004**

# Roman Peter Melnyk

I was born in my grandfather's mill in Ladychyn on July 5, 1941.

Two weeks before, on June 22, 1941, Germany launched Operation Barbarossa, the invasion of the Soviet Union, and the German army was moving eastward rapidly. On June 30, 1941, Ukrainian nationalists in Lviv proclaimed the formation of an independent Ukraine. For a brief, glorious period, Ukrainian flags were flying in towns and villages in Halychyna (Galicia).

My father, Bohdan, and my mother, Bronyslawa, were living in the town of Pidhaijci, where my father was employed with the Ukrainian cooperative. As my mother was close to giving birth, they were anxious to get her to a safer place, either with her family in Ivanivka or my father's family in Ladychyn. As fate would have it, the Melnyk homestead was to be the venue.

My parents lived in Pidhaijci for the next two and a half years. As the fortunes of war turned, the Soviet Army beat back the German forces and was proceeding westward. It was clear that it was not safe to remain in the path of this advance. In our little family, it was particularly precarious as my brother, Andrij, was just born on February 28, 1944. Eleven days later, on March 10, 1944, along with other members of our family and coworkers, we set out on an unknown journey that would last over five years until our arrival and settlement in Canada.

The entire journey was later chronicled by my mother in a letter to her grandchildren. There were brief stops in Stryj and Gorlice (where we were welcomed by the Boyko family) and longer stays in Walda, Kulmbach, and Bayreuth, until we were settled in the displaced persons camp in Regensburg in 1947. This was one of the largest camps in the American zone and had established rather good community facilities. It was here that I started kindergarten and completed the first two elementary grades in school.

Because my mother had relatives living in Canada—her cousins of the Martyniuk family—Canada was the settlement destination of choice. Finally, we embarked on our ocean journey on the SS *Samaria* and arrived in Quebec City on August 15, 1949. We proceeded to Montreal . . . and a whole new world. I was eight years old.

Montreal of that period was a great place to grow up. It was still the biggest city in the country, a multilingual and multicultural society, before these concepts were defined, with a majority French Canadian Catholic population, dominant Anglo-Scot economic elite, a vibrant Jewish community, and growing ethnic groups. The city was experiencing a postwar transformation that would take it through the Quiet Revolution, the Quebec separatist movement, and the redefinition of the face of the Province.

Our family settled first in the Hochelaga district of Montreal. The predominant population was French Canadian, but immigrants had settled there for some years. A Ukrainian Catholic church, St. Michael's, had been established in the area as early as 1911. This area now attracted quite a number of new immigrant families. We attended the local French Catholic school, St. Anselm, but, curiously, in a separate English-language wing. We soon became altar boys at St. Michael's and later joined the Ukrainian Catholic Youth. And we had an added bonus: the Parish owned a wonderful property in the Laurentians, "Camp Ukraina," and we quickly developed an entitlement to it.

We were always active in Plast. We went off to summer camps at "Baturyn" in the Eastern Townships and ski camps in the Laurentians. We went off to jamborees in Canada, the United States, and Europe and created a formidable network of friendships that have lasted all these years. For some years, we played soccer with S.T. Ukraina in Montreal, winning the city juvenile championship in 1958.

In 1954, I enrolled at Cardinal Newman High School. It was an exciting time. We were encouraged to succeed academically by our teachers and our parents. As a sizable all-boys school, we had football and soccer teams that won city championships and provided us with bragging rights. I graduated in 1958 and, under an existing option, did "fifth year" for university credits.

The next step was McGill University. I chose political science and economics as my major subjects and graduated in 1962 with a bachelor of arts (honours) degree. My years at McGill provided a window to a broader world. In the winter of my senior year, I wrote the Canadian Foreign Service Exams along with hundreds of other hopefuls. As fate would have it, in the spring of 1962, I was advised that I was one of the successful applicants and the course of my life set off in a new direction.

I left Montreal in May 1962 for a training period in Ottawa and a cross-Canada tour. After a year, I was given my first posting with the Canadian Embassy Visa Office in Cologne, West Germany. On August 16, 1963, (exactly fourteen years after my arrival in Montreal), I sailed for Europe.

It was a great time to be in Germany, which was undergoing its Economic Miracle. Because I was single and mobile, I was a useful officer for temporary assignments in Hamburg, Stockholm, and Helsinki. After a year, I was appointed officer-in-charge of the Visa Office in Stuttgart. I was twenty-three years old.

This could only happen in Canada.

In the summer of 1965, I was in Paris on a holiday trip and, through a series of chance encounters, met a bright young lady from Toronto named Tania Boyko, who was in Paris for the summer on a student exchange. We had a drink at the Café de la Paix, she continued on her journey and I on mine. But it was a fateful encounter because a year later, after she returned home to Toronto and I found myself in Toronto to study law, we met again and our destiny was sealed.

In mid-August 1965, I received a telegram from home that my father was very sick and close to dying. I returned to Montreal and had some time with him before he died on September 3, 1965. I had applied for educational leave to do a Master of Arts degree in public administration at Carleton University in Ottawa. It was there that I decided that I wanted to go to law school. I completed one more assignment for the government, a trip that took me to the Caribbean and South America. Then it was back to school.

For the next three years, I attended the University of Toronto Faculty of Law graduating in 1969. This was followed by an "articling period" with the law firm of Gardiner, Roberts, the Bar Admission Course, and, finally, the Call to the Bar in 1971.

But, more significantly, Tania and I had rekindled our "brief encounter" in Europe and this blossomed into our marriage in Toronto on June 6, 1970, our own special D-Day. We first settled on Claxton Blvd. in Toronto, Tania worked for the Government of Ontario and I started practicing law with the firm of Gardiner, Roberts on Bay Street. We were soon blessed with our first daughter, Marichka, who was born on November 6, 1970.

By sheer chance, I noticed an ad placed by the Canadian Broadcasting Corporation (CBC) looking for lawyers. I replied and was offered a position as legal counsel. I accepted. This small event went on to define my working life and career.

We first moved to Ottawa in the fall of 1971. Tania took a position with the federal government and we developed ties to the community. Our daughter, Melanie, was born on August 22, 1974. We were to spend eight years in Ottawa, which was a great place for our little girls to grow up, and we remember it with great fondness.

The next major step occurred in 1979. I had an opportunity to return to Toronto as senior legal counsel of the CBC, Tania was ready for a change, and we felt that Marichka and Melia would benefit from the larger Ukrainian community in Toronto. We bought a house at 169 Princess Anne Crescent on a flying visit from Ottawa. We moved in August, 1979 and this was to remain our home to this day, thirty years later.

Tania rejoined the Government of Ontario, Marichka and Melia enrolled at the nearby St. Demetrius School and later continued at St. Joseph / Michael Power High School in our borough of Etobicoke.

In early 1980, a seemingly casual conversation led to a significant change of direction for me. I was offered the opportunity to establish the Department of Independent Production at CBC. This meant that I would leave the law department and get involved in television programming.

This was an exciting prospect and I embarked on this new direction on April 1, 1980. It was a stimulating period during which an amazing amount of original television programming was produced by a host of creative young producers. Among these was the classic Canadian miniseries *Anne of Green Gables*; the comedy series *SCTV*, with the improbable breakout success of Bob and Doug Mackenzie in the "Great White North"; and the short film *Boys and Girls*, which went on to win the Oscar at the Academy Awards in 1984.

In 1984, I moved on to the position of TV network programme director and in 1989 to director of network television. The CBC was always reorganizing and changing. By 1993, it was time to seek other alternatives. So, in September 1993, I "went private" as executive vice president of William F. Cooke Television, which was involved in the distribution and production of television programmes. Things turned again in 1996 when I was offered the position of vice president for business affairs at CTV, which was then expanding quite rapidly. I spent five years there, before retiring in 2001.

With that work backdrop, life in Toronto proceeded apace. Both Marichka and Melia were involved in Plast with its various activities, summer and winter camps, and jamborees. They each went off to Queen's University in Kingston and each returned to Toronto for postgraduate studies. Tania and Marichka were also involved with Help Us Help the Children and traveled to the summer camps for orphan children in Ukraine.

I was invited to the board of St. Demetrius Development Corporation, which ran the Seniors' Residence (where my mother lived from 1981 to 2004) and which was embarking on the building of a nursing home. I was president of the corporation for four years. We were also involved in a number of Ukrainian community organizations, some of which provided us opportunities to return to Ukraine. Tania and I were in Ukraine in September to October 1989, when Tania coordinated an Ontario Trade Mission. I traveled there later as an advisor on television projects and hosted an internship program for Ukrainian journalists in Canada. I was in Kyiv for the Orange Revolution as an election monitor in December, 2004.

In 2002, Tania and I decided to do an unencumbered trip to Ukraine and Poland to visit some of the places of our lives' journey. We visited Gorlice, where we had stayed with the Boyko family in 1944, and where my cousin, Daria Stulkowsky, was born, and where Tania was intended to be born. We visited Pidhaijci, where our family lived and my brother was born, and where Tania's family had lived. We drove through Ternopil, where my parents had gone to school, and on to Ladychyn, the Melnyk homestead. We stopped by the small river, just over the bridge. This was where my grandfather's mill once stood, on this pastoral river bank, filled with geese bickering in the sun of a summer afternoon.

Up the road, on a hill, is the village church where I was baptized. In the cemetery behind the church, is the Melnyk family burial plot, with a large monument of red sandstone. There are no more Melnyks left in Ladychyn, and the progeny are scattered far and wide.

In the circle of life, Melia married John Stetic on September 30, 2000. On July 30, 2004, their son Will (Vasylko) was born, and on July 11, 2007, their little girl, Katya, was born. I now have the proud title of *Dziadzio* (grandfather).

**Vasylko (Will) with proud Grandpa Roman
Toronto, 2008**

**Etobicoke Melnyks
Marichka, Melanie, Tania, Roman
Melanie and John Stetic's Wedding, September, 2000.**

# Tania Boyko Melnyk

I came into this world in a coal car on a moving train traveling through Eastern Europe towards Vienna. The date was July 30, 1944. The train, moving westward just ahead of the advancing Soviet armies, was carrying the remnants of my immediate family who had managed to survive the Second World War: my father, Osyp Boyko, a lawyer; my very, very pregnant mother, Halyna Spunder Boyko; my maternal grandmother, Anna Gellhorn Spunder; my maiden aunt, Lucia Spunder; and my uncle, the Rev. Myron Holowinsky, a widower who had been married briefly to another aunt, Olha Spunder.

As related to me by my aunt and grandmother, because the train was unable to stop, I was bathed initially in melted butter and subsequently in water that my father was able to collect from the dripping train engine when the train made a brief stop to refuel. With my aunt Lucia as my godmother, I was christened quickly by my uncle Myron when we reached Vienna.

In Vienna, my mother and I were taken to a hospital. My uncle found lodging at St. Barbara's Ukrainian Catholic Church. My father was left to take care of my aunt and grandmother (and eventually my mother and me). Somehow, he managed to connect with an Austrian gentleman named Althausen, who had a small textile factory in a town near Salzburg called Zell am See. Herr Althausen offered my father a position managing his factory and we all moved to Zell am See where we lived for the next four years.

The town was located on a lake in the Alps near a number of displaced persons camps, allowing for active contacts with other refugee families of Ukrainian background, including the Tatomyr and Melnyk families.

In 1947-48, as the Berlin Crisis/ Airlift was getting under way, my family became convinced that another war was imminent in Europe and applied for emigration to Canada. Luckily for us, we were all accepted

My aunt Lucia left first, in early 1948, for employment as a hospital worker in a TB sanatorium in what was then the town of Weston, just outside of Toronto. My parents and I followed in the summer of 1948 on a converted freighter, "The Beaver Brae." After a harrowing trip full of nausea and sea sickness, we arrived in Canada on July 18, 1948 and settled in Toronto. My grandmother stayed on in Austria and joined our family in Toronto six months later.

At first, my parents, my grandmother, and I lived in an attic apartment at 90 Dewson Avenue. In 1949, we bought a newly constructed house at 422 Salem Avenue where my aunt Lucia also joined us. While my parents and aunt went to work, my grandmother looked after me until I was old enough to go to St. Clement's (now St. Mary of the Angels) School.

My mother and aunt worked in the garment industry and my grandmother helped out as best she could by doing some decorative beading at home. After a brief stint as a worker in an oven factory, my father found a position with the Ukrainian Catholic Eparchy of Eastern Canada under the newly appointed young Bishop Isidore Borecky. Then, after two years with the eparchy, my father secured his license to sell real estate, a field in which he was employed for the rest of his life: first as a partner in J.J. Ellis Real Estate and later as sole proprietor of J. Boyko Real Estate.

After a year or so on Salem Avenue, we moved in the late 1950s, to 11 Nairn Avenue, where I attended St. Clare's School for grades 2 and 3. As our fortunes improved, we moved again in January 1952, to a fine home at 62 High Park Boulevard. I lived there for the next eighteen years.

My grandmother developed gangrene shortly after our last move and passed away on February 2, 1952. My Aunt Lucia lived with us for a few more years before buying her own home nearby.

While at High Park Boulevard, I attended St. Vincent de Paul School (1953-57), later St. Joseph's High School (1957-62), and then the University of Toronto (1962-66).

My life changed significantly in 1957 with the confluence of three major events.

On August 19, 1957, shortly after my thirteenth birthday, my mother gave birth to my sister, Dana. I graduated from St. Vincent's and went on to St. Joseph's High School, and I joined PLAST, a Ukrainian Scouting Organization.

All of these events had a large impact on my life. Suddenly, I was no longer the center of my parents' attention and was able to move about more freely without their close scrutiny. My high school, though a relatively small convent school of some 600 girls, offered the opportunity to meet a peer group of interesting girls from other parts of the city. And, perhaps most importantly, PLAST brought me into the centre of the Ukrainian community in Toronto. I now had a wide circle of friends, male and female, with whom I was able to bond in a very special way and, in the process, have a lot of fun.

In 1962, I graduated from St. Joseph's and went on to the University of Toronto (U of T). That summer, I spent two months in Lausanne, Switzerland, studying French at the University of Lausanne. At the University of Toronto, I majored in political science and economics, graduating in 1966 with a Bachelor of Arts (Honours) degree.

In 1965, a year before graduating, I again had an opportunity to spend a summer in Europe, this time in Paris, working at the Galeries Lafayette as an *hotesse-interprete* (hostess-interpreter). 1965 proved to be a watershed year in my life. I have often felt that I found my soul that summer in Paris, and, in the process, also my fate in the person of one Roman Peter Melnyk, eldest son of the same Melnyks that had crossed paths with my family in Gorlice in 1944. Roman had been posted in Germany with the Canadian

Foreign Service and was passing through Paris on a holiday. Although we did not marry for another five years, the die was pretty well cast that June day in Paris over a glass of wine at the Café de la Paix.

Roman moved to Toronto in 1966 to study Law at U of T and I, having graduated, found myself happily ensconced in a career with the Province of Ontario. We were married on June 6 (the anniversary of D-Day) 1970.

After a year and a half of married life in Toronto, and the birth of our daughter Marichka, we moved to Ottawa. In late 1971, Roman was hired by the legal department of the Canadian Broadcasting Corporation (CBC) headquartered in Ottawa. Having discovered that I was not happy as a stay-at-home mom, I went back to work with the Federal Civil Service, initially with the treasury board and later at the Department of Finance.

Our eight years in Ottawa allowed us to put down roots as a family. We started out by renting a townhouse on the Rideau River at 20 Marco Lane—a lovely home, except for the fact that it tended to get flooded every spring by the swelling Rideau. We quickly realized that rowing to our front door was not how we wanted to live, and bought a townhouse—our first property—at 3328 Southgate Road in South Keys Village. Our second daughter Melanie (Melia) was born there in 1974. Space soon became an issue so we rented out our townhouse to a coworker and bought a second property just two blocks away at 1344 Pebble Place. During those years in Ottawa, we became close with a number of young families in much the same situation as we—most originally from Toronto, Montreal, or Winnipeg. It was busy but happy times, during which, close relationships were formed that are sustained to this day.

In 1977 I was given the opportunity of a lifetime with the Department of Finance as assistant director, international programs—a job that involved developing Canada's policy and relationships with the International Development Banks (the World Bank, Inter-American, Asian, and African Banks). This job took me to virtually every corner of the world. At about the same time, Roman was asked to set up an office of the CBC's legal branch in Toronto, a job that required him to be in Toronto four days a week! Needless to say, maximum flexibility was required, but somehow we did it—thanks largely to some excellent babysitters and two wonderful little girls, Marichka and Melia, who rolled easily with anything that came their way.

However, by the middle of 1979, it was becoming clear that this situation could not be sustained indefinitely. My job, great though it was, was taking more time away from my family than I was prepared to give.

In late 1979, with Roman being offered a position in Toronto, I took a one-year leave of absence from the federal government and we moved back to Toronto.

We bought a home at 169 Princess Anne Crescent in the west end of Toronto. It has remained our home for the past twenty-nine years.

Our return to Toronto allowed us to be reunited again with my family and with Roman's brother, Andrew and his family (his wife Chrystyna and their two boys, Markian and Roman, who lived nearby in Newmarket).

When my leave of absence was up, I returned to work fulltime with the Province of Ontario. Unfortunately our reunification with my family proved to be short-lived. My father, mother, and Aunt Lucia, by now in their 70s, were ailing. My father passed away in 1982 of heart failure and my aunt and my mother in 1983 and 1984, respectively, both as a result of complications from a stroke. These were very difficult years. Our girls were both very much involved in their schooling at St. Demetrius and in Plast and Ukrainian school. I was trying to reestablish my interrupted career and Roman was developing a new career as director of independent production at the CBC.

By the late 1980s, our lives began to settle down. I was busily involved in economic development with the Ministry of Industry Trade and Technology, Roman was advancing his career in programming at the CBC, and the girls were quickly working through their studies in St. Joseph's/Michael Power High School (my old alma mater).

By the early 1990s, Marichka had moved on to Queen's University with Melanie not far behind. I became director of community development with the Ministry of Municipal Affairs and Roman, after twenty-two years, left the CBC to work in the private sector.

In 1997, after thirty years of employment, I became eligible for early retirement. I left my job to launch the most recent and fulfilling phase of my life.

While still undertaking some part-time assignments and projects, I am now able to give my full attention to my family.

The past ten years have included working in Ukraine with the Children of Chornobyl Canadian Fund, management of the Competitive City Regions project for the Canadian Urban Institute, six years as a member of the Committee of Adjustment for the City of Toronto, and annual participation in the provincial literacy testing program.

With Roman's retirement in 2001, we have actively pursued our first love—world travel. In the past ten years, we have been to Greece, Turkey, Portugal, Spain, Egypt, China, England, France, and Italy on a number of occasions, as well as the United States of America and the Caribbean, Most recently, we toured South America, traveling through Brazil, Argentina, Chile, and Peru.

Despite all this, my family remains the center of my world, and I rejoice in their success and accomplishments. Marichka is a successful producer with CBC Radio, producing a daily three-hour show, *Here and Now,* in Toronto. Melia, an urban planner with the city of Toronto, is married to John Stetic, an accomplished software executive with Novell Corporation. Melia and John have two children, Vasylko and Katya, my grandchildren and the source of my ongoing joy and delight. We keep close contact with our ever-growing extended family—Andrew and Chrystyna, their boys and grandchildren, my sister, Dana, and the Stetic family, spending Christmas, Easter, Thanksgiving, and most significant family events together as one large, noisy but caring family.

This summer, in July 2008, I will mark the sixtieth anniversary of my arrival in this great country.

Toronto, Canada
May 2008

**Boyko Family: Three-year-old Tania with mother,
Aunt Lucia, grandmother, and father.
Zell Am See, Austria, 1947**

**Zell Am See, Austria, 1940s**

**Preschool children, Zell Am See**
**Tania Boyko (second from left), Marta Tatomyr, Chrystyna Tatomyr**

**Marichka Melnyk, B.A., Queen's University**

**Melanie Melnyk, B.A., Queen's University**

# Ostap George Tatomyr

Ostap George Tatomyr, son of Alexander and Sophia, was born in Philadelphia on March 3, 1949, less than a year after the Tatomyr family arrived in the United States. Ostap was the apple of his mother's eye because he strongly resembled his mother's beloved oldest brother, Osyp, and he was a joy for his sister, Chrystyna, who was five years older than Ostap. Shortly after his birth, the family moved to Bristol, Pennsylvania to be closer to his father's brother, Jaroslav, and to avoid the heat, pollution, and traffic of a big city. Four years later, in 1953, Ostap's younger sister Lesya was born.

As a child, Ostap showed many talents. He was identified as a gifted learner in Grade 6, excelled in all sports from an early age, and showed promise of musical/artistic talent. Ostap had a wonderful sense of humor and brought great joy and laughter into his family home and social circles. As he grew older, Ostap developed a muscular physique and became a magnet for young ladies.

At the height of the Vietnam War, Ostap turned eighteen and registered for the draft. In 1969 a lottery was held to determine the order that young men born between 1944 and 1950 would be called up for service, according to their birthday. The 366 days of the year were written on pieces of paper, placed in plastic balls and drawn in order. Each date was assigned a number. That year, 195 of the 366 birthdates were called. Ostap's number was 267.

His number wasn't called, but because he did not believe in the merits of this war, Ostap suffered a great deal of anguish while waiting.

In his late teens, Ostap was a member of the Ukrainian Boy Scouts, Plast, and of the prestigious fraternity, Burlaky. His friends included Roman Mychalewsky (a cousin), Ihor Chenstukh (who would be best man at his wedding), Oleh Ciuk, Roman Novakiwsky, Oleh Bak-Boychuk, and the Chajkiwsky brothers, Bohdan and George. Known as the "Young Burlaky," they were particularly active at the Lehighton Resort in Pennsylvania, organizing sports festivals, Ukrainian social activities, Plast activities, and making their presence known at the weekly dances under the stars. They spent a great deal of time at this resort, a former estate of a landowner who loved rare trees and had built an exquisite home on the property.

As the Burlaky grew older and went through the "passages of life" they maintained their friendships. Most of them got married and had children. Sadly, of the eight good friends, four of them died prematurely: Oleh Bak-Boychuk (1992), Ostap (2005), Bohdan Chajkiwsky (2007), and Oleh Ciuk (2008).

Ostap attended Temple University and West Chester University, graduating with a Bachelor of Science degree in education. He was employed by the Bensalem Township District School Board for a number of years as a teacher and coach. At the same time, Ostap became involved with the Philadelphia Flyers hockey team in media relations and as a member of the training and physical conditioning staff. During his three years with the Philadelphia Flyers, the team won two Stanley Cups, in 1974 and 1975. Ostap also had a brief involvement with the Philadelphia "Fury" Soccer Club in the North American Soccer League as a sports administrator and a signed player. In addition, he sang in the all-male Prometheus Choir in Philadelphia for a number of years and was involved with the Tryzub soccer team in a number of capacities.

In 1978, Ostap made the decision to move to Canada because there were few teaching positions available in the United States and there were more teaching opportunities in Ontario. For a while, he lived in Newmarket, Ontario, with his sister, Chrystyna, her husband, Andrew, and nephews, Markian and Roman. This was a joyous time for Chrystyna as she and her brother had been very close growing up and she missed him. Ostap was also a wonderful, doting uncle to Markian and Roman, who adored him and tried to copy "his walk, his talk and his great sense of humor."

While living in Newmarket, Ostap was employed as a teacher for a short period of time. Eventually he decided to explore the field of business and was hired as director of human resources at Xerox in Toronto. Ostap moved to Toronto, where he had easier access to his job. Later in his career, he was a strategic executive with IBM. With his intelligence, innovative spirit, and creativity, Ostap excelled in business.

At this time he was also involved with the Toronto Blizzard professional soccer team as an official. Always a caring uncle, Ostap arranged for Markian and Roman to be involved in a pre-game shootout at a Blizzard game, when his nephews were seven and four years old respectively. It was a dream come true for the boys and one that they would remember forever.

During the early 1990s, Ostap wrote a book, *Beyond the Uke Line*, a study of fifty-five National Hockey League players of Ukrainian descent. The book was published in 1992 on the one-hundredth anniversary of Ukrainian refugees coming to Canada. Since Ukraine had declared its independence the previous year, George was planning to translate the book into Ukrainian and make it available for distribution in Ukraine.

While in Toronto, Ostap met Christine Holubinsky, herself a daughter of Ukrainian immigrants, a math teacher with the Toronto Catholic District School Board. Ostap and Christine were married in 1979. Their first child, Daniel, was born in 1982. Daniel developed into a bright and talented student, and graduated from the University of Toronto in 2005. Like his father, he is an extremely capable athlete, particularly in baseball. Daniel was involved with the Toronto Blue Jays for five years and was also drafted by a minor league baseball team.

In 1986, a daughter, Melanie, was born to the Tatomyr family. She was a precocious child, who excelled in the arts. She was a student at the prestigious National Ballet School for a number of years and graduated from Toronto's Ryerson University.

Daniel and Melanie are the last to carry the Tatomyr name that has endured through Ukrainian history from the thirteenth century. It is a family name that is synonymous with service to the community, political activism, and a strong sense of nationalism.

Following his retirement from IBM, Ostap continued to pursue his business interests as a private entrepreneur.

Suddenly and unexpectedly, Ostap died on May 25, 2005. His death was a tragic blow to his family and friends. Ostap is mourned by those who loved him for his wit, intellect, innovative spirit, and loving nature.

Written by his sisters, Chrystyna Melnyk and Lesya Horodysky.

Aunt Christine and Uncle Ostap at Markian's first communion

**Christine and Ostap Tatomyr, 1987**

**Daniel, Christine, Melanie, Ostap Tatomyr, Marta Lukasewycz, Roman Melnyk, Stephan Lukasewycz, and Chrystyna at Markian's wedding, 2001.**

# Alexandra Marie Sas-Tatomyr Horodysky (Lesya)

## Bordentown, New Jersey

I was born January 13, 1953, at the Bristol General Hospital, Bristol Pennsylvania, the youngest of three children of Sophia and Oleksander Tatomyr. My older sister, Chrystyna, was born in Ukraine in 1944, and my brother, Ostap, in Philadelphia in 1949. We grew up in the suburbs of Philadelphia and Trenton, New Jersey, and were able to experience the best of Ukrainian and American cultures.

As children, we were exposed to *kazky*, fairytales and stories of our ancestors, as told by our parents, grandmother Olha, and our *Teta* and *Vuyko*, Aunt Luba and Uncle Jaroslav, who lived just down the street. Joining us were our cousin, Marta, and our neighbors, the Suchenko sisters.

To further our cultural knowledge and to better understand our heritage, we attended Ukrainian school on Saturdays and joined several youth groups—Ukrainian Youth Association (SUM) and later Plast, the Ukrainian Scouting Organization where I became a counselor and helped other youngsters learn about their past.

I was educated in the Bristol Township public schools, attended Bucks County Community College and graduated from Temple University with a Bachelor of Science degree in elementary education. Every summer during my college years, I worked at Soyuzivka, the UNA estate in upstate New York, as camp counselor, waitress, and participant in the various cultural programs featured weekly at the resort. This estate, set in the beautiful Catskill Mountains, gave ma a wonderful opportunity to interact with other Ukrainian teens from all over the United States and Canada.

For eight years, I taught at the Bordentown Regional School District as a substitute teacher and was an active member of the Bordentown Parent Teachers Association. I also taught Saturday school at St. Josaphat Ukrainian Catholic School in Trenton. After college, I was employed at a Philadelphia law firm for several years, and for the last eleven years, I have been employed by the New Jersey Superior Court in Trenton.

On May 28, 1977, I married my knight in shining armor, Roman T. Horodysky. Our son, Andrij, was born on Feb. 11, 1978, and our daughter, Laryssa, on Nov. 6, 1981.

For many years, I have been active as a member and office holder of Ukrainian National Women's League and the St. Josaphat's Ukrainian Catholic Church in Trenton.

I enjoy Ukrainian arts and crafts, and learned to write pysanky and the fine art of Ukrainian embroidery from my mother, Sophia, and Ukrainian ceramic making and painting from my mother-in-law, Maria, who is well known in the Ukrainian community for her excellent ceramic products.

# Roman Taras Zenoviy DeBratko Horodysky

## Bordentown, New Jersey

I was born on March 10, 1946, in Kaufbeuren, West Germany, to Zenon Horodysky and Maria Lewitska. My father, Zenon, was born in 1915 in Semakiwciw near Kolomyja, and my mother, Maria, was born in 1924 in the town of Yavoriw in western Ukraine.

My father, Zenon, completed his secondary education in 1935 and took up the study of law and theology at the University of Lviv. Just before the Bolsheviks invaded Galicia in September of 1939, Zenon was working as an assistant to Father Joseph Slipyj. Father Slipyj was later appointed Archbishop of Lviv, and, in 1963, after eighteen years of imprisonment by the Soviets in Siberia, was released and ordained a cardinal by Pope John XXIII. Zenon witnessed many attempts by the Bolsheviks to intimidate Father Slipyj and the Metropolitan of Lviv, Andrij Sheptytsky. A few years later, Metropolitan Sheptytsky was poisoned by the KGB and died November 1, 1944.

Zenon resumed his study of law at the University of Prague, where he received a Doctor of Law degree in 1943.

That summer, he returned to Ukraine, and while visiting the resort town of Krynitsia, he met nineteen-year-old Maria Lewitska, who, with a friend, was celebrating the completion of her teacher training courses. Maria recalls that in an attempt to get to know her, Zenon pushed Maria into the swimming pool.

They were married the following year, but as the Red Army advanced on Kolomyja, the young couple moved westward to Bratislava, Slovakia. When it became inevitable that the Red Army would retain control of much of eastern Europe, including Slovakia, Zenon and Maria took the last train out of Bratislava, heading west.

Soviet aircraft spotted the escaping train and began to strafe it. The conductor pulled the train into a tunnel and stopped. My mother recalls that the tunnel quickly filled with smoke and that all the passengers were having difficulty breathing. When the aircraft finally flew away, the train continued on its westward journey but was strafed several more times. When the train reached the small German town of Kaufbeuren, the conductors said they were going no further. They abandoned the train along with all the passengers. My parents decided to take up residence in this town.

When the war ended in the spring of 1945, my parents thought they were finally safe. During that time, however, the Soviets had set up a camp near Munich to hold all the people they designated for repatriation to the Soviet Union. Zenon was arrested and brought to this camp along with several of his colleagues. It was only through the efforts of a U.S. army captain of Ukrainian origin that he was released. It was then that Zenon knew for sure that he wanted to emigrate to the United States of America.

I was born in Kaufbeuren in 1946 and shortly thereafter, my father obtained a job with the United Nations Refugee Relief Agency (UNRRA) and later the International Refugee Organization (IRO), where he assisted Ukrainians in their attempts to emigrate to North America. Finally, in 1951, after most of the displaced persons had left Germany and Austria, our small family was ready to leave.

At age two, we relocated to Munich, where we lived until 1951. Earliest childhood memories include visits to the zoo park in Munich, winter sledding down some slopes, and running across the open fields by our apartment building to the American GI convoys and asking for, and getting, gum and chocolate from the U.S. troops.

In September 1951, we emigrated to the United States. Unlike the majority of immigrants, we flew to the United States, landing in New York. After landing, we were processed through Ellis Island and were free to do whatever we desired. We headed to Northampton, Pennsylvania, to my father's sister's house, where we lived for several months. We eventually moved to Trenton, New Jersey, where we joined the active Ukrainian community.

I was educated in the Catholic school system in Trenton and attended Rutgers, the state university of New Jersey. While there, I joined the ROTC and received a commission in the U.S. Air Force as a Second Lieutenant when I graduated with a bachelor's degree in 1968.

In the meantime, my father was also attending Rutgers University as a graduate student. He was granted his master's degree on the same day that I received my bachelor's degree. My father continued with his graduate studies and received his PhD in Byzantine Studies from the same university. My father worked in the library at Rutgers University and initiated the Ukrainian Section of that library.

In July of 1968, I reported for active duty, and, after finishing training, was stationed at Wright-Patterson Air Force Base in Ohio with the 17th Bomb Wing, Strategic Air Command. This wing had the last B-52 ever built. This was indeed an awesome aircraft. While serving in the USAF, I traveled to California, Louisiana, and England. In 1972, after attaining the rank of captain, I left the air force and returned first to Chicago and eventually to Trenton.

I enrolled in graduate courses in public administration at Rider College and earned thirty credits towards a master's degree.

In 1974, under the pretext of picking up books donated to the Rutgers Library, I met Lesya Tatomyr. We fell in love and, a few years later, I married my Ukrainian princess. The original meeting of the young couple was arranged by the fathers of the two families through a mutual friend.

We honeymooned in Dauphin, Manitoba, where we attended the annual Ukrainian Festival. Accompanying us on this trip was my college roommate, Dr. Yuri Medwid, and his wife, Nina. Neither Yuri nor I knew that our wives were pregnant at the time. Both couples shared a 1974 VW pop-top camper during the Dauphin trip.

In 2007, I retired from the New Jersey Department of Transportation after thirty-three years. Currently, I am enjoying fishing, amateur woodworking projects, and renovating our house.

I'm an active member of OUN, the Olzych Research Foundation, ODWU (Organization for the Democratic Rebirth of Ukraine), and the Ukrainian National Home of Trenton, where I have been the treasurer since 1982.

**Roman Horodysky's great-grandfather (on mother's side) and family c.1900.**

# Andrij and Laryssa Horodysky,
# Roman and Lesya's children.

**Andrij** was born on February 11, 1978, between two major blizzards. From an early age, Andrij was a consummate lover of nature, catching his first fish at age four. This event set the course for the rest of his life. He was educated in the Bordentown Regional School District, participated in soccer, baseball, band, and theater. Andrij attended and graduated from the Ukrainian Heritage School in Philadelphia for which he received his language requirement credits at Eckerd College. After graduating from Eckerd College, Andrij worked for the Florida Marine Research Institute and entered the graduate program at the Virginia Institute of Marine Science (VIMS), which is part of the College of William and Mary. He received a Master of Science degree in 2004, and is currently pursuing a Ph.D. at the same school.

As part of his training, Andrij has visited countries all over the world including Honduras, Micronesia, Australia, Venezuela, Alaska, Canada, and numerous Caribbean countries. While in Alaska, he tangled with a grizzly bear that destroyed his very expensive fishing rod. He dreams of exploring the Amazon and the Orinoco Basin and hopes to one day discover a new species of organism and to publish one article as a lead author in *Science* or *Nature*.

**Laryssa** was born November, 6, 1981, in Trenton, New Jersey, a beautiful little girl who resembled both her grandmothers, Sophia and Maria. She was a very good student in elementary and secondary school, and, from an early age, showed an interest in the arts, particularly, theatre. She is known for her strong sense of humor, wit, and intelligence, and the ability to enjoy life to the fullest.

Laryssa attended Quinnipiac University in Connecticut and graduated with a Bachelor of Arts, magna cum laude, in psychology in 2004. She also started graduate course work towards her master's degree. Currently, she is working as a clinical child psychologist at Bancroft Neuro Health Center in New Jersey.

**Grandfather Zenon, Andrij, parents, Lesya and Roman,
Grandmother Maria and Laryssa Horodysky, 1988**

**Laryssa in Ukrainian traditional garb at dance recital**

**Maria, Roman, Laryssa, Lesya, Andrij at Laryssa's graduation
Quinnipiac University, 2004.**

# Marta Tatomyr-Lukasewycz and Omelan Lukasewycz

## Duluth, Minnesota.

### Marta

Marta was born in Starij Sambir, on October 29, 1943, to Jaroslav Tatomyr and Luba Fedevych. In that part of Ukraine, in the grips of the German occupation, it was a very dangerous and terrible time. During her labor, Marta's mother could hear rifle fire as the Nazis were executing prisoners in the town square. Marta's first months of life were spent in the relative quiet of a small Ukrainian village, Luzhok, where Marta's mother was a school teacher and her grandfather, Julian Tatomyr, was the parish priest. Marta and her parents left Ukraine in 1944 with the rest of the Tatomyr family. They settled at first in Philadelphia, and, in 1951, they bought a little house in Edgely, Pennsylvania, where they lived for the next thirty-five years.

Marta attended Drexel University in Philadelphia and graduated with a degree in chemistry in 1966.

### Omelan

Omelan was born in Mostyska, Ukraine, on September 28, 1942, to Olha and Stephan Lukasewycz. His father was a director at a food cooperative and his mother worked in a bank. Omelan's family left Ukraine in 1944 and traveled west by rail in open boxcars. The family was forced to work in a munitions factory, and Luba, Omelan's sister, was born on VE Day, May 9, 1944. On that day, the Lukasewyczs heard cannon fire. Mistakenly, they thought that troops were approaching, but in fact, the firing was to commemorate the end of the war.

The family ended up in the Enwangen DP camp in Germany and left for the United States in 1949. They came to Philadelphia where they were sponsored by Olha's uncle, who had immigrated to the United States in the 1920s. Times were hard in the beginning. Stephan worked in a sugar factory while Olha sold hotdogs from a pushcart on Marshall St. in Philly. The family lived in cold water flat with no indoor bathroom; they had to use an outhouse. Eventually, Stephan left the sugar factory, Olha abandoned the pushcart, and they opened a luncheonette. They prospered, and in 1962, they bought a grocery store in the Ukrainian neighborhood known as Twenty-Fourth Street.

For the first time, they had a nice home of their own. They renovated the house, bought new furniture, and life was good. Their grocery store supported the family for twenty-five years, until Stephan died and Olha sold the store in 1984.

Omelan graduated from St Joseph's College in Philadelphia and went on to get a PhD in microbiology and immunology from Bryn Mawr College in 1972.

Omelan passed away in 2006 after a long and courageous battle with multiple myeloma.

## Family

**Omelan and Marta** met in 1961 on a Greyhound bus headed to Montreal to attend a Plast ski camp in the Laurentians. At that ski camp, they met many Canadian "Ukey" kids with whom they would go on to become lifelong friends. On that fateful bus trip, Marta broke the ice by mooching a cigarette from Omelan. Omelan, always the gentleman, supplied her with cigarettes the entire trip and the seeds of a great friendship and future romance were planted. By 1964, friendship grew into love, and in the evening of Valentine's Day 1968, in her parent's garden, Omelan, asked Marta to marry him. The wedding took place three months later, on May 25, 1968, in Levittown, Pennsylvania. Marta and Omelan were very happy when so many of their friends, from far and wide, were able to attend their wedding. It was especially important to them that their best man was Andrew Melnyk and their maid of honor was the then Chrystyna Tatomyr.

At that time, Omelan was working toward his Ph.D. and Marta was working as a chemist for the Department of Agriculture. In 1970, they left their families, friends, and Ukrainian community, and moved to Austin, Texas, where Omelan followed his professor to finish his PhD. The move from Philadelphia to Texas was a cultural shock, forcing Marta and Omelan to assimilate into the American culture and find their place in it. In 1972, after Omelan received his degree, they moved to Ann Arbor, Michigan, where Omelan received a post doctoral fellowship in immunology. In Ann Arbor in 1973, a daughter, Anne (Anya) Kathryn, was born. In 1975, Omelan accepted a faculty position at the University of Minnesota Duluth Medical School, and the family moved to Duluth, Minnesota. Omelan went on to teach immunology to medical students for the next thirty years, until his death in 2006. Omelan was an enthusiastic and gifted teacher, and is well known in the Minnesota medical community, having helped educate, over the years, many of the physicians practicing in Minnesota today.

In 1976, in Duluth, a son, Stephen John, was born. The family put down roots, wove itself into the fabric of the Duluth community, and lived an interesting, active, and fruitful life. There was no Ukrainian community in Duluth, the closest being in Minneapolis, 150 miles of northern woods away. In spite of that, the family managed to retain its Ukrainian identity and everyone in Duluth, who knew the Lukasewyczs, knew that they were of Ukrainian heritage.

Anya and Stephen attended public schools, were active in sports, and emerged as Midwesterners of Ukrainian heritage. Anya and Stephen both went on to graduate from Harvard University in Boston and both went on to graduate from the University of Minnesota Medical School in Minneapolis in 2000 and 2004 respectively.

After completing her undergraduate work, and before attending medical school, Anya received a Rockefeller Fellowship to study foreign cultures. She chose to spend her time in Ukraine, working with disabled children under the auspices of the Children of Chernobyl Fund.

Stephen married Christine (Christy) Stalker, his high school sweetheart, in 2000. Their son, Andrew Omelan, was born on February 20, 2006.

Currently, Anya is a physician specializing in internal medicine in Minneapolis and Stephen is completing a residency in urology at the University of Minnesota.

**Stephen, Omelan, Marta, and Anya Lukasewycz**
**with Nana Duluth, 1990s**

**Stephen, Omelan, Christie, and Marta, Toronto, 2001**

**Brother and sister medical team: Dr. Stephen and
Dr. Anya Lukasewycz with Stephen and Christie's son, Andrew, 2008**

# Oksana Stulkowsky-Winstead

## (daughter of Olga Melnyk and Dmytro Stulkowsky)
## Seattle, Washington

I was born in Bamberg, Germany, on June 12, 1947. My parents and sister, Daria, fled Ukraine shortly after my sister's birth on May 30, 1944. Prior to and after my birth, we lived in DP camps in several German cities—Bamberg, Bayreuth, and Pforzheim. My green card states we arrived in New York on July 2, 1949. I was two years old and three feet tall. My first recollections are from Philadelphia, where we moved in 1951, and I remember a visit to the tobacco farm in Barstow, Maryland, where we first lived, having been sponsored by a kind farmer and given housing in exchange for my father's labor in the tobacco fields.

Our parents bought their home at 4811 North Sydenham Street in Philadelphia for $5,000 in 1953, and I remember walking to kindergarten at Logan Elementary School and bringing a blanket-bed I could lie on during naptime. And I remember Jimmy, who was my first crush; he had freckles and a big smile. Once St. Basil's School opened, my sister and I walked an extra block and up a hill to the school. Wister Woods nearby and played a part in my childhood fantasies as well as a hiding place when playing hooky from high school. My public high school experience was multicultural, multiracial, and multireligious, something I had been sheltered from in my Ukrainian upbringing. In 1965, I graduated from Philadelphia High School for Girls and enrolled at the Community College of Philadelphia, where I earned an associate degree in 1967. The CIA recruited students at that time so I applied just before embarking on a three-month European trip with my sister.

A CIA job offer awaited my return from Europe, and at age twenty, I moved from Philadelphia to the Washington DC area. Already at that time, my goal was to travel, and I thought the CIA would afford me that opportunity. Travel I did, but not as I had thought: I met and married Darian Diachok in 1969 and followed him to Munich, Germany, where he was stationed with U.S. Army Intelligence. We lived and worked there for two years and traveled extensively with month-long trips to Spain and Greece. While I worked at the U.S. Army and Air Force European Exchange System in Munich,

I met a woman from Eugene, Oregon, who talked about the Northwest and put the thought in our heads that we should head west.

Indeed, in 1972, Darian and I moved to Seattle after he was accepted in the architecture masters program at the University of Washington. During the four years in Seattle, while Darian studied and I worked in special education at the experimental education unit of the university, I completed my bachelor's degree in anthropology and archaeology, realizing my goal of a college education. Upon completing my studies, I was hired by a tour company, Society for the Preservation of Archaeological Monuments, and escorted tours to ruins in Chile, Easter Island, Peru, and Ecuador. My dream of travel was again realized, but change was in the wind; Darian and I parted a year after we returned to Washington DC, and I returned alone to Seattle and once again worked for Tom Lovitt, a special education professor at the University of Washington.

Many close friends awaited my return to Seattle in 1977, and on January 21, 1978, I married one of them, Ricord Winstead, a fourth-year medical student. Our daughter, Nadia, was born on October 21 that year while we lived at 3-1/2 Smith Street on Queen Anne Hill. Six months later, we drove to New Orleans for passage to Panama aboard the SS *Cristobal* for Ric's first year of family practice residency at Gorgas Hospital. While there, in 1980, we witnessed the turnover of the Panama Canal to Panama and viewed the eruption of Mt. Saint Helens on armed-forces television. We returned to Seattle, after our fourteen-month stay, to the Swedish Hospital residency program and bought our first home at 9206 Palatine Avenue North in the Greenwood neighborhood. Having bought a small two-bedroom home, and with the imminent arrival of our son, Alex, on August 19, 1981, we moved to 3040-164th Place NE in Bellevue, Ric's parent's rental home, where we lived for twenty years.

Those were memorable years, with motherhood as my primary focus. When Nadia and Alex were in school, I volunteered my time in various capacities: teaching computers in their elementary school, working in the middle school nurse's office, mentoring high school creative writing, assisting a family with quadruplets, working at the 1990 Goodwill Games, and working with the Beyond War Foundation to further the critical message that war does not solve problems.

In 1995, Ric and I embarked on our cohousing adventure. With a small group of families, we undertook to build an intentional community where we would know all our neighbors, share meals, and cooperate together to manage and maintain our dwellings. We hired an architect and development consultant and designed our community to build on surplus land purchased from the city. This was a six-year endeavor, one on which I worked full time without pay. The big payoff was that this is where Ric and I moved in 2001 and where we currently live at 828 Hiawatha Place South at Jackson Place Cohousing in Seattle.

My experience with the cohousing project and work with our development consultant were the stepping stones to the job I have today at the King County Housing Authority, redeveloping a ninety-acre public housing community into a mixed-income community called Greenbridge (www.kcha.org/hopevi).

—April 2008

# Ricord Burton Winstead, MD,

## (son of Verna Tennessee Stover and Maurice Burton Winstead, MD)
## Seattle, Washington

The first Winsteads on American soil were among the late-1600s Virginia settlers. They eventually moved to coastal North Carolina and had land holdings in pine forests, a saw mill, and tobacco production in Winsteadville, North Carolina, by the 1900s.

My father left Winsteadville to attend medical school and met my mother in Chapel Hill. After they married, and following the birth of my sister, Olivia, on February 28, 1941, he commanded Detachment A of the Ninth Field Hospital during World War II. His hospital supported the first army going ashore on D-Day + 3 at Utah Beach in the Normandy invasion. He followed the battle fronts across France and Belgium, where his clearly marked hospital was destroyed by German shelling during the Battle of the Bulge. He then set up an evacuation hospital during the Rhineland battles in Kirchhellen, Germany, where 800-1,000 wounded moved through daily for air evacuation from the European Theater of Operations. After Germany's surrender, his Ninth Field hospital set up in Babbenhausen, a German prisoner-of-war camp, where 50,000 prisoners were cared for by German physicians and medical personnel.

After the war, my father completed two years of internal medicine training at Baltimore's Johns Hopkins University Hospital and was assigned to Walter Reed Army Hospital in Washington, D.C., where I was born on July 7, 1947, and my sister, Lee, was born on May 1, 1949. Our family bought a brick home in the new suburb of Chevy Chase, Maryland. In 1952, my father was assigned to Ft. Clayton U.S. army hospital in the Panama Canal Zone, where we moved prior to my brother, Spencer's, birth on January 25, 1953. He was then assigned to Gorgas Hospital in Ancon, which served civilian Panama Canal employees and their families plus the military from the fifteen Canal Zone bases. My father practiced at Gorgas Hospital for the rest of his medical career and my parents stayed in Panama for thirty years. My mother received her master's degree in library science and worked at the Canal Zone Library for twenty years. In her seventies, she explored genealogy and traced our family line back my generations.

I lived in the Chevy Chase house the first five years of my life, but my childhood was truly shaped by growing up in the Canal Zone at 288 Gorgas Road, Ancon. Built of insect-resistant California redwood, with a copper roof, the four-bedroom two-story house sat on top of a concrete foundation with a large two-car garage and a maid's room. It had large screened porches and tall ceilings to catch the tropical breezes. The house was a block from the city of Panama, and during two serious riots, the next-door cement Cathedral of St. Luke sheltered our home from incoming sniper fire.

With my father's encouragement, I came to love the tropics and spent much of my childhood and adolescence outdoors—camping in the jungle in jungle hammocks or shooting rapids on the Chagres River in a dugout canoe carved with an adz and axe for me by an Embera Indian. I twice paddled through the canal in a four-man dugout in the annual Boy Scout Ocean-to-Ocean Cayuco Race, and I hiked from the Pacific to the Atlantic on the old Spanish trail. Our family spent time in the interior enjoying the country homes and hospitality of Panamanian friends at the Pacific beach in Coronado, in the cooler mountains of El Valle, two hours by rough road from Panama City, and in El Volcan near the Costa Rican border.

I graduated from Balboa High School in 1965 and spent three months touring Europe with a friend, in a Simca I picked up for my parents at the Paris factory. We drove through France, Spain, Italy, Switzerland, Austria, and Germany, including an adventurous side trip through East Germany to Berlin, then Holland, England, and Scotland, before shipping the car back to Panama and returning home by air. I attended Canal Zone College and earned an associate in arts degree. At that time, my father developed a severe paralytic illness, Guillain-Barre syndrome, and was completely paralyzed for six months. He did eventually recover and return to work but had lost much of his muscle strength and was no longer capable of the active outdoor activities of boating he so much enjoyed. At about that time, my mother purchased a five-acre finca, Mirasol, in El Valle, and this became the family country home. As Maurice's strength returned, he enjoyed many building projects, directing his carpenter and mason. Eventually, my parents retired at Mirasol and lived in this tropical paradise for five years, two hours from Panama City and without a phone—until their health deteriorated to the point they realized they needed to be closer to medical facilities.

In 1967, I traveled by Tica Bus through Central America to the United States and then spent the rest of the summer crisscrossing the United States on a Greyhound bus pass. I passed through most of the states and stopped at the major national parks, ending up in Baltimore for the next two years to earn my Bachelor of Arts in History at Johns Hopkins University. I frequently visited my sister, Olivia, her husband, and two children in the D.C. suburbs, and on one trip, met up with a friend of my sister, Lee's, from the Canal Zone, Michelle Meyers, who was working as a secretary in D.C.

After graduating from Hopkins in 1969, I returned to the Canal Zone to apply for a conscientious objector status instead of facing the army draft and the inevitability of Vietnam. With the firm support of my father, I was granted CO status. I also was deemed 4-F and so had a permanent physical exemption from military service (due to hyperurecemia—my attacks of gout these days are reminders of those days). Being completely free of the draft, Michelle and I were married later that year at St. Luke's Cathedral next door to my Ancon family home.

Michelle and I spent three years traveling in a variety of campers through Central America and spent time in Guatemala, learning back-strap weaving from Catchequel Indians in the small village of San Antonio de las Aguas Calientes outside of Antigua and in Monteverde, the Quaker community in the Costa Rica highlands. We eventually bought forty acres of land with a section of ancient cloud forest, a small patch of coffee and some cleared pastures—but no road, water, electricity, or house. We returned to the United States to earn enough money to develop the dream of a farm. Ending up in Seattle, I decided to attend medical school with the idea of returning to Monteverde as a physician (the very remote area was visited by a government physician, nurse, and dentist once a month). I was accepted at the University Of Washington School Of Medicine in 1975 and trained my first year in Pullman in Eastern Washington as part of an innovative expansion of the medical school to provide training for students from surrounding states without medical schools. Michelle remained in Seattle during this year—the strains of medical school significantly contributed to the marriage ending the next year. We divorced in 1976, and I returned to the Seattle campus to complete my training.

During our time in Seattle, Michelle worked at the University of Washington's Experimental Education Unit where she met a Ukrainian couple, the Diachoks. Darian attended the School of Architecture and Oksana was completing her BA and also worked at the EEU. They returned to the East Coast—Oksana had always complained about how parochial and uninteresting Seattle was compared to the vibrant D.C. scene. Their marriage also ended, and Oksana returned to Seattle alone to her job at the EEU.

Oksana and I married on January 21, 1978, during my third year of medical school. We took a quick trip to Panama to introduce Oksana to my family and celebrated Carnival with my brother Spencer's family in Penonome. Nadia Verna was born at Group Health Hospital in Seattle on October 21, 1978, and I returned to Panama with my new family for the last year of the Gorgas Hospital postgraduate program and completed my first year of flexible internship. We lived in a government duplex in Ancon, not far from my old family home, and our daughter learned to walk on the uneven flagstones of my parent's country home, Mirasol, in El Valle. Spencer's son, Alan, was a few months younger than Nadia so the grandparents had an opportunity to enjoy both grandchildren.

I was accepted in the Swedish Family Medicine Residency in Seattle and we bought our first small home in the Greenwood district. With a second child on the way, it was clear a larger house was needed so we moved into my parent's Bellevue rental across a Lake Washington floating bridge from Seattle, just three weeks before Alex was born on August 19, 1981 at Swedish Hospital. Alex's birth occurred on one of those long days when I had been up all night attending the labor of one of my patients and was scrubbing to go into the delivery room when I saw Oksana waddling down the hall in early labor.

After completing my residency and becoming a board-certified family physician, instead of going back to Costa Rica, another residency doctor and I opened a new practice in Bellevue across the street from Overlake Hospital. Building a new practice was hard work, involved many hours and moonlighting in emergency rooms and walk-in clinics to make ends meet. It was during this time that I volunteered as summer camp doctor at Camp Parsons Boy Scout camp on Hood Canal. The camp provided a small beach cabin and our family enjoyed an economical vacation for several years—until Oksana explored the area with a real estate agent and found our beach house in Brinnon, five miles south of the camp. It became our year-round weekend sanctuary from work and the bustle of the city. We enjoy the panorama of the Dosewallips River delta, we watch the resident bald eagles raise their young, we canoe, and eat oysters from the beach.

Starting in 1982, we became very active in Beyond War, working on the global threat of nuclear war. We met many of our lifelong friends doing this work. Oksana also developed a network of friends through the children, the playgroup, and we have enjoyed these friendships over the past thirty years.

I left my Bellevue practice after three years and worked at the Sea Mar Clinic, a Hispanic community health center, and became involved in the emerging managed care movement. Eventually, I secured a job as a medical director for a national company setting up a new operation in Washington. Medical management appealed to my growing understanding of the importance of a systems approach to population health. I became a full-time physician executive. This path led to an interesting variety of opportunities and an equal measure of disappointments as the harsh realities of medical economics often trump doing the right or reasonable thing in the larger best interests of society and patients. One of the key skills of a physician executive with the handicap of fearless integrity is to be able to pick oneself up and start over—many times. This pattern seems to describe the arc of my career in medical management.

When nearing the empty nest stage, Oksana and I embarked on a seven-year odyssey to find an alternative to the isolation of suburban living. We founded a cohousing community with a group of like-minded souls and became owner-developers of a twenty-seven-unit condominium on a 1.25-acre site near Seattle's International District. We have a large common kitchen and dining room and an active meals program with community meals five days a week. Since we live so close to downtown, many of us walk, bike, or bus to work. We have a good mix of ages, from infant to the eighties, and we make decisions by consensus so there is great commitment to communication and problem solving. Our community members are active and involved not only in the life of Jackson Place Cohousing but also in the larger surrounding community. Together we have created a vibrant and engaged community in an urban setting. We feel fortunate to live in community with people who are committed to participating in the life of the community and not just buying a condo.

A lifetime has passed in a flash. Parents have died and children have been raised to become their own independent wonderful people. Life continues to be an adventure.

—April 2008

The Winsteads of Seattle:
Alexander Burton Winstead, Oksana Stulkowsky-Winstead,
Nadia Verna Winstead and Dr. Ricord Burton Winstead

# Daria Stulkowsky-Kulchycky

## Philadelphia

I was born on May 30, 1944, in Gorlice, Poland, to Olga Melnyk-Stulkowsky and Dmytro Stulkowsky. My parents, along with my mother's sister, Lucia, and brother, Bohdan Melnyk, and his family left Pidhajci, Ukraine, in March just ahead of the advancing Red Army. When I was just a few weeks old, we continued our journey through Austria to Germany.

We lived in a displaced persons camp in Bamberg, Germany, where my sister, Oksana, was born on June 12, 1947. From there we moved to Bayreuth and on to Pfortzheim, where we lived until our eventual emigration to the United States. My father was an officer in the Pfortzheim DP camp police and helped keep order among the Ukrainians awaiting permission to travel to the United States. Being three or four years old then, I recall standing in line with other children, all of us holding metal bowls, while waiting to get soup—it was split pea. My father knew the art of *rizba* (wood carving) and he carved beautiful plates, frames, album covers, and cassettes, which my mother painted. He sold his creations to earn extra money for food for our family. In late June 1949, we were approved for immigration to the United States via a U.S. military ship. I remember dolphins swimming alongside the ship, that I wanted to sleep in the top bunk, and that a woman passenger gave me a little ring, which I lost. As we pulled into New York Harbor on July 2, 1949, I saw the Statue of Liberty.

After vaccinations and paperwork, my father had a choice to remain in New York or to look for work elsewhere. He was approached by a tobacco farmer looking for workers to take to Maryland. Dad agreed, and we were driven to Barstow, Maryland, and provided a house on the farmer's property. We lived there for one year with no heat, electricity, or water—with only a potbellied stove in the kitchen that also heated the house, a well for water, and an outhouse.

My father bought several dozen chickens and built a chicken coop. Mom grew vegetables and also raised a pig. Dad worked very hard picking and hanging tobacco leaves in the barns. Mom took care of us, tended to the garden and animals, and cooked a lot of egg—and chicken-based meals. During that time, my father sponsored my maternal aunt, Emilia Melnyk Mychalewsky, her husband, Nicholas, their two children, as well as Nicholas's brother, Zenon. Later, we also sponsored the Leskiw family.

With a borrowed $100, my father purchased an old car in 1950 and taught himself how to drive. When the year was up, we packed and moved to Philadelphia where we first stayed with the Soviak family and then rented a house on North Sixteenth Street with the Wapowsky family. An apartment on Wingohocking Street was our next home and then, finally, we bought our own house at 4811 North Sydenham Street in 1953. During that time, my father worked as a carpenter, joined a union, and moved up to the position of superintendent. My mother first worked evenings cleaning offices in center city Philadelphia and then worked with other Ukrainian women at Kodak "Perfect Photo," cutting negatives.

I attended Steel School, then Logan Elementary School for a year, after which my sister and I attended St. Basil's School on Lindley Avenue, run by Ukrainian Catholic sisters of St. Basil the Great. During these and my high school years, I was a member of Plast, the Ukrainian scouting organization, attended weekly meetings, and four-week summer camps in East Chatham, New York—these are some of my favorite memories. I attended Saturday Ukrainian school and was active in the student organization and choir. My best friends were and still are Maria Rosola Panczak and Lida Dymicky Pakula.

I attended St. Basil Academy in Fox Chase where I took the business course and graduated in 1962, and after high school I worked as a clerk typist. For two years, I took secretarial finishing classes in the evenings at Pierce Business School to qualify for executive secretarial positions and worked for the Pennsylvania Railroad, Robert Bruce Sportswear Mills, and the Internal Revenue Service.

In 1967, I took a leave of absence from work and my sister, Oksana, and I took a memorable trip to Europe sailing to England on the MS *Aurelia*. With our Eurail passes, we traveled for two months from England to France (Bastille festival in Paris), then through Holland, Belgium, Germany, Italy, Monaco, Switzerland, and Austria.

During the sixties and seventies, my close friends were Bohdan Kulchycky, Bohdan "Bobby" and Halina Woloszczuk, Jarema and Oksana Rudakevich, and Joe and Kathy Fylypowycz. On February 15, 1969, I married Bohdan "Dan" Kulchycky.

After I left home, my mother purchased a duplex and moved out of our Sydenham Street home, while my father remained there. Their marriage had been strained for many years and they had stayed together for the sake of the children. Mom worked, was active in the Ukrainian National Women's League and painted Ukrainian ceramics. My father continued construction work, sang in the Ukrainian mixed choir, *Kobzar*, and was active in the Ukrainian community and the Bensalem Seniors Association.

After our wedding, Dan and I lived in Maryland for a year, then moved back to the Philadelphia area and bought our first home at 842 Cornwells Avenue, an old 1850s three-story fourplex in Bensalem. We were once again close to our family and friends.

On May 4, 1973, our daughter, Roxolana Mira (Lana) Kulchycky, was born two months premature and had a very difficult beginning in life. We brought her home from the hospital after two months. One year after her birth, we received the heartbreaking diagnosis that Lana had cerebral palsy. These complex times contributed to our marriage slowly falling apart.

In 1977, Dan was promoted to branch accounting manager and transferred to Buffalo, New York, and our family of three moved. We rented out all of the units in the Bensalem house and purchased a home on 49 Scamridge Curve in Williamsville, New York. Lana attended a United Cerebral Palsy infant stimulation program and I spent time caring for her, keeping a garden, painting Ukrainian ceramics, and writing *pysanky* to sell. Regrettably, the marriage did not work out, and, after the worst Buffalo blizzard ever, in 1978, I moved back to Bensalem with Lana into the fourplex. During this time, my mother moved into Ascension Manor, a retirement community in Philadelphia built by Ukrainians.

Unfortunately, Lana did not show improvement and was diagnosed with profound mental retardation. In 1979, the program she attended at the Bucks County Association for Retarded Children (BARC) told me about a wonderful organization, Life Path, in Sellersville, Pennsylvania. I knew I could not provide Lana with all the advantages for her improvement, and, after the hardest decision of my life, she became a permanent resident of Ridge Crest in Sellersville, Pennsylvania. There, she receives excellent care, including physical, occupational, and speech therapy—all provided by Life Path and the state of Pennsylvania (she is still with them today). Over the years, Lana has had weekly visits from my mother, Sonia, her father, and me.

In 1980, I met Peter Gatta, an immigrant from Italy, who I believed would be my future husband. On September 8, 1982, our daughter, Sonia Giuliana Gatta, was born. Sonia's father continues to live in Bensalem and has been involved in his daughter's life.

In 1983, my father had cardiac bypass surgery and lived with me and Sonia in Bensalem to recuperate. He then sold the house on Sydenham Street and moved into his own unit in the fourplex. It was wonderful having him around, and he helped me very much. During the 1980s, I was active in the Philadelphia Ukrainian Women's League and served as president of my branch for two years. I also painted Ukrainian ceramics and Christmas ornaments, which I sold during various holiday bazaars.

Sonia attended St. Charles Elementary School in Bensalem and Ukrainian school on Saturdays at the Ukrainian Educational and Cultural Center in Jenkintown, Pennsylvania. She was a member of Plast and went to the same summer camp in East Chatham, New York, that I had attended in my youth.

On March 19, 1996, my father died at eighty. Later that year, my mother moved into a unit in the Bensalem fourplex, and in September of 1996, I took the job of secretary and marketing coordinator for Ukrainian Selfreliance Federal Credit Union, where I am still employed.

In 1998, I sold the Bensalem house and purchased a home at 1034 Henrietta Avenue, Huntingdon Valley, Pennsylvania, for my daughter, mother, and me. Sonia attended St. Basil Academy in Fox Chase, a short walk from home, and graduated in 2000. She received a scholarship to the University of Scranton, where she majored in biology/premed and spanish. During her junior year, Sonia attended a semester at the University of Valparaiso in Chile and lived with a host family in Vina Del Mar. During that time, she traveled with friends through Peru, Bolivia, Argentina, and down to the tip of Chile. I was able to vacation there, and, together, we visited Santiago and Buenos

Aires, Argentina. Sonia graduated from college in 2004, and she and I traveled to Portugal and Spain to celebrate (her graduation gift).

While taking a one-year break from school, Sonia worked as an optician and then entered Pennsylvania College of Optometry. She will graduate in 2009. She then hopes to complete one year of residency prior to starting her career as an optometrist.

In 2004, at age ninety-one, my mother moved into Willow Lake Assisted Living and currently lives there.

I am a member of the Annunciation of the Blessed Virgin Mary Ukrainian Catholic Church and am active in the Ukrainian community. My faith has helped me through many hard times, and I am grateful for my family and two children. I thank God for Lana, who has given me so much strength and has brought out the best in me and everyone who knows her; and for Sonia, who gave me a chance to experience motherhood and who is so loving and smart and makes me so proud. I enjoy traveling with friends and have visited many interesting destinations on the East Coast. As of this writing, I am sixty-four years old, Lana is thirty-five, and Sonia is twenty-five. After retirement, I would like to travel and, hopefully, enjoy grandchildren.

**Mychalewsky and Stulkowsky Families, Philadelphia, 1954**
**Nicholas and Emilia (Melnyk) Mychalewsky, Olha (Melnyk)**
**and Dmytro Stulkowsky**
**Christine Mychalewsky, Oksana Stulkowsky,**
**Roman Mychalewsky, Daria Stulkowsky**

With visitors from Canada and three-month-old Peter Bak-Boychuk. 1966
Roman and Andrij Melnyk, Christine and Oleh Bak-Boychuk,
Oksana and Daria Stulkowsky
Bronyslawa Melnyk, Emilia (holding baby Peter), Roman Mychalewsky, Olha
Stulkowsky, and Nicholas Mychalewsky

**Daria Kulchycky with daughters, Sonia Gatta and Lana Kulchycky, 1994**

# Emilia's Family

## Our Journey through the last half Century

By **Christine Mychalewsky Bak-Boychuk**, her daughter

In August of 1944, my mother, Emilia Melnyk, was taken as a forced laborer to Germany where she worked in the German "Reimag" undertaking in Kahla, Germany. She was liberated by the U.S. Army in April 1945. In June, 1945, she traveled to the DP camp in Bamberg, Bavaria, Germany. There, she met my father, Mykola Taras Mychalewsky. They were married on January 25, 1946. My father is from the Kolomyia region of Ukraine, which at that time was called Galicia, Poland. At the DP camp Mom worked as an Administrative typist and Dad was registered with the military government of the camp as a sanitation engineer.

This is where I was born, on December 13, 1946.

In August of 1947, my family moved to the Ukrainian DP camp, Leopold Caserne in Bayreuth, Germany, where my brother Roman was born on March 9, 1949. At this camp, mom worked as an artistic embroiderer.

Later that year, our family was moved to the DP camp in Ludendorff, Germany, to await immigration, which was delayed because I became ill. I was hospitalized under quarantine for a month in November 1949 and wasn't approved for immigration until April 22, 1950.

We were sponsored by my maternal aunt, Olga, and her husband, Dmytro Stulkowsky, and together with my father's brother, Zenon Mychalewsky, traveled on the U.S. navy ship *General R. L. Howze*, entering the United States at New York City on June 15, 1950. I don't remember anything from this time or my family's immigration to the United States.

We stayed briefly with my maternal aunt's family on a farm in Maryland and then moved to Chester, Pennsylvania. There we rented a house together with the Korchynsky family at 303 Hayes Street. We lived on the first floor.

In October 1953, my parents purchased their first home and we moved to 3023 West Sixth Street. Many Ukrainian families lived in the area. We attended Holy Ghost

Ukrainian Catholic Church and all of the children attend the Holy Ghost School, located next to the church. All social, religious, and cultural activities revolved around the parish.

Mom was an active member of the Ukrainian National Women's League of America Chapter 13. Dad belonged to the Ukrainian Engineer's Society.

Dad was very gifted. He did wood engraving and taught me how to make *pysanky* (Ukrainian Easter eggs). Mom loved to embroider. Both painted beautiful *hutsul*—and *trypillian*-style ceramics, many of their pieces decorate my home today.

After school and on Saturdays, I attended the Ukrainian Catholic Institute. I took ballet and piano lessons at the Ukrainian Music Institute. I remember poetry recitals and playing piano duets with my best friend Marusia Zbyr at holiday concerts.

On June 7, 1956, we all became naturalized U.S. citizens and Dad's name was officially changed by court order from Mykola to Nicholas. In October of that year, Dad started working for the General Electric Company as an electrical engineer. He worked for the GE Company until his retirement in January 1972.

I was a member of Plast. Every summer from 1957 through 1963, I spent a few weeks at the Ukrainian Plast camp in East Chatham, New York, where I was active in sports. I played on the volleyball team. I earned a first place medal for high jump and second place for running. In 1960, I graduated and began attending the Notre Dame Academy High School located in Moylan, Pennsylvania, near Chester. In July 1961, we all traveled to Niagara Falls and then to Toronto, where I finally got to meet my godfather, Bohdan Melnyk, and my Canadian cousins, Roman and Andrew. In 1962, we all met again at the Plast Jamboree in East Chatham, New York.

So that my father would be closer to his job, in August of 1963, our family moved to 5347 North Camac Street in Philadelphia, Pennsylvania. I graduated from Girls High School and moved on to Temple University, majoring in English. Starting in 1959, my family began spending summer vacations at the Ukrainian Homestead in the Pocono Mountains near Lehighton, Pennsylvania. This is where I met my husband, Oleh Petro Bak-Boychuk. Oleh's father, Theophil Bak-Boychuk, was one of the founders of the Ukrainian Homestead, named in honor of Oleh Kandyba-Olzhych. In 1958, he worked together with the Philadelphia and Allentown branches of ODWU to purchase the five-hundred-acre Bauer estate with historic Lentz Mansion, which became the "Ukrainian Homestead." Oleh was very well known in the Philadelphia area as the goalie for the Ukrainian Nationals Tryzub amateurs soccer team. We were both members of the Temple University Ukrainian Club and sang in the Temple Ukrainian Club Choir.

Oleh and I married at the Ukrainian Catholic Cathedral on Franklin Street on May 1, 1965. We lived in an apartment over his parent's store, MODA, on Girard Avenue, near the Cathedral. In June of 1967, we purchased our home at 5733 North Sixth Street in Philadelphia. We were both active in the Ukrainian youth organization, ZAREVO. In 1966, we had purchased a printing press at an auction and began to publish the *ODWU Bulletin* for the National Executive of the Organization for the Rebirth of Ukraine.

At the Homestead, Oleh helped organize the Ukrainian Youth Federation of America MUN. In 1976, MUN began to publish *VESZHI*, a quarterly magazine. Oleh was the editor. A close friend, Ostap Tatomyr, was on the editorial staff. All of us were enthusiastic soccer and hockey fans. Ostap also worked for the FLYERS organization and we were able to attend the victory banquet celebrating their Stanley Cup win.

In April of 1977, we organized the MUN conference at the Homestead. Besides the meetings dealing with the primary concerns of our organization, a program of sports activities was scheduled throughout that summer. We held a car rally, as well as tennis and golf tournaments. The volleyball tournament between the team from Tryzub and the MUN team, calling themselves the "Lehighton United," was the most popular event of the conference.

On May 13, 1977, my father, Nicholas Mychalewsky, passed away. He was killed in a freak accident on my parents' property in Lehighton.

In 1978, we purchased a store front building at 5738 North Fifth Street and officially opened our company "B & B Printing Service." Our primary business was the computer typesetting, printing, and publishing of Ukrainian books and magazines. In Philadelphia, 1979 was dedicated as "The Year of the Child." That year, we worked on Hanna Cherin's book, *Little Schoolgirl Mila's Diary* and Iryna Dybko's *White Eagle Narratives*. We were printing the *St. Sophia* bulletin for the Religious Association of Ukrainian Catholics, Inc., USA, and *The Patriarchate* magazine for the Ukrainian Patriarchial World Federation. We worked with Dr. Petro Mirchuk on his two volumes *My Journeys in Israel*. Dr. Lew Pylypenko's book of poetry, *Friends of my Life*, and Volodymyr Bilajiw's book of poetry, *Beyond Happiness*. We worked with Dr. Bohdan Romanenchuk of Kyiw Publishing, who was chief-editor of many Ukrainian books and mazagines. We printed anniversary and jubilee books for Plast, SUM, and many area churches and schools. We printed *The Ways of Golden Podilla*, a book of historical essays for the Shevchenko Scientific Society. Our biggest and longest project was published by the society *Boykivshchyna*. We worked with chief-editor, Myron Utrysko, for over three years on the large hardbound collection of historical and ethnographical materials about this region of Ukraine.

Both of our sons were born and grew-up during these years. Peter Theophil Bak-Boychuk was born October 6, 1965, and George Michael Bak-Boychuk was born July 25, 1969. Our family summers revolved around the many activities at the Ukrainian Homestead. My parents and Oleh's sister had summer homes there. In 1978, we took the boys to Disney World in Orlando, Florida, our first time on a plane.

Peter was a happy baby. He met all of his early childhood developmental milestones on schedule. At six years of age, he began to suffer from multiple seizures. It took three years for the doctors to find the right combination of medications to finally bring the seizures under control. The doctors thought Peter must have suffered some minimal brain damage when he had emergency surgery at three months of age. After this, Peter was left with some physical and intellectual disabilities. He attended special education classes at McClure Elementary School. He was a student at Delta Middle School and Ashbourne Academy. He loved to sing, and at middle school, he appeared in the play

*Grease*. Through a special works program, he has worked as an assistant in a print shop at the Fox Chase Cancer Center, and as assistant of social activities at the Cheltenham Nursing Center.

George attended Lowell Elementary School and Cardinal Dougherty High School. He also attended Ukrainian school on Saturdays at the Ukrainian Educational and Cultural Center. At Temple University, he majored in biology and anthropology and graduated in 1992. He works in the pharmaceutical industry as a project manager.

In the years after my father's death, Mom continued to live in Lehighton most of the year. Many Ukrainian families had retired there, and she had a large group of friends. They were all active at the Ukrainian Homestead and belonged to the senior citizen's club in town. During the summer months, the boys and I would visit almost every weekend. There were Saturday night dances, many festivals, potato baking, and swimming at the pool. Mom would return to her home on Camac Street for the winter months. She was a member of Christ the King Parish on Cayuga Street. She belonged to Chapter 43 of the Ukrainian Women's League and Ukrainian Senior Citizen's Organization at the Ukrainian Center. Every spring, she would spend a few weeks in Florida with one of her friends. Mom, who loved to travel, went on many tours and pilgrimages.

Oleh and I separated in the late 1980s. He closed and sold the business and I went to work for the Providence Association of Ukrainian Catholics on Franklin Street, across from the Ukrainian Cathedral in Philadelphia. I worked as business manager of America Publishing. At that time, we were publishing and printing the daily paper *America* and the weekly Archdiocesan paper *The Way*. Mstylav Dolnycky, Dr. B. Romanenchuk and Bohdan Katamay were associate editors of the paper, *America*. In 1986 and 1987, the Schevchenko Scientific Society published the thousand-page book *Kolomyia and Its Region*

Since my father's family comes from this area of Ukraine, my mother and uncle, Zenon Mychalewsky, who was living at the Homestead at that time, were able to contribute information and pictures for the publication.

In 1988, I sang with the Philadelphia Ukrainian Millennium Choir, under the direction of Maestro Michael Dlaboha. We had concerts at Carnegie Hall, in the State Capitol in Harrisburg and in Toronto, Canada, all commemorating the one thousand years of Christianity in Ukraine.

In early 1991, I started working for Trident S & L Association on Twenty-third and Brown Streets in the Fairmount section of Philadelphia. I had gone back to night school to study economics and finance. I got my real estate license in 1992 and also worked part-time for Trident Realty.

In 1996, the State of Pennsylvania decided they would no longer offer deposit insurance to the 144 small community-based S & L Associations. We organized a new board of directors and Trident Credit Union was chartered in August 1997. We were the first S & L in the state permitted by the Department of Banking to convert to a credit union. I was one of the founders of the credit union and worked as treasurer/managing officer. At that time, I was also on the board of Rossini Savings, Cornerstone Savings Association, and treasurer of the United Ukrainian American Relief Committee, Inc.

Emilia Madylus was on the board of Trident Credit Union. In her last will and testament, she instructed that a *"Trust was to be established for the benefit of those children . . . in need of medical treatment and care due to injuries or harm suffered as a result of Chornobyl, Ukraine nuclear disaster . . . "* She named me as sole trustee. I organized a board of trustees, bylaws were enacted, and the Stefan and Emilia Madylus Trust Inc. was established in 1995. Another member of the board, and a good friend, was Larry Mazepa. Mr. Mazepa was president of the Ukrainian Self Reliance Credit Union of Philadelphia and a board member of the Sister Cities International organization in his hometown of Boyertown, Pennsylvania. The Boyertown-Bohodukhiv sister cities program was already involved in aiding the city of Bohodukhiv, in the Kharkiv region of Ukraine. Aid was being funneled in the form of medical supplies and medicine. Containers were shipped yearly providing clothing, medical supplies, an ambulance, glasses for the elderly and orphans. A successful student, teacher, and doctor exchange was in operation. As it turned out, Bohodukhiv is an area where a large number of former Chernobyl residents resettled. Many children living in the area were suffering from diseases and maladies secondary to radiation exposure. There was no adequate health care. The area was being served by a rather primitive medical clinic. Construction on the local hospital, begun during the Soviet Era, had been halted due to the worsening economic situation in Ukraine. The Madylus Trust, with the help of the Boyertown Sister Cities Organization and the newly established Bohodukiv Building Committee hired the architectural/construction firm of SITAL from the city of Kharkiv, Ukraine. Together, we established the Bohodukhiv Hospital Construction Project and funded the continuing construction of the hospital. Because of our project, the committee was able to secure matching funding from the government, and today, the Bohoduchiv Regional Hospital is open and serving the residents of the area.

In 1996, Dr. Alexander Chernyk, of the Ukrainian Federation of Greater Philadelphia sponsored Bohdan Gyrych, a ten-year-old resident of Kyiv, Ukraine, for hip replacement surgery and chemotherapy at St. Christopher's Hospital of Philadelphia. The Madylus Trust funded his treatment.

In 1999, the trust paid for a large shipment containing medical instruments, eye glasses, clothing, and over 3200 pounds of school supplies collected by the Sister City Committee of Boyertown.

In 2000, a large contribution was given to the Ukrainian Gold Cross Children's Camp in Lehighton to sponsor children from Chornobyl to summer camp at the Ukrainian Homestead.

In July 1992, I purchased 934 Chandler Street in the Fox Chase area of Philadelphia.

Oleh was living with his parents at the time. The boys and I were constantly in touch with him. He had been chronically ill for over six years and passed away on October 18, 1992. In April 1995, mom sold her house on Camac Street and came to live with Peter and I at our home on Chandler Street. George was working and had his own apartment in Conshohocken, Pennsylvania.

During these years, I was able to join Mom and her close friends, Sonia and Roman Melnyk from Chester, Pennsylvania, in their travels. In 1989, we toured the Hawaiian Islands; in 1999, we took a Caribbean Cruise. In September 1991, when Ukrainian artist Bohdan Mehyk opened his first art exhibit in Lviv, Ukraine, Mom and I traveled with his group. This was my first time in Ukraine. We were able to spend two days with my cousins, Nanka and Iryna, in Ternopil. They are the daughters of mom's oldest sister, Ulia. We saw the land where *grandfather's mill* stood and visited the Melnyk family crypt, built by grandfather Petro, at the cemetery in Ladychyn.

In 1993, we took a cruise to the Bahamas; in 1994, we traveled to Alaska. In 1995, we took a Scandinavian cruise and visited Norway, Sweden, Estonia, and Denmark. The highlight of the cruise was our visit to the Hermitage Museum in St. Petersburg, Russia.

In 1996, Peter stayed with mom in Lehighton, and I travelled with my friend, Charytina Lytwyn, to the Greek islands of Santorini and Crete, to Ephesus in Turkey. We visited the Old City in Jerusalem, the Parthenon in Athens, rode on camels at the pyramids in Giza, and attended the opening of the Tutankhamen Exhibit at the Cairo Museum in Egypt.

Mom was involved in a car accident on Easter Monday, March 1, 1997. She injured her hip, broke her right foot and both of her hands. She was hospitalized for a week, in rehab for three weeks, and then required home care for two months. Mom was back in Lehighton as soon as her recovery allowed. A mammogram that summer showed a lump in Mom's breast, which led to the diagnosis of breast cancer. Mom underwent two operations and six months of extensive radiation treatments. She refused to let anyone know about her illness. Her grandsons and I were the only ones aware of her situation.

In October 1998, in an effort to assist in the reintroduction of credit unions in Ukraine, the Ukrainian National Credit Union Association (USA) held their annual conference in Ukraine. I attended the conference. During the conference, I met with the mayor, chief doctor, and members of the Bohoduchiv Hospital Committee. After the conference, I was able to spend three days with my fraternal cousin, Oksana Mychalchuk, in Kolomyia. Oksana is the daughter of Antin Mychalewsky, Zenon's twin brother. We toured many of the places where my father grew up. Uncle Zenon had passed away that year on March 22, 1998.

On August 31, 1999, Peter had a terrible accident. He was hit by a bus and suffered crush injuries to his face and both feet. He endured facial reconstruction surgery and extensive rehab for his foot injuries. Despite all of his hardships, he has grown into a pleasant and kind young man. Peter lives with me. In September 2000, he began working full time in a sheltered workshop run by PATH Industries. He has become a very capable worker and one of their highest producers. He loves to do word puzzles, go camping with his friends, and anything that has to do with home improvement. We go to home improvement shows so that he can meet and collect autographs of his heroes Dean Johnson, Norm, and Tom Silva from *This Old House*, his favorite TV Show.

In December of 2000, I went to work as branch manager for Earthstar Bank. The office was closer to home, the hours were shorter, and I had more time to spend at home.

In the fall of 2001, Mom, my brother, Roman, and I traveled to Toronto, Canada, for the wedding of Roman Melnyk's daughter, Mila.

In the summer of 2002, Peter, George, his fiancé, Alexandra, and I traveled to California to attend the wedding of my youngest niece, Laura. We stayed on the beach at Malibu and the boys were able to visit with their four Bak-Boychuk cousins, Nadia, Gregory, Andrew, and Laura, and meet all of their families.

On July, 12, 2003, George married Alexandra Babanskyj. Alexandra was born on July 29, 1973. She grew up in Watchung, New Jersey, where she attended Watchung High School. She graduated from Yale University in 1995 with a degree in English. In 2006, Alex graduated from Temple Law School and currently practices law in Center City, Philadelphia, Pennsylvania.

After the wedding, Mom and I had to stop our travels due to her age and worsening heart condition. She had a damaged heart valve, but refused to get a pace maker. She tried to remain active by attending various church and Ukrainian community functions. We stayed at the Homestead in Lehighton often. In 2005, Mom began to experience episodes of confusion and was diagnosed with early signs of Alzheimer's. She fell asleep and passed away on October 18, 2005. She was eighty-three years old.

I have had some health issues of my own to deal with the past few years. I try to remain active in ODWU and at the Homestead. In January 2008, I resigned as manager of the Bridesburg branch of Earthstar Bank and am working on a part-time basis in the loan department. God has given me many blessings and some trials during my life. Every person and experience have added something unique to my life. I am thankful for every moment.

The latest blessing is my grandson, Nicholas Victor Bak-Boychuk, born August 4, 2006.

George, Alex, and Mykola live nearby in Lafayette Hill, Pennsylvania. They visit Baba and Uncle Petro often. As our family continues its journey through the next fifty years, I look forward to retirement, spending time in my garden, and more grandchildren.

## Important Dates

Emilia Melnyk Mychalewsky was born January 5, 1922, deceased October 18, 2005
Nicholas Taras Mychalewsky was born January 29, 1907, deceased May 13, 1977
Christine Helen Mychalewsky Bak-Boychuk was born December 13, 1946
Oleh Petro Bak-Boychuk born June 16, 1945, deceased October 18, 1992
Peter Theophil Bak-Boychuk was born on October 6, 1965.
George Michael Bak-Boychuk was born July 25, 1969
Alexandra Babanskyj Bak-Boychuk was born July 29, 1973
Nicholas Victor Bak-Boychuk was born August 4, 2006

**Proud grandmother Christine with Nicholas Bak-Boychuk**

# Roman Mychalewsky

The youngest of the Littlest Exiles from our families is Roman Mychalewsky.

(Based on a telephone interview with Roman)

I was born, March 9, 1949, in the Bayreuth DP camp in Bavaria, at a time when the majority of refugees had already made plans to leave. My mother's sister, Olha Stulkowsky, and her family left for the United States in June1949, and her brother, Bohdan Melnyk, and family left for Canada in August of the same year. My mother, Emilia Melnyk Mychalewsky, and father, Mykola, weren't quite ready to leave, and wanted to stay until I was a little older. I was baptized at the camp. My godmother was Bronyslawa Melnyk.

Finally, our sponsors, Aunt Olha and family, had made arrangements, and our papers were in place. We arrived in New York City in November 1949, when I was eight months old.

Much of my early family history is similar to my sister, Christine's.

We lived in Maryland where Father worked on a tobacco farm. Later, we moved to Chester, Pennsylvania and finally to Philadelphia.

When I was in high school, I joined Plast and befriended a group of like-minded adventurers who became my lifelong friends. One of my friends was Chrystyna's brother, Ostap Tatomyr. Other close friends included, Oleh Ciuk, Oleh Bak Boychuk, Bohdan and George Chajkivsky, and Roman Novakivsky.

We all joined the Plast fraternity, Burlaky, and during the 1970s, organized ski camps in Canada and upstate New York. I attended Pennsylvania State University and later was employed by the U.S. Postal Service.

During the 1970s, and after I retired, I traveled to Ukraine where I established contact with the Melnyk family members who did not leave in 1944: Uncle Roman and Aunt Julia.

My uncle, Reverend Roman Melnyk, remained in Ternopil. When the Soviets took over, he was presented with a choice: become an Orthodox priest or be deported to Siberia. He converted to the Ukrainian Orthodox Church and continued to provide spiritual care to his flock under extremely difficult postwar circumstances.

I also visited the oldest Melnyk sister, Julia Nenych, and her family, and made contact with the Mychalewsky family of Kolomyja.

Nadia and I continue to live in Philadelphia, enjoying our retirement.

**Roman (second from left) with best friends and girlfriends**

# To Leave a Legacy

# To Live, To Love, To Learn, To Leave a Legacy

*There are certain things that are fundamental to human fulfillment. The essence of these needs is captured in the phrase,' to live, to love, to learn, to leave a legacy'.*
—*First Things First*, Stephen R. Covey

**To Live:** *The need to live is our physical need for such things as food, clothing, shelter, economic well-being and health.*

Both Chrystyna and I had a somewhat shaky start in life—Chrystyna's harrowing first year and a half of life is described in Grandfather Julian's diary. I was born "on suitcases" in a war zone, and when I was eleven days old, we left on a year-long journey through Poland, Czechoslovakia, Austria, and Germany. We moved from shelter to shelter, food was scarce, there were few luxuries. We survived detentions, bombings, and narrow escapes—all before our first birthdays.

Despite that, Chrystyna and I have been blessed with excellent health.

We were fortunate to be in the right place when opportunities presented themselves and our parents made choices which turned out to be best for our families.

Our parents made the hard decision to leave our homeland and we managed to escape Stalin's totalitarian nightmare just in time.

My parents were in the area that became part of the Soviet Zone after the war and would have been trapped were it not for the tragic bombing of Dresden. This convinced my parents to flee to the safety of the American Zone.

The Tatomyrs, exhausted by their journey, considered staying in Vienna, where Father Julian could have found a position as a church pastor, but decided to leave for Western Austria at the last minute, just ahead of the advancing Red Army.

We were fortunate to have family members in North America who sponsored us when we were stranded in postwar Europe, and communities that helped us settle into our new countries. Our parents made sure that we had the best education they could afford and encouraged us to be professionals. We prospered in our new countries and were able to give back and to share our good fortune with others.

As adults, Chrystyna and I have had incredible, enjoyable careers; we were able to travel, see, and appreciate various cultures, teach in eight countries on five continents and, with humility and awe, experience the complexities of our world.

**To Learn:** *The need to learn is our mental need to develop and grow.*

Early in my adult life, I made a decision to become a teacher. It turned out to be the right choice for me. It defined me.

People become teachers for different reasons.

Some like the hours: all major holidays and summers off, job security, good pay, and an excellent pension.

Others enjoy teaching because they possess certain specific skills and, on a daily basis, have the privilege of sharing these skills, whether it's mathematics, history, or basketball, with young people.

Although these two aspects of teaching were important to me, I didn't begin to really develop as a teacher until I made the discovery that changed my approach to teaching and took me to a higher level as an educator.

Early in my career, I was teaching a Grade 11 remedial math class. My group consisted of a dozen or so boys who had failed the subject the year before. They were bored and they hated math. I tried to get them motivated. I tried to dazzle them.

One day, I set aside the curriculum and decided to teach them something I thought would be fun. I decided to teach them some basic trigonometry and took them outside to show them that just by knowing the angle of elevation and the distance to a flag pole, using trigonometry, we could calculate the height of that flagpole.

I thought that would be exciting. I explained the sine, cosine, and tangent ratios and was about to show them how to find the angle of elevation to the top of the flagpole when a boy raised his hand and asked, "Will I need to know trigonometry to get a job as a pizza delivery man?"

Everybody, including me, thought that was quite funny. My lesson was destroyed and I was brought down to earth.

That night, I had an epiphany. I realized that I was being selfish. I love math and, believe it or not, trigonometry can be fun (really!), but that afternoon, I had been trying to teach the *subject*. What I needed to do was to teach the *student*.

The next day, I changed everything about my teaching. I decided that instead of teaching facts, I would try to make a positive difference in the life of every child every day, by letting them enjoy learning. Once we achieve that, knowledge will follow.

I began to thrive on teaching.

A few years later, when I became a principal, I found a quote that inspired and guided me. I printed and distributed this quote to all my teachers every year, hoping that this philosophy would inspire them in their daily teaching.

*"I've come to the conclusion that I am the decisive element in the classroom. It is my personal approach that creates the climate. It's my daily mood that makes the weather. As a teacher, I possess a tremendous power to make a child's life miserable or joyful. I can be a tool of torture or an instrument of inspiration. I can humiliate or heal. In all situations it is my response that determines whether a crisis will escalate or de-escalate and a child's life humanized or de-humanized."*—Haim Ginott.

After paying my dues as vice-principal for seven years in three very different high schools, my superintendent decided I was ready for the next step and although I really enjoyed teaching, I felt everything that happened to me in life—all my experiences, from the DP Camps to altar boys to Plast, and all my experiences as a student and, of course, as a teacher and vice-principal—prepared me to be a high school principal. I was ready.

But I was determined not to become, 'THE PRINCIPAL', the scary, final arbiter, man in a suit, sitting in the office who is only seen at parent-teacher meetings and during graduation ceremonies. I was determined to be different—the type of principal I wish I had had.

**Sutton DHS** In 1988, I was appointed principal of Sutton District High School. SDHS was considered a tough school—1,400 kids, a high absentee rate, a high drop-out rate, a high percentage of unmotivated students and with many characteristics often associated with inner-city schools. My superintendent instructed me to "turn the school around."

The next seven years were the most challenging and most rewarding of my career. I was fortunate that there were dedicated teachers, department heads, vice principals and office staff, at the school who welcomed me and eagerly participated in all the changes that were needed to make the school a better place for students. I was also fortunate that my new superintendent, John MacLaughlin and the school board's director of education, Bob Cressman, were so supportive of all our initiatives. Together, we were able to make a lot of good things happen.

We opened a Child Care Center so that single teen mothers could continue their education while their babies were well cared for on site; we started a re-entry program for adult high school drop-outs; we opened a First Nations Study Center and held annual Pow-Wows right in our school gym to show our native students the importance of their culture and to make them feel more welcome. We even bought our own school bus (funded by the community) so that our students could more easily travel to sports competitions and field trips. Our students got involved in various community projects which also brought the community closer to the school. If we strayed from Board Procedures from time to time, our supervisors usually forgave us because they knew we were doing all this in the best interests of the kids.

To build school spirit and to get the whole school involved in a single activity, I asked the owner of a local airfield to fly over our school to take an aerial photo of all our students. The editor of the local paper was invited to go along on the flight to take the picture. We managed to get 1,500 students and staff to stand on the football field to spell out S D H S. The picture appeared on the front page of the local paper and a tradition was started. For the next seven years, we took an aerial picture of the students spelling out various words on the field and hung the framed photographs in a place of honor in the library. On the days we took these pictures, we usually had almost perfect attendance at school. With time, school spirit soared, attendance improved and so did our test scores and graduation rate.

When it was announced that I would be transferred after seven years at Sutton, the student council asked me to fly over the school one more time to take one last picture.

They wanted to say good-bye. As I flew over the school, I was really touched. The fourteen hundred students had spelled 'ANDY' and all of them were waving madly.

**University of Toronto** While I was at Sutton District High School, I received an offer to teach at the Ontario Institute for Studies in Education (University of Toronto). For five years (summers and weekends) I instructed aspiring school administrators at the Principals' Qualification Program. This was an incredibly rewarding professional experience and a great honor.

The director of this program was Professor Ken Leithwood, one of North America's top experts in Educational Leadership practices. At the time, he was doing research on Transformational Leadership practices and asked to visit my school. After his visit he decided to use Sutton High to study how leadership practices influence school change.

His report was very positive and highly supportive of the work we had done at the school. This case study was later published as four chapters of a graduate level text book on educational leadership (*Changing Leadership for Changing Times,* Leithwood, Jantzi, Steinbach) that is still in use today at the University of Toronto.

**Denison SS** After seven years at Sutton, I was transferred to Dr. Denison Secondary School, in Newmarket. I was so happy that I was finally going to be a principal in a school in my own town. Everywhere I went I ran into students, their parents or teachers. It created a very different dynamic for me. The parents of my students were my neighbors and friends. My students worked part time as servers in restaurants and as clerks in stores we frequented. Wherever we went in town, I could always expect to hear, "Hi, Mr. Melnyk."

Dr. Denison, a highly regarded community leader for whom the school was named, was still alive during my tenure there. Although it was difficult for him physically, he visited the school at least twice a year—for graduation and for the annual aerial photo.

**Williams SS** Three years later, I was transferred to Dr. Williams Secondary School in Aurora. This again was an extremely positive experience. I have so many fond memories of the many outstanding people with whom I worked and the students we served. I also continued the tradition of taking aerial photos at my schools.

In 1999, after almost thirty years with the York Region School District School Board, I was eligible for retirement but wasn't ready to leave teaching. Chrystyna and I decided to apply for teaching positions overseas. With that in mind, my friend, Adel Kamel, a chemistry and physics specialist and I traveled to Boston for an international school hiring fair. We each had several interviews with overseas school but neither of us was offered a position.

The next year, at another international hiring fair in Toronto, a school in Madrid, *International College Spain*, had an opening for a secondary principal. They also had an opening for a special needs teacher. Chrystyna and I applied for these positions.

This school had an excellent reputation and was in a highly desirable location. Seventy-six people from all over the world applied for the principal position in Madrid. I didn't think I had a chance. Six finalists were asked to come to Madrid for three days of interviews. I was one of them. Seeing the other candidates, all with international experience, I again didn't think I had a chance. After two days, only three candidates remained—a young man from Britain, an American, and me. Somehow, I was chosen.

Chrystyna and I were offered the positions and we started an amazing adventure that lasted several years.

Just before we left Dr. Williams Secondary School for Spain, the students again surprised me. My going-away gift from them was a flight in a light aircraft over Toronto and York Region so I could see the three schools in which I served as principal—from the air. When we flew over Williams, the twelve hundred students and staff again surprised me. They had spelled out 'FELICIDAD' on the football field and as the airplane flew over, everyone was waving and cheering. That was another unforgettable moment and the best going-away present I could have hoped for.

**Spain** Our first international school experience at International College Spain started in September 2000. We loved Spain—the Euro lifestyle, the "ex-pat" experience, the relaxed Spanish attitudes to work and the fun, the music, the castles, the cathedrals, and the history. Once we understood the tradition and passion involved, we even got hooked on bullfighting. We *ran with the bulls* in small town fiestas and almost ran in Pamplona—but wisely changed our minds and watched the silly tourists from the stands of the arena. We became huge fans of the *Real Madrid* football team, watched their games and celebrated after every victory. We spent every peseta we earned to travel to every corner of Spain, including Tenerife, Ibiza, and Ceuta, the tiny Spanish enclave in northern Africa, and to Portugal and France.

We had many visitors while we were in Madrid, including our sons who kept telling us that since we came to Spain, we were acting like teenagers.

Just before we left Spain, we decided we wanted to complete "The Camino," the famous Santiago de Compostela pilgrimage. The pilgrimage trail starts in the village of St. Jean Pied-du-Port in southern France and runs 780 kilometers (almost 500 miles), across the northern part of Spain through Pamplona, Burgos, Leon, and dozens of villages and towns to the cathedral in the town of Santiago de Compostela. Pilgrims usually take thirty days to walk this trail, visiting ancient churches, and staying in shelters along the way. We only had a week. We decided to walk a few parts of the trail but mostly, we did the pilgrimage by car and instead of staying in humble shelters, we stayed in luxurious Paradores (Spanish-style hotels located in castles and other exotic settings). It was still a beautiful and memorable religious experience. (After we left Spain, we found out that David Beckam and his wife, 'Posh Spice' moved into a house very close to International College Spain and visited our school with their sons. Chrystyna would have enjoyed meeting them. The Beckams later decided to register their children in a nearby British School.)

**China** After two years in Spain, we returned to Canada, where I became principal of a small private school in Toronto. After only a few weeks in the position, the school owners asked Chrystyna and me to represent the school at a student fair in China. We traveled to Beijing and Hong Kong, visited schools and worked very hard at the student conventions. We visited all the tourist places of interest like the Great Wall, the Forbidden City, Tiananmen Square, Mao's tomb and Victoria Peak but most importantly, we learned a lot about Chinese culture and how business is conducted in that country.

We also discovered how incredibly well the communist government in China was able to keep news about unpleasant events from the world. We were in Hong Kong while the SARS epidemic raged just north of the city, foreign visitors knew nothing about this. Weeks after we returned to Toronto, we learned about all the deaths that occurred in the area just north of Hong Kong while we were there, but only *after* that epidemic had spread to Toronto and several people had died.

No precautions were taken in Hong Kong because the Chinese government elite decided to keep it secret. That was unforgivable. We were wandering through the crowded outdoor markets of Kowloon, we ate with the locals at the height of the epidemic, but even though officials were fully aware that an epidemic was spreading, nobody bothered to warn us. After that experience, we became a little less enthusiastic about the "Chinese Economic Miracle."

**Trinidad** The following spring, I received a phone call from an agent searching for a vice-principal for a Canadian school in Trinidad. At first, I said no. I was concerned that after being a principal all these years I wouldn't do well as a vice-principal. But they offered tempting incentives and we couldn't resist. We were provided with a car and a lovely four-bedroom mansion on a hillside in Port of Spain, overlooking the bay. From our balcony we could watch the sailboats and tour ships in the bay. Every morning, we could see the green and yellow parrots flying to their feeding grounds, and in the evening, the scarlet ibis returning from Venezuela. At night, we could see the twinkling lights of Port of Spain and Levantile.

We loved the beaches, got hooked on calypso music, joined a calypso band, and "played" Carnival. We attended live shows featuring legendary performers like Sparrow and David Rudder and listened to dozens of steel bands. Chrystyna celebrated her sixtieth birthday dancing on the streets of Port of Spain in the carnival parade wearing a beautiful carnival costume.

It was great to live in a tropical climate, but we found it difficult when we came down from our opulent hilltop home every day and had to pass through the slums below, seeing people living in tin shacks in abject poverty. Trinidad has huge oil reserves and all their oil profits could easily provide for the basic needs of all Trinidadians. Unfortunately, a small group of people have become very rich while the majority has remained poor. The rich lament that there is so much crime and are constantly fearful that they, or members of their families, will be kidnapped for ransom. They spend huge amounts of money on security but haven't figured out that life would be so much better if only they could learn to share their wealth with their fellow citizens.

**Japan** Our next posting was Columbia International School in Tokyo, Japan. I was appointed principal and Chrystyna was hired as special education coordinator. We loved Japan. The people were wonderful, the sights were exotic, and the country was safe, interesting, and orderly. We could see Mt. Fuji from our apartment balcony, but only on days when sacred Fuji-San decided to show itself. We learned to travel everywhere by train, to line up quietly, and to endure the crowds. We were fascinated by "salarymen," young working men, usually uniformly dressed in black suits, having lifetime job security but little individualism. We explored dozens of temples and climbed Mt. Fuji (though not to the top). A Japanese saying warns that someone who climbs Mount Fuji is a hero. Anyone who climbs Fuji twice is a fool. We didn't want to take a chance on being considered fools.

We travelled on the *Shinkansen* (bullet train) to Kyoto to explore the Geisha district and the famous Kyoto temples and attended sumo matches at the sumo shrine in Tokyo. We skied in Sapporo, marveled at the cherry blossoms in Tokyo in spring, and regularly attended the fascinating and unique Kabuki theatre presentations in the Ginza district.

Before we left Japan, I was somehow convinced to participate in a Japanese TV reality show—an afternoon I'd rather forget.

**Kuwait** We had a small taste of life in the Middle East during the six weeks we spent helping to set up a new Canadian international school in Kuwait. Arriving from Frankfurt, our flight path took us along the Danube River, across the Black Sea, then along the Iraq-Iran border with the forbidding Zagros Mountains on the Iranian side and the Iraqi desert and oilfields on the Iraqi side, and with Baghdad just out of sight to the west. As we reached the *Arabian* Gulf (not the Persian Gulf, please), the aircraft made a quick descent into Kuwait City. Flying so close to a major war zone was an unnerving experience.

Less than a generation before, Kuwait was a desert dotted with Bedouin tents. Today it's a growing cosmopolitan city with too many modern and elegant air-conditioned shopping malls, hotels, apartment buildings, and western-style fast food restaurants. Women in traditional black *abayas*, covered from head to toe with only tiny slits for their eyes, browsing through expensive shops in the air conditioned supermall, mingle with elegant women dressed in western clothing. Kuwaiti men in white robes lounging over coffee mingle with the foreign Western workers temporarily living in Kuwait.

Our hotel in downtown Kuwait was used by a British outfit, which provided "Security Guards" for truck convoys that traveled daily from Kuwait to Baghdad. These mercenary soldiers worked for six week in Iraq and then were allowed two weeks rest in our hotel. A "soldier" we befriended told us that of his original twenty-four-man detail, only sixteen remained. The others had been killed in Iraq—but their deaths will never be recorded among the war fatalities. For these mercenaries, the pay was excellent but life expectancy was low.

The look in the soldier's eyes indicated he would have preferred to be home instead of preparing for another mission, but since his pay was withheld until the completion of his two year contract, he and his friends had to go back to Iraq.

**Egypt** Our next posting was at the Canadian International School of Egypt in Cairo. Once again I received a phone call asking if I could come to Cairo to replace a principal whose wife had become ill. It sounded like a wonderful opportunity. We lived in Maadi, a suburb of Cairo where many ex-pats live, and on a good day, could see the Great Pyramid of Giza from my office window at school. Chrystyna and I spent many evenings in our favorite restaurants on the banks of the Nile River, watching feluccas sailing by in the setting sun.

We rode camels in the desert, snorkeled in the Red Sea, and basked in Sharm el Sheik. We cruised down the Nile from Luxor to Aswan twice; the second time, with our three-year-old granddaughter, Anya, and her mother, Kristine.

Seeing the temples of Karnak through the eyes of a child was priceless.

But the highlight of our stay in Egypt was climbing to the top of Mount Sinai to catch the sunrise after spending the night in a Bedouin camp at the base of the mountain. That was a spectacular spiritual experience.

*        *        *

**Twelve hundred students from Dr. G.W. Williams Secondary School
in Aurora wishing us luck
June 2000**

I've had a long and amazing educational career. I was a math teacher for sixteen years, a vice principal for eight years, a principal in Ontario for twelve years and overseas for another six years for a total of forty-two years as an educator. I have been a teacher and a principal in schools on five continents and loved every minute.

Few have been fortunate to have had such a rewarding career.

Many years ago, Saint Augustine stated that "the world is a book, and those who have not traveled have read only one page."

Our travels, to incredibly interesting places all over this world have allowed us to experience volumes.

**To Love:** *The need to love is our social need to relate to other people, to belong, to love and to be loved.*

My parents nurtured me, gave me love, support, and every opportunity to succeed. My big brother protected and guided me (when I needed protection and guidance), and I had wonderful friends as a child. As I grew older, I met other friends who made my life interesting and purposeful.

But the greatest gift of love came to me as I approached adulthood. I met a beautiful woman, a soul mate, and friend. She is intelligent, loving, interesting, passionate, and exciting. We've been on a honeymoon for more than forty years. The best decision I ever made was kissing her in the bus station in Montreal, pursuing her, marrying her, and loving her ever since.

In the summer of 1969, I proposed to Chrystyna, rented a nice flat not far from downtown Montreal, and invested $5,000 (borrowed from the same Ukrainian Credit Union where my father had worked) in a restaurant venture, La Steppe.

On December 27, 1969, on a day that a record thirty-six inches of snow fell on Montreal, Chrystyna and I were married at St. Michael's Church and had our reception at La Steppe's very recently finished reception hall. (Workers were installing the plumbing and carpets the day before our wedding. They just made it.) Our wedding was the first event at *our* restaurant. In spite of the snow, almost all of our guests made it. It was a party!

Since we held Canadian and American passports, we could have lived and worked anywhere in North America. We decided we wanted to live in Montreal. It was a vibrant and exciting city, we had many friends, and teaching opportunities were plentiful. (A month or so before we got married, I called my school board office to see if there were any openings for elementary teachers. I told my superintendent I was about to marry a teacher from Pennsylvania. He hired Chrystyna, on my recommendation, sight unseen, over the phone.)

When we returned from our honeymoon in January, Chrystyna taught a Grade 6 class at Corpus Christie School in Baie-d'Urfe, a few kilometers from my school, St. Thomas High School in the West Island area of Montreal.

After less than two years in Montreal, with the political situation in Quebec heating up, we joined thousands of other English-speaking Quebecers and headed down Highway 401 to Ontario. We loved Montreal and never thought we'd leave, but we agonized over our loyalties. I considered myself a *Canadian* living in Quebec, not a *Quebecer* somehow stuck in Canada. A few months earlier, my best friend, George Wesolowsky, opened his medical practice not far from Toronto, in Paris, Ontario and my brother married Tania Boyko from Toronto. Somehow it felt like Toronto would be an interesting destination.

Teaching positions were available in Ontario, exciting opportunities existed for both of us in that province, and the salaries were very good. We thought we'd give it a try for a year or two, and then return to Montreal. I picked up the *Globe and Mail*, found a school searching for a math teacher in Newmarket, a growing suburban town just north of Toronto. Without so much as calling ahead, we drove to the school. I asked to see the principal, told him I was a math teacher and that I'd accept the job. He asked me a few perfunctory questions and hired me.

Just before we got married, Chrystyna's doctor told her that it would be difficult for her to have babies, and if we wanted to have children, she should have them as soon as possible. Almost exactly one year after our wedding, on December 18, 1970, our first son, Markian, was born at St. Mary's Hospital in Montreal. He was a beautiful, happy, and healthy baby with an excellent disposition.

When Chrystyna was pregnant with our second baby, we moved to our first real house on Sunnidale Road in Barrie, Ontario. Our second son, Roman, was born March 16, 1974. He too was beautiful, happy, and healthy. We enjoyed the Barrie lifestyle for a few years but finally, tired of the daily commute, we moved to Newmarket—closer to our jobs and closer to Toronto.

Our two children, Markian and Roman, are the best expressions of our love. We enjoyed every minute of their childhood. They continue to enrich our lives. We love them and they love us back. They married wonderful, dynamic, intelligent women, Kristine Chandler, a lawyer, daughter of Ken and Shan Chandler, and Tammy Jones, a financial analyst, daughter of Bruce and Carolyn Jones, and gave us three gorgeous granddaughters, Anya, Ava, and Julia. They are our pride and joy every day. They give us more love than anyone can imagine.

**To Leave a Legacy** *The need to leave a legacy is our spiritual need to have a sense of meaning, purpose, personal congruence and contribution.*

Our children, Markian and Roman,
our grand-children, Anya, Ava, Julia,
our family everywhere
all the students whose lives we touched
and this book.
That is my legacy.

# EPILOGUE

## Tributes, Memoirs and Images

1. *Portrait of a Child Soldier,* Volodymyr Tatomyr

2. *Babcia—Grandmother,* Bronyslawa Martyniuk Melnyk

3. *Eulogy,* Sophia Tereshkevych Tatomyr, 1984

4. *Eulogy,* Jaroslav Tatomyr, 1994

5. *Growing up in Montreal*

6. *My Uncle's Trunk:* Vasylko and Erna Martyniuk

7. *The Tatomyr Clan, Open Letter to his children,* O. Tatomyr

8. *Autobiography,* O. Tatomyr

# 1. Tribute

## *Portrait of a Child Soldier,* Volodymyr Tatomyr

Following are a few short excerpts from Volodymyr Tatomyr's book, *Youth in Defense of Their Homeland* published in Philadelphia in 1960.*

- **Philadelphia, 1958.** I sit at my desk in my residence in Philadelphia writing my memoirs. My writing is accompanied by the steady rumble of subway cars transporting passengers to distant parts of the city. Often during my daily work, in the evening or in the loneliness of the dark night I am suddenly consumed by an escalating, overwhelming force. Frequently it is distant, unclear, incomprehensible . . . but its aftereffect on me is familiar.

  Forty years have passed since I was a 16 year old youth fighting for the liberation of my homeland. The images overcome my heart still, intrude on my peace of mind and senses with memories of despair and tragic deeds, and haunt my consciousness with the memories of the deaths of my friends and comrades.

  These tumultuous, painful moments slowly vanish as my imagination is calmed by the whisper of winds from my beloved homeland and the gentle rustling of vast fields of wheat covering the steppes of Ukraine. The stillness of my soul is abruptly awakened by the staccato burst of rifle fire . . . . and the screams of the dead and dying . . . my friends breathing their last breath as I try to will them to live. The blood spilled by the dead is recorded for posterity by the countless poppies wilting in the fields and meadows of my homeland . . . . and at the height of my anguish I recall my beautiful wife, Oksana, fighting and losing her life to a powerful enemy, tuberculosis . . . . burying her in the rich black soil of Ukraine after such a short time together and eventually leaving her to fight another war, and to wander the world in search of a peaceful safe haven. As I remember and grieve, I become aware of the contrast between my youth and my advancing years. Yet, in the security of my new homeland, I grieve for my childhood friends, my comrades in battle, my family left behind and my beloved Oksana.

May the memories of my youth speak to others through the voices of those who witnessed and experienced the brutality of a war fought for freedom."

- **Spring, 1914:** "In March of 1914, as twelve year old students and members of Plast in Strij, we had an opportunity to participate in a celebration of the one hundredth anniversary of the birth of Taras Shevchenko, the beloved poet-laureate of Ukraine. Among thousands of joyful Ukrainians of Galicia, we participated in a massive procession of peasants in their white garb, villagers, town and city people in their magnificent local costumes of every style and color, Plast groups (including ours), Prosvita* societies, choirs, orchestras, sports organizations and political leaders and clergy led the procession. The songs, the music, the laughter and the emotions overwhelmed everyone present.

  Shortly after this celebration World War I began. Many of my friends and comrades died but others arose to replace them and to continue the relentless fight for our freedom."

- **In 1918,** we were fifteen and sixteen year olds. It was a pivotal year. In January, hundreds of Ukrainian students volunteered to help save Kyiv from the advancing Russian Armies. Poorly equipped and untrained, they made their stand in the town of Brody. Three hundred young men were killed by the Soviets but they slowed them enough to give the new Ukrainian government a chance to form. On January 22, 1918, The Ukrainian National Republic was declared in Kyiv. On February 9th, Germany, Austria-Hungary, Bulgaria and Turkey recognized the new Republic. We were overjoyed but the Poles were terrified that they would lose Eastern Galicia and increased their oppression of our lands. Polish authorities banned Plast and warned of severe consequences for anyone caught participating in Plast activities. At the same time, the Polish scout group was allowed to function and was ordered to spy on us and to track our movements. This was a signal for us to increase our activism. Our elders held meetings, created secret committees and began to collect guns, rifles and other armaments.

- **The Pledge.** One evening, our Plast group was told to meet in the basement of the Prosvita building where we received instructions. First, all of us raised our

---

\*     Prosvita means 'enlightenment' in Ukrainian. The Prosvita society was created in 1868 to preserve and develop Ukrainian culture and education and as a counterbalance to anti-Ukrainian colonial and Russophile trends in Ukrainian society. In 1913 Prosvita had 77 affiliate societies and more than three thousand reading rooms, as well as, libraries, theatre clubs, choirs, orchestras and study groups. In 1939 Prosvita was shut down by the newly-arrived Soviet rulers but continued operating outside the borders of Ukraine, in Europe and North America. It was renewed in Ukraine in 1988.

right hands and with voices filled with emotion, in the dim light we repeated the following words: "I will serve the Ukrainian nation and am ready to die for the cause, so help me God." We were officially soldiers of a new Ukraine! We were told to be prepared. We began gathering uniforms, rifles, pistols and other armaments from the Austrian army depots which were abandoned when the Austrian and German troops were demobilized and were retreating. We hid the armaments in safe places around town.

- **On October 31, 1918, at night,** we were ordered to report to a designated spot. All forty or fifty of us sat quietly on the floor—the only sound was the sound of forty or fifty hearts beating—thinking about the following day when we might actually become citizens of our own nation. This was no longer a game, but a life and death battle for freedom. The hours passed by very slowly. It was after midnight and outside it was raining. At three o'clock in the morning we were directed to another room where we received rifles and ammunition. In the dark corridor, 15 and 16 year old soldiers stood in two rows, waiting for sunrise.

- **November 1, early morning.** The rain pounded the concrete, the wind whistled through the orchards and scattered chestnuts everywhere. We approached the fenced-in train station. One section of our group disarmed the guards and after an endless half hour, the lights finally came on in the station. We had succeeded. At exactly seven o'clock one of my classmates ran out of the station with a Ukrainian flag in his hand. He ran quickly to the town hall and in minutes climbed the tower and hoisted the blue and yellow flag from the highest point. Behind the autumn clouds, the sun rose and powerful calls of joy, and pride resounded among the victorious young soldiers. I looked around. We were all so young. We were children but we could not go back. We were committed to total victory. This scene was repeated countless times in villages and towns throughout western Ukraine. The West Ukrainian National Republic was formed.

- **Spring 1919.** (Volodymyr, at the age of 17 had been appointed leader of a Plast-Youth unit within the Ukrainian Galician Army. They were often sent on scouting expeditions in support of the Army. Following is an eyewitness report): In the Spring of 1919 the Galician Army was advancing toward Lviv. The scouts reported that several enemy divisions on horses had appeared in Stanislav and were spending their evenings in a coffee house. As I approached the Dnister River, I met our 14 year old scout who identified the enemy as Poles. I received an order to find a number of boats to be positioned on our shore. A number of 14-15 year old boys crossed the river to Romania and returned with a number of rowboats. Unfortunately four young boys died in this dangerous mission.

- **August 1919.** We were about 80 miles from Kyiv. I was assigned three scouts, a wagon and a driver, grenades and a small machine gun to try to intercept communiqués from Bolsheviks regarding the strategies of their infantry against tanks. The three scouts entered the village to find food. Unexpectedly a Bolshevik squad on horses galloped into the village surprising them. The driver and I were able to retreat through a cemetery into the forest but the three scouts were captured. As evening approached the driver and I returned to try to find our scouts. We spotted six or seven Bolsheviks leading one of the scouts. They demanded that he dig his own grave and one of the Bolsheviks from a distance of a few centimeters shot the scout in the face and shattered his jaw. We started firing our machine guns and sprayed the Bolsheviks. Some got away but we killed several of them. We pulled our friend out of the grave. He was still alive. We then threw the dead Bolsheviks into the grave and took our scout to a shelter. The boy could not speak but he asked for a piece of paper. He wrote that he was from Pidhajci and begged that we kill him because he knew he could not live with the injuries. We told him we could not kill him. He was bleeding profusely and died before our eyes soon after. The next day, villagers brought us a second scout. The villagers told us the Bolsheviks let the scout go because they were convinced that he had gone insane from the torture. All his fingers were cut off, they smashed his nose and gouged out one eye. Mercifully, blood poisoning ended the scout's life. Later, we discovered that that scout was a 17 year old girl. The third scout was found the next day. He had been tortured, tied to a log and thrown into the river where he drowned. All three had died refusing to pass any secrets to the Bolsheviks. They did not betray their homeland.*

Volodymyr survived the typhoid epidemic that decimated the Ukrainian armies in 1919 in the 'Quadrangle of Death', south of Kyiv.

In 1920, at the age of 18, Volodymyr was a young officer in the Ukrainian Galician Army. His unit was surrounded and captured by the Polish Army. Several of his comrades died in the Polish prison camps. He was released in 1921.

During the late 1920s he married his sweetheart, Oksana. She died one year later of tuberculosis.

In 1938 Volodymyr was imprisoned by the Poles and sent to the Bereza Kartuska Prison. He was released in September, 1939 and returned to Sambir.

A year later, in 1940, Volodymyr's younger brother, Evhen, died after prolonged torture in a Bolshevik prison in Sambir. (Please see "Torture NKVD 1" in Chapter 9).

In 1942 his sister, Eleonora died when the train in which she was traveling with her young daughters was fire-bombed by the Nazis just a few kilometers from Strij.

In 1944, his best friend died while fighting with the Ukrainian First Galician Division against the invading Soviet forces at Brody.

---

* translated and collated by his niece Chrystyna Tatomyr Melnyk.

In 1948, he emigrated to the United States along with his cousins, Jaroslav and Oleksander and their families and settled in Philadelphia where he helped organize Plast and Prosvita Reading Rooms in that city and published three books about his war experiences.

He died in 1962 at the age of 60 and is buried at the Ukrainian cemetery in Fox Chase, Pennsylvania. He never remarried.

# 2. Tribute

## *Our Babcia—Grandmother, Bronyslawa Martyniuk Melnyk*

She is often referred to as the "glue" of our family, for her ability to bring us all together on holidays and special occasions. Due to the wisdom, determination and character forged through her 96 years, the woman we call simply *Babcia*—Bronyslawa Melnyk—is so much more than the typical Ukrainian grandmother evoked by her moniker. Sure, she embroidered each of us our own traditional shirts and made sure we always had more than enough to eat, but our Babcia has always stood as a figure of solidity, consistency and unconditional love for as long as our family can remember. Most remarkable has been her capacity to quietly endure a lifetime of challenges, most of them unimaginable to her grandchildren today.

Bronyslawa's (Bronia's) life began peacefully enough on January 7, 1912, when she was born in the village of Ivanivka, part of the Terebovla *Oblast* (province) of the Halychyna region. She was the third child of five children born to Justina and Mykhajlo Martyniuk. Showing an early interest and aptitude for education, young Bronia was sent to the town of Ternopil at the age of 10 to attend one of the few Ukrainian girls' *gymnasia* (high schools) in Halychyna. She excelled in her studies and in 1930 became the first Martyniuk to achieve *matura* (graduation). She had to complete her final oral and written exams in Polish—a feat most of her classmates could not accomplish.

Bronyslawa continued her education through post-secondary courses, and after completing a Home Economics Certificate program at the Institute in Ternopil, she found work with the Ukrainian Cooperative in her home town, Ivanivka. While attending a summer seminar for Cooperative employees in 1938, she was re-acquainted with a handsome young man from her school days, Bohdan Melnyk. Within two years, she and Bohdan were married.

Bronyslawa's first son, Roman—my father—was born in Ladychyn in July 1941, in the midst of advancing German occupation forces. She gave birth to her second son, Andrij, in February 1944, and eleven days later, with the Soviet front bearing down on their town, she and Bohdan packed up their toddler and newborn son and headed to unknown destinations westward. Meanwhile, Bronyslawa had also learned of the capture and presumed death of her dear brother Vasyl, with the whereabouts of other family members virtually unknown. Over the next five years, relying on the good graces of relatives, acquaintances and family friends, the young Melnyk family found refuge in Horlyci, Austria, and various Displaced Persons' camps throughout Germany.

Growing up, I was always aware of the circumstances under which my father and uncle were born and raised in their early years. Simple math and basic history led me to realize that this all occurred during wartime, which I figured must have been difficult but I didn't give much more thought to it. Today, as a mother of two small children myself, I am utterly amazed that my grandmother's young family was uprooted, moved westward to new and foreign places, relying on fragile social networks for work and shelter, during such a turbulent period. I am left to wonder if I could have found her strength to weather it as gracefully as she did.

Always recognizing the value of education, Bronyslawa took advantage of the opportunity to learn English, earning a Translator's certificate. This stood her in good stead when the Melnyks eventually landed in Canada on August 16, 1949, otherwise penniless and with few apparent prospects for supporting their two children. Eventually she found work as a seamstress in Montreal. Her abilities and attention to detail with clothing was quickly recognized, promoting her to the more regarded and lucrative position of sample maker. At the same time she contributed to her community by joining the Ukrainian Catholic Women's League and other women's associations in Montreal and seeing her sons through their Plast and academic endeavors.

Bronyslawa would be challenged once again when Bohdan, her husband of twenty-five short years, died at the age of 55. Her sons now grown and moved away, she maintained her family's Montreal apartment on her own for nearly twenty years. During this time, she celebrated the marriages of Roman to Tania Boyko, and Andrij to Chrystyna Tatomyr, and in the years that followed, the birth of her four grandchildren: Marichka, Markian, Roman and Melia. At that point Bronyslawa officially became Babcia.

The early years for us four cousins were regularly marked by the five-hour road trips to Montreal to visit Babcia (and the promise of a Kit Kat bar once we got there). Quite often she would return the visit with even longer bus rides to see us in Ottawa, Toronto, Barrie and Newmarket—trips she insisted on taking by herself, and sometimes overnight. In an effort to maximize her time with us and to broaden our understanding of our Ukrainian heritage, Babcia began taking us for yearly two-week excursions to Soyuzivka, the Ukrainian National Association property in upstate New York. With Babcia at the helm, the Melnyk grandchildren felt like we had the run of the resort, attending Ukrainian dance camp in the morning and inhabiting the pool in the afternoon while Babcia caught up with her contemporaries on the deck. For four or five years in the prime of our childhood, this became our summer tradition and strengthened the bond between all of us.

Inevitably the long trips to and from her children and their families proved too demanding even for Babcia. Fortunately, St. Demetrius Parish in Toronto had undertaken an ambitious building project and opened its Seniors' Residence in 1984 (immediately adjacent to the elementary school attended by Roman's daughters). Babcia packed up her belongings once more and left her beloved adopted hometown of Montreal to take up an apartment much closer to her grandchildren. This allowed Babcia to become a more established fixture in all of our lives and cemented her status as Melnyk family matriarch. She has presided over every Christmas and Easter celebration our combined family has held since, and has been the guest of honor at countless recitals, concerts, graduations, weddings and baptisms over the years. Through it all she chronicled every press clipping, program and leaflet that made mere mention of any of our names, and despite her modest pension she managed to put away a substantial amount for each of her grandchildren for the betterment of their futures. And every year without fail, until her sons could convince her she was no longer fit to do so, she boarded an overnight bus bound for Montreal to attend to the grave of her true love, Bohdan. In the new millennium Babcia watched the fourth generation of her family emerge with the birth of her great-grandchildren: Anya, Will, Ava, Julia and Katya. by Melania Melnyk, granddaughter.

# 3. Tribute

## *Eulogy: Sophia Tatomyr, by Oleksander Tatomyr*

Sophia was born in the foothills of the beautiful Carpathian Mountains in Ukraine. The region is lush with dense pine forests, meadows ablaze with delicate, wild flowers, and the gurgling rapids of the Dnister River. At her birth, the mystique of this area danced across her face, reflecting the light, the lush green of the forests, the swaying wild flowers and grasses blowing in the wind. She was lulled to sleep by the hum of the nearby Dnister and the numerous creeks flowing from the mountains into the mighty river.

To her doting parents, older brothers and sisters, neighbors, and visitors to this resort region, Sophia resembled a beautiful, delicate wild flower. They often commented on her beauty and delicate features.

Sophia was the seventh child of the Tereshkevych family. As the youngest child she basked in the attention of her loving family. Unfortunately, in her early years, her father became ill with an undiagnosed disease. Many of the family's responsibilities fell on the shoulders of her mother to feed, clothe, and parent a large family. Soon, the older children began to help their mother to sustain the family. As the youngest child, Sophia was somewhat oblivious to the difficulties that faced them.

Suddenly, World War I exploded. The eldest son, the pride and joy of his father, volunteered to join the army. A brave soldier, he was killed by a grenade in the Alps toward the end of the war. A pervasive sadness blanketed the family after his death. The health of Sophia's father, after the death of his son, declined rapidly. His only solace came from his second son, Osyp, who tried to be a father to his siblings and a support to his mother. Sophia tried to lift her father's spirits with her lilting, melodious chatter and infectious laughter.

From an early age, Sophia loved the outdoors. She was captivated by the glistening brooks that flowed down the mountain into the Dnister. However; during thunderstorms, the majestic Dnister became a ferocious force that endangered the homes of nearby villagers. During these storms in the mountains, the echoes magnified the sounds of thunder and lightning. As the waters of the Dnister began to rise to the shoreline, Sophia would run home and find reassuring hugs from her mother.

In fair weather, Sophia was drawn to the majestic mountain, *Knyaza Hora* (Prince's Mountain), behind her home. With pure joy, Sophia would gaze at the mountain that shimmered in the sunlight. Her greatest desire was to climb to the mountain peak when she got older.

Sophia's mother often entertained her children with magical stories from the past. She said that long ago, a castle stood on this mountain. Wealthy princes and princesses of the nobility resided in this stately castle. Over a period of time, a monastery replaced the existing castle. It was occupied by many religious monks, who developed illuminated manuscripts, tilled the soil, worked in producing arts and crafts, and constantly prayed to God Almighty to protect the mountains and villagers scattered through the mountains and valleys of this region,

In ancient times, Sophia's mother continued, a famous king had lived in Spas and ruled Ukraine. Following his death, he was buried under the altar of the famous monastery. Her stories contained episodes in the history of Ukraine, its invaders, and the hardships of the villagers in withstanding their assaults.

A creative and highly imaginative child, Sophia began to dream of a handsome prince who would descend from the mountain peak and arrive at her doorstep. In her dreams, Sophia would run to him, but as she woke, the prince would not be there. This dream reoccurred many times in her sleep, but she was always disappointed that her wishes did not come true.

Many of the villagers worked in the fields at hard labor. It soon became evident to the Tereshkewych family that their youngest daughter did not have the physical strength to work the fields, as she often fainted from exertion. Her family decided that the best course of action for Sophia was to get an education and work as a professional in her later years. She attended a local school and then a teaching seminary in Sambir.

As Sophia began to attend the teaching seminary, her father suddenly died—he fell asleep at the table for unknown reasons. It was difficult to determine the cause of his death. Grief descended on the family once again. Even though Sophia grieved for her father, she had little time for tears. She was working very hard in her teaching studies and had great support from her fellow students. Her friends enjoyed her company because she had a compassionate nature, natural intelligence, quick wit, and laughter that would cascade through the halls of the seminary. In particular, the male students were captivated by Sophia's beauty, her auburn hair, hazel eyes, vivaciousness, and lithe figure. She had a sensitive and sensual nature, great aesthetic appeal, and a wonderful sense of humor. Her male friends were attracted to her and competed for her attention.

Although Sophia was flattered by all of this male attention, she also had a serious, reflective side to her. With a deep love for her homeland, she became a member of the underground, a cell of the Organization of Ukrainian Nationalists. Frequent meetings were held to plan strategies for protecting the homeland from invaders and infiltrators.

Upon completing her education studies, Sophia found to her dismay that no jobs were available for Greek Catholics of Ukrainian origin in education. Sophia was devastated by the blatant discrimination toward Ukrainians. Determined to find employment, Sophia found jobs in nursery schools in neighboring villages. Creative and artistic, she excelled in preparing recitals and dramas for her talented "tots." Eventually, aware of her keen intellect, the bishop's chancellery employed her as an administrator in Peremyshl.

In September 1939, World War II began; Sophia was twenty-four years old. After two weeks of bloody battles, Poland was destroyed and the Bolsheviks occupied Ukraine. During this time, Sophia returned to Spas and found employment as a teacher. She loved music and taught her students Ukrainian songs, Cossack songs, and patriotic songs of the Ukrainian Sich Rifleman. Soon, a Bolshevik official paid Sophia a visit and warned her to discontinue the nationalistic education of her students or her life would be in danger for opposition to authority. He said, "Tovarysh, your teaching is counterrevolutionary and you will be deported to the labor camps in Siberia. Cease this type of teaching immediately!" Although shaken by this Bolshevik visit, Sophia, a rebel by nature, continued to teach her Ukrainian program.

Not long before the German Invasion of 1941, the NKVD began lengthy and frequent interrogations of Sophia and other suspected nationalists. The Bolsheviks demanded that Sophia provide them with a list of all subversive nationalists in the village of Spas.

Clever by nature, Sophia gave the NKVD a list of all people living in Spas, Ukrainians, Poles, and Jews. This outward defiance enraged her interrogators and they threatened to execute Sophia on the spot.

Sophia returned from these interrogations pale, visibly shaken, and emotionally exhausted. However, she vowed that she would never give the NKVD the information they wanted. Sophia decided that in order not to betray the nationalists in Spas, she was prepared for imprisonment, deportation to Siberia, or death. The explosion of the German-Bolshevik war and the flight of villagers into the forests saved Sonia's life at a very precarious point.

With the invasion by the Germans, many Ukrainians hoped that this occupation would not be as oppressive as that of the Bolsheviks. All Ukrainians hoped that the Germans would free Ukraine from Soviet tyranny.

The Ukrainians proclaimed their independence. This was a historic moment, as Ukrainians wept and embraced each other. A formal Declaration of Independence was proclaimed in Sambir in June 30, 1941. In attendance were countless Ukrainians, including Sophia.

But the elation of independence was short-lived. The German invaders arrested and deported the leaders of the newly independent Ukraine to concentration camps. They brutally curtailed the freedom of all Ukrainians. Following the euphoria of independence, Sophia returned to her hometown of Spas.

Evil flourished; an informant directed German troops to Sophia's home. The soldiers scattered family belongings in chaotic disarray, searching for valuable objects—beautifully embroidered Ukrainian blouses, new clothing, kitchen appliances and utensils.

Incidentally, the Gestapo found a small handgun hidden behind a painting. At the time of this home invasion, a rather unpleasant forestry engineer happened to be living in Sophia's home and the family insisted the gun belonged to him. No explanations were acceptable to the Germans. Promptly, they arrested Sophia's brother, Osyp, and told her that the family would never see him alive again. In despair, Sophia rushed to Sambir to find help for her beloved brother. Fortunately, the forestry engineer appeared and showed the Gestapo official permits for ownership of the handgun. Osyp was released and returned home. Following this terrifying incident, it took Sophia a long time to overcome her anxiety and foreboding of future events.

For a brief time, good fortune shone on Sophia. With the recommendation of the director of an agriculture school, she began to teach at this new educational facility. Located in a beautiful mountain range, the rustling of the forest and the tranquil sounds of mountain brooks soothed her agitated soul. This educational estate had wide walkways, towering trees, stately buildings, a beautiful orchard, and an enchanting meadow. The estate was filled with the youthful, joyous sounds of several hundred young children and teachers from various regions of the Carpathians.

Sophia flourished in this stimulating setting. She met and fell in love with the director of this facility, Oleksander Tatomyr. Sophia found much fulfillment in her married life and teaching profession. A daughter, Chrystyna, was born on January 28, 1944. Sophia devoted herself to her family. With her gentle and loving nature and her talents as a teacher, Sophia doted on her first born child.

This idyllic interlude did not last long; the war fronts were rapidly approaching the Carpathian Mountains. Daily, the villagers residing in the mountains could hear the deafening roar of cannons. For families who had been targeted as nationalists, a most difficult decision had to be made immediately. In order to survive the oncoming invasion and to protect their villagers from interrogation and death from "guilt by association," many Ukrainian activists had to leave their families and homes. The Tatomyr family was high on the list of undesirable political agitators, and they had no choice but to flee. The departure of those who decided to leave and those who stayed behind was heartrending. The future of all of these people was a total, uncharted mystery. After saying farewell to her family and friends, Sophia was overcome with sadness and despair. The last words spoken by the villagers who remained were, "Do not forget us in the foreign lands. We will pray for you."

Throwing the last of their essentials into their wagon, Sophia, her husband, and baby Chrystyna climbed into their wagon to begin the long journey across the Carpathians to the west. This journey took them across the Carpathian mountain range, Slovakia and Hungary and to a resting place at the border of Czechoslovakia, which had been devastated by the Germans. Daily, they were exposed to the elements, to insufficient meals, to searches for night lodging, to hostility from people in the countries through which they traveled, and to the life-threatening air raids that dogged their route from the beginning of their journey. It is a tribute to their resourcefulness, strength of character, and longing for freedom that the Tatomyr family, and countless others, survived the horrors of war.

Finally, the Tatomyr family reached Austria and settled in the rocky, frigid Alps in Sankt Georgen. All of them suffered from battle fatigue, but they managed to carve out a life for themselves in this tiny hamlet. In spite of the circumstances of the war, the refugees developed a vibrant Ukrainian community and actively participated in the cultural and social life of Sankt Georgen. Sophia, as in the past, was involved with the Ukrainian nursery schools. Unfortunately, great sadness descended on the family with the death of the patriarch, Rev. Julian Tatomyr, following an operation for stomach cancer in 1946.

But the journey did not end in Sankt Georgen. Fate destined many DPs to seek their freedom and fortune in a foreign land across a vast ocean, in the United States and Canada. The journey across the ocean was very rough, and Sophia spent a great deal of the journey below deck, sick to her stomach. Luckily, the journey did not affect the children, Chrystyna and Marta (first cousins), who spent time cavorting on the large deck of the ship, the *Marine Tiger*, whenever the weather was good.

Approaching the shores of the United States of America, the Tatomyr family was riveted by the site of the Statue of Liberty and intimidated at their first glimpse of Ellis Island. Their identity cards showed the price that they had paid in their struggles for survival in a brutal war; they were all emaciated from the challenges they had endured for three long years.

Settling in Philadelphia for two years, Sophia and her family coped with the hardships of all refugees: integration into an alien culture, loss of identity, loss of economic and social status, loss of profession, and loss of loved ones. Sophia was extremely homesick during this time, while Oleksander took any job that was available to make ends meet. The heat of the city was oppressive and their living accommodations were very humble. Sophia's second child, Ostap, was born on March 3, 1949. Sophia adored her son because he reminded her of her beloved brother, Osyp, in Ukraine.

There was one more transition in Sophia's long journey from her beloved Spas to the United States. It was not a long journey from Philadelphia, to Edgely where Oleksander and Sophia bought a home in a small town that later grew into the large city of Levittown, Pennsylvania. Sophia's third child, Lesya, was born here.

Maternal obligations occupied much of Sophia's life. She participated actively in the social life of the community. She was vigilant in having her children attend church and parochial school. Sophia was a member of an organization that promoted the development of youth through summer and winter camps.

A passion for flowers was Sonia's hobby. Her home was ablaze every spring in a rainbow of luscious flowers—petunias, azaleas, zinnias, roses, and primroses. Oleksander, who loved gardening, made a huge productive vegetable garden in the backyard.

One day, a sad message arrived from Ukraine. Sophia's brother and his family had been deported to Siberia to the labor camps for ten years. Distraught with worries over her family in Siberia and in foreign lands, Sophia's mother died in her eldest sister's arms.

After Osyp returned from Siberia, he and Sophia exchanged letters. She was overjoyed when she received a letter from him. He told her about the fate of their family and friends left in Ukraine. When she could, Sophia would send parcels to her brother and his family. One day, a letter arrived from an unknown correspondent with the wrenching news that her brother, Osyp, had died of a heart attack after a short illness.

This was the most tragic and painful episode in Sophia's life. It was only through the strength of her character, her belief in God, and the support of her loved ones did she survive this most personal grief. For a long time after Osyp's death, the joy of life vanished from Sophia's gentle, beautiful face. Her devotion to her children and her husband's love sustained her during this difficult time.

After her children left home, Sophia's strength and joy came in the anticipation of the birth of grandchildren. It was then that her smile, her wit, and her laughter returned.

Severe chest pains sent Sophia to the hospital on March 1983, but despite the vigilant care of doctors and nurses, and a desire for a speedy return to her home, a massive heart attack claimed her life on the day she was to be released from hospital. Immediately before her death, she asked that her children, grandchildren, and family be told of her eternal love for all of them.

After her death, she traveled to a better world, to those who she had loved and missed during her years in her adopted homeland. She was at last truly safe, under the loving care of God.

In a foreign land, having survived the brutal hardships of war and deprivation, my beautiful wife wilted, as a wild flower wilts under harsh conditions, far from the exquisite Carpathian Mountains and the majestic Knyaza Hora of her youth. A fresh grave surfaced in our adopted land, decorated with American flowers. This is the final resting place of Sophia Tereshkevych Tatomyr, an exquisite wild flower from Ukraine.

*     *     *

This tribute to Sophia Tatomyr was written by her loving husband, Oleksander, one year after her death.

March 7, 1984

**Sophia and Oleksander, Levittown, Pennsylvania**

# 4. Tribute

## *Eulogy, JAROSLAV TATOMYR, 1994*

Jaroslav Tatomyr was born in Sambir, Ukraine, in 1910.

A former graduate of the Lviv Polytechnic Institute, Jaroslav was the second son of Olha Khomytsky and Rev. Julian Tatomyr, former senator of the Polish Parliament. His older brother, referred to as Yunyo, died when he was two years of age following a typhoid epidemic in the Sambir region. Jaroslav's brother, Oleksander, was almost four years younger.

Jaroslav was a member of Bahryanij Kvit, whose membership consisted of many students from Lviv Polytechnic Institute. Among the group were the three handsome Kosiv brothers—Mykhajlo, Roman, and Anatol, a well-known composer whose future pseudonym would be Kos-Anatolsky; the Makariv brothers—Modest and Orest; Roman Chaykivskij; Ivan Kulchitskij; and Jaroslav Tatomyr.

The group referred to Jaroslav as 'the Boyar', a reference to the noble roots of his ancient clan and for his dignified manner, idealism, and problem-solving talents within this group. He was credited with developing the motto of the group, "Ukraine Above All Else!" Unfortunately, none of the members of Bahranij Kvit are alive today.

After completing their studies at the Lviv Polytechnic Institute, fate scattered the graduates in many directions. During his studies, Jaroslav was imprisoned for his nationalistic fervor on several occasions, like his father, Rev. Julian, and his brother Oleksa.

Continuing his education, Jaroslav traveled to Paris, France, to study engineering. After completing his first year of study in Paris, Jaroslav returned home for the summer holidays. Unfortunately, his engineering studies abroad were interrupted permanently by the Bolsheviks, who refused him a travel visa to continue his studies.

Shortly thereafter, he met and fell in love with Luba Fedevich, daughter of Reverend Ivan Fedevich (1883-1939), a pastor and community leader in the town of Turka. Following their marriage, their first and only child, Marta, was born in 1943. Luba was a gifted artist, and in later years she would pass her artistic talents to her child, Marta.

Luba also had a flair for fashion, designing and sewing beautiful gowns for Marta for the annual ball held in Philadelphia, the Engineer's Ball.

As the Bolshevik front approached the Sambir area, Jaroslav and his family joined his father, his mother, his brother with his family, his cousin Volodymyr and three servants in their flight from the Bolshevik terrorists. The Tatomyr family was well-known for their activism against the Red Army and was high on the list for execution or deportation to the labor camps of Siberia.

The Tatomyrs traveled in four horse-drawn wagons through Carpathian Ukraine, Slovakia, Hungary, and Czechoslovakia. The harrowing journey is described in detail in the war diary of Jaroslav's father, Rev. Julian Tatomyr.

In 1948, along with the rest of his family, Jaroslav left for the United States from the city of Bremen on the *Marine Tiger*, a large passenger ship assigned to ship refugees to foreign countries.

At first the Tatomyrs lived briefly in one room, later settling in separate tenement homes in the ghettos of Philadelphia. Jaroslav was the first to leave the oppressive heat and pollution of the city in 1951. He found a small house on a beautiful corner lot in Edgely, Pennsylvania that was to become the sprawling suburbs of Levittown in a few short years. At the time of their move, Edgely lay in a pastoral setting surrounded by corn and asparagus fields. Unlike the mighty Dnister River, a tranquil canal flowed near their property.

Shortly after Jaroslav moved to the country, his brother, Oleksander, and his family, moved into a smaller home down the street from them. At that time, there were ten families of refugees living on an L-shaped street. The children living there included Marta, Chrystyna, Ostap, the Suchenko sisters—Manya, Katya, and Ivanka, who was in her early teens.

These early years in a new country were challenging for the Tatomyrs, as they were for all refugees. With little or no knowledge of the English language, few contacts, difficult economic conditions (based on the end of World War II and the shift of production from war materials to resources for peace), and social-emotional adjustments as new immigrants, Jaroslav and his family experienced a challenging integration into the mainstream of American society. For them, as for others, the loss of status—from the top of the ladder in Ukraine to the lowest rung in the United States—was a most difficult adjustment.

Jaroslav, along with his brother, found work in construction as their small hamlet of Edgely began to expand into the colossus of Levittown. Jaroslav helped a friend, Lev Yuskevich, to find work in construction.

After working just one month in construction, Yushkevich found employment with the Westinghouse Electric Company in Lester, near Philadelphia. He helped other immigrants, including Jaroslav, by teaching them the concepts and skills necessary for future employment at Westinghouse.

With Jaroslav's rapid acquisition of English, Yushkevich helped his friend get a job in the company as assistant to a mechanical engineer in the division of gas turbines. In part, Jaroslav was offered employment because he was an excellent mathematician and a charismatic leader. People in the company were drawn by his charm and leadership abilities.

Following his retirement, Jaroslav received a contract from Westinghouse as a private consultant which enabled him to double his income—a significant achievement for an immigrant.

Jaroslav was tall, blond, and handsome, gifted and empathetic toward others. His leadership abilities served him well as an employee of the Westinghouse Electric Company. Always a nationalist, Jaroslav tried to help his brothers and sisters in Ukraine by writing numerous articles to newspapers exposing the tyranny of the past and present situation in Ukraine.

Eventually, Jaroslav and Luba sold their home and moved to the Assumption Retirement Home in Philadelphia. It was there that Luba died, following a fall in 1989. The loss of his wife after many years of marriage left Jaroslav lonely and sad. His daughter, Marta, and her husband, Dr. Omelan Lukasewycz, associate dean of the medical school at the University of Minnesota in Duluth, visited as often as they could. Jaroslav became a grandparent with the birth of Omelan and Marta's first child, Anya, and again with the birth of their second child, Stephen. Jaroslav was overjoyed that both his grandchildren completed their undergraduate studies at Harvard University and obtained their degrees in medicine in Minnesota.

Jaroslav Tatomyr died in January 1994 and was buried at St. Mary's Cemetery, Fox Chase, Philadelphia, alongside his wife, brother, sister-in-law, and his parents. He was eighty-three years old. He will be remembered as a modest, dignified man who was dedicated to preserving the traditions of his Ukrainian heritage in his adopted country, America.

# 5. Memoir

## Growing up in Montreal

### Saint Michael, Saint Anselme, and Saint Laurent

## SAINT MICHAEL

Shortly after we arrived in Montreal, our family joined St. Michael's Ukrainian Catholic Church. St. Michael's, one of the oldest Ukrainian parishes in Canada and the first one to be established in Montreal, is located in a relatively poor working-class area of "east-end" Montreal. The parish has a history dating back to 1899 when a group of "First Wave" Ukrainian immigrants (those who arrived in Canada before World War I) met, with the intention of starting a church of their own. The first mass was celebrated by a visiting priest in 1902, and in 1910, Metropolitan Andrij Sheptytsky of Lviv visited the young parish. In 1911, the first pastor was appointed, a property was purchased on Iberville Street, and, in 1916, the cornerstone of the church was laid by Bishop Budka. The following year, on Easter Sunday, the first mass was celebrated in the newly constructed building.

In 1930, the Parish Hall was built, and when the next wave of immigrants arrived after World War II, the original church was razed to make room for a large Byzantine-style church that was constructed in 1954 under the direction and supervision of the new pastor, Father Nicholas Kuchniryk.*

The parish quickly became the center of our religious and social activities. Our "wave" of immigrants, officially labeled the Third Wave, had injected new life into the parish, which was slowly losing members to other churches being established in other parts of Montreal.

The existing First and Second Wave (those who arrived between the wars) parishioners, whom we called the *Staro Prybuli*, or Previously Arrived, warmly welcomed

---

* Adapted from an article by Jaroslaw Panasiuk (my former classmate) on the fiftieth Anniversary of St. Michael's parish.

us *Novo Prybuli*, or Newly Arrived. They helped our parents find accommodations, schools, and jobs, and sometimes hired them to work in their businesses.

My father was asked to join the church building committee, my mother joined the Women's League, and my brother and I became altar boys.

With the arrival to our parish of Father Ted Harasymchuk as auxiliary priest, our lives centered on the church even more. Father Ted had us convinced that being an altar boy at St. Michael's was the highest privilege a boy could hope to achieve. To keep us interested, he bought us new vestments, taught us old church traditions, and made up some new ceremonies. He didn't want us hanging around pool halls, so he found a ping-pong table, a couple of pool tables, and an old jukebox, and placed them in the church hall basement for our use. He constructed a club room and allowed access to the church hall to altar boys at anytime. (At one point, as president of the altar boys, I was entrusted with having my own key to the church hall.) It worked. We spent most of our free time around the church.

Every young boy in Montreal was a fan of the Montreal Canadiens hockey team. We all dreamt of one day playing for the fabled team, and even though we didn't necessarily own a pair of ice skates, we believed it was possible. After all, Bernie "Boom Boom" Geoffrion, one of the great Montreal players at that time, grew up in our neighborhood.

Father Ted, however, was a Detroit Red Wings fan. We couldn't understand this at first, except that we knew he originally came from "out west" and Detroit, we knew, was somewhere "out west."

Detroit and Montreal were the two best teams in hockey. During a nine-year period from 1952 to 1960, Montreal won the Stanley Cup six times and Detroit three times.

One day, when the Red Wings were in town, Father Ted gathered a few of the altar boys and told us we were going to see a game at the Montreal Forum. We didn't know how he did it but somehow, he got tickets to the hottest game in town. With great anticipation, we entered the Forum through the underground parking garage, past the maintenance entrance, and suddenly came face to face with the rink end-boards while the players were warming up.

All our heroes were right there, in bright, living color. My first sight of Maurice Richard, Gordie Howe, Boom Boom Geoffrion, Ted Lindsay, and Jean Beliveau just inches away is a memory etched permanently in my brain.

I don't remember who won that night, but the icing on the cake came after the game. The Detroit goalie was the legendary Terry Sawchuk, a Ukrainian from "out west". When the game ended, we were taken to the Detroit Red Wings dressing room to meet him. We were in awe. He joked around with us and told us Father Ted was his best friend. We understood why Father Ted was a Red Wings fan.

I too became a Red Wings fan after that game (even though I could never let anyone in my neighborhood know my secret).

# CAMP UKRAINA

St. Michael's was unique among the Ukrainian parishes in Montreal because the parish owned a beautiful property in the Laurentian Mountains north of Montreal. The property was donated to our church by the Roman Catholic Church hierarchy in Quebec during the 1930s (perhaps to ensure that Ukrainians in Quebec stayed within the Catholic Church and not, God forbid, join with the Orthodox). Camp Ukraina consists of hundreds of acres of virgin forest, a beautiful lake, and excellent facilities. During the thirties, the property was remote and was not easy to reach because the roads weren't very good; but today, the camp can be reached from the city in about an hour.

Every summer during the 1950s, St. Michael's Church organized a three-week camp for children at Camp Ukraina. It was so inexpensive that even immigrants who struggled financially could afford to send their children to these camps. If a family could not afford to pay the modest fee, the church, or someone from the established Ukrainian community, was always more than happy to sponsor a child. For the first nine years after we arrived in Canada, we spent most of our summers "up north" at Camp Ukraina. During the early fifties, immediately following the three-week church camp, Plast held its own three-week scout camp in the same location. As a child, I thought it was normal that all children spent six weeks at summer camp. I was surprised to find out that most of my classmates stayed in the hot city all summer and rarely had a chance to swim in a clear Laurentian lake.

When Plast bought its own property in the Eastern Townships in the mid fifties, we would spend three weeks in the Laurentians, bid a tearful farewell, and after spending a day, or less, at home in Montreal, would take another bus for a few more weeks at the new Plast camp in the Eastern Townships. Few children from our neighborhoods had an opportunity to have such wonderful summers.

# SAINT ANSELME

Although it seemed that just about everyone who lived in our east-end neighborhood was Catholic, there were three very distinct groups: The French Canadians, who mostly belonged to the Roman Catholic Eglise St. Anselme, where services were held in Latin and French; the Polish Catholics, who belonged to St. Mary's Roman Catholic Polish Church a few blocks away, where services were in Latin and Polish; and the Ukrainians, who belonged to St. Michael's Ukrainian Catholic Church, an easy five-minute walk from the other two churches, where services were in Ukrainian.

We Ukrainians celebrated all the Ukrainian holidays according to the "old" calendar and always took a day or two off school for Ukrainian Christmas and Good Friday and any other holiday we could get away with. Rarely did any member of one church visit any of the other churches. Three solitudes lived side by side in our neighborhood and in our classrooms.

We lived separately though there was very little animosity among the groups. Political correctness had not yet been invented and there was a significant amount of name-calling in the school yards but nobody got overly upset over this. It was expected.

We were usually called *Maudi DP* (Stupid DP) or *Maudi Polak* (Stupid Pole), but that didn't bother us too much. We knew we weren't stupid and we knew we weren't Polish, so they were wrong on both counts!

We had a few choice names for our tormentors as well, so it all evened out. We also called the Polish kids *Maudi Polak*, which really confused the French Canadian kids, and we called French Canadians "pea soup" or "Pepsi" but that too was all rather tame since they called themselves those names as well.

All in all, the ethnic groups got along reasonably well.

Right after World War II, there had been a debate in Canada about whether Eastern European and Jewish refugees should be allowed into the country. By the time we arrived, however, the debate was over. The postwar economy was strong, workers were needed, and immigrants were prepared to start at the bottom. Ukrainians were law-abiding, generally kept a low profile, and rarely made demands on the social services. (It is also possible that we were tolerated because for once, the poor French Canadian residents of our neighborhoods had someone even poorer than themselves to look down upon.)

We picked up English and French very quickly and soon we were just like all the other people in the neighborhood. We knew that our poverty was temporary and that we would soon move out to a better neighborhood.

Although there were three thriving parishes in this small area, we all attended the same school—the French-English, Ecole St. Anselme School operated by the Montreal Catholic School Commission. We English speakers always felt that we were forgotten and ignored by the school board higher-ups. For one thing, the school was primarily French with only a small portion of the enormous school building walled off to allow for an English section.

The English section of the school had only seven classrooms, Grade 1 to 7, and nine staff members, two French Canadian nuns (the principal and vice principal), who belonged to the same order of nuns that ran the French section of the school, two Polish nuns (Grade 1 and 3), two Ukrainian nuns (Grade 2 and 4) and three "civilians," Mr. Langue, Miss O'Hagen, and Mr. Janusus, who taught Grades 5, 6, and 7.

Two weeks after we arrived in Canada, my mother brought my brother and me to the English section of the school to register us into Grade 3 and Grade 1 respectively. Although we did not speak a word of English, my mother reasoned that my brother completed Grade 2 in Germany and I had two years of kindergarten and knew how to read and write so we deserved to be in Grade 3 and 1.

Sister Therese, the principal, thought differently.

She reasoned that though my brother was eight years old, he couldn't speak English, and therefore should start at the beginning, in Grade 1. And, since I was only five and a half, I was too young to attend school. My mother pleaded with the nun (in her best English) and with the Grade 1 teacher (in Polish) but to no avail.

After two months, my brother mastered a fair amount of English and was performing at the top of his Grade 1 class. In November, he was promoted to Grade 2. My mother saw an opportunity, and with the help of our parish priest managed to convince the principal to let me take my brother's spot. I started Grade 1 two months late, in November.

There were thirty-six desks permanently screwed into the floor of the Grade 1 classroom—six rows of six desks. Twenty-four students filled the first four rows of desks while three other students sat in the next row. Although there was room nearer the front of the class, I was placed in the last desk in the last row, by the window. There was no one in the desk in front of me and no one else in my row. I reasoned they did that so that I would not infect anyone else with my lack of knowledge.

The Polish nun occasionally spoke to me in Polish, which I pretended not to understand, and I spoke to her in Ukrainian, which she pretended not to understand. For most of the day, I sat in the back, mute, trying to follow the class in English. At the end of the month, I received a report card. I was given *F*s in all subjects. At the bottom of the report card was my class rank: I was ranked twenty-eighth out of twenty-eight students.

The following month, another DP, my friend, Orest Kucharsky, who also spoke no English, joined the class. He was placed in the opposite corner of the class and we were warned *not* to communicate with each other. We would glance at each other and giggle once in a while and would get stern looks from the teacher. At the end of the next month, my friend Orest performed even worse than me. This time, I ranked twenty-eighth out of twenty-nine students. I saw that as an improvement.

Seven or eight other Ukrainian children attended our Grade 1 class; most of them were "second generation" and spoke English. There were about the same number of Poles and the rest of the students in the class were mostly French Canadians whose parents wanted them to learn English before enrolling them in French schools for high school.

I made friends with some of the Ukrainian second-generation students. They were bilingual and were able to help me when I couldn't understand the instructions. I soon became best friends with Freddy Shlapak, a second-generation classmate. He too was an altar boy at St. Michael's and together we managed to get into a lot of trouble with our teacher and the principal.

## The Strap

By the end of Grade 1, I understood and spoke reasonably good English and because, unlike most of my classmates, I already knew how to read and write, I soon ranked near the top of the class. By Grade 4, I was consistently ranked second or third.

One student in the class always ranked higher than me: my nemesis, Vera Mischuk.

No matter how hard I tried, she always ranked first . . . . until May of our Grade 4 year. I had a great month, or perhaps she had a poor one, but when the report cards were handed out, I was ranked first and she second.

At St. Anselme, the person who ranked first at the end of each month was given a gold medal to wear. That medal had *always* hung on Vera's tunic. I felt bad taking it away from her. The principal reluctantly presented the medal to me and reminded me that I better not lose it. She may have even reminded me that it was made of solid gold and was very expensive.

My parents were very pleased with my ranking and immediately took out their Brownie camera and took a picture. That same month, my brother, Roman, had placed first in his class as well. The picture of the two of us wearing medals was framed and sat on the living room table for years.

My friends, of course, gave me a hard time for wearing "Vera's medal." A few days later, I somehow managed to lose the medal while I was playing soccer or climbing a tree or wrestling with my friends. When we couldn't find it, I was sent to the principal's office.

I received a long lecture and then Sister Therese called Mr. Langue, the Grade 5 teacher. She informed me that because I had lost the medal, I would never, ever, be awarded a medal no matter how well I ranked and as punishment, I would receive "The Strap"—once on each hand.

I felt there was something very wrong with this form of justice and that the punishment didn't fit the crime but reasoned that Sister was taking this opportunity to punish me for all the other "crimes" I had committed so far in my school career.

I had had an encounter with Sister just a few months before this 'medal incident'.

On March 5th 1953, rumors that Josef Stalin, the Soviet dictator, had died started to filter through the news media. My parents received a phone call very late that night from one of their friends who told them to listen to the radio. Reports were coming in slowly and at first there were few details about whether Stalin had been poisoned, was murdered in a coup or had died of natural causes but by late the next day, it was confirmed that he was dead.

I recall my father's reaction . . . . He turned his head to the side and pretended to spit. That was the first time I had ever seen him make this gesture but there was no confusion as to what he meant. My mother clasped her hands and murmured, "May he rot in hell."

I was just nine years old at the time, but I was already quite politicized. I had heard enough about the horrors committed by Stalin while sitting around the dinner table, during Plast assemblies and during Sunday afternoon concerts to have formulated an opinion about 'the most evil man who had ever lived'

Three days later, at Sunday mass, with Freddy and I serving as altar boys, Father Nick's sermon was dedicated to a solemn review of Stalin's crimes. Immediately after the service, a *panachyda* (requiem mass) was held to commemorate all the people Stalin had murdered.

The following day, on Monday morning, Sister Therese, came into our Grade 4 classroom to give us the 'news' that Stalin had died. All the Ukrainian kids looked at each other in surprise. We had all known about this for days. This wasn't news. Sister Therese then announced we were all going to say the rosary and pray for Stalin's soul.

I couldn't believe what I was hearing. How could anyone suggest praying for such an evil person?

I yelled out, "He's already in hell."

Sister took great offence at this. She reminded me that only God decides who goes to heaven or hell and that I had blasphemed.

I insisted that Stalin was a murderer and that he was definitely in hell and I wasn't going to pray for him.

I looked to my teacher, a Ukrainian nun who was in church the previous day and had heard the same sermon I heard. She was in an awkward position but surely would support me. I also knew my Ukrainian classmates would support me and my parents and Father Nick and anyone else of importance in my life would support me.

Sister Therese was furious. She yanked me out of class and dragged me to the office. She demanded an apology, made me kneel and tried to make me say the rosary. I refused.

That night, uncharacteristically, I told my parents what had happened. I wanted them to hear it from me before the school called with their version. My parents sat me down and we had a discussion. My father defended me and said he was proud of what I had done but wished I had expressed myself differently. My parents punished me for being rude to authority but the next morning, my mother took time off work, brought me to school and in front of me told Sister Therese that I did not have to pray for Stalin.

I gained a huge amount of respect for my parents that day . . . . and the rosary was never said for Stalin in our Grade 4 class.

I don't think Sister Therese ever forgave me for this.

Mr. Langue was a large man who smelled of cigar smoke and alcohol. Everyone feared him. The nun handed him the regulation school strap: eighteen inches long, one and a half inches wide and a quarter-inch thick, made of reinforced rubber. I took my punishment, flinched, and then smiled at Mr. Langue and the nun and told them it didn't hurt at all. I was determined to not give them any satisfaction. Later, I excused myself from class to spend the rest of the day in the bathroom, running cold water on my hands so my mother wouldn't notice the red welts.

I never again tried to be *first* at that school. Even when a test was easy and I knew all the answers, I would always make one deliberate error so I wouldn't stand out. Vera Mischuk wore the medal most of the rest of the time until we graduated. I didn't mind.

She was really smart and deserved it. Years later, she became a successful politician in the City of Montreal and as Vera Mischuk-Danyluk was elected and reelected mayor of the Town of Mount Royal several times. To my knowledge, she is still serving in that capacity.

Freddy Shlapak and I, on the other hand, were in trouble with Sister a few more times in our elementary school career. Eventually, Freddy went off to university, became an engineer and a successful corporate executive.

Years later, when I became a principal at Sutton District High School, I found a regulation school strap in the bottom drawer of my desk. All forms of corporal punishment had been banned a few years earlier but the Strap was left there for me by the previous principal. I called my superintendent and told him I was taking the strap home. I had no intention of ever using it and I didn't want anyone in the school to ever have a chance to use it either. He agreed with me. Today, the strap still sits on my bookcase at home.

In a very strange way, Sister Therese helped me formulate my personal philosophy of education. It has served me very well for more than forty years as a teacher and principal.

In 1956, I entered Cardinal Newman High School, an all-boys school run by Christian Brothers. It was, of course, a Catholic school, with the student body consisting mostly of Irish and Italian Catholics, with a smattering of Poles and Ukrainians and just about every other ethnic group imaginable—as long as they were Catholic.

In high school, I was mostly interested in sports, and my report cards reflected my lack of academic effort. My marks were just good enough to get by but I was one of the top athletes in the school by the time I graduated, *lettering* in soccer, basketball and track.

Academically, I was just average in most subjects but my one strong subject was mathematics. I found the subject easy and usually had the answer to the question the teacher put on the board before he finished writing it down and before the "new concept" was taught. To keep me out of his hair, the teacher would often ask me to help other kids with their math or, if I irritated him enough, to leave the class during his lessons.

In Grade 10, my math teacher bet me a dollar that I could not get one hundred percent on the Provincial Math Exam. I won the bet. As he paid me my dollar, he told me he knew all along that I could do it. He was just trying to motivate me. It worked!

Earlier that year, the Soviets succeeded in sending the first object into space—a beach-ball sized satellite named *Sputnik*. The Soviet-United States space race was on. Many North American politicians were quite upset because we weren't producing enough scientists and were losing the Space Race. I was caught up in the rush to educate more scientists. Since I was good in math, I was advised by my teachers to go to university to study science. For the first time since Grade 4, I had an academic goal.

# SAINT LAURENT

Just as we were starting to outgrow "Altar Boys" and were old enough to use the public transit system on our own, Plast purchased a clubhouse on Esplanade Street, on the other side of "The Main" (St. Laurent Boulevard), not far from downtown Montreal. The clubhouse was across the street from a park with soccer fields and tennis courts, which stretched all the way to Park Avenue and across that road blended into the biggest park in Montreal, Mount Royal Park. We had "The Mountain" at our doorstep. Church and school were huge influences in my early life, but the biggest impact on my life from an early age was being a member of this scouting group.

Ukrainian children, almost all former DPs from all the different DP camps of Germany and Austria who were now living in different parts of Montreal, would gather at the clubhouse once or twice a week to socialize, listen to stories of the old days, learn scouting skills, play sports, and meet members of the opposite sex (this list is not necessarily in priority order).

For half the year, plans were being made for summer camp in the Eastern Townships and for the other half of the year, for the ski camp over the Christmas holidays, in the Laurentians.

Growing up, my very best friends were members of my scout troop.

Although we lived in different parts of the city, George, Bobby, Mickey, and I were inseparable, and George Wesolowsky remained my best friend until he died in 1997.

# 6. Memoir

## *My Uncle's Trunk, Wasyl (Vasylko) and Erna Martyniuk*
### (1993-1993)          (1921-2007)

### Vasylko

My mother's youngest brother, Wasyl, who all his life was called by the diminutive Vasylko, was born in Ivanivka, Galicia, Ukraine, in 1915 as World War I raged in Europe. The relative calm that existed a year earlier when the Austrians were in power evaporated as various armies fought for control of this part of Ukraine. In 1918, western Ukraine enthusiastically joined the Ukrainian Republic, which had been formed the year before in Kyiv, but three years later, eastern Ukraine was annexed to the Soviet Union and Galicia fell under the control of Poland. By the time Vasylko completed Grade 4, the Poles had taken control of schools and entry to further education in the gymnasia became more difficult for Ukrainians. He did not follow his sister, Bronyslawa (the only member of the Martyniuk family to complete her matura and to graduate from gymnasia), and instead joined his father working on their small plot of land.

In 1938, he married his childhood sweetheart, Maria (Marynia), and two years later their son, Bohdanchyk, was born. In September 1939, the Germans invaded Poland and World War II broke out. A few weeks after, the Bolsheviks took control of his province.

Vasylko and Marynia were both active politically, and, along with many of their friends, joined the anti-Bolshevik resistance movement. When the Nazi armies crossed into Ukraine in June of 1941, the Bolsheviks retreated eastward. Before they left, however, they received orders from Moscow to kill their prisoners and to capture any anti-Bolshevik agitators and to send them to Siberia.

Vasylko was not at home when the Bolsheviks came for him, but they took his wife, Marynia, and his son, little Bohdanchyk. They placed them in a crowded cattle car along with hundreds of other known anti-Bolshevik agitators and sent them to Siberia. The only good news for Vasylko was that in the last minute, his son, Bohdanchyk, had been saved by some quick thinking by Marynia when she threw their infant son into the arms of his grandmother who was running along side the train as it pulled out of the station. Marynia was never heard from again. She may have died with so many others on the long journey, or she may have died in the harsh tundra of Siberia after arrival.

Still, Vasylko always maintained the hope that she may have survived and would return home someday.

In 1943, as the Germans were retreating, they passed through Ivanivka; Vasylko's son, three-year-old Bohdanchyk, was playing in the ditch in front of grandmother's house and was cut by a piece of shrapnel from a recently exploded German bomb and died from the resulting infection.

Vasylko was devastated.

A few months later, Vasylko was captured by the Germans, tortured for several months, and then sent to the Buchenwald Concentration Camp, where he was assigned to forced labor.

## Erna

Erna was born January 1, 1921, in the Bukovina region of southern Ukraine, in Dubivka, a small village not far from the provincial capital, Chernivtsi. During that time, Bukovyna was occupied by Romania. Erna's mother died when she was nine years old, and since her father worked long hours outside the home, Erna had to stop attending school in order to take care of her younger brother and help her father with household chores. They were very poor, had little to eat, and eventually lost their home.

Erna often spoke of how she and her younger brother would go to neighboring farmers' fields at night, after the potatoes or other vegetables had been harvested, to look for small pieces of discarded or unpicked vegetables so they could have something to eat. On good days, they were able to collect enough to sell or exchange for other necessities. On other days, they barely had enough food for even a few bites.

In desperation, Erna's father decided he could no longer take care of his two children. He tried to give them to an orphanage but orphanages were overcrowded and could not take children who still had a parent. Erna claimed that her father tried to "sell" her and her brother. In fact, Erna's father managed to "give" his children to a wealthy German settler in Chernivtsi. The settler needed someone to cook and clean his house and to take care of the animals. In exchange for food and a place to sleep, the two young children worked in his home.

Erna did not have a great deal of formal education, but by the time she was a teenager, she was fluent in German, Romanian, and Ukrainian. When the Nazis invaded Chernivtsi in 1941, the German settler, perhaps to gain favor with the army, offered the then twenty-year-old Erna to the German commanding officer. At first she worked as a translator, but when the officer moved on, Erna was sent to Germany as an *arbeiter,* along with thousands of other young men and women, to work as a slave laborer. Erna never talked about the three years she spent in Germany as an arbeiter.

When the war ended, Erna wandered alone around Germany, not knowing if she was Romanian or German or Ukrainian. Eventually, she ended up in a refugee camp designated for Ukrainians and in 1949, as a single twenty-eight-year-old, she made her way to Canada.

*   *   *

In 1950, while attending a church social in Montreal, Erna was introduced to Vasylko. She was single and Vasylko considered himself a widower, even though he wasn't completely certain if his wife, Marynia, was alive or dead.

Erna was attractive and gregarious, and, in spite of all she had been through, had a cheerful attitude to life. Vasylko was quiet, even morose most of the time, still grieving the loss of his wife and son and he never fully recovered from the horrors of his incarceration in Buchenwald. Erna was a ray of sunshine in his life.

During those early years in Canada, Vasylko worked on house construction and eventually became a successful contractor. Erna cleaned houses.

In 1951, ten years after Marynia disappeared and he had given up hope of ever hearing from her, Vasylko asked Erna to marry him.

My mother, Bronyslawa, did not approve of this arrangement. Back in 1938, she and my father attended Vasylko and Marynia's wedding, they doted on little Bohdanchyk and later mourned his death. My mother had difficulty accepting the fact that Vasylko wanted to marry someone else. Vasylko persisted, and after checking with a priest and after contacting their home village to make sure there was still no word from Marynia, my mother accepted that life must go on. My parents, brother, and I attended Erna and Vasylko's wedding ceremony.

Vasylko, once a very healthy, strong young man, had not been in good health since the war. He was tired of the city and decided to sell his house and his business and move to the country. He found a hundred-acre farm in VanKleek Hill, Ontario, about an hour's drive from Montreal, and, in 1958, became a gentleman farmer.

My uncle and I always got along very well. When I was fifteen years old, he took me for a drive through his property in his new 1959 Buick. When we got to the furthest point of his farm, he turned the car around and let me drive it back to the farmhouse, to the astonishment of my parents.

One hot summer day, as I was helping my uncle in the barn, I noticed that he had numbers tattooed on his left arm. I hadn't noticed before then that he always wore long-sleeved shirts. This day, his sleeves were rolled up. I asked him about the tattoo. At first he didn't want to talk about it, but then we sat down on a bench inside the barn, and with almost no emotion, he told me about Buchenwald. By the end of his account, however, we were both in tears.

When Chrystyna and I were dating, we heard that Vasylko's dog had been killed by a car. As we were traveling in Vermont, we noticed a sign: Free Puppies. We stopped, picked one, and managed to cross the border without the puppy being noticed by the border guards. We gave the dog to my uncle. Over time *Aza* proved to be a good guard dog and it gave us another reason to go visit my aunt and uncle.

When we were getting married in 1969, Chrystyna and I asked Vasylko to stand in for my father at our wedding.

## *My Uncle's Trunk*

My uncle died of cancer in 1993, on the very day that Chrystyna and I were in his home village, Ivanivka, visiting his son's grave.

In 2002, Erna began showing signs of dementia. She had difficulty taking care of herself and living on her own. My brother, Roman, and I decided that it was time to move her into a full-service home.

When we were closing down Erna's house in VanKleek Hill, Ontario, we held a large yard sale. As is customary in Ontario small towns, all the neighbors came by; most saying they just wanted to have a small token to remember Vasylko and Erna.

The sale was going well when a man pulled up in a truck and asked if my uncle's old wooden trunk was for sale. When I said it was, he offered fifty dollars for it.

After he put the trunk in his truck and left, another man, who identified himself as my uncle's good friend, approached me. He stated that I had just sold the trunk my uncle had used to ship all his possessions when he came to Canada in 1949 and that the trunk was very precious to my uncle. I felt terrible that I had sold it.

That night we had to return home to Toronto but for the next few days, I couldn't stop thinking about what I had done. The next weekend, Chrystyna and I drove the 500 kilometers back to VanKleek Hill, found the person who had bought the trunk, and offered him one hundred dollars for it.

On October 6, 2007, we received a phone call from the Hawkesbury Nursing Home. Erna died peacefully in her sleep.

Today, my uncle's trunk sits by the window in our living room. It's the most precious object we have to remind us of my uncle and aunt.

Vasylko Martyniuk and Erna Martyniuk

# 7. Memoir

### *The Tatomyr Clan, Letter to His Children*
### OLEKSANDER TATOMYR
(Translated by his daughter, Chrystyna Tatomyr-Melnyk)

Dear Children,

You are asking that I write the history of the Tatomyr family of Sambir. I am overjoyed that you are interested in your ancestors-their spiritual and physical attributes, their contributions, successes and challenges and their involvement in the religious, political, cultural and economic life of the Ukrainian homeland.

I am not surprised, that you, the descendents of one of the most sophisticated nations of Eastern Europe and of an ancient family, want to understand the past.

Frequent invasions by wild tribes, barbaric Tatars and Muscovites, among others, made it difficult to preserve familial and national memories, facts and treasures. Therefore, I face significant challenges in searching for necessary materials to support an objective analysis of the Ukrainian nation and our family genealogy.

The task that is facing me is most difficult beyond the boundaries of Ukraine, because I have no access to the archives, museums, libraries, cemeteries and other places where your forefathers lived and their descendents continue to reside.

At this time no one in our family has attempted to write a comprehensive chronology of the family clan. My father, Julian, had made efforts to document the experiences of our family during World War I and World War II in his diary.

My history of our family will contain omissions and gaps because of the absence of quantitative and, at times, qualitative resources. From the misty past I have managed to gather some historical data. It is imperative to further research data at the Library of Congress in Washington, D.C. and major libraries in the West. Correspondence with some of my esteemed colleagues, who are interested in the genealogy of families, has been helpful to me.

I have relied on my memories of treasured significant moments from the past, my early childhood and the present. My memories include the places in which we were destined to live, the village of Silec (in the Sambir region) that was the epicenter of our clan from ancient times, the village of Cherkhava, our family 'Mecca', where festive family gatherings occurred at my grandfather's estate with family relatives in attendance, the city of my birth, Sambir, the creation of an independent Ukraine in 1918, our exodus to the east and life in Kamyanezt-Podilsky when I was a young child, our return to the lush Carpathian mountains, my law studies in Lviv and seminary studies in Peremyshyl, the appointment of my father to the Senate of the Polish Parliament, my intermittent imprisonments, our exodus beyond the Syan River, the chaotic events of World War II, our travels through foreign lands, the death of my father in Austria from cancer, and, ultimately, our exodus to the U.S.A. on the SS Marine Tiger. My first glimpse of the Statue of Liberty filled me with hope for the future. The experiences at Ellis Island for strangers in a new land, gave our family the opportunity to live in freedom in our adopted homeland.

My memoirs will be supported by copies of selected historical materials and articles, which mention the Tatomyr clan and copies of my personal documents and numerous photographs. Unfortunately, our most treasured possessions were buried in a trunk under an old oak tree adjacent to my home in Topilnicia, as we left our families and villages hastily before the advancing front.

The most ancient document in my possession depicts a well-attended family reunion in 1892 in Sambir. Family members in attendance included the Nestorovich's, the Tatomyr's, the Rabij's and the Kozanevich's with their children.

Conversations with my father were most helpful to me in understanding our clan. In particular, he cited a vital family document with family statistics and chronology that traced the genealogy of our clan over the past two hundred years. This document was in the possession of my grandfather in Cherkhava. I discussed this document with my cousin Oleksander Berezhnysky from Buffalo, whose father became the parish priest in Cherkhava following his father's death. Oleksander was unable to give me a satisfactory response as to the whereabouts of this significant document concerning the longevity of our clan.

My father emphasized to me that we were descended from Ukrainian nobility and that at some point we were granted a family crest and the title of SAS. Our family name, Tatomyr means 'father of peace' in Ukrainian. This information developed a feeling of dignity within me and a sense of responsibility for the well-being of our nation through personal dedication and activism. My father was an outstanding role model in this regard, with superior leadership abilities.

Stories told to me by my mother, Olha, familiarized me with her family, Khomytsky. I remember my mother as a young woman, a blond and blue-eyed beauty, who was very talented musically.

MY GRANDFATHER'S MILL

Eventually the greatest assistance in tracing our family roots came from my father's cousin, Dr. Julian Rabij. From him I received the most ancient photographs of our family branch and the Nestorovych family from the 1700's.

Further light on our lineage was shed by my conversations with Maria Tatomyr Bereznyska, the daughter of a teacher from Pidbiza in the Carpathian Mountains, a distant relative of my father. She shared information with me about our family roots and the village of Silec.

Editor Lev Lepky, in his invaluable conversations with me, emphasized that for families of ancient lineage and noble roots, a unique responsibility rested on their shoulders-to protect the fate and destiny of Ukrainian nationhood.

Dr. Bohdan Korzmaryk, a close family friend, focused my attention on the significant historical documents of Hrushewsky that cite our family on several occasions. Further details were provided by Oleksander Berezhnysky and Evhen Turyansky, my second cousin.

In particular, it was the interest of my children Chrystyna, Ostap and Lesya that has motivated me to write my memoirs of our family. It is my great desire that my grandchildren will become familiar with the long and illustrious history of the Tatomyr clan. It is my hope that my memoirs will inspire them to appreciate their heritage and associate with other Ukrainians in their 'milieu', though they live far from the homeland of their forefathers. Given an opportunity to visit the beautiful country of Ukraine, I hope that they will support their brothers and sisters there in any way they can.

Correspondence with Adam Hordynsky, a school friend, encouraged me to continue tracing our family roots. If God Almighty, because of my advanced age, prevents me from gathering further data on the Tatomyr clan and organizing it into a historical compendium, at least I will have attempted to explain briefly to my descendents the significance of their familial historical past. Finally I hope that from my research my descendents will continue to research and document our family history.

Knowledge of the past history of our ancestors and the Ukrainian nation by my descendents will give our family opportunities for growth in an appreciation of their cultural heritage and, perhaps, renew a sense of responsibility in them to expand and preserve the history of this distinguished clan for future generations.

## TATOMYR CLAN OF SAMBIR

The Sambir clan of the Tatomyr family had its roots in the village of Silets. The village is located in the picturesque Carpathian Mountains on the river, Bystrytsa, twenty kilometers from Sambir in western Ukraine.

Here, in Silets, my grandfather, **Ivan**, son of Reverend **Evhen** Tatomyr (1815-1870), was born in 1842. He completed his seminary studies, married my grandmother, **Karolyna** Nestorovych, and became a priest. Initially, my grandfather was the pastor in Spryni, followed by forty years of pastoral service in Cherkhava, a mecca for Ukrainians.

My grandfather was a consummate gardener. He had a beautiful orchard with a variety of apple and cherry trees, along with twenty cows and four horses. The family deeply loved their grandfather and celebrated his birthday annually on July 7 (*na Ivana*) with a boisterous celebration. Family members who attended this celebration included Rev. Mykhajlo, Rev. Julian Tatomyr and family, Borkowsky, Berezhnysky, and Rabiji; later, other family members were included in the annual celebration, such as Turyansky, occasionally, Rev. Peofil Tatomyr from Pidbuza, Mykhajlo Tatomyr from Silets, and more distant family and neighboring priests.

On the first day of the birthday celebration, there was a banquet that lasted late into the night with numerous toasts to my grandfather. On the second day, there was a Mass and *panakhyda* for departed family members. There was also a separate panakhyda for my grandmother, Karolyna, near the church.

In stature my grandfather was of medium height and mesamorphic build. He was very energetic and active. He showed a great love for his family. My grandfather paid for the engineering studies of his oldest grandchild, Volodymyr, in the city of Danzig on the Baltic Sea.

Rev. Ivan died at eighty-four years of age in Cherkhava in 1925 and was laid to rest next to my grandmother. His surviving children included **Mykhajlo, Eleanora, Olena, Julian,** and **Maria.**

**Mykhajlo** completed his seminary studies and married Sophia Sozanska, an exceptional beauty, artist and gifted musician. Mykhaylo became pastor in the village of Kavska in Stryjzchyna. Mykhajlo and Sophia had three children: Volodymyr, Eleanora, and Evhen.

**Evhen** was a gifted athlete (like his mother). He joined the Ukrainian Galicia Army at sixteen and served on all the fronts in the east. At twenty-six years of age, he was murdered in a Bolshevik prison in Sambir.

**Volodymyr,** as a soldier in the Ukrainian Galician Army, fought in countless battles against Poles and Bolsheviks. Following his army service, he organized Prosvita reading rooms for children and adults to promote Ukrainian literacy skills and nationalism. He married, but his wife died of tuberculosis after one year of marriage. Eventually, he became the director of youth for all of Galicia through the Ukrainian Central Committee in Lviv and Krakow. During World War II, he became a mentor to Ukrainian youth in the service of his country, focusing on artillery training. After he emigrated to the United States of America, Volodymyr became an active member of Prosvita, organizing reading libraries for the children of refugees, and was one of the founding members of the sports organization Tryzub. Volodymyr published three books. He never remarried. He died of a heart attack in 1962 in Philadelphia.

**Eleanora** married Rev. Yakiw Turyansky. They had three children, two daughters and a son. Their son, Evhen, lives with his family in Detroit. Eleanora and Yakiw died in Ukraine.

My grandfather's third child was **Olena,** who married Myron Borkowski, an employee of the postal system. They had two daughters, Melania and Ivanka. Melania excelled in artistic abilities. From an early age, she loved to paint flowers, especially roses that adorned the front of their family home. Her sister, Ivanka, had a soft, melodious voice and an affinity for domestic pursuits. Behind their attractive family home, was an exquisite orchard with a variety of fruit, trees and, shrubs. At the present, only Melania is still living in Starij Sambir.

My grandfather's fourth child was my father, **Julian**, a well-known religious leader and social activist in Galicia. Julian married Olha Khomitska, the daughter of Rev. Petro in Husakove in Peremyshyl. Olha was a blue-eyed beauty, musically gifted in piano and, extremely hardworking by nature. She was devoted to her two sons. She suffered many illnesses throughout her life. My father, through his service as pastor in the churches of Galicia, was elevated to a high position in the Peremyshyl eparchy. For his political and social activism in the Ukrainian National Democratic Unification movement, Rev. Julian was appointed to the Polish Senate.

During World War II, my father was chaplain of a national high school and director of a religious organization with other church officials, Ryznyza, in Sambir. In 1918, Rev. Julian was director and chief organizer of ten thousand peasants who took over Sambir and included it in the Western Ukrainian National Republic. During the period of independence in Ukraine, my father fulfilled the function of school inspector in the Sambir region. He helped create the Ukrainian army and worked to improve the administrative capabilities of its leaders.

When the Polish Army under General Haller—assisted by France, England, and the United States of America (who provided weaponry)—invaded Galicia and approached the borders of Sambir, Rev. Julian and his family fled eastward. They arrived at the river Zbruch in Kamyanetz-Podylski and settled there for a time. Upon the return of the family to western Ukraine, Rev. Julian became pastor in Hrozovi in the Carpathian Mountains, Torchynovykhach, Luz, and then again in Luzok-Horishny in the Carpathians. In Starij Sambir, he organized cooperative and agricultural associations. In particular, Rev. Julian focused on youth, sports groups, and on children, by initiating children's libraries as a buffer against "Polonization."

Rev. Julian was imprisoned several times for providing birth certificates in Ukrainian (rather than Polish) to his parishioners and for his bravery and leadership abilities in protecting the Ukrainian nation from the Polish occupiers.

When the Bolsheviks occupied Galicia in 1939, Julian and his family escaped to Peremyshyl, where he became director of the Ukrainian Relief Committee. For his energetic and dedicated efforts in helping the people of this region, Rev. Julian received a citation signed by all the villagers in his care.

In 1941-44, Rev. Julian returned to the Carpathians where he continued to be an activist for the rights of Ukrainians, prior to his emigration to Austria. Rev. Julian was director of the religious order of St. Andrij and succeeded in his efforts to unite the two Ukrainian rites—Catholic and Orthodox.

My mother, **Olha**, had a brother, Jaroslav, from Sambir, who relocated to Vanevych, where he built a beautiful villa. He was married to Sabina Popel, the daughter of a city dweller. Although Sabina's mother was of Polish descent, Sabina became a Ukrainian patriot and active participant in Soyuz Ukrainok, a feminist organization committed to creating a new nationally conscious, culturally developed, and socio-economically progressive woman.

The fifth child of Rev. Ivan was **Maria**, who wed Rev. Oleksander Berezhnysky, pastor of Mschanzia in the Carpathians. Following the death of Rev. Ivan, Rev. Berezhnysky moved to Cherkhava, the family center.

Maria and Oleksander had four children: Julian, Eleanora, Oleksander, and Maria. Julian and Eleanora died in their teens. Oleksander died five years ago in Buffalo, leaving his wife, Oksana, of the Zayatz family. Rev. Ivan's daughter Maria still lives in Ukraine. She was deported to Siberia for ten years of hard labor. Upon her return, she married and had two sons. Upon the death of her husband, Oleksander, she moved to Sambir. In Cherkhava, the priest became Rev. Osyp Turyansky, husband of Eleanora of the Tatomyr clan from Kavska.

Until our departure to foreign lands in 1944, the pastors of Cherkhava were all members of our family.

My father died in Salzburg on March 26, 1946, and was buried in Salzburg, Austria. There was a massive attendance of religious leaders and Ukrainian refugees at the funeral. A moving tribute was given by the well-known Ukrainian poet Mykola Matiiv Melnyk. In 1978, Rev. Julian's remains were transported to Fox Chase, Philadelphia, where he was buried at St. Mary's cemetery in Philadelphia. My father was buried next to his wife, Olha, who died in Levittown in 1968. She outlived my father by twenty-two years.

# 8. Memoir

## *Autobiography,* Oleksander Tatomyr

I was born in Sambir, Ukraine, on May 9, 1913. My parents were Rev. Julian Tatomyr, a prominent religious leader and social activist, and Olha Khomitska, whose father was also a priest.

As an infant, I experienced my first emigration to Czechoslovakia during the invasion of Galicia by the Bolsheviks in 1914. After the dissemination of the Red Army in Horlyza in the Lemko region and its subsequent retreat in 1915, our family returned to my birthplace, Sambir.

In the spring of 1919, when the Polish army of General Haller advanced toward Sambir, our family again fled, this time to the east. Following some dramatic adventures en route, we arrived at Kamyanetz-Podilski. We found ourselves in a "quadrangle of death." Typhoid spread like wildfire in this area and relentlessly destroyed our army and many civilians.

As a six-year-old boy, I gazed with awe at the discipline, order, and fighting spirit of the Ukrainian Galician Army. I was dismayed by the shoddily dressed battalion of the Ukrainian National Republic Army, which was then stationed in Kamyanetz-Podilski. In contrast, the Polish Army, under the leadership of Pilsudski, was well-dressed and well-equipped for battle.

With the destruction of Ukrainian fronts, our family returned to Sambir, which was now under Polish occupation. With the permission of the bishop of our region, our family fled deep into the Carpathian Mountains to avoid the scrutiny of the Polish spies and the political instability in Sambir and surrounding areas. When the political situation became more stabilized, we returned to Sambir.

In 1930, I joined the Organization of Ukrainian Nationalists (OUN) and became very active in propagating illegal literature (banned by the Polish occupiers) and organizing new partisan groups. At the same time, I worked for a gymnastics and firefighting society called Sokil. Based on a successful Czech model, the society gave village youth the opportunity to take part in parades, and develop personal qualities of discipline, cooperation, patriotism, and education. Concurrently, I also was employed at Prosvita as one of its members, a society that was devoted to "the learning and enlightenment" of Ukrainian youth against Polonization. Reading rooms spread quickly across Ukraine. Their goal was to teach young people to read and speak in their own language and to appreciate the history, culture, and arts unique to their country.

In 1931, I completed gymnasia in Sambir and entered law school at the University of Jan Casimir in Lviv. Unfortunately, my law studies were interrupted when I was imprisoned for fifteen months for my activism in the Ukrainian nationalist movement. I spent those fifteen months in cramped quarters, taking a daily tally of cockroaches scurrying around me, and making a chess set from paper. I played chess daily with other prisoners to keep my mind sharp and to pass time. Luckily, due to lack of concrete evidence of my activism, I was released from prison.

I returned to my law studies in Lviv. At the same time, I became commander of the nationalist movement in our region and regained my persistent, energetic activism. The Polish police constantly tracked my movements. I endured frequent lengthy interrogations and further periods of imprisonment.

After completing my second year of law at the University of Jan Casimir, I was again sentenced to prison in Sambir and eventually released. These frequent prison terms did not diminish my spirit; on the contrary, I became a more determined and passionate freedom fighter.

Ignoring the ban on leadership activities in OUN, I helped organize the celebration of Ukrainian Youth in Christ held in Lviv. With thousands of young Ukrainians eager to participate in this celebration, the Polish government issued a ban for travel on trains by Ukrainians. Ignoring the Polish ban, we traveled to Lviv in wagons, where a massive demonstration by one hundred thousand nationalists was held in Sokola Square. Here the people of Ukraine swore their allegiance to God, while at the same time, the heartless, godless Bolsheviks were effectively creating a man-made famine in Eastern Ukraine.

This famine resulted in the systematic starvation of seven million men, women, and children in the east from 1932 to 1933. Many Ukrainians believed that this was Stalin's way of attempting to weaken Ukrainian nationalism. Attempts made by the Bolsheviks and some members of the foreign press to deny this human disaster proved futile. The nationalists sprang into action. In 1933, I visited many villages in Ukraine to inform them of the mass murders being perpetuated in Ukraine. Other members of OUN also spread out over Ukraine to educate the people about the atrocities committed by the Bolsheviks on our innocent brothers and sisters in the east.

Repeated imprisonments fragmented my law studies and I had to abandon them. In 1933, I became a seminary student to continue the priestly traditions of our clan and to improve my chances to help my countrymen in this position.

During the summer holidays, after the dissolution of Sokil by the Polish authorities, I worked in *Luh* (the old Sich), a popular prewar youth organization. It spread rapidly in the foothills of the Carpathian Mountains. Within this society, I organized national festivals, which were massively attended by young Ukrainians from western Ukraine, gave political speeches, and organized theatrical productions. My aim was to motivate young people to take pride in their heritage and to protect their homeland through active nationalism. In my free time, I researched ancient Ukrainian literature in various churches. Based on the study of these sacred books, I prepared a chronicle of the history of the villages of Luzok-Horishny, Busovysko, and Starij Sambir.

With the political awakening of Carpathian Ukraine, I was promptly arrested by the Polish authorities after four year of seminary studies. With time for reflection during my imprisonment, I underwent a deep personal crisis. I began to experience serious doubts about my commitment to the priesthood. My father visited me in prison several times to discuss my personal difficulties and concerns, but finally, I decided that the priesthood was not my destined vocation. I know that my father was deeply disappointed by my decision because it broke the continuity of this vocation in our family clan.

Eventually I volunteered to the Ukrainian Army Tank Division, which was located in Perevorsk. I developed a course manual for participants, which was published in Krakov. After I completed the theoretical and practical courses of army discipline, taught by former leaders of the Ukrainian National Republic Army, the Germans suddenly liquidated our school.

I made a decision to attend a one-year pedagogy course in Krynyza, completed the course and received my teaching diploma. During the Bolshevik-German war, I returned to Sambir and worked as a teacher and organizer of youth groups in Luzok. There were 600 members in the youth group, who yearned to fight for the freedom of Ukraine.

In 1942, I completed agricultural studies in Bereznysi and Chernyzy in the region of Stryj. This diploma enabled me to open a regional agricultural middle school in Topilnicia, where I was director and a teacher. There were 500 students and six additional teachers on staff. The students were housed in a boys and girls dorm.

During this time I fell in love and married Sophia Tereshkevych. Having completed her pedagogy degree in Sambir, she had been unable to work as a teacher under the Polish occupation of Ukraine. When Sophia married me, I hired her as a teacher at my agricultural school. We lived in a spacious home near the school. On January 28, 1944, our first child, Chrystyna, was born. As newlyweds, we enjoyed our home, our family, our child, and my prospering school. The winds of change would bring dark, dangerous clouds into our lives.

Immediately before the invasion of the Bolsheviks, Sophia, Chrystyna, and I left our homeland as political escapees in late July 1944. After a long, arduous journey by wagon through Carpathian Ukraine, Slovakia, Hungary, and Czechoslovakia, we arrived at our final destination (or so we thought)—Sankt Georgen in the Austrian Alps. Our dwelling was not far from Zell am See, where there was a large DP camp of Ukrainian refugees.

For two years, I worked for the Ukrainian Relief Committee in Zell am See, assisting Ukrainian refugees in thirty villages. In 1947, I worked at construction for some time. I learned many invaluable skills that would help me to find work following our emigration to the United States.

Tragically, my father died in Salzburg following an operation for stomach cancer in 1946. This was a blow for the whole family, particularly my mother, who had not been well for many years. Since I had been very close to my father and admired him immensely, his death left a deep chasm in my soul. We had survived so much brutality and hardships during the war as a family that it was unimaginable that we would have to leave him in Salzburg alone, buried on foreign soil.

In 1948, we left for the United States, through the city of Bremen on the *Marine Tiger*. Upon our arrival in New York, we were greeted by the Statue of Liberty and the inspectors at Ellis Island. Weak from the voyage and exhausted by the events of the last three years, we managed to pass inspection and received our entry into New York.

We arrived in Philadelphia in the heat of late spring. At first, many refugees lived in a small room and eventually, I found a small home in a tenement district near Second Street and Logan Avenue. We had a very tiny yard in the back of the house. Our second child, Ostap, was born in 1949.

Challenged by the English language upon arrival, I worked in a butcher shop, then a sugar refinery, and completed a course in electricity and welding trades. In our Ukrainian community, I was active in the diaspora centre and in *Samopomych*. My wife and I helped thirty people to emigrate from Austria to the United States of America, assisting them with finding housing and employment.

As my wife yearned for the beauty of the mountains and fresh air of her hometown, Spas, we decided to leave the crowded, hot tenements of the city and moved to a tiny hamlet in Bristol, Pennsylvania.

Eventually, I obtained a job with General Motors in Trenton, New Jersey, in piecework. My eldest daughter once asked me how I survived the repetitive boredom of this job. I told her that my soul returned to my homeland where there were so many happy memories, but that my mind was active in considering options to help our brothers and sisters in Ukraine. So in that time at work, I would compose numerous letters and articles in my head, focusing on the plight of the Ukrainian people, and publish them in local papers. The *Levittown Courier Times* arranged an interview with my wife and I. "Journey of a Patriot" was a lengthy feature of our emigration. It included photographs during my studies, as a freedom fighter, and as an activist in religious celebrations in my homeland.

Our youngest daughter, Lesya, was born in Levittown in 1953. My daughters were active in Plast, Ukrainian school, and music lessons. My son had a passion for athletics, journalism, and music.

Always an activist, I organized a new Ukrainian parish, formed and taught in Ukrainian schools, initiated a dance group and a drama group.

In 1969, I became a member of Boykivshchyna, a committee of former refugees from the Boyko region. I was also coeditor of a monthly journal by the same name and frequently submitted articles on various topics.

I retired from General Motors in 1979, after twenty-five years at the company. I wanted to devote more time to my wife and literary pursuits. I was proud, that from humble beginnings in our adopted land, all of my children graduated from university as teachers. They married, left home, and began new lives in Toronto, Canada, and in Bordentown, New Jersey. My family is my pride and support in my waning years. I believe that they will faithfully observe the traditions of the Tatomyr clan. This the fervent wish of both my wife and I.

On March 11, 1983, my lifelong friend and dear wife, Sophia, died of a massive heart attack at sixty-seven years of age. She slipped away quietly, telling me to tell her family that she loved them deeply. She was the heart and soul of our family, and I was inconsolable after her death. My deep faith in God sustained me to continue to support our family and work for Ukrainians, both in the diaspora and in my homeland of Ukraine. May the Almighty protect my family and allow them to continue to work for the good of the church and our homeland, Ukraine.

*       *       *

Oleksander Tatomyr died peacefully at home on June 27, 1987, having outlived his wife by four years. His last years were deeply affected by the loss of his life partner, his true love, Sophia. He was buried at St. Mary's Cemetery in Fox Chase, next to his beloved wife, his father, and his mother. Eventually, he was joined at St. Mary's Cemetery by his sister-in-law, Luba Fedevych Tatomyr, and his older brother, Jaroslav Tatomyr.

At Fox Chase, they were also surrounded by friends with whom they had survived the horrors of World War II.

We are very fortunate that records of the lives of our family were preserved through the efforts of our grandfather and father, and that they did not disappear in the ashes of the "history of man's inhumanity toward man".

**Oleksander Tatomyr (center), at Seminary in Peremysl, Poland, 1939.**

**Julian and Oleksander at "Chornyj Stav," a partisan meeting place, August, 1940.**

# Final Thoughts

# *Imperialism in the Twenty First Century*

For most of the twentieth century and for two hundred years before, Ukraine was occupied by various foreign regimes. The Russian Empire and later the Russian dominated Soviet Union ruled eastern Ukraine. The Austrian Empire, Poland and the Soviet Union occupied western Ukraine. All Ukrainians suffered during the Nazi invasion and occupation of 1941 to 1944.

At various times, these foreign regimes banned the Ukrainian language, destroyed Ukrainian churches and tried to convert Ukrainians to Roman Catholicism or to Russian Orthodoxy. During the first half of the twentieth century millions of Ukrainians died in combat in Polish, German and Russian concentration camps and in deliberately engineered genocidal famines.

Throughout all this time, the concept of Ukraine somehow survived. The Ukrainian language, distinct from Russian and Polish, survived. The Ukrainian Catholic (Uniate) and Ukrainian Orthodox Churches were persecuted, but survived. Though they did not have their own state, the people still called themselves Ukrainians and at every opportunity during the twentieth century fought to create their own sovereign nation.

The horrific nuclear accident at Chornobyl in 1986 exposed everything that was rotten and corrupt about the Soviet Union. That, and pressure for change from within and from without eventually caused the regime to disintegrate. Countries that throughout the cold war had been kept in Moscow's orbit by force chose to leave the 'union'.

Central European countries like East Germany, Poland, Hungary, the Czech and Slovak Republics and the Balkan countries broke all political ties with the old Soviet regime and turned westward. Soon after, accompanied by much protest from Moscow, Latvia, Estonia, Lithuania, Georgia and Ukraine democratically decided that they wanted to be independent and to set their own course. Asian Republics followed. Other republics, like Chechnya, tried but failed to escape Moscow's grip.

Previously, Ukrainians tried to create an independent state in 1917, 1918 and 1941 but each time, lacking international recognition and military support, they failed.

Finally, in 1990, Ukrainians chose by a majority of more than 90% to leave the Soviet Union. Currently, Ukraine is enjoying its longest period of independence since the seventeenth century.

Our grandparents, parents, aunts and uncles and their generations did not accept foreign domination and struggled against it. Many died, all suffered unspeakable brutality and a few lost everything. The lucky ones managed to escape to the West. Sadly, most of our family members who survived and made it to freedom in North America, didn't live long enough to witness Ukraine's ultimate independence from the Soviet Union. They worked so hard all their lives for that moment and would have given anything to visit their homeland again, but it wasn't to be.

## ORANGE REVOLUTIOIN

The birth of a renewed independent Ukraine in August 1991 did not bring instant success. In-fighting, corruption, greed, power grabs, genuine internal differences of opinion and especially, foreign interference from Russia caused Ukraine's democracy to remain very fragile. The government often became paralyzed and came very close to collapse on a number of occasions.

In 2004, Ukraine was experiencing another major political crisis. A corrupt, Kremlin-backed political party tried to steal the election. The people wouldn't stand for it.

The world watched as Ukrainians once again tried to define their country. Day after day, thousands braved the winter cold of Kyiv to protest the corruption, foreign interference, lack of democracy and the attempted assassination of their political leader. Against all odds, and in spite of Russian interference, the Orange Revolution succeeded and a fragile democracy was re-instated in Ukraine.*

Four years later, in 2008, after seventeen years of existence, Ukraine still has political and economic problems and is still experiencing intimidation and interference from Moscow, but there is hope that as the old Soviet era elite 'that prospered under the old conditions' dies off, Ukraine will be able to forge a strong, independent European democracy.

Poland has made peace with Ukraine and Ukrainians and was one of the first European nations to recognize Ukrainian independence in 1991 (Canada was the first western nation to do so). Poland supported the Orange Revolution and in recent years has been one of the most ardent supporters of Ukraine's desire to become a member of NATO and the European Union (EU).

Germany has acknowledged its terrible Nazi past and was one of the first countries in Europe to invest in Ukraine and to otherwise contribute positively to Ukraine's

---

* My brother, Roman, was in Ukraine at this time. He was sent by the Canadian government as an 'observer' to ensure that the new elections were conducted fairly. Our niece, Marichka, also took time off work to go to Kyiv to experience this exercise in democracy.

economic development. Unfortunately, in recent years, Germany, along with much of the rest of Europe, has become dependent on Russia for its energy supplies, and thus has lost a measure of its own independence. Germany supports, at least in principle, Ukraine's eventual integration into Europe but cannot make its decisions independently. Russia has them 'over a barrel.' Germans must do what they are told by Russia or risk losing access to Russian gas and oil.

Germans will have to take some courageous measures if they want to regain their ability to act like an independent nation.

Most countries in the world have recognized Ukraine and accept its right to exist as an independent sovereign state.

Only Putin's Russia is still lamenting the breakup of the Soviet Union and only Russia is still endangering Ukraine's independence. Russia continues to meddle in Ukraine's political process, threatens economic punishment by withdrawing oil and gas supplies and continues to deny Ukraine's sovereign right to choose its trading partners and political alliances. In one way or another, it still hopes to ensnare Ukraine.

Civilized countries don't behave this way.

Imperialism, as it is being practiced by Russia in the twenty first century is an antiquated, evil concept and is destined to fail—although the lure of an easy military victory over a weaker opponent is very tempting for a rich, militarily powerful country.

During the summer of 2008, for example, when the United States was pre-occupied with its presidential election campaign and was entangled in two protracted wars in Iraq and Afghanistan, and while the world was distracted by the opening ceremonies of the Beijing Olympics, Russia used its military might and its well oiled propaganda machine to attack and occupy Georgia.

Georgia, like Ukraine, dared to seek closer ties with Europe. Russia decided to send a strong message to all its former satellites and to assert its hegemony in the area. Putin felt confident of success because he knew the West has no stomach for a confrontation and will do nothing because of Europe's dependence on Russia's gas and oil.

## APPEASEMENT IN THE TWENTY-FIRST CENTURY

Putin's actions in Georgia in 2008 are reminiscent of Hitler's actions in the Sudetenland seventy years earlier:

In 1938, German newsreels showed 'evidence' of Czech 'atrocities' against Sudeten Germans and Hitler threatened to use military force.

In 2008, after issuing Russian passports to separatist Georgians living in South Ossetia, Putin claimed Georgians committed atrocities against 'Russian citizens' justifying an invasion.

In 1938, Hitler convinced British Prime Minister Neville Chamberlain, that Sudetenland was 'the last problem to be solved.'

Chamberlain decided Hitler was 'a man who can be relied upon' and decided that Czechoslovakia was not one of the 'great issues' which justified war, but just 'a quarrel in a far-away country between people of whom we know nothing.'

Chamberlain returned to England and declared, 'I believe it is peace in our time.' In 2008, will similar sentiments be expressed?

In 1939, Hitler asked 'Who still talks nowadays about the Armenians?'

In 2008, Putin can boast, 'Who still talks nowadays about the Chechens?'

As well, Putin justified the death and destruction his armies inflicted on tiny Georgia by comparing Russia's actions to those of the United States when they invaded Iraq.*

# IS UKRAINE NEXT?

Ukraine desperately wants to become a member of one of the most successful association of nations in history, the European Union. The EU has grown in power, territory and numbers of nations and, in many ways appears to function as an empire. But this 'empire' is very different from all the previous empires that enslaved Ukrainians. The EU represents the modern concept of empire, one that expands not by force, but by invitation.

Ukraine *wants* to be a member of this empire and as a sovereign democratic country has that right under international law.

And so does Georgia. Moscow's continuing destabilization efforts in Georgia and Ukraine are designed to make their membership in the EU much more difficult.

Shortly after the Russian invasion of Georgia on August 7, 2008, former United States national security advisor Zbigniew Brzezinski stated: "Ukraine could well be

---

\* Senior US government officials now admit what everyone suspected all along, that the Iraq war was mostly about oil. "In short: A cabal of oil profiteers who came to power by dubious means in the world's mightiest nation took advantage of the September 11 attacks to start an unrelated war that it has wanted to wage for years. The consequences to world peace are still unfolding and may yet become more serious. The suffering has far outweighed the benefits of deposing Saddam Hussein: more than 4,000 Americans dead, perhaps ten times that number of Iraqi battle deaths, more than 150,000 civilian deaths and over two million Iraqi refugees driven into exile—one tenth of the countries population. The damage to human rights and to the moral standing of the United States has been incalculable. Ancient freedoms such as habeas corpus, a foundation of English-speaking democracy for a thousand years, were lightly brushed aside. The so called war on terror will breed only more war. Our only hope is to build a new world order in which everyone has a say and shares the rewards". (Ronald Wright *What is America? A Short History of the New World Order.* 2008)

the next flashpoint. The Russian leadership has already openly questioned whether it needs to respect Ukraine's territorial integrity. Russian leaders have also remarked that Crimea, a part of Ukraine, should once again be joined to Russia. Baltic nations such as Lithuania, Latvia and Estonia have been the object of various threats from Russia, including economic sanctions and disruptive cyberwarfare.

The stakes are high. Ultimately the independence of the post-Soviet states is at risk. Russia seems committed to the notion that there should be some sort of supernational entity, governed from the Kremlin, that would oversee much of the former Soviet territories. This attitude reflects in part the intense nationalistic mood that now permeates Russia's political elite. Vladimir Putin, former president and now prime minister, is riding the nationalist wave, exploiting it politically and propagating it with the Russian public. Some now even talk of a renewed Russian military presence in Cuba as a form of retaliation against the United States for its support of the independence of post Soviet states.*

The United States and the West must take a strong stand.

I believe that the United States will return to its long standing principles and will again be seen as a positive force in the world. Russia will not be successful in blackmailing European countries and its attempt to intimidate its neighbors like Ukraine will fail, as well.

On our first trip to Ukraine in 1993, Chrystyna and I found that the Russian language, especially in Kyiv and Odesa was paramount. It was hard to find anyone who spoke Ukrainian and, as westerners, we were looked upon with a great amount of suspicion. When we returned to Kyiv and Odesa a year later, things had already changed. Increasingly, young people understood and were able to respond to us in Ukrainian and they seemed more comfortable with our presence in their country. On our last trip to Kyiv in 2007, we found that servers in restaurants and salespeople in shops, especially the younger ones, quickly and seamlessly switched to Ukrainian when we spoke to them. They were comfortable in Russian and Ukrainian and they no longer viewed us with suspicion. Perhaps, it is even more significant that many young Ukrainians were also reasonably fluent in English and were eager to have conversations with us because we were westerners. Attitudes of Ukrainians in Lviv and the rest of western Ukraine are even more Euro-focused.

Ukrainians have tasted freedom. There is no going back.

"For most of Ukraine's population born during or after the perestroika era of the 1980s, there is no trace of Sovietism; they know full well about the famines and political tragedies inflicted on Ukraine by the 'foreign' revolution in Russia (in 1917) and by two of the most terrible dictators of the twentieth century, Lenin and Stalin. With only the current generation of ex-Soviet apparatchiks separating them from leadership, they are cynically optimistic about their country's European future."17

Brzezinski proposes a more enlightened path for Russia: "Ukraine's very existence as an independent country transforms Russia. Indeed, Russia's eventual acceptance

---

*       New York Times, August 9, 2008

of Ukraine's Europeanization could make Ukraine a model for Russia itself, both geographically and psychologically."

Putin will have to change his nineteenth century thinking and abandon Russian imperialism or he will increasingly be viewed as a dinosaur. I am convinced that Russians will soon tire of Putin and will look to the west for a brighter future for themselves . . . . perhaps even embrace democracy.

Forty years ago, in 1968, Russian tanks entered Prague to crush an attempt by the people to free their country of Soviet tyranny. For a short time, the Soviets were able to subdue the population, but eventually the occupiers were thrown out and today nobody thinks of Prague as anything but European and there is no fear that the Czech Republic will ever again fall under Russian control.

I believe Ukraine will follow a similar path.

At the very beginning of this book, I quoted Gandhi:

> *"When I despair, I remember that all through history the way of truth and love has always won. There have been tyrants and murderers and for a time they seemed invincible, but in the end they always fail."*

History will repeat itself.

# Documents and Images, 1930-2008

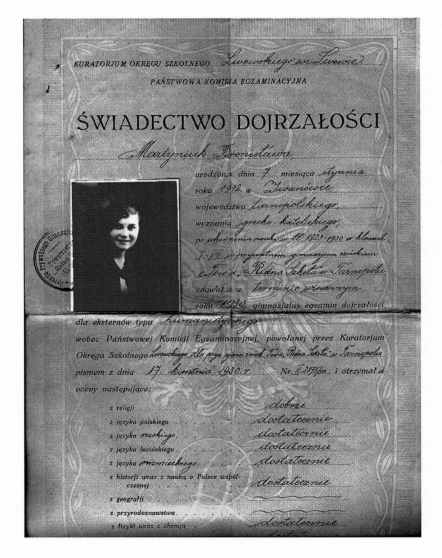

**Bronyslawa Melnyk's matura graduation certificate, 1930. Although she graduated from a Ukrainian school, the final exams (oral and written) had to be completed in Polish. She was one of only a few of her classmates who were successful.**

( Gen.-Gouv. )

# MILITARY GOVERNMENT OF GERMANY

TEMPORARY REGISTRATION     Zeitweilige Registrierungskarte

Name
Name    M e l n y k  Bronyslawa     Alter   33   Geschlecht   weibl.
                                                        Age        Sex

Ständige Adresse
Permanent Address    Podhyce / Westukraine     Beruf   Hausfrau
                                                        Occupation

Jetzige Adresse
Present Address    Kulmbach, Wolfskehle 31

Der Inhaber dieser Karte ist als Einwohner von der Stadt    Kulmbach     vorschriftsmäßig registriert und ist es ihm oder ihr strengstens verboten, sich von diesem Platz zu entfernen. Zuwiderhandlung dieser Maßnahme führt zu sofortigem Arrest. Der Inhaber dieses Scheines muß diesen Ausweis stets bei sich führen.

The holder of this card is duly registered as a resident of the town of               and is prohibited from leaving the place designated. Violation of this restriction will lead to immediate arrest. Registrant will at all times have this paper on his person.

Kennk. Gen. Gouv. A 00676
        Legitimations Nummer                                     Capt. H. Moore
        Identity Card Number                                    Name und Rang
                                                      Mil. Gov. Officer, U.S. Army

      Unterschrift des Inhabers                                          30. April 1946
        Signature of Holder                                            Datum der Ausstellung
                                                             Date of Issue

(Dies ist kein Personal-Ausweis und erlaubt keine Vorrechte.)
(This is not an identity document and allows no privileges.)                  Right Index Finger

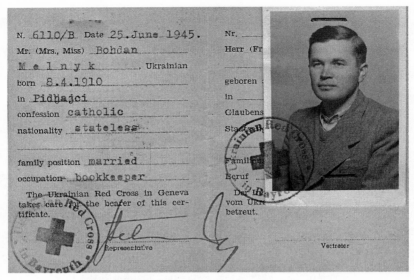

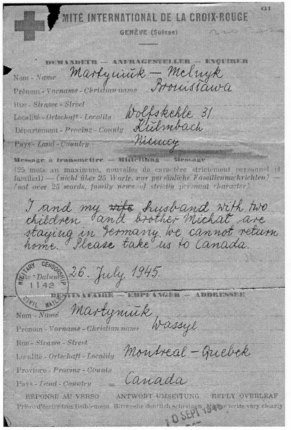

# PHISICAL EXAMINATION AND
# IMMUNIZATION REGISTER OF DISPLACED PERSONS

*Melnyk   Andrij*

| Last Name | First Name | Male Female |

*2*

| Nationality | Age |

## THYPHUS

| Date | Amount | Init | Date | Amount | Init |
|------|--------|------|------|--------|------|
| 29. 10. 45 | | | | 0,5 | B |
| 1. 11. 45 | | | | 1,0 | M |
| 12. 11. 45 | | | | 2,0 | B |

## DIPHTHERIA

| Date | Amount | Init | Date | Amount | Init |
|------|--------|------|------|--------|------|
| | | | | | |
| | | | | | |
| | | | | | |

## SMALLPOX VACCINE

| Date | Amount | Init | Date | Amount | Init |
|------|--------|------|------|--------|------|
| 29. V. 46 | | | | | B |
| 31. VII. 46 | | | | | B |

## TRIPE TYPHOID VACCINE

| Dates of Administration | | | | Init |
|------|------|------|------|------|
| Series | 1st Dose | 2d Dose | 3d Dose | |
| 1st Ds. | 7. 9. 45 | | 0,5 | B |
| 2d Ds. | 23-9. 45 | | 1,0 | M |
| 3d Ds. | 21. 9. 45 | | 1,0 | B |
| Booster | | Init | 2,0 | |
| Booster | | Init | | |

## PHYSICAL EXAMINTATION

| Date | General | Special* | Init |
|------|---------|----------|------|
| | | | |
| | | | |
| | | | |

*enote type

Buchdruckerei Emil Mühl, Bayreuth

**1021**

Serial Number

Resettlement Centre Amberg Area No. 4

**X-Ray Certificate** C 55

Name: MELNYK Audrij

Sex: M    Age: 5    DP. No.: 821422

Findings on attached film:

Lungs and heart : no pathologic changes noted.

Film:

Fingerprint forefinger right hand:

Date: 24. Jun. 1949

Signature of X-Ray Spec.

Amberger Zeitung - 3. 49 - 26 000 - 2136

**IMMUNIZATION    RECORD**
**UNRRA    TEAM 1046**

Name: Melnyk Audrij

Age: 28. II. 44.

Index No.: 433348 ) 821422

Typho d    Date 1
2
3

Typhus    Date 1  6.8.81
2 13.X. 47. 20.10.48

Diphteria    Date 1  12. IX. 47.
2 14. X. 47.

Small Pox Date
Reaction

(CABIN CLASS)

# 540 IMMIGRATION IDENTIFICATION CARD

### THIS CARD MUST BE SHOWN TO THE EXAMINING OFFICER AT PORT OF ARRIVAL

Name of passenger MELNYK, ANDRIJ

Name of ship SAMARIA

Name appears on Return, sheet 18     line 30

| Medical Examination Stamp | Civil Examination Stamp |
|---|---|
| | CANADA AUG 15 1948 QUEBEC. P.Q. |

(See back)

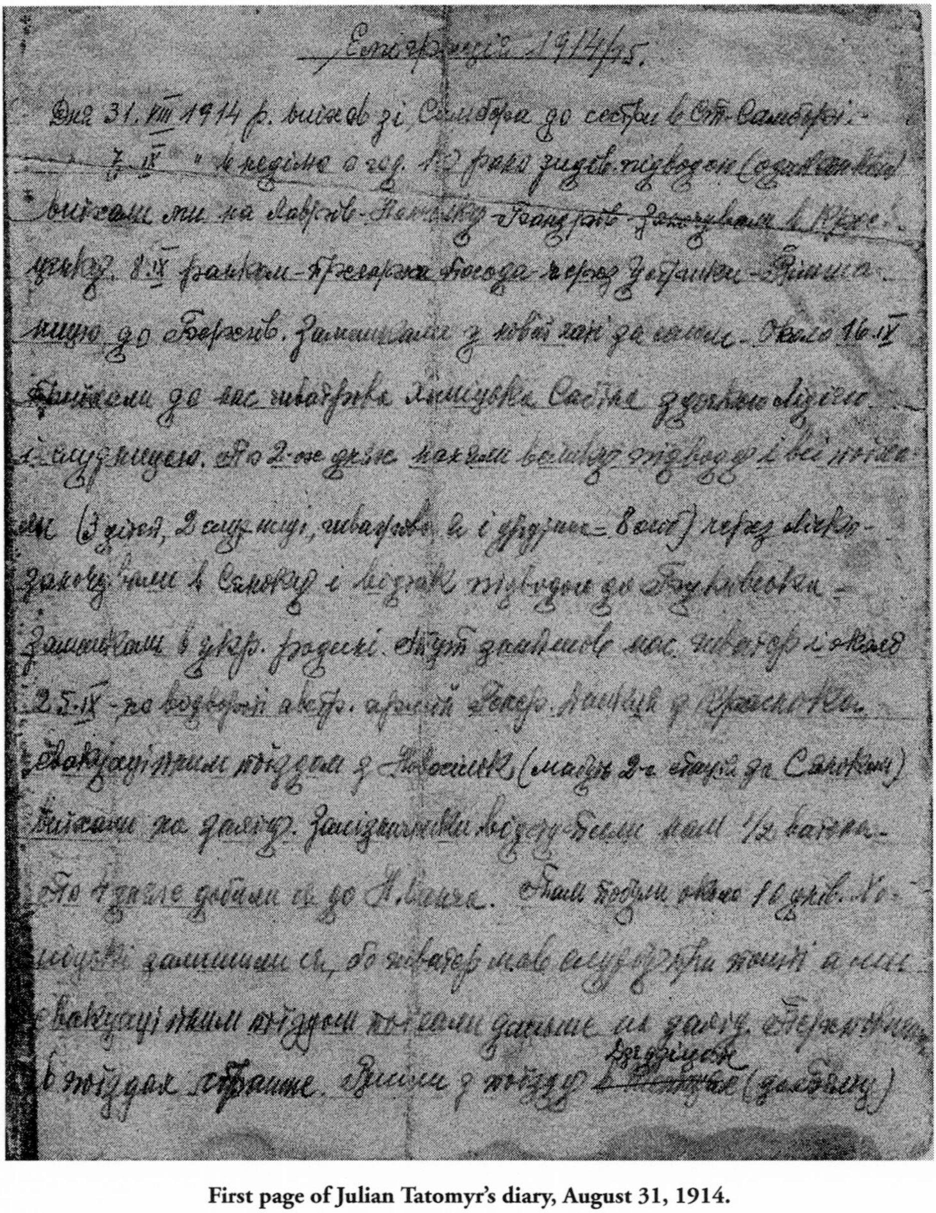
Евакуація 1914/15.

Дня 31.VIII 1914 р. виїхав зі Самбора до сестри в Ст. Самборі.

**First page of Julian Tatomyr's diary, August 31, 1914.**

Last entry in Julian Tatomyr's diary, just before his death in 1946,
with a postscript written by his son, Oleksander, March 26, 1946.

**Melnyks in Regensburg, 1946.**

Martyniuk-Hrycyk wedding, Montreal, 1952.
Top row: Vasylko Martyniuk, Bohdan Melnyk, Stefan, Nicholas,
and Mykhajlo Martyniuk
Middle row: (second from left) Erna Martyniuk, (third) Bronyslawa Melnyk.
Front row: Hrycyk family, bride, Anna Martyniuk, Vasyl Martyniuk,
(our prime sponsor to Canada), his wife Anastasia, and Vasyl's mother,
recently arrived from Ukraine.
Sitting on floor: Roman Melnyk, Vera Martyniuk, (girl) Hrycyk,
and Andrew Melnyk.

**Grandmother Bronyslawa Melnyk
with cousins Marichka, Melanie, Markian, and Roman
Soyuzivka Resort, New York, 1980.**

**Cousins: (l to r) Roman Melnyk, Stephen Lukasewycz, Melanie Tatomyr, Markian Melnyk, Daniel Tatomyr, Anya Lukasewycz, Andrij Horodysky, Laryssa Horodysky. Family Reunion, Newmarket, Ontario, 1989.**

**Next generation: Markian, Kristine, Anya, and Ava Melnyk, 2008.**

**Roman, Julia, and Tammy at Julia's christening, January 2008.**
**Julia Alexandra Melnyk was born January 3, 2007. We didn't realize until months**
**later that Julia's great-great grandfather, Reverend Julian Tatomyr**
**was also born on January 3**
**. . . 124 years earlier, in 1883.**

**Cousins Vasylko (Will) Stetic and Anya Melnyk, 2008.**

Great-grandmother Bronyslawa Melnyk with Will, (born July 30, 2004), Katya (July 11, 2007), Anya (June 26, 2004), Ava (August 16, 2006), and Julia (January 3, 2007)

Four generations of Melnyk women:
Great-grandmother Bronyslawa, Mother Melanie, Grandmother Tania, Aunt Marichka, with Katia (2008).

**Four generations of Melnyk women:**
**Great-grandmother Bronyslawa, mother Kristine, Ava,**
**Grandmother Chrystyna, and Anya.**

*In memory of*

*George Wesolowsky (1997)*
*Ostap Tatomyr (2005)*
*Omelan Lukasewycz (2006)*

Dr. Omelan Lukasewycz (1943-2006) and
Dr. George Wesolowsky (1945-1997).
My two very best friends.
On fishing trip near Sioux Lookout, Northern Ontario, 1996.

**Ostap George Tatomyr (1949-2005) with sister, Chrystyna,
holding nephew, Will O'Keefe.
Portrait of his daughter, Melania, by aunt Chrystyna sits on the piano.**

**Best friends.
With George and Irene, Lake Ontario, 1995.**

# Important Dates in Ukraine's History

| | |
|---|---|
| 988 | Prince Volodymyr of Kyiv accepts Christianity from Constantinople, baptizes citizens in Dnieper River. |
| 1200 | Danylo, Prince of Halycz, takes up residence in Halychyna (Galicia). |
| 1240 | Invasion of Kiev by Golden Hordes led by Batu Khan. Kyiv sacked. |
| 1648 | Khmelnytsky rebellion begins. Khmelnytsky elected Hetman, enters Kyiv victorious. |
| 1654 | Treaty of Pereyaslav. Khmelnytky seeks protection of Russian Tsar. Tsar betrays Khmelnytsky. |
| 1657-86 | Wars among Poland, Russia, Turks, and Cossacks for control of Ukrainian lands. |
| 1772 | Eastern Ukraine becomes part of Russian Empire. |
| 1772 | Partition of Poland. Austro-Hungarian Empire creates province of Galicia consisting of present day southern Poland (Krakow), western Ukraine (Lviv), and south along the Carpathian Mountains to the Romanian border. |
| 1848 | Abolition of serfdom in Austrian Empire, including Galicia. |
| 1914 | World War I breaks out. Ukrainian Halytska (Galician) Army formed. Battle Polish, Russian, Austrian, and Romanian armies. |
| 1917 | Ukraine declares independence in Kyiv after collapse of Russian Empire |
| 1918 | Western Ukraine declares independence as Austria collapses. |
| 1922 | Eastern Ukraine incorporated into the Soviet Union. |
| 1923 | Treaty of Versailles formally grants sovereignty over all of Galicia to Poland resulting in Polish rule in predominantly Ukrainian eastern Galicia. |
| 1926 | Polish governor of Galicia closes Ukrainian language schools and newspapers, Orthodox churches demolished, twenty-thousand Polish settlers brought into eastern Galicia. |
| 1929-33 | Stalin's collectivization campaign results in man-made famine that kills 5-7 million Ukrainian peasants in Eastern Ukraine. |
| 1937 | Mass deportations and executions in Stalinist purges. |
| 1939 | Ribbentrop-Molotov nonaggression Pact signed between Hitler and Stalin. Nazi forces invade Poland. World War II begins. Russian forces occupy Eastern Galicia. |
| 1941 | Hitler breaks pact. German forces occupy Ukraine. Millions die, including five hundred thousand Jews. |
| 1942 | Ukrainian Insurgent Army formed to fight first the German and later Soviet invading armies. |
| 1943 | Ukrainian Divisia of SS formed. Fight first battle against Soviets in town of Brody in Galicia, sustain high casualties, sent to Slovak front, captured by British. |
| 1944 | Soviet armies reoccupy Ukraine, mass exodus of Ukrainian intelligentsia to the West. Mass deportations to Siberia and Gulags of escapees found in Soviet controlled territory. |
| 1945 | Allied victory leaves Ukraine in Soviet hands, but resistance continues. Creation of enlarged Ukrainian SSR including eastern Galicia. |
| 1945 | Ukrainian SSR becomes founding member of United Nations |
| 1954 | After nine years Ukrainian Insurgent Army is defeated by the Soviets. |

# Modern History of Ukraine

| | |
|---|---|
| 1986 | Radioactivity spews across Europe after accident at Chornobyl nuclear station. |
| 1988 | RUKH, the Ukrainian People's Movement for restructuring, is established. |
| 1991 | Ukraine declares independence after abortive putsch attempt in Moscow and referendum in Ukraine with more than 90-percent support for independence. Krawchuk becomes first president of Ukraine. Starts reforms including reestablishment of the use of the Ukrainian language in all government agencies. |
| 1994 | Kuchma becomes president. Closer ties with Moscow ensue. Corruption becomes a way of life in government. |
| 1997 | Kuchma signs Friendship Treaty with Russia |
| 1999 | Kuchma appoints Victor Yushchenko, head of the central bank, as prime minister. |
| 2000 | In early November, police discover the decapitated corpse of investigative journalist Georgiy Gongadze, who had been looking into high-level corruption. Tapes subsequently appear, allegedly of Kuchma discussing ways to get rid of Gongadze. |
| 2001 | Yushchenko loses a nonconfidence motion in April. Kuchma appoints Anatolliy Kinackh as prime minister. |
| 2002 | Mass demonstrations against Kuchma. Kuchma appoints Victor Yanukovich as prime minister. |
| 2003 | Further mass demonstrations against Kuchma. |
| 2004 | In run-up to the October 31 presidential elections, opposition leader Yushchenko is hit by a disfiguring illness. Yushchenko alleges he was poisoned by the regime. Opponents say he ate bad suchi. |
| | First round of voting leads to runoff election on November 21 between Yushchenko and Yanukovich. Observers report widespread fraud, but official count gives victory to Yanukovich. Opposition launches street protests. Occupy Kyiv's Maidan (Square). Orange Revolution (so called because of the color Yushchenko used in his campaign) begins. |
| | About 2,000 to 15,000 people camp in tent city on Kyiv's Maidan. Up to a hundred thousand people come out daily, wearing orange clothing, banners, and scarves in support of Yushchenko. Coverage of peaceful demonstrations beamed around world. Russian President Putin throws his support behind Kuchma's candidate, Yanukovich. Accused of interfering in internal affairs of sovereign nation, Putin backs down. European countries get involved as does the USA and Canada in support of fair elections and democracy. Thousands of election observers arrive in Ukraine, including five hundred from Canada. |
| | December 26, Yushchenko wins election decisively. Offers olive branch to Yanukovich supporters and makes one-day visit to Moscow as his first foreign trip. |
| 2005 | Yushchenko appoints his strongest supporter, Julia Tymoshenko, prime minister. |
| 2005 | Yushchenko dismissed Tymoshenko. |
| 2006 | Parliamentary elections take place in March. Yanukovych block takes highest percentage of votes. Yushchenko remains as president, appoints Tymoshenko prime minister. |
| 2008 | President Yushchenko visits Canada, addresses joint session of Commons and Senate. On May 29, 2008, Parliament unanimously proclaims that the Holodomor Famine-Genocide in Ukraine was an act of genocide. The last Saturday of November declared Holodomor Memorial Day in Canada. |

(Adapted and updated from *Maclean's* magazine, December 13, 2004.)

# Sources and References

Much of the material in this book is derived from primary sources: stories my parents told us; stories heard around the dinner table; speeches at Sunday-afternoon concerts (which seemed to occur with great regularity in Montreal during the 50s and 60s); discussions with my uncles, aunts, friends of the family; and, of course, our own memories of the early days. As a child, I didn't really want to hear stories of my homeland—I thought they were boring—but as I grew older I wanted to hear more and more. When I finally became interested, my mother, Bronyslawa Melnyk and father-in-law, Oleksander Tatomyr gladly offered a great amount of information.

Among the translated written material I used (indicated by * or number in my text) are the following:

*1.    Memoirs and letters to her grandchildren by Bronyslawa Melnyk

*2.    Diaries of Rev. Julian Tatomyr (1914-1946)

*3.    Newspaper articles and letters by O. Tatomyr (1970-1986)

*4.    Records, Church of Latter Day Saints, Mormons, Salt Lake City, Utah

*5     Encyclopedia of Ukraine

*6.    Subtelny, Orest. Ukraine: A History. 3rd ed., University of Toronto Press, 2000.

*7.    Davies, Norman. Europe: A History, Norman Davies, 1998.

*8.    Magocsi, P.R. A History of Ukraine, University of Toronto Press, 1996.

*9.    Regensburg, Articles and Documents, (Ukrainian text), 1985.

*10.   Redlich, Shimon. Together and Apart in Brzezany, Indiana University Press, 2002.

*11.   Luciuk, L., Hruniak, S. Canada's Ukrainians: Negotiating an Identity, 1991.

*12.   Luciuk, L. The Oxford Companion to World War II, Dear and Foot eds. (P.1159-65)

*13.   Utrysco, M. Boykiwshchyna, (Ukrainian text), Philadelphia, 1980.

*14.   Davies, Norman, No Simple Victory, Viking Press, 2006.

*15.   Isajiw et al., The Refugee Experience, Ukrainian DPs after World War II, CIUS Press, 1992.

*16.   Tatomyr, Wolodymyr, Ukrainian Youth in Defense of Their Native Land, Philadelphia, 1960.

*17.   Khanna, Parag The Second World, Random House, 2008

# Acknowledgments

When I started this project, I feared a book about the Ukrainian DP experience would have limited appeal and thought of simply writing down a short chronology for my children.

I was enthusiastically encouraged by my family to expand the scope of this book and to gather as much information as possible. My wife, **Chrystyna (*Xrystia*),** was with me throughout the process. I owe her huge thanks for the hours she spent translating her father's and grandfather's writings into English, checking for accuracy of place names and characters, and for presenting all materials in a readable typed format. She read and re-read every word in the manuscript, corrected and advised me, made valuable suggestions but most of all encouraged me every step of the way.

My son, **Mark**, currently the head of the history department in a large high school in Markham, Ontario, inspired me by his description of his pupils' reactions whenever he deviated from the prescribed curriculum and retold *my* stories about the war to them.

My younger son, **Roman**, currently working as a senior researcher at Merck Pharmaceuticals in Montreal, almost daily reminded me to "keep writing." His visit to Ukraine in 2001 "blew him away."

Sincere thanks to my sister-in-law **Lesya Horodysky**, of New Jersey, who spent a summer, sometimes with a magnifying glass, transcribing her grandfather Julian Tatomyr's diary (written in pencil for the most part in a faded notebook with missing pages and illegible words) into a readable typed format.

Thanks to my brother, **Roman,** who continually gave me excellent information, helped me remember names and events from our early days in Montreal and who guided me through events from the hazy past.

I was encouraged to consider a wider audience by my dearest and best friend since childhood, **Dr. George Wesolowsky,** a physician in upstate New York, who died tragically in 1997 but lives on in my thoughts. We talked about this book while on a fishing trip in Northern Ontario just days before he died. Thanks also to **Dr. Omelan Lukasewycz,** of Duluth, Minnesota, a dear friend who became family when the two of us married the Tatomyr cousins. He was an inspiration to me. He died in 2006 and is missed.

I received guidance and encouragement from my friend **Dr. Orest Subtelny**, a history professor at York University and author of the much-quoted book *Ukraine: A History*. I burdened him with the first and second draft of my book. His suggestions were invaluable.

Thanks to my first cousin, **Oksana Winstead**, for editing the final version of this book and for translating and transcribing my aunt Olga's recollections about our journey from war-torn Ukraine to the displaced persons camps in Germany, and to my niece, **Melania Melnyk**, who did a final accuracy check of this book before publication.

As a high school principal, I offered my services as guest speaker to my senior history and geography classes on a regular basis. The reaction of suburban Canadian teenagers (who almost always have other things on their minds), as well as of students in Spain, Trinidad, Japan, and Egypt, to my stories about our war experiences has been overwhelming.

Thanks, **teachers,** for inviting me into your classrooms; and thanks, **students**, for your enthusiastic feedback.

Finally, thank you, **America and Canada,** for giving us the opportunity to live and to be free citizens in these two wonderful countries.

**Kyiv Airport, 1995**

*The year 2008 marks the sixtieth anniversary of the arrival
of the Tatomyr family in the United States of America.
The year 2009 marks the sixtieth anniversary of the arrival
of the Melnyk family in Canada.*

# Name Index

# General Index

## C

# I

IBM   249-50
Immigrants
  in millions   73-4
  in the United States of America   73
Institute for the Professional Development of
    Teachers   92
International Refugee Organization (IRO)
    7, 256
Iraq war   155, 347
Iron Curtain   15, 27, 215
Ivan Franko University   60
Ivry Inn   221

# J

Jews   140, 142
  in Buchenwald Concentration Camp   196
  in Galicia   102
  hidden in Lviv   60
  mass murders of   155
  Nazi genocide against the   141
  in Odesa   98
  registered as Austrians   74
  tensions between Ukrainians   109
  wearing armbands   140
Josaphat's Ukrainian Catholic School   253
Julian calendar   47, 221

# K

Kabuki theatre presentations   295
Kamia'nets Podilsky   83
Kamin Sokil   63, 68
  raid on Bolsheviks   63
Kazky   253
Khrushchev era   34
Kiev   16, 19, 367 See also Kyiv
Kniaz   48
Knyaza Hora   310, 314
Kobzar   273
Komsomol Youth   30

Kosice, clinic in   170
Kremlin   89, 90, 348
Kreshchatyk Boulevard   151
Krynitsia   255
Kulaks   90
Kuwait   295
Kyiv   16, 19, 46, 82, 84, 97, 151
  acceptance of Christianity in   46, 367
    anniversary of   16
  captured by Poland   84
  captured by Russia   84
  clearing of Germans in   164
  formation of central council in   82
  as Hetman   41
  invasion by Golden Hordes   367
  Khmelnytsky rebellion   367
  Kyiv Patriarchate   154
  Maidan   368
  Pecherska Lavra   152
  settlement of   40
  signs in   151
  Ukrainian Republic   213, 328
    unity with Western Ukrainian Republic
    83
  under Russia   41
  World War I   89

# L

La Steppe Restaurant   223
Ladychyn   45, 74, 76, 105, 129, 158, 236,
    239, 283
  liberated by the Red Army   162
  Ukrainian cemetery in   158
Laurentians   220-1, 223, 231-2, 237, 262,
    321, 327
Lavra   152
League of Nations   91
Lebenstraum   134
Lemberg   19
Lenin, seeking to control Ukraine   89
Levittown   262, 313, 315, 317, 337, 341
Liechtenstein   15